BICYCLE DESIGN

BICYCLE DESIGN

An Illustrated History

TONY HADLAND AND HANS-ERHARD LESSING

with contributions from Nick Clayton and Gary W. Sanderson

The MIT Press   Cambridge, Massachusetts   London, England

MIT Press books may be purchased at special quantity discounts for business or sales promotional use. For information, email special_sales@mitpress.mit.edu.

Set in Helvetica Neue by The MIT Press. Printed and bound in the United States of America.

Library of Congress Cataloging-in-Publication Data
Hadland, Tony.
Bicycle design : an illustrated history / Tony Hadland and Hans-Erhard Lessing; with contributions from Nick Clayton and Gary W. Sanderson.
pages cm
Includes bibliographical references and index.
ISBN 978-0-262-02675-8 (hardcover : alk. paper) 1. Bicycles—Design and construction—History. 2. Bicycles—Parts—History. I. Lessing, Hans-Erhard. II. Title.
TL400.H33 2014
629.2'31—dc23
2013023698

10 9 8 7 6 5 4 3 2 1

I'M MORE INTERESTED IN A WORLD THAT WORKS THAN WHAT SELLS.
Paul MacCready, pioneer of human-powered flight

CONTENTS

....

PREFACE

With more than a billion (that is, 10^9) machines produced so far, the bicycle ranks among the world's most numerous vehicles. Yet the automobile has received much more attention. Indeed, few areas within the history of technology have been as neglected as the history of the bicycle. In this book we attempt to dig a bit deeper into its history than was done in the earlier scattered literature.

It took the oil crisis of 1973 to renew interest in the bicycle and its history. Interest was, however, already being nurtured by special-interest groups in various countries—notably the Veteran-Cycle Club, founded in England in 1955 by John and Derek Roberts. The V-CC's journal, *The Boneshaker*, has long been a major resource for cycle historians. Since 1990, an International Cycling History Conference has been held in a different country every year, and the proceedings have been published under the title *Cycle History*. The impressive research material accumulated by the Veteran-Cycle Club and the International Cycling History Conferences (founded by Nick Clayton) proved very useful to us. We also used many other sources, especially technical literature and patents. This does not mean, however, that all the questions have been fully answered. Many of the early manufacturers are long gone, having left no traces in any historical archive. It is also a sad fact that, thus far, few contributors from Asia, Africa, and South America have found their way to one of the International Cycling History Conferences, so our perspective is necessarily that of the developed countries of the West. A complete world encyclopedia of bicycle inventions remains to be compiled.

We begin by focusing on the early evolution of the bicycle in the days before it achieved its most successful and enduring form, the diamond-frame safety bicycle. We then look at the further development and refinement of the bicycle for specific purposes, such as racing, portability, and all-terrain use. We also examine the evolution of bicycle components with specific functions, such as the enhancement of speed, comfort, and luggage carrying. We use patent drawings where we can, because they are more instructive than manufacturers' illustrations. We are well aware, however, that patent drawings leave the social implications of inventions obscure. As the title of an Open University module once put it, "invention is not enough," and just because something was patented doesn't mean that it was widely adopted or even that it was put into production. It does, however, show that a problem and a solution were understood by someone at a particular time and in a particular place. A patent may also have influenced later inventors and stimulated change. We therefore consider not only the commercially successful designs, but also many noteworthy designs that failed to find widespread acceptance. In some cases, lack of success was due to inherent weaknesses of concept. But many designs failed because of other factors, such as cost, fashion, poor marketing, or a lack of appropriate manufacturing techniques. For example, a perfectly feasible bicycle disc brake was patented 100 years before such devices became commonplace, reliable, and affordable. Sometimes an invention is ahead of its time.

We concentrate on the technological aspects rather than the sociological. We don't provide histories of companies, our feeling being that this should be done at a national level.

The rise of personal mobility was a strangely resistible process. Despite booms in 1817–1820, 1867–1870, and 1895–1900, seven decades elapsed before the arrival of a practical vehicle for the masses. Widespread adoption of the bicycle was thwarted by the interplay of the learning curve for balancing, various clampdowns by authorities, and competition from roller skating. After its strictly utilitarian beginnings as a replacement for starved horses, the bicycle could survive the later gaps between booms in its popularity only as a piece of sports equipment. In the twentieth century, this link with sport turned anti-progressive when technically conservative racing professionals displaced sewing-machine mechanics as prominent retailers of bicycles. Racing-oriented dealers were accustomed to the Union Cycliste Internationale's policy of suppressing "unfair advantages." And bicycle manufacturers haven't always served the needs of commuters, who, unlike the UCI, want as many "unfair advantages" as they can get. Since 1976, the International Human-Powered Vehicle Association, founded by Chester Kyle and Jack Lambie, has nurtured novel designs, unconstrained by the dead hand of the UCI.

We also discuss some of the myths that bedevil bicycle history. For example, while browsing the Internet we have read that Leonardo da Vinci invented the bicycle, that Frank Bowden of the British bicycle firm Raleigh devised the Bowden cable, and that Messrs. Sturmey and Archer designed the first Sturmey-Archer three-speed hub gear. We counter such falsehoods wherever we can.

We hope that the reader will find many interesting and surprising facts in this story of humankind's fascination with the bicycle, which according to a 2004 poll by the *Times* of London is the most important of inventions. It is perhaps better described as "the freedom machine," and 2017 marks the bicentennial of the start of its remarkable evolution.

ACKNOWLEDGMENTS

We are indebted to Nick Clayton, the founder of the International Cycling History Conferences, and Gary Sanderson, the organizer of the twentieth conference, for generously sharing their research on British and American themes, respectively. Our special thanks go to the artists Geoff Apps, Alan Osbahr, and R. John Way, who generously permitted us to use their illustrations to embellish our book. We also acknowledge the support of numerous bicycle researchers and enthusiasts worldwide, many of whom having become not just colleagues but friends. You will find them identified among the comprehensive sources and references listed at the back of the book. In particular, we wish to thank the following people, whose contributions have been especially significant: Sven Altfelder, Alessandro Belli, Nadine Besse, Gerd Böttcher, Mike Burrows, Alan Clarke, Colin Davison, Pryor Dodge, Michael Embacher, Bruce Epperson, Walter Euhus, Alastair Florance, Renate Franz, Jeremy Garnet, Paul Grogan, Michael Grützner, Anne Henry, Raymond Henry, Mike Hessey, Kris Holm, Karin and Jan Hult, Matthias Kielwein, Keizo Kobayashi, Kazusuke Koike, Jan Králik, Herbert Kuner, Nigel Land, Scotford Lawrence, John Macnaughtan, Michael Mertins, Ray Miller, Gertjan Moed, the late Alex Moulton, Nicholas Oddy, Rob van der Plas, Claude Reynaud, Andrew Ritchie (the cycle historian), Francis Robin, Brian Rosenberg, Florian Schlumpf, Arnfried Schmitz, Helge Schultz, Jacques Seray, Lorne Shields, Robert Sterba, Roger Street, Howard Sutherland, Tilman Wagenknecht, and—last, but not least—our understanding and patient wives.

A NOTE ON SPELLING AND ON THE NAMES OF COMPONENTS

Because the book is published by an American press, American spelling is used in most places. British spelling and punctuation are retained in quotations from British sources.

A few bicycle components have different names or spellings in the United States than in the United Kingdom. Most of these differences are well known—for example, "tire" (US) vs. "tyre" (UK) and "fender" (US) vs. "mudguard" (UK). Where we feel that confusion might arise, we have tried to clarify. The table below and the diagram in appendix D may also be helpful.

Etymology. (Words in parentheses are nicknames.)

	This book	German	French	British	American
1817–	Early velocipede	Draisine, Laufmaschine	Draisienne vélocipède (célérifère)	Draisine, velocipede (hobby-horse)	Draisena, velocipede
1866–	Cranked velocipede	Veloziped	Vélocipède bicycle	Velocipede bicycle	Bicycular velocipede
			Véloce, vélo bicycle	Bicycle (boneshaker)	Bicycle
1880s	High-wheeler	Bicycle	Grand-bi	Bicycle	Bicycle
		Hochrad (since 1885)		Ordinary (penny-farthing)	High-wheeler
1890s	Bicycle	Niederrad	Bicyclette	Safety bicycle	Safety bicycle
		Fahrrad		Safety bicycle	Safety bicycle

VELOCIPEDES AND THEIR FORERUNNERS

1

....

MOBILITY BEFORE THE VELOCIPEDE

Ice skating

A period of unusually cold weather at the end of the eighteenth century made a new kind of personal mobility fashionable throughout the Old World: ice skating. Even the Thames in London was frozen over in 1788–89, and again in 1812–13. On the European continent, only in the Netherlands, where there were narrow canals and ditches, had ice skating been commonplace in the past. Period reports describe Dutch farm women skating from marketplace to marketplace on frozen canals while balancing milk cans on their heads and knitting (Ginzrot 1830, volume iii, 328).

Figure 1.1 Clockwise: German students with girl on ice (Zindel 1825); outdoor roller-skating demonstration in The Hague, 1790 (Swiss Sports Museum); one-wheeled Hoppa in Paris, 1771 (Ginzrot 1830); Chinese wheelbarrow with sail, 1798 (Houckgeest 1798).

In the eighteenth century ice skating was a pastime of Dutch nobles and commoners alike, but after a while it was abandoned by the upper classes. Though it soon became clear that a man on skates could travel faster than a man on a horse, only a small fraction of the adult population—a daring few—learned to balance on skates (Zindel 1825).

Early roller skating

To simulate ice skating in theatrical productions, four small wheels were added to the skates. (See, e.g., French 1985.) This worked well on the boards of a stage, but not on the streets (Nieswizski 1991). A few more instances of indoor skating on wheels before 1800 are known, as is one heroic outdoor attempt (on the road between The Hague and Scheveningen in 1790) involving early in-line roller skates.

The wheelbarrow

The wheelbarrow was a military invention of Chuko Liang in the third century. Called a "miu niu" (meaning "wooden ox"), the early Chinese wheelbarrow, with one large central wheel, was meant to carry a soldier's food supply for a whole year while enabling him to travel 20 feet in the time it would have taken to go 6 feet (Needham 1991). The wheelbarrow was a common means of transportation for passengers and goods in China until recent times. Thus, China, like the Netherlands, had a horseless form of personal transport before the advent of the bicycle.

The wheelbarrow didn't appear in Europe until the twelfth or the thirteenth century. Builders of castles or cathedrals could halve the number of laborers needed to haul small loads by substituting a wheel for the front man of a hod or a stretcher. With that technique, however, half the load had still to be carried by the man who pushed. The Chinese design had the wheel below the center of gravity, so there was no burden on the pusher. Somehow the Chinese design crept into British agriculture, or was reinvented in Britain. A report on a Chinese-style barrow appeared in the London journal *Museum Rusticum et Commerciale* in 1765.

Carriage makers in Paris took to the idea of a single-track wheelbarrow around 1771. A one-wheeled cabriolet called a "Hoppa," its inventor unknown, had as its single wheel a wide roller; it also had skids as stabilizers for emergencies (Ginzrot 1830, volume iv, 49).

In the 1790s, Lord George Macartney of Britain and Andreas van Braam Houckgeest of the Netherlands traveled to China. Upon returning, each of them published drawings of a center-wheel wheelbarrow equipped with a sail (Lessing 2001). That idea doesn't appear to have been adopted in Europe, except for dune carts and rail vehicles.

Wheelbarrow design was a subject of technology courses at the University of Heidelberg, where a design by Johann Gottfried Borlach (now lost) was kept in the sample collection (Lessing 2001).

An early Japanese human-powered vehicle

In Japan, a country that had a long tradition of foot-powered irrigation for the cultivation of rice, a remarkable boat-shaped land vehicle with three wheels was built in 1732 (Koike 2013). This Riku-Hon-Sesya ("impulsive land boat") is described and pictured in a chapter of *Hiraishi-Ke Monjyo*, a manuscript written by the scholar Kuheiji-Tokimitu Hisaishi. Built at the behest of a local lord, it had two four-wheeled predecessors, one built in 1729 by a man named Monya Shoda and one in 1730 by a man named Takeda. The latter two vehicles are not as well documented as the Riku-Hon-Sesya, but it is recorded that locals called Monya Shoda a "long-distance man" (Senri-Sha-nohito).

Between the rear wheels, the Riku-Hon-Sesya had a kind of composite crankshaft, which was fastened to both sides of a central wooden flywheel. The cranks, like those in local irrigation mills, had wooden sandals as pedals. The front steering system consisted of a vertical steering pole around which a rope was wrapped several times, both ends going to levers on the front-wheel column. (A similar system was used by local fishermen to pull their boats from the water onto the beach.) The operator stood upright on the sandals and turned the steering tiller by hand. Eighty years later, a German inventor named Karl Drais used the same sequence from treadmill to crankshaft in his four-wheeled Fahrmaschinen.

In his manuscript, Hisaishi reported that his three-wheeled boat ran better than the earlier four-wheelers. On reaching the bottom of an incline, a four-wheeler had to be carried; the new one could run up the slope. The cover of the manuscript featured a poem praising the machine's ability to go anywhere with dancer-like movements while giving the pleasure of freedom. Whether more land boats were built after Hisaishi's isn't known.

Niches for human-powered vehicles

From the seventeenth century on, there were two niches for human-powered personal transport in the Western world: vehicles for people with disabilities and garden phaetons made to travel on pathways.

Wealthy disabled people could get hand-cranked wheelchairs. The cheaper Bath chair usually had to be drawn or pushed around by another person. In 1725, a German named Gärthner

Box 1.1   **BOOKS ON CARRIAGE THEORY**

The physics of the carriage became better understood toward the end of the eighteenth century. However, Charles Camus' *Traité des forces mouvantes* (1722) was erroneous on the proper disposition of loads on carriages with front wheels of smaller size. The correct theory, arrived at by Johann Lambert and published after his death, calculated that the load should be shifted toward the larger rear wheels (Lambert 1778).

Further research was encouraged by prizes offered by learned societies. In 1763 the Swedish Academy of Sciences asked "if the carts could not be improved in such a way, that the same horse could pull 70 liesspounds as easily as 40 liesspounds on a conventional cart"—i.e., an improvement of 75 percent (Treue 1986). A gold medal was won by the two-wheeled (side by side) cart of Jacob Faggot, a model of which was kept at the University of Heidelberg. Another entry was a wagon wheel with a hub of solid brass to reduce friction on the axle.

In 1797 the Royal Danish Society of Sciences published (in Latin) a challenge to show, on mechanical principles, why a four-wheeled wagon should be preferable to a two-wheeled cart. First prize was won by Nicolaus Fuss, a professor of mathematics in St. Petersburg. He published his work as *Versuch einer Theorie des Widerstandes zwey- und vierrädriger Fuhrwerke* (*Essay of a Theory on the Resistance of Two- and Four-Wheeled Carriages*) (Fuss 1798). According to Fuss, a four-wheeled wagon should have less resistance to surmount under all conditions than a two-wheeled cart. His model, according to which rolling resistance depended linearly on how deep a wheel sinks into the surface of the soil, was theoretical and had not been tested in practice.

In 1813, Franz Josef von Gerstner, director of the Prague Polytechnic Institute, published two treatises on freight wagons and streets (Gerstner 1813). Equated the work done against rolling resistance to the compression work done on the soil, he arrived at a nonlinear relation between rolling resistance and weight. So did Thomas Tredgold in *A Practical Treatise on Railroads and Carriages* (1835). Coulomb's law of friction suggests a linear relationship such that a four-wheeler and a two-wheeler of equal weight would have the same rolling resistance (Lessing 2003a).

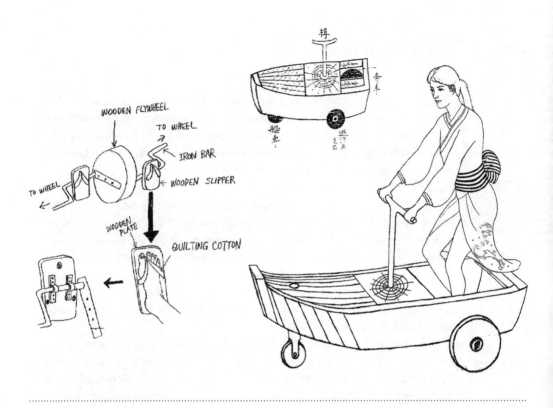

Figure 1.2 Hisashi's Riku-Hon-Sesya (impulsive land boat) and its pedal drive unit (Shiga State Library; photo and reconstructions by Kazusuke Koike).

designed a self-propelled chair, with hand-operated rims on both wheels and a small trailing wheel with caster effect, that was similar to those in use today (Leupold 1725).

Replacing the Bath chair with a carriage and putting a lackey on board to tread the rear wheels was suggested by a Frenchman, Dr. Elie Richard of La Rochelle (Ozanam 1696). The heavy coach technology and the rutted, muddy, dirty carriageways of the time may have been the main obstacles to wider adoption. In 1774, when the lightweight two-wheel curricle pulled by a single horse became popular in London, Richard's idea made a comeback. A mechanic named Ovenden, presumably of the wheelwrights Bushnel & Ovenden, published *A New Machine to Go without Horses* the following year (Ovenden 1775). This time the idea found uses not on the carriageways but on the grounds of stately homes. In 1775, when a garden architect employed by Carl Theodor, Elector of the German Palatinate, visited London, he purchased a

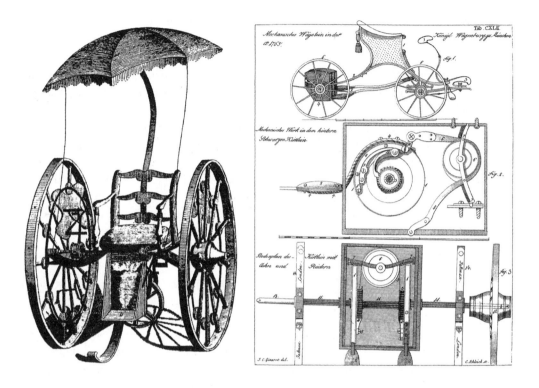

Figure 1.3 Left: a hand-cranked wheelchair from Diderot's *Encyclopédie* of 1751. Right: a garden phaeton of 1775 (not 1765), marked "Jackman London" (Ginzrot 1830).

lever-powered garden phaeton for the Elector's summer residence and garden in Schwetzingen. It is thought that this beautiful phaeton, which had "Jackman London" engraved on one of its steel springs, was ordered by Queen Charlotte, and that she canceled the order (Wackernagel 2002, volume i, 112; personal communication from Rudolf Wackernagel). It seems to have remained in Schwetzingen until 1803, when it was moved to Munich, where it is now preserved in the Deutsches Museum.

Personal transport still relied on the horse and was therefore expensive. In a lecture at the Royal Military Academy of Woolwich, the mathematician Thomas Stephens Davies estimated the cost of a horse over its entire lifespan at £1,700 (Davies 1837). For that sum, one could buy a house in London. Less affluent people used donkeys, goats, or dogs to pull carts.

A SHORTAGE OF OATS NECESSITATES HORSELESS TRANSPORT

In 1812, during the Napoleonic Wars, Europe and New England experienced the first of five bad harvests. The passing armies had raided Germany's grain stores, and as a result that country suffered particularly badly from the soaring price of corn and oats. In October of 1813, only ten days after Napoleon's defeat at Leipzig, the 28-year-old Baron Karl von Drais, a state-employed forester and former forestry teacher, applied to the Grand Duke of Baden for a "privilege" on a four-wheeled human-powered wagon. (During the short Badenian revolution of 1849, the Baron preferred to be called simply Citizen Karl Drais.) In Baden, which had no patent law at the time, a "privilege" granted the right to become the only seller of an item within the Grand Duchy. Drais, a civil servant not allowed to do any side business, was refused the "privilege." In any case, the experts who were called upon (Tulla 1813) doubted the novelty of the idea, citing the garden phaeton at Schwetzingen.

Drais's Fahrmaschinen

Drais may have seen the servant-powered garden phaeton at Schwetzingen or may have encountered it while studying technology at the University of Heidelberg (Lessing 2003a, 122). In an article that appeared three years later in *Neues Magazin*, he criticized its deficiencies: "There have been earlier attempts to self-propel a carriage via some machinery. But that machinery was ponderous in surmounting friction, complicated, and therefore never suitable for any noticeably practical use." He also referred to the bleak situation that prevailed at the time: "In wartime, when horses and their fodder often become scarce, a small fleet of such wagons at each corps could be important, especially for dispatches over short distances and for carrying the wounded." (translated from Drais 1816)

No pictures of Drais's two Fahrmaschinen (driving machines) exist, but Drais left written descriptions (Lessing 2003a, 117). Fahrmaschine 1, intended to carry as many as five people, had a treadmill fastened to a shaft between its rear wheels. The driver sat, facing backward, on a suspended saddle, and operated the treadmill with his feet. Fahrmaschine 2 had a forged crankshaft between the rear wheels that allowed the driver to be seated facing forward while treading the crankshaft. Fahrmaschine 2 attained a speed of 4 miles per hour. "On arriving at steep hills, or a very bad road," Drais wrote, "one takes on a horse as an extra team member—just as wagoners do—by letting down the steering rods . . . to become shafts within which to harness the horse."

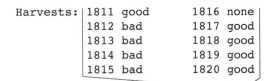

Harvests: | 1811 good 1816 none |
| 1812 bad 1817 good |
| 1813 bad 1818 good |
| 1814 bad 1819 good |
| 1815 bad 1820 good |

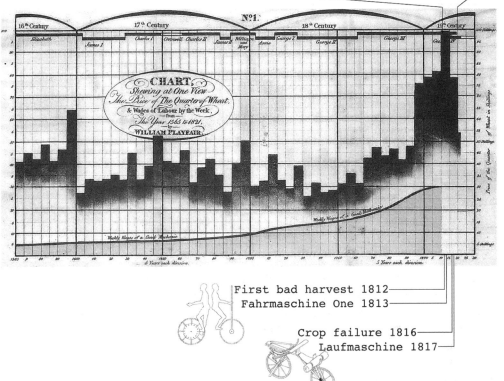

First bad harvest 1812——
Fahrmaschine One 1813——

Crop failure 1816——
Laufmaschine 1817——

Figure 1.4 Five-year averages of wheat price (Playfair 1822). The true peak occurred in 1817. Drais's inventions follow the first and the worst crop failures, respectively.

Encouraged by the acclaim of Tsar Alexander I, for whom he had demonstrated Fahrmaschine 1 in Karlsruhe while the Tsar was visiting there, Drais took Fahrmaschine 2 to Vienna in 1814 to demonstrate it during the Congress. The princes who had assembled in Vienna for the purpose of dividing up Europe seem to have shown no interest in Drais's Fahrmaschine, despite the increased price of oats.

"Difficulties not yet overcome by the inventor," Drais acknowledged in a handwritten note, "include becoming very tired on bad roads and in the mountains." Of course, the treadmill could be made larger for better leverage, but treading the largest possible treadmill would be the same as simply treading on the ground. Having arrived at that depressing conclusion, it seems, Drais decided to try direct propulsion in his next invention: a two-wheeler.

The "year without a summer," and a breakthrough

The 1815 eruption of Mount Tambora, a volcano east of Bali, was called "the last big subsistence crisis of humanity" by the American historian John Post (1977). Volcanic ash reached the Northern Hemisphere in 1816, the "year without a summer." Snowstorms and continual thunderstorms destroyed harvests both in Europe and in New England. There were widespread shortages of food, especially among the lower classes, and corn hastily bought in the Netherlands or in Russia couldn't be distributed from Mannheim's Rhine harbor into the interior because there were no horses left—those that hadn't been slaughtered had starved. Thus, there was a need for a horseless means of transport (Lessing 2001). We have no statement from Drais on this, but we have circumstantial evidence from his inventions after conspicuous crop failures (see figure 1.4) and from newspaper voices of the period (translated in Hamer 2005).

Two wheels replace four hooves

The earliest mention of public use of Drais's two-wheeler, initially also called a Fahrmaschine but later called a Laufmaschine ("running machine"), dates to June 12, 1817 (see Drais 1817a)—not to July, as some period newspapers asserted. In the literature, the year is often reported as 1816, but that appears to be a misinterpretation of Drais's delayed article on his four-wheeled Fahrmaschine 2 (Drais 1816).

By June of 1817, Drais had been living in the city of Mannheim for six years. His first spin on the two-wheeled Laufmaschine was taken on the best road in the Grand Duchy: the road that went toward the Elector's summer residence at Schwetzingen. Halfway to Schwetzingen, Drais turned around and rode back home. He traveled 8 miles in slightly less than an hour.

Figure 1.5 Reconstructions of Drais's Fahrmaschine 1 and Fahrmaschine 2 (Lessing 2003a).

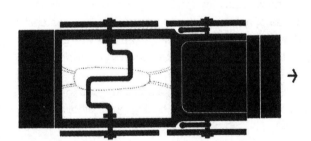

It has been speculated that Drais reduced his four-wheeled Fahrmaschine to the two-wheeled Laufmaschine in order to accommodate it to the narrow forest paths on which the machine was to be used (Dunham 1956, 4). In fact, the only testimony by Drais on how he arrived at the two-wheeler principle can be found in a brief notice he submitted to the weekly *Badwochenblatt*: "The main idea of the invention has been taken from ice skating." (translated from Drais 1817a) Later, Drais published several articles on the invention (Drais 1817b,c). His three-page description (1817c) included two plates and was available from booksellers. (For an English translation, see Lessing 1991.) Using brief reports they read in newspapers, or using the engraving that Drais generously mailed to people who expressed interest, craftsmen in many places built their own versions of the Laufmaschine (or Draisine, as the press began to call it). (The railway draisine got its name because the earliest one was a two-wheeler made to travel on a single rail.) Dresden became a center of draisine production; at least five tradesmen in that city pirated Drais's invention.

With the help of his father, a learned jurist, Drais again applied for a "privilege," this time on exclusive use of the machines. (A license badge was nailed to the draisine's tiller—see figure 1.7.) He obtained a ten-year "privilege" in 1818 thanks to the Grand Duchess Stephanie Napoleon. That same year, he obtained a French brevet (patent) for five years; he also obtained a patent of some sort in Prussia. In Bavaria, in Austria, and in the city of Frankfurt, Drais's applications were declined to protect local pirate builders.

The design of draisines

Draisines were, in many ways, similar to present-day bicycles. Their wooden wheels, held together with iron hoops, were equal in size, each about 27 inches or 675 millimeters in diameter. One early draisine, now preserved at the Deutsches Museum in Munich, weighed only 45 pounds; it was made of well-seasoned ash wood. However, the ergonomic characteristics of a draisine differed considerably from those of a present-day bicycle. Balancing was easily mastered only by young people used to skating on ice; indeed, riding a draisine was described as "skating on the road." The difficulty of balancing ruled out the use of indirect propulsion by means of cranks as in Fahrmaschine 2. To make it easier for the rider to put his feet on the ground, the seat was lower than that of a modern bicycle. Having a draisine made to measure by a local cartwright required getting one's inseam measured. Resting one's elbows on the upholstered balancing board relieved strain on the crotch. The tiller, which carried the license badge, was directed with the fingers. Brass bushings around the axles reduced friction and could be oiled through a radial bore in the hub.

The steering mechanism, intended to be self-righting, made use of the caster effect. The front axle trailed six inches behind the vertical pivot, and curved sliding billets were used to keep the front bogie from wedging with the perch. Two letters from users reveal that white soap was used to lubricate the sliding billets (Lessing 2003a, 257). The tiller could be tilted forward and used to pull the draisine uphill.

In a magazine article, Drais—who had studied physics at Heidelberg—correctly described the methods of regaining balance and turning:

> If one . . . has inadvertently lost balance, one can help oneself by using the feet or by steering. Specifically, one steers a bit towards the direction to which the point of gravity of the whole tips over. And if one wants to make a turn, one should move the point of gravity to the inner side immediately before, and shortly after, steering thereto. (translated from Drais 1820)

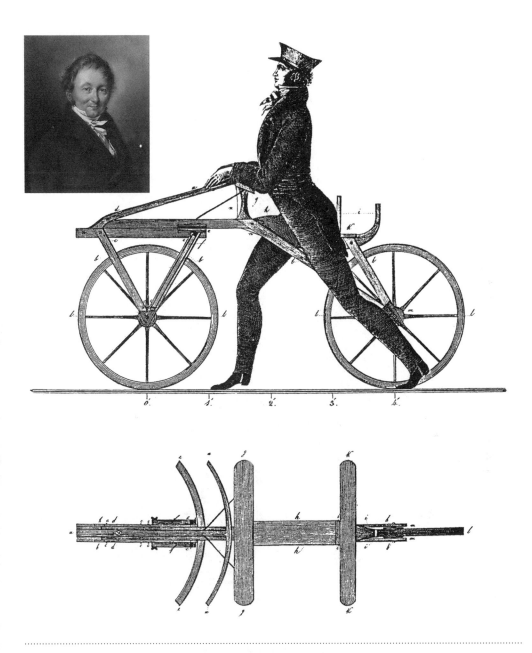

Figure 1.6 Karl Drais circa 1820 (H.-E. Lessing) and a Laufmaschine (Drais 1817c). Scale is in feet.

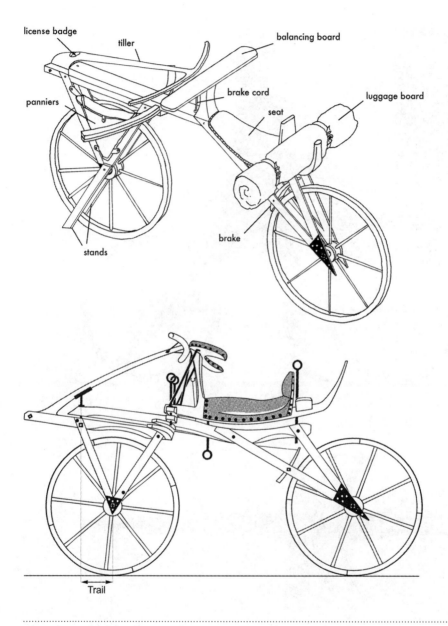

Figure 1.7 An isometric drawing of a draisine with options added (Lessing 2012).
Figure 1.8 An adjustable draisine of 1817 (Lessing 2003a).

The first bit of advice can be summarized as "steering into the undesired fall" (Meijaard et al. 2011). It utilizes centrifugal force to tilt the rider and the machine upright again. The advice on turning reminds us that in order to turn left on a single-track two-wheeler one must briefly steer to the right. Drais speaks of leaning to the left, but with the hands on the tiller that is tantamount to steering to the right.

It is a modern misconception that riding a draisine was just like walking while sitting, and that all a rider could do was coast downhill. (See, e.g., Herlihy 2004, 24.) Speeds of 8 miles per hour and more could be sustained with occasional rapid thrusts of the legs. Reporters were surprised that Drais could roll 60 feet or more without touching the ground.

To foil pirate builders, Drais positioned the cord-operated brake so that the rider's leg would conceal it. Period carriages had no such brakes; they were stopped by the draft animals alone, or, when going downhill, by a skid shoe.

In 1817 Drais offered a range of Laufmaschinen, including a tandem and several "ladies' draisines" (some with three wheels, some with four). A ladies' model had a comfortable seat between the front wheels. Drais maintained that a female passenger could "sit deeply enough not to get sick" (1817c).

downhill

Figure 1.9   A period method of braking a carriage (Ginzrot 1830).

FIRST GENERATION 1817

SECOND GENERATION 1820

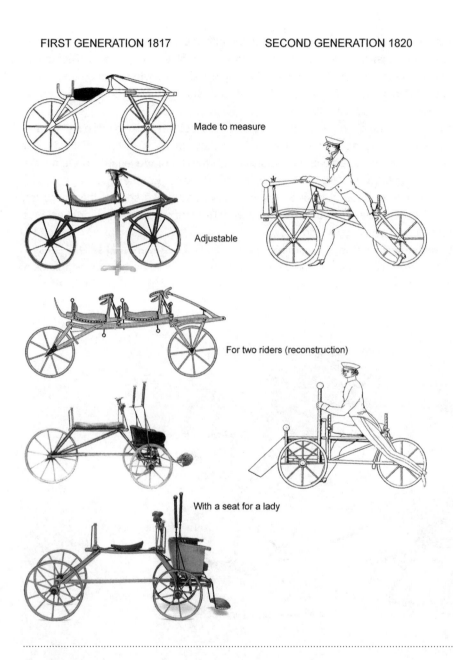

Made to measure

Adjustable

For two riders (reconstruction)

With a seat for a lady

Figure 1.10 Drais's range of draisines (Lessing 2003a).

Box 1.2

COMMENTS BY RIDERS OF DRAISINES

Two letters and a diary entry written by riders of draisines have surfaced. The letters are quoted here as translated from pages 252–257 of Lessing 2003a:

> For more convenience the seat can be suspended from springs—I myself own such a machine. And if the front wheel is higher by half a foot than the rear wheel, one moves very easily, since the front wheel and not the rear wheel has to carry the main load, as experience will teach you. Moreover the machine should not be shorter, that is the wheels shouldn't be brought nearer to each other, because the machine then moves not as easily, as I have learned by experience already.
> —Peter Maurenbrecher (postmaster, Cologne), 1818

> Before starting, one has to screw the saddle just to such a height that the feet still stand on the ground and then sit down upright, hold the tiller bar ahead with both hands and strive for both wheels to be in line. Then, quite slowly at first, set the machine in motion by alternately positioning the feet, and then strive to keep this straight run of the wheels. And the run will go constantly faster and better, especially downhill. And if one has to climb a hill, this effort will not cause more tribulation than to mount a hill on foot. To screw the saddle up higher, I had a spanner made for me, such that tall and small people can operate this Laufmaschine. (Jaspar von Oertzen, chief administrative officer of the district Roggow in 1818 to his grand-duke Franz I. von Mecklenburg when presenting him with a Draisine. It was a successful ploy, as von Oertzen soon became minister of finance.)

> Riding the fast curricle (Tresenne [i.e., draisine]) works out for me quite fair already. Daily I make a small commotion in the apartment and ride around through all rooms, until I shall dare once—being more experienced in the art—to go outdoors. It is entertaining. . . .
> —Michael Gäßler (attorney, Straubing), who had won the draisine in a lottery in Regensburg 1819

Box 1.2
(continued)

In a letter dated 1833, the inventor Karl Drais recalled the fear of balancing among the populace. The entry is quoted here as translated from page 163 of Lessing 2003a:

> Nearly everywhere my performance on this instrument was attributed to my personal skill rather than to the invention itself. People imagined the manipulation of it much more difficult than it is, usually by saying: "Well, if everybody had the skill to use it like you, the thing would be very useful indeed." But they did not dare to sit on it, although I have taught several persons very well in four lessons.

Return of the horses

In the autumn of 1817, the first good harvest in several years was brought in, breeding and selling of horses resumed, and the window of opportunity for Karl Drais's invention closed. Draisine riders fell into disfavor, especially because they used the sidewalks rather than the carriageways. Riding on the sidewalks was forbidden in Mannheim by December of 1817 (Lessing 2003a, 290 and 364) and presumably in other German towns. Drais's hopes of finding a manufacturer went unfulfilled. However, he was named a member of two scientific societies, and the new Grand Duke granted him an early retirement from the forest service with the title of Professor of Mechanics. Drais and his machines lost favor among students in 1820 after his father, Baden's most senior judge, declined to grant clemency to a student who had committed a political murder. Facing public harassment after the young man was executed, the inventor left the country for six years and worked as a land surveyor in Brazil.

Several notable feats were accomplished on draisines. In 1820 a British engineer rode one 300 miles over the Pyrenees, from the French town of Pau to Madrid (Drais 1820). In 1829, in a semi-clandestine race of 26 draisines in Munich, the winner averaged 14 miles per hour for 30 minutes. But newspaper articles on draisines gave way to articles about railways.

DIFFUSION OF THE SINGLE-TRACK VELOCIPEDE

Despite a clampdown on draisines in Germany, the idea of a two-wheeled human-powered machine soon spread to the entire Western world. Christian Schenk, a mechanic in the Swiss city of Bern, had built one such machine by September of 1817 (Lessing 2003a, 158). In Austria, Anton Burg and Son, manufacturers of agricultural machinery, began to build velocipedes, and early in 1818 they opened a riding school in Vienna. In order to protect Burg and Son, an Austrian patent was denied to Drais. Burg and Son patented three-wheeled velocipedes as late as 1824, and their catalog of 1857 still showed a children's draisine (Ulreich 1993). They may also have produced a simplified velocipede (Ulreich 1999).

Figure 1.11   Burg's riding school in Vienna, 1818 (*Briefe eines unvoreingenommenen Eipeldauers* 7, 1818). Purportedly one could learn to ride within 10 hours for 10 guilders.

Le vélocipède in France

At the end of 1817, France, which had been allied with the Grand Duchy of Baden until four years earlier, was Karl Drais's first choice as a place to sell a license and apply for a patent. A recently discovered letter to Grand Duke Carl August of Saxony-Weimar (Reissinger 2011), for whom Drais had procured a draisine from a cartwright in Mannheim, confirms that Drais engaged Jean Garcin, a famous ice skater in Paris who had written a book on skating (Garcin 1813), to establish manufacture in Paris and to open a riding school.

Because Drais, although retired, was still technically a civil servant on paid leave, he could not travel to Paris without approval. He used intermediaries to deal with Jean Garcin and his associate Tournus. In an analogy to the high-speed coach called the "vélocifère," a new name—"vélocipède" (literally "quick foot")—was created for the Laufmaschine. "Vélocipède" was probably derived from the old German expression "Schnellfusz machen" ("make the quickfoot," meaning "run away") (Lessing 2012). "Draisienne," a French variant of "draisine," was also used.

To apply for a French patent, Drais sent his servant to the Ministry of the Interior in Paris. It seems that the servant, who spoke only broken French, repeatedly identified himself as Drais's Diener (the German word for "servant"). The clerk, using phonetic spelling, wrote down "Dineur" as the name of the applicant (Durry 1982, 20). In the subsequent cycling literature, a man named Dineur was said to have been Drais's patent attorney; however, the profession of patent attorney didn't exist in Paris at that time, and the period Paris directory doesn't list a Dineur at the given address (Keizo Kobayashi, personal communication). Among the signatories to the patent application was the president of the patent commission, the famous scientist Joseph Louis Gay-Lussac, who raised no objections to the novelty of the velocipede. In 1818 a five-year brevet (number 1,842) was granted.

In March of 1818, Drais's servant and some other men rode a small fleet of draisines from Mannheim via Strasbourg to Paris, a distance of about 300 miles. Drais wasn't able to join them, having been invited on short notice to give a lecture before the Polytechnic Society of Frankfurt, of which he had become an honorary member. On a Sunday the French partners presented the draisines in the Jardin du Luxembourg. The park's long avenue de l'observatoire was an ideal setting. Press opinion of this event was divided (Kobayashi 1993, 41). At least the *Journal de Paris* of April 14, 1818 reported that its reporter had walked a considerable distance "to see these peculiar carriages intended to abolish the luxury of horses and to lower the price of oats and hay."

French craftsmen modified the design of the draisine in a way that had already been demonstrated by an anonymous mechanic at a Frankfurt fair in 1817 (Lessing 2003a, 295). Drais's front wheel and fork assembly was a separate bogey, pivoted at the front and supported at its rear by a quadrant. It was turned by a steering bar called a Leitstange. That arrangement, common on carriages, was necessitated by the trail for self-alignment of the front wheel. The French machine's front wheel and fork simply pivoted in a bushed socket through the frame, but kept the trail by bending the fork backward (Lessing 2012). The wheels now turned within a solid iron fork and rear stays of similar construction; that alteration resulted in a more elegant look, but presumably also in more weight; Drais criticized it (1820).

The skater Jean Garcin rented two-wheeled and three-wheeled draisines to visitors to the amusement parks in the outskirts of Paris by the hour. One benefit of the new personal mobility was immediately evident to males who rented ladies' draisines for their female companions: one could ride off with one's darling to a secluded spot within the park.

Figure 1.12 Wooden stays are replaced by wrought iron in France in 1818 (Wikimedia Commons; Tietze 1925; Tony Hadland).

Pirate copiers in Paris and in the countryside deviated from Drais's designs in some ways. From period newspapers we know of a wood turner in Beaune, named Lagrange (Kobayashi 1993, 59), who may have been the supplier of the velocipede owned by the inventor Nicéphore Nièpce in nearby Chalon-sur-Saône. The museum there holds Nièpce's machine, some of whose parts are made of turned parts. That machine has bores in the beam to which Nièpce intended to attach mechanical legs for propulsion, as we know from letters to his brother.

In October of 1818, Drais himself rode the 300 miles to Paris via Nancy, where he gave a demonstration of the draisine. The reason for that trip isn't known, but there may have been difficulties with the licensee. Drais brought along a three-page leaflet describing the vehicle in French and using the term "vélocipède" (1818). After a demonstration in the Tivoli amusement park, the gazettes reported that the idea for the draisine had come from ice skating, as was stated in the leaflet.

The velocipede in England

We are indebted to Thomas Stephens Davies, a teacher of mathematics at the Royal Military Academy in Woolwich, for a lively report of the early days of the velocipede in England. Davies had been a devotee of the velocipede in his younger years. In 1837 he gave a lecture titled "On the Velocipede." (See appendix B below.) Reportedly one of his acquaintances, a citizen of Mannheim named Bernhard Seine, had brought Drais's leaflet to Bath early in 1818, had had a draisine built there, and "did not hesitate to run on his velocipede at a violent rate down some of the steepest streets in that city over the pitching of the road." Davies found the fact that he had "never heard of [Seine's] meeting with any accident" amazing, because Seine's velocipede appeared to lack a brake. (As was mentioned above, Drais's design concealed the brake.)

In the autumn of 1818, Denis Johnson, a coach maker who had just opened a workshop at 75 Long Acre in London, applied by petition to be granted a patent on a "Pedestrian Curricle or Velocipede" "in consequence of a communication made to [him] by a certain foreigner residing abroad." He had recently "procured" one of these "very useful machines" from "abroad." The fourteen-year patent he was granted cost Johnson £100 (Street 2011, 19). There were no international patent agreements; citizens could patent foreign inventions with slight alterations or "improvements" with impunity. Johnson's patent drawing shows that his velocipede was modeled after a French one, so the unidentified foreigner could have been Jean Garcin as easily as Karl Drais. Johnson dispensed with trail altogether and used what has been called "indirect steering." The steering bar shown in his patent drawing looped out over the front wheel, attaching loosely to the front axle; presumably it could be rotated 120° to serve as a stand for parking.

Figure 1.13 Denis Johnson's patent specification drawing of November 1818.

In Johnson's second-generation velocipedes, the steering arrangement was different. Similar to the French style, a short handlebar was bolted directly to the top of the fork stem. Trail remained absent. Steering was still accomplished partly by means of body movement. There was no brake on the rear wheel.

Johnson inscribed his machines with production numbers styled as roman numerals. (The highest numeral on a surviving machine is CCCXX, meaning 320.) He opened two riding schools in London. His illegitimate son John served as an instructor, and also demonstrated the machines in various English cities. Ludicrous names for the vehicles sprang up—Hobby, Hobby-Horse, Dandy-Horse, German Horse (Shields 2012).

The price of a velocipede ranged from £8 to £10, equivalent to about £590–£740 in present-day currency according to the Bank of England's inflation calculator. There was widespread unauthorized copying. In Dublin, two Irish builders operated riding schools (Street 2011, 171).

Figure 1.14 Johnson's ladies' velocipede of 1819 (Roger Street).

Johnson's ladies' velocipede had the armrest extended downward to form a stomach support. An example is held by the Science Museum of London.

With the once-pressing need to replace the horse already forgotten, the velocipede found new uses in the United Kingdom. Davies commented on some of these in his 1837 lecture:

> I am acquainted with individuals who went with their velocipedes from twenty to thirty miles in a day on excursions into the country, and many young men were in the habit of riding sixty miles or more in the course of a week. It is easy to see how beneficial this exercise must have been to the health of the riders, who were generally inhabitants of cities, and often occupied during the day in sedentary pursuits connected with the business. . . . Some cases were presented for admission at the public hospitals, arising from mismanagement and falls. . . . Men who might have been perfectly secure if they had been content to go at an easy pace at first, until they got accustomed to the motion, would mount and try to run as rapidly as possible along a gravelly road full of loose stones, and suffered from the violent exertion.

This account puts into perspective the argument that ruptures or hernias were the main reason for the demise of the velocipedes, as Roger Street supposed in his book *Dashing Dandies* (2011, 91). But not every contemporary account shared that view. "Mr. Roberts says that the great objection to its general use was the 'tendency it had for rupturing,'" Charles Spencer wrote (1883, 19), "but I used it, more or less, for years."

Because their prices (£8–£10) put them beyond the reach of the working class, velocipedes soon became status symbols among young noblemen. Riding on the sidewalks and colliding with pedestrians didn't win the young dandies many friends. Envy and resentment were partly responsible for opposition to velocipedes and their riders. Caricatures were also partly responsible. Reportedly the caricaturist Robert Cruikshank and his printer, James Sidebethem, clad as dandies, collided while riding their velocipedes down Highgate Hill, and Sidebethem later died. This unfortunate chain of events was seen as the main reason for the velocipede's loss of popularity. Cruikshank's numerous droll sketches of dandies on velocipedes made the machines and their riders a laughing stock (Spencer 1883, 15–17; also see appendix B below).

On the basis of a Pavement Act already in force, magistrates forbade riding on the sidewalks (known in Britain as "pavements"), fining violators £2. Yet velocipedes couldn't be ridden safely on the carriageways. "Why, the steam engine itself never could have stood against so powerful and united a body!" Davies commented (1837). When Drais traveled to England to demonstrate his punched-tape stenographic machine in 1832, he authorized construction of a second-generation draisine in the forlorn hope of convincing the editor of *Mechanics' Magazine* that the time had come for a revival (Drais 1832).

Figure 1.15 A second-generation Johnson velocipede of 1819 (Alan Osbahr).

Early velocipedes in the United States

An early report of Drais's earliest spin out of Mannheim and back appeared in the Philadelphia newspaper *Poulson's American Daily Advertiser* on November 7, 1817; apparently it had no practical consequences. The first American advertisement for a velocipede seems to have appeared in the *Baltimore American and Commercial Daily Advertiser* on May 5, 1819; in it one James Stewart, renowned for his fine piano workmanship, offered a new mode of travel under the name Tracena (derived from a phonetic spelling of "Drais"). Apparently inspired by Stewart's ad, Charles Willson Peale, a famous portraitist of American presidents, built himself a velocipede, using iron taken from a threshing machine on his farm near Philadelphia. Peale was also inspired by an illustrated article in the *Analectic Magazine* of June 1819, which had been copied from a British booklet put out by a London printer (Fairburn 1819). The velocipede became the star attraction at Peale's museum in Philadelphia, and soon his sons were building lighter wooden velocipedes and riding them on the farm and in Germantown. The novelty was replicated by wheelwrights along the East Coast as far north as Boston (Dunham 1956, 35). According to the few surviving advertisements, all the machines were similar to Johnson's. According to an unidentified period source, Denis Johnson sailed from London to New York to promote his velocipede (Street 2011, 54). An inventor named William Clarkson obtained a patent (alas destroyed in a fire at the patent office) for "an improvement in the velocipede" on June 26, 1819. According to Norman Dunham (1956, 42), an amphibious velocipede was built in Kentucky.

Upon its introduction in New York, the velocipede created great excitement. Evidently manufacturers were unable to meet the demand for some time. Daring individuals rode at nightfall along the Bowery to Vauxhall Gardens, and even bolder ones descended the hill from the beginning of Chatham Street to City Hall Park. An exhibition center for the new machines was opened near Bowling Green. Many riding schools started up in nearby eastern cities. In upstate New York, newspapers reported appearances of velocipedes in Troy, Saratoga, and Hoosick Falls. In New Haven, Connecticut, "sundry wild riders" were reported to be "in the habit of dashing along the side-walks . . . after dark, with such heedlessness and impetuosity, as to annoy all who have not, like themselves, the good fortune to be mounted on wooden horses" (Dunham 1956).

In June of 1819, after news of London's clampdown on velocipedes had arrived in the United States, an old pavement ordinance was invoked and a young man in Philadelphia was fined $3 for riding on a sidewalk. Although the offense had hardly been within the intent of the law, that case brought an end to the use of velocipedes in Philadelphia. The use of velocipedes was prohibited in New York, and New Haven threatened similar action. Reports that Harvard University students rode velocipedes on the bridge between Boston and Cambridge at night suggest that riding may have been forbidden there too.

THE CLAMPDOWN ON TWO-WHEELERS AND THE RETURN TO MULTI-TRACK VELOCIPEDES

The suppression of riding by the authorities seems to have been the main reason for the demise of the velocipede, not—as Herlihy (2004, 30) supposed—the vehicle's technical inferiority. Bans are known to have been instituted in the following places (Lessing 2003b):

Mannheim (by December of 1817)

Milan (in September of 1818)

London (in March of 1819)

Philadelphia (in June of 1819)

New York and New Haven (later in 1819)

Calcutta (in May of 1820).

The tendency of historians to neglect the ugly aspects of administration may explain the brevity of the above list. Blocking the use of sidewalks forced velocipede riders onto the carriageways, where balancing their machines was difficult. This same pattern of suppression repeated itself in a clampdown on cranked velocipedes in 1870.

THE FIRST ROLLER-SKATE PATENTS

Though its own initial success was short-lived, the velocipede encouraged an alternative mode of personal transport: roller skates. In 1819, a year after the arrival of draisines in France, a mechanic named Petibled tried three-wheeled roller skates on the boulevards of Paris (Ginzrot 1830, volume iii, 329). However, the wording of his patent indicates that Petibled's main aim was for the skates to be used in a more controlled environment. French patent 383 of 1819 included a "description of skates to perform indoors everything that can be done by the skaters on ice with ordinary skates." The rollers were made of metal, wood, or ivory. Five years after the arrival of draisines in England, a fruit merchant in London, Robert John Tyers, patented an in-line roller skate, called the Volito (Latin for "I am floating"), with five copper or cast iron rollers in series and a stop or brake at the end (British patent 4,782 of 1823). Tyers is reported to have set up a roller-skating school on a tennis court near London's Haymarket (Nieswizski 1991, 20).

In 1825, seven years after the debut of draisines in Vienna, a Viennese watchmaker named August Löhner obtained a patent (Austrian patent 598) for three-wheeled "mechanische Räderschuhe" ("mechanical wheel shoes") (Norden 1999). In 1828, Jean Garcin, who ten years earlier had imported draisines into France, invented a three-wheeled in-line skate (French patent 2,026), which he called "patin à éclisses" ("skate with splints"). The rollers were made of

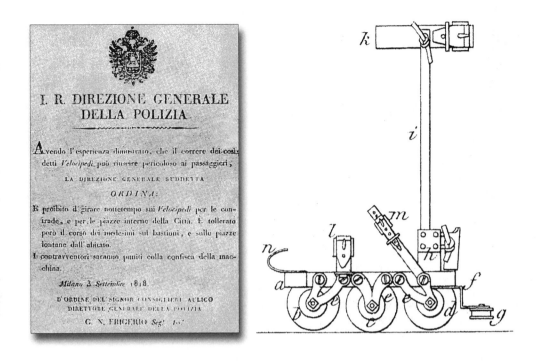

Figure 1.16 Left: A police poster from 1818 announcing that the velocipedes of those riding at night in Milan would be confiscated (Gardellin 1941). Right: Jean Garcin's "Cingar" in-line roller skate of 1828 (patent drawing).

copper or horn. Although his patent was voided four years later because of the prior claim of Petibled's patent, Garcin manufactured his "Cingars" (a play on the spelling of his name) until 1839 and taught roller skating in his own school (Nieswizski 1991, 21). But except for some bold early adopters, roller skating appears still to have been restricted to indoor halls and to theatrical simulations of ice skating.

The velocipede seems to have stimulated the invention of what later would become the scooter (Lessing 2003a, 368). The German theater architect Carl Ferdinand Langhans, a son of the architect of Berlin's Brandenburg Gate, experimented in 1817 with a three-wheeled draisine, which he steered while standing on it with one foot and propelling it with the other (Krünitz 1850). In 1825 an anonymous contributor sent the editor of *Mechanics' Magazine* a picture showing a kind of rigid in-line skateboard on which one foot is placed while the other foot scoots forward.

STABLE VELOCIPEDES FOR ANXIOUS RIDERS

Although young ice skaters took to draisines or velocipedes easily, the majority of Europeans weren't athletic and were extremely timorous about balancing on two wheels. After all, they hadn't learned to do so as children, as most people now do. As early as the summer of 1817, a Nuremberg mechanic named Carl Bauer turned his attention to the old idea of a three-wheeler moved by arm power and levers, with the legs inactive in stirrups. Bauer produced a booklet on Drais and his machine (Bauer 1817) that included a copy of Drais's copper plate before Drais himself could publish such a booklet. We have two letters in which users of drai-sines mention that they or their acquaintances had tested Bauer's three-wheeler and that the results had been poor. Apparently three-wheelers were expected to be more stable than two-wheelers without too much of an increase in driving resistance. Mechanics also came up with designs for a four-wheeler driven by a hand-cranked belt and levers and for a three-wheeler with a high seat (Lessing 2003a, 166).

In May of 1819, a London coach maker named Charles Lucas Birch built a three-wheeler that he called a Velocimanipede. A man at the front scooted it along with his feet while another man on a low seat at the back turned the rear wheels by means of hand cranks, and there was a high seat for a lady. Birch demonstrated the Velocimanipede before the royal family in Kensington Palace (Street 2011, 143). After the clampdown on riding velocipedes on side-walks, Birch felt encouraged to build some hand-lever-operated three-wheelers. He called one of them a Manivelociter (it had one operator and one passenger), one a Bivector (it had two operators), and one a Trivector (it had three operators). According to a report published in September of 1819, a Trivector covered the 67 miles from London to Brighton within 7 hours. Its large-diameter wheels (3 feet at the front, 5 feet at the rear) allowed it to roll better than a two-wheeler on the carriageways.

Even before the ban on riding on sidewalks, a machine called the Pilentum appeared. A tricycle for ladies made by Hancock & Company in London, it had treadles and handles work-ing on a crankshaft between the rear wheels; "the direction is managed by the centre handle which may be fixed as to perform any given circle" (Street 2011, 137). It isn't known how long such tricycles were used in Britain; interest in railways diverted the interest of the press away from them, so the lack of media coverage is inconclusive.

THE QUADRICYCLE YEARS

The furor that greeted the two-wheeled velocipede in 1819 testifies to Regency England's enthusiasm for new ideas and for the possibility of cheap personal transport. Over the next fifty years, newspapers continued to publish reports of velocipedes' being invented or demonstrated, yet the state of the roads made multi-track machines, like single-track ones, impractical for daily use. By the 1840s, the railway boom had caused the roads to be neglected even more than before. Road maintenance would show no improvement until the late 1870s, when riders of high-wheelers would begin to lobby for better conditions. Despite the lack of any technical breakthrough in velocipede design in these years, a few names from the period deserve mention.

Between 1819 and 1822, Dr. Edmund Cartwright, inventor of the power loom, came up with two designs for what he called a "locomotive carriage" or a "Centaur" (Strictland 1843). Worked by two standing men, it was reported to have carried a load of 16 hundredweight (about 1,650 pounds) a distance of 27 miles. Despite Cartwright's hopes, his experiments died with him in 1823. More than twenty years later, a correspondent to *The Mechanics' Magazine* confused Cartwright's machine with a contemporary quadricycle (probably one made by Willard Sawyer), misleading later cycle historians.

Willard Sawyer, a carpenter in Dover, began to build velocipedes around 1830 (Clayton 2005). His catalogs describe "Velocipedes, double-action self-locomotives, and hand-propellers" — that is, quadricycles driven by foot, hand, or both. Sawyer was awarded a medal at the Great Exhibition of 1851 and subsequently supplied elegant, lightweight machines to the Prince of Wales and the young Prince Imperial of France. He claimed more than forty titled or distinguished patrons, and his marketing was clearly aimed at the country gentleman in his park rather than the artisan. Other quadricycle makers targeting the same small market, including J. Ward of Leicester Square, never quite attained the elegance and lightness of construction that Sawyer did.

Sawyer's quadricycles were expensive. Amateur enthusiasts in country districts saved money by building their own machines (*The Field*, November 15, 1862). By 1860, double-crank rear-axle drive was favored. The debate over the advantages of hand propulsion and foot propulsion continued.

Sawyer's bread and butter was the rental trade at pleasure grounds such as the Crystal Palace in London and at England's South Coast seaside resorts (Clayton 2005). In 1868, Dover magistrates declared his velocipedes a nuisance, so he closed his Dover factory and decamped to nearby Deal. He seems to have achieved little technical progress over a forty-year career. His 1863 catalog showed a "Newly invented Sketching, Angling or Shooting Carriage" with

Figure 1.17 Willard Sawyer on his quadricycle, circa 1851 (Dover Museum).

special fittings for carrying an umbrella, a gun, fishing rods, and sketching apparatus, but this was merely his standard carriage dressed up to appeal to a different market. His machines could be driven by either the rear or the front wheel. As late as 1868, amateur velocipedists were still debating the ideal layout and whether foot or hand drive, or a combination of the two, was to be preferred.

Three-wheeled and four-wheeled velocipedes appeared in rural districts in the 1860s. Their builders shared technical specifications and performance data with other amateur mechanics through local Mechanics' Institute meetings or through specialist magazines. (The earliest of the latter, *The English Mechanic*, published its first issue in November of 1865.) In 1863, Joseph Goodman patented a tricycle that became well known as the Rantoone (British patent 1,280 of 1863, American patent 44,256 of 1864). Manufactured by several licensees, it was propelled by hand and foot levers cranking the rear axle, one of the large rear wheels running free to facilitate turning. The Rantoone had considerable success, winning a race in 1869 at the Crystal Palace against the new French two-wheeled velocipedes (Street 2006).

"THE RANTOONE,"

A SELF-PROPELLING CARRIAGE

(SECURED BY ROYAL LETTERS PATENT),

Manufactured of Wrought Iron in Different Sizes.

DESIGNED FOR YOUTHS AND ADULTS.

Figure 1.18 Detail of advertisement for the Rantoone (Light Dragoon 1870).

Scotland has a long engineering tradition, and Mathew Brown's Edinburgh Tricycle was one of the first tricycle velocipedes to be commercially produced in the British Isles. It was contemporaneous with the arrival of the Parisian two-wheeler (Dodds 1999, 18). Its layout was the reverse of the Rantoone's; it had two steered wheels at the front and a single driving wheel at the rear.

Inspired by articles and letters in *The Mechanics' Magazine* and *The English Mechanic*, enthusiasts in northwest England began experimenting with different styles of velocipedes. In 1860, Mr. A. Rosse of Oswestry encouraged progress by offering a reward to anyone who could design a machine — "preferably a three-wheeler with large diameter wheels" — that "could spin along at seven or eight miles an hour" (*Mechanics' Magazine*, December 14, 1860). In 1862, Mr. Goddard of Stalybridge journeyed 200 miles to the London International Exhibition on a two-man back-to-back hand-lever velocipede. By 1868, a group of riders in Goddard's area had formed England's first cycling club, the High Peak Velocipede Club (Clayton 2006a). From 1867 on, James Hastings and others engaged in lively magazine correspondence, detailing their progress and exchanging ideas. Half-round solid rubber tires for winter use were proposed even before the iron-tired two-wheeled velocipede arrived from Paris (*English Mechanic*, December 27, 1868). Nevertheless, all these ideas for multi-wheeled velocipedes would be swept away by the Michaux two-wheeler, which had already been captivating Paris for a year.

In the years 1820–1860, velocipedes remained a largely British preoccupation. We have very few reports of their use in the United States during those years. (E. W. Bushnell of Philadelphia introduced small coaches for children around 1835; see Herlihy 2004, 57.) In Baden, where Karl Drais had first patented his groundbreaking idea, interest flagged as a consequence of the various bans, although after Drais's return from Brazil there was a revival of children's draisines (Lessing 2003a, 433). Drais continued to promote his draisines as late as the 1830s (*Mechanics' Magazine*, September 29, 1832), by which time he was working on a typewriter, a punched-tape stenographic machine, and a wood-saving stove.

ROLLER SKATING GAINS MOMENTUM

Georges Meyerbeer's opera *Le Prophète*, in which ice skating was simulated on roller skates, scored a European triumph in 1849. A Parisian butcher, Louis Legrand, provided two-wheeled in-line skates—to provide extra stability for ladies and beginners, the rollers were doubled. Covered by a French patent (number 8,758 of 1849), these "Prophète skates" were sold to the public for use in roller-skating schools. How many such schools there were in Paris at the time isn't known. A French book on ice skating published in 1853 includes a picture of a roller-skating couple on a sidewalk (Paulin-Désormeaux 1853).

The increasing popularity of figure skating on ice created a desire to perform the same maneuvers on roller skates. The roller skates that had been constructed so far worked well only in a straight line, and taking curves required the application of great force. An American mechanic and furniture dealer named James Plimpton solved the problem with his "rockable" four-wheeled skates (US patent 37,305 of 1863). Two pairs of parallel wheels, one under the ball of the foot and another under the heel, working on rubber blocks, allowed the user to steer by

....

Figure 1.19 Above: Couple on Legrand rollers on sidewalk (Paulin-Désormeaux 1853). Below: Plimpton rollers were leased at rinks and were not sold (National Museum of Roller Skating).

PLIMPTON'S

CIRCULAR RUNNING ROLLER SKATES

PATENTED:

In United States,	January 6, 1863
Reissued "	April 5, 1870
Reissued "	March 7, 1871
Improved "	June 26, 1866
In England,	August 25, 1865
In France,	October 10, 1865
Improved	October 29, 1869

Also, Patents pending for Mexico, Argentine Confederation, Bolivia, Brazil, Chili, Colombia' Peru, Venezuela, Cuba, Jamaica, Porto Rico, Trinidad, Austria, Belgium, Denmark, Prussia. Saxony, Baden, Bavaria. Wurtemberg, Italy, Portugal, Russia, Spain, Sweden, Switzerland, British India, Ceylon, Cape of Good Hope, New Zeland, &c., &c.

LEASE OF SKATES
FROM
James L. Plimpton,

PLIMPTON BUILDING,
Intersection of Stuyvesant and Ninth Streets, New York.

AND RECEIPT

for amount deposited for rent of same,

B Y

....

....187

No. ....

shifting weight or just by pressing on one side of the foot. This made cornering and curving great fun. Through worldwide licensing of skating rinks at which his roller skates were rented but never sold, Plimpton maintained a monopoly and became a multi-millionaire. Europe's first Plimpton skating rink opened at London's Crystal Palace in 1865 (Nieswizski 1991, 27). The new generation of roller skaters learned to balance with rollers under both feet. For them there was no need to have at least one foot repeatedly in contact with safe ground, as on the draisines of old.

Box 1.3   **PERIOD NON-FICTION PUBLICATIONS UP TO 1823**

German

Johann Carl Siegesmund Bauer. *Beschreibung der v. Drais'schen Fahrmaschine und einiger daran versuchter Verbesserungen*. Nuremberg: Steinische Buchhandlung, 1817. (For a facsimile reprint, see Bauer 1817.)

Die Laufmaschine des Freiherrn Carl von Drais. Mannheim: Schwan & Götz, 1817. (A French edition was published in 1818; for a facsimile reprint, see Drais 1817c.)

British

William Pinnock, *A Catechism of Mechanics: Being an Easy Introduction to the Knowledge of Machinery. By a Friend to Youth*. London: Whittaker, 1823.

Curiosities for the Ingenious: Selected from the Most Authentic Treasures of Nature, Science and Art, Biography, History, and General Literature. London: Thomas Boys, 1821.

Fairburn's Whimsical Description of the New Pedestrian Carriage. London: Fairburn, 1819. (Facsimile reprints are included in Lessing 2003a and in Street 2011.)

FRONT DRIVE

The origin of the idea of attaching cranks to the front axle of a velocipede is the most fiercely debated topic in cycle historiography, and not merely because of the lack of period documentation. As Tom Rolt said (1965), "the reason why the question of priority is so often the subject of heated debate is that an historic invention is never wholly original."

What really was new was balancing while cranking, not the crank itself. And roller skating must have been the forerunner of balancing while cranking: a person who had survived skating with rollers under both feet no longer feared lifting his feet off the ground and putting them on pedals (Lessing 1996). Hand-cranked and treadle-driven sewing machines may have had some influence (Merki 2008, 48).

UNRESOLVED QUESTIONS ABOUT THE ORIGINS OF FRONT DRIVE

Period sources before 1867

A delegation of high-ranking Chinese officials traveled through Western Europe between March and July of 1866. On returning home, Bin Chun presented his travel notes to the court; they were printed in 1868–69. He reported the presence of draisine-style velocipedes in Paris, and also the presence of a new type of velocipede:

> On the avenues people ride on a vehicle with only two wheels, which is held together by a pipe. They sit above this pipe and push forward with movements of their feet, thus keeping the vehicle moving. There's yet another kind of construction which is propelled by foot pedaling. They dash along like galloping horses. (as translated in Moghaddass 2003)

The passage shows some structural similarity to the entry on the velocipede in Littré's 1865 *Dictionnaire de la Langue Française*:

> a sort of wooden horse, placed on two wheels, on which one put oneself into equilibrium, while one gave oneself a forward impulse by the feet. On the modern velocipede the feet are put onto stirrups formed as cranks that make the big wheel turn and provide a high speed. (translated from Robin 2010)

In neither case can we be sure that the "modern velocipede" referred to here had two wheels or three. Many authors, eager to reserve the term "velocipede" for the new cranked two-wheeler, ignored the fact that before 1867 "velocipede" meant a vehicle with three or four wheels unless one specified otherwise. Evidence that the draisine-like two-wheeled velocipede was in use in France a bit later is provided by a patent (French patent 82,137 of 1868) awarded to two citizens of Troyes, Denis Bouvin and Louis Hubert Gilles, for a "vélocipède-parachute"—an "ordinary velocipede" with toe steps and eccentric stabilizer wheels.

The idea of using parallel cranks for propulsion of tricycles had appeared in French patents decades earlier. Jean-Henri Gourdoux of Paris proposed using parallel cranks, not cranks set off 180°, to drive the front wheel directly (French patent 1,585 of 1821), but his design would have encountered a dead-center problem in spite of the sprung strings drawing the pedals upward. A design by Rolland Hubert, also of Paris, used the rider's up-and-down motion for additional drive. The unilateral cranks ended in conventional stirrup irons. Obviously

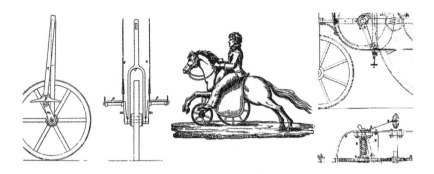

Box 2.1   **THE ORIGIN OF THE ENGLISH WORD "BICYCLE"**

"Les tricycles" had been known in Paris since Christmas 1828, when a new species of carriage, mounted on three wheels and drawn by two horses, had been introduced. (See figure 2.3.) That same year, the noun "bicycle" was used for a cabriolet, a light cab for one to two passengers drawn by a single horse and having two wheels on a single axle (*Journal des Artistes*, July 6, 1828). The earliest use of "tricycle" as an adjective was in an 1867 French patent for "un vélocipède tricycle." The French adjective "bicycle" appeared in the formulation "un vélocipède bicycle" (meaning a two-wheeled velocipede). The English analogs "bicycular" and "tricycular," first used in the United States in formations such as "a bicycular velocipede," gave way to "tricycle" and "bicycle" early in 1868.

the feet pushed these down in unison. Thanks to a ratchet, the rider could bring the stirrups up while pressing the saddle down, thereby operating another crank (French patent 7,243 of 1837). No contemporary report on these tricycles is known.

The earliest evidence of a two-wheeled velocipede with pedal cranks on the front axle is found in the April 6, 1866 edition of *Le Journal de l'Ain*, a newspaper published in Bourg-en-Bresse (Salmon 2012). Le vélocipède bicycle (soon to be nicknamed the boneshaker) might today be seen as leading down the wrong road of front-wheel propulsion. It was, however, a defining step toward surmounting the fear of losing balance or losing contact with the ground. Improvement was rapid thereafter, and cycle development has progressed more or less continually to the present day despite periodic bans by the authorities. The situation before the advent of the cranked two-wheeler is hardly documented at all. We don't know whether draisines and early velocipedes had been in use in Paris, unhampered by any clampdown, since 1818, or whether they had been reinvented in Paris—perhaps because roller skating had become fashionable, or because the young Prince Imperial Napoleon IV had been given a Sawyer quadricycle in 1862 (Lessing 2007). One can only list the small number of sources and discuss their problematic nature.

One trusted source is US patent 59,915, granted to a French immigrant named Pierre Lallement and his American partner James Carroll in November of 1866. A rather ambiguous source is an application by Georges de la Bouglise, a 25-year-old student, to exhibit a

Laissant la rive gauche, qui jusqu'au Jardin-des-Plantes ne nous aurait offert que le vaste entrepôt des vins, établissement vraiment digne d'une grande capitale, nous gagnâmes la rive droite. A défaut de *Tricycle*, autre voiture d'un genre nouveau qui nous est annoncée, nous prîmes un *Bicycle* ou cabriolet, qui après nous avoir conduits dans l'île Notre-Dame, nous remit sur la ligne que suivent les *Omnibus* de la rive droite, par la rue St.-Antoine jusqu'à la Bastille.

SCHNELLFUSZ, *m. schneller fusz, in der wendung* sich auf seinen schnellfusz machen, *fersengeld geben, entfliehen:* der leutenant aber machte sich unverweilet auf seinen schnellfusz. *Simpl.* 1, 204, 7 *Kurz.*

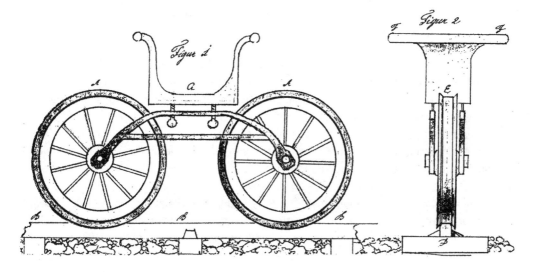

Figure 2.3 Earliest known mentions of "Bicycle" (alias Cabriolet) and "Tricycle" (*Journal des Artistes*, July 6, 1828); entry for "Schnellfusz" in Grimm and Grimm's *Deutsches Wörterbuch* (1854); patent drawing of Bernard's railroad draisine of 1837.

"vélocipède à deux roues" at the upcoming World's Fair in Paris in 1867. That application—dated October 6, 1865, and declined—doesn't mention pedals. The specified size, 1.8 × 1.1 × 0.2 meters, allows only enough space for toe rests, not enough for pedals. We can't exclude the possibility that Bouglise was applying to exhibit a modernized draisine-like velocipede with one-meter solid-spoke wheels and the seat on a serpentine frame, though it has been speculated that he wanted to exhibit a cranked two-wheeler (Kobayashi 1993, 92; Lessing 2007). An American source (Pratt 1883) confirms that French draisine-like velocipedes "lingered, until entirely supplanted, in 1868."

Then there are the letters written to the editor of *The Irish Cyclist*, in the myth-fabricating 1880s and 1890s, by J. Townsend-Trench, who claimed to have bought a cranked two-wheeler from the blacksmith Pierre Michaux in July of 1864 while visiting Paris. But Townsend-Trench was so eager to be acknowledged as the first person to have imported a cranked velocipede to the British Isles (another letter writer had made the same claim) that he paid to have a sketch published. Townsend-Trench may have merely visited the 1867 International Exposition in Paris (Lessing 2007).

A recently discovered 1:10-scale drawing of a velocipede in a notebook for the 1863–64 school year by Aimé Olivier, one of the founders of the Compagnie Parisienne, has been interpreted as representing a prototype of the Compagnie Parisienne's cranked velocipede (Herlihy 2001). It shows no cranks, though, and seating a 1:10-scale manikin on what is interpreted as a saddle proves that this was a draisine-like velocipede to be pushed by the feet contacting the ground. Moreover, the swept-back handlebar served to support the underarms, as the balancing board of a draisine did. (The manikin is unable to spread its elbows.) Putting one foot onto a virtual pedal shows that operating it would have entailed a painful rise of the thigh (Lessing 2002). The conclusion is that the Oliviers first worked on a draisine-like velocipede in 1863–64, perhaps as a preliminary effort or perhaps just for the purpose of learning to balance. Besides, the drawing wouldn't show a third wheel if there was one on the rear axle, so even a foot-pushed tricycle may have been intended. The associated calculations speak of wheels of fir and spokes 10 millimeters thick. The scribble of a front fork in an October 1864 entry in the diary of Aimé Olivier's father, Jules, titled "fourchette du vélocipède" (Reynaud 2008), doesn't make clear whether the vehicle for which the fork was intended was to have two wheels or three. It shows a toe rest 23 millimeters wide, not a pedal on a crank arm. (See figure 2.5.)

Figure 2.4 Pierre Lallement and his US patent of 1866 (portrait from *Outing and the Wheelman*, October 1883).

P. LALLEMENT.
VELOCIPEDE.

No. 59,915.

Patented Nov. 20, 1866.

Inventor.
Pierre Lallement
Bhis atty
John E. Earle

N. PETERS CO., PHOTO-LITHO., WASHINGTON, D. C.

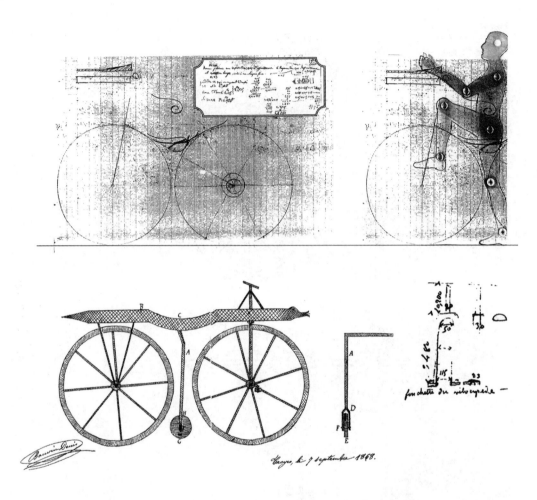

Figure 2.5 Above: A notebook drawing made by Aimé Olivier in 1863 or 1864, with notes and a manikin added. The manikin proves that the machine had draisine ergonomics. Below left: a 1868 velocipede/draisine patent drawing showing toe rest and starter wheels. Below right: a 1864 entry in Jules Olivier's notebook showing a fork and a toe rest. (Drawings from Sanderval collection; photo by Claude Reynaud.)

At the London International Exhibition of 1862, the catalog of the London exhibitors J. La Roche & J. Mehew included an entry reading "Velocipede: all the iron-work of tubular iron," which could have meant anything from a draisine-like two-wheeler to a lever-driven quadricycle. Two decades later this was characterized in a journal as follows: "a distinct improvement on all its predecessors, inasmuch as it had the germ of the true principle—a rotating axle, worked by crank action. This machine had three wheels, a large one in front and two small ones behind." (*One and All*, April 17, 1880) That description wouldn't exclude applying levers to a crankshaft between the rear wheels (and Drais had already used such a crankshaft in his Fahrmaschine 2), but a decade later it was interpreted by Lacy Hillier, a racer turned journalist, as follows:

> All the "self-moving carriages" of this early date were to be propelled by levers, but there seems every probability that the credit of first applying the crank action to velocipedes belongs to an English firm, as Messrs. Mehew of Chelsea showed in the Exhibition of 1862 a three-wheeled velocipede, the front wheel steering as in a modern bicycle or the old dandy horse, the other two wheels, which of course were somewhat smaller, being placed side by side behind. . . . This English-made machine was fitted with a pair of cranks to the front-wheel. (Hillier 1891)

This statement should be regarded with caution. Hillier was six years old at the time of London's International Exhibition. His description was summarized in 1928 as follows: "Messrs. Mehew of Chelsea showed a three-wheeler at the Great Exhibition, with a pair of cranks on the front steering wheel." (Lightwood 1928) One would need a picture of a LaRoche & Mehew velocipede (also said to have been present at the exhibition) to be sure that it had cranks with pedals on a single front wheel.

Ex post narratives of the invention

One school of thought suggests that the tricycle with a single crank-driven front wheel originated around 1855–1860, and that the first cranked two-wheeled velocipede probably was developed from one of these around 1862 (Clayton 2006b). Another school suggests that foot-pushed two-wheeled velocipedes abounded, and that one of them was provided with pedal cranks on the front wheel.

With so many questions still open, the best approach—until more evidence for one of the various narratives is unearthed—is to list the narratives in chronological order of appearance. There are, essentially, four written narratives. Two of them go back to times when nationalist priority quibbles were still unknown. Even then, claiming priority or a patent was a matter of dazzling customers and deterring competitors, with no legal consequences if one's claim was untrue.

Narrative A (Pierre Lallement, 1866)

The earliest narrative is attributed to a French immigrant to the United States, a cartwright named Pierre Lallement, who obtained, with an American partner named James Carroll, a patent titled "Improvement in Velocipedes" (US patent 59,915 of 1866). The claim begins as follows: "My invention consists in the arrangement of two wheels, the one directly in front of the other, combined with a mechanism for driving the wheels, and an arrangement for guiding; which arrangement also enables the rider to balance himself upon the two wheels." The patent drawing shows a velocipede that is strikingly similar to later pictures of the first-generation Michaux velocipedes. The Lallement-Carroll patent became important when it was bought by a New York carriage maker named Calvin Witty in February of 1869 and then by the high-wheeler tycoon Albert Pope in 1879. The generality of the Lallement patent allowed Witty and then Pope to collect licensing fees not only from their American competitors but also from every individual importing a bicycle from abroad. In the absence of international patent agreements, it was easy for French manufacturers to ignore this US patent, but presumably its existence prevented the granting of an identical patent in France.

Charles Pratt, a Boston lawyer representing Pope, offered Lallement (who had returned from Paris after an unsuccessful attempt to manufacture velocipedes there) a job with Pope's company. In his notebooks, an English price list of The Patent Velocipede Manufactory P. Lallement is preserved, expressing the claim "Original patentee and manufacturer"—but not "inventor." In his testimony in an 1882 court case, *Pope vs. McKee & Harrington*, Lallement said that in the summer of 1863 he had scrapped his first unsatisfactory prototype in Paris while working for a carriage maker named Strohmaier, had started building a second one in 1865 for his new employer, Jacquier, and had completed the latter in the United States. Earlier he had seen a mechanical horse in a toy shop and a draisine in Nancy, where he had grown up. In response to a blunt question from the examiner, he admitted to having heard of similar designs:

Q: Will you swear that no one at that time ever said anything to you about there being other velocipedes with cranks?

A: Before I made that velocipede I did not see or hear anything about velocipedes with cranks. I did not take the machine and put it in my pocket, I took it on the boulevard and all the people saw it. Some did say they seen some like that before mine. (US Circuit Court, New York, quoted in *The Wheelmen Magazine*, May 1993)

Upon this relativization of Lallement's priority, Pope opted for an out-of-court settlement with his opponents McKee and Harrington (Sauvaget 2000), and in America Lallement's claim to be the inventor was thrown into doubt (*Wheel World*, June 1881).

Narrative B (Pierre Michaux, 1868)

An advertising leaflet that can tentatively be dated to 1868 describes Michaux (who customarily omitted his first name) as "inventor and manufacturer of the velocipede with pedals - patents S.G.D.G. [sans garantie du gouvernment]." The cranked velocipede pictured has two wheels. The claim specifies only a velocipede with pedals, with no hint that Michaux also built three-wheelers. Presumably this publicity was financed by René Olivier (Aimé's brother). A patent application based on the Oliviers' ideas was filed in 1868 under Michaux's name. In 1867, identical short advertisements without the addendum "à pédales" appeared in French gazettes. In fact, at that time Pierre Michaux had no velocipede patent at all; he had only a single patent on articulated shears (French patent 23,576 of 1855), and the pictured prize medals appear to relate to that invention (Herlihy 1994). Perhaps later statements by René Olivier and Henry Michaux that Pierre Michaux had begun building velocipedes in 1855 were intended to steer those who heard them toward that patent. From 1868 on, René Olivier supported Michaux financially, apparently because he needed a front man for his plans. In May of 1868, René registered a company, together with his brothers Aimé and Marius, under the name Michaux et Cie. One explanation for this procedure may be that their father, Jules Olivier, who owned chemical plants around Lyon, would provide funds for his sons only if they didn't use the family's name in their risky enterprise (Herlihy 2010). Presumably the same condition was imposed by René's and Aimé's father-in-law, Jean-Baptiste Pastré, an owner of shipyards in Marseille, who invested even more. In hindsight, the marriages of the Olivier brothers appear to have been strategic ones. Soon Pastré's shipyards were forging the frames of the Oliviers' second-generation velocipedes.

The members of the Michaux family involved are listed as follows:

father Pierre Michaux, blacksmith (1813–1883) Paris

son Ernest Michaux, blacksmith (1842–1882) Paris

son Henry Michaux, manufacturer (1845–19??) Paris.

The better-off southerners are listed as follows:

> father Jules Olivier, chemist (1804–1885) Avignon
>
> son Marius Olivier, engineer (1839–1896) Villeneuve
>
> son Aimé Olivier, engineer (1840–1919) married 1866 a daughter of Pastré
>
> son René Olivier, engineer (1843–1875) married 1867 a daughter of Pastré
>
> father-in-law Jean-Baptiste Pastré (1803–1877), shipping magnate, Marseille
>
> cousin Raymond Radisson, assayer (1831–1903) Lyon.

Also listed—not a relative, but a classmate of René Olivier—is Georges de la Bouglise, engineer (1842–1911).

Narrative C (René Olivier, 1869)

By 1869 there was a rift between the absent Olivier brothers and their *de facto* foreman, Pierre Michaux. The Oliviers' friend Georges de la Bouglise had taken a leave from his studies at the École des Mines to design production tools. The Oliviers dissolved Michaux & Cie. and founded La Compagnie Parisienne des Vélocipèdes in June of 1869. The new company's slogan was "Time is money." Georges de la Bouglise, who had worked without salary but received 5 percent of profits, went back to the École des Mines to complete his studies; reportedly he had no interest in investing (Olivier 1869). Pierre Michaux, who had sold all rights to the new company, founded (with a partner) the Société Michaux-Père et Cie., and continued to produce Michaux velocipedes. The Oliviers sued. In a note to his lawyer, neatly written by a clerk, René Olivier stated his view of the origins of the cranked velocipede:

> A number of years ago a workman [un ouvrier] imagined fitting cranks to the velocipedes of bygone times. I do not know if Mr. Michaux's son had knowledge of the case. What is certain is that, having had at hand a tricycle (velocipede with three wheels), the front wheel of which was fitted with cranks, he dismantled it and transformed it into a bicycle. That is the only invention he ever made, i.e., transformation of a tricycle with cranks into a bicycle with cranks. (translated from Olivier 1869)

Here it was balancing while cranking that was new, not the crank itself. The son was Ernest Michaux, and this version differs completely from narrative E by the younger brother Henry

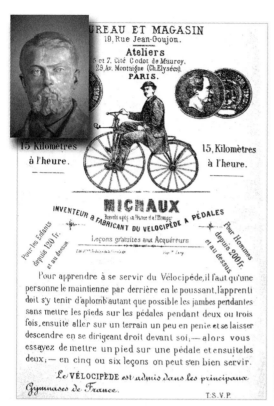

Figure 2.6 René Olivier (shown in photo) used Pierre Michaux as a front man to camouflage his business. (Photo by Claude Reynaud.)

Michaux three decades later. (See below.) But it was repeated in a book only five years later, decades before the nationalist priority quibbles of the 1890s:

> We are told that one day one of those tricycles was brought to the Michaux house, less well-known several years ago, to be repaired. The son of the house plays with the apparatus. Instead of three wheels he puts there only two, and he gets the front wheel going with his feet. He tries, he starts and he falls. He starts again, and his run gets more stable. Each fall fires his courage. (translated from Deharme 1874)

Looking for a plausible invention story, René Olivier apparently had the Compagnie Parisienne's tricycles in mind. The rear fork of one of these was long enough to accommodate a single rear wheel, converting the tricycle to a bicycle once its rider had acquired some confidence. Other tricycles had rather wide and short forks that wouldn't take a large rear wheel; conversion could be done only with a smaller wheel, which resulted in an awkward appearance. In the aforementioned note to his lawyer, René asserted that "all this took place around the year 1854 or 1855" (Olivier 1869). That seems much too early, and Ernest Michaux was only 12 or 13 years old at that time.

Narrative D (Louis Baudry de Saunier, 1891)

In 1890, German cycle journals appealed for donations to support the transfer of Karl Drais's remains to a new cemetery in Karlsruhe and the erection of a tombstone. This generated mixed reactions in France, which had been defeated by Prussia in the French-German war of 1869–70. A journalist named Louis Baudry de Saunier quickly wrote a booklet titled "Histoire de la Vélocipédie" (Baudry 1891) in which he created a fictitious French counterpart to Karl Drais—a Comte de Sivrac, who was said to have preceded Drais by riding a rigid two-wheeler as early as 1791. (An unsteerable two-wheeler can be ridden only by a circus performer.)

Baudry writes about Michaux's repairing a draisine in 1855 and trying to add a drive system to it. A first attempt allegedly involved a rod operated by one hand and linked to a wooden spoke of the rear wheel. This was an approach hitherto unknown even on multi-track velocipedes; it resembled the drive system of a contemporary steam locomotive. Baudry describes the next attempt as again involving a hand-operated rod but this time driving a crank on the front wheel. For the feet not to remain useless, the final step would have been to drive the crank by the feet by means of pedals. The scribble illustrating this is said to be by Michaux and from a German source, cited as *Revue Allemande*. A publication titled *Deutsche Rundschau* contains no pictures at all, and the report is not in it. Another hint led to a letter to the editor of Berlin's *Tägliche Rundschau*—published on August 31, 1890 under the heading "Who has invented the Velocipede?"—that merely reported the four-wheeled carriage of Trexler in 1784 (Matthias Kielwein, personal communication). Thus, again there is a preliminary supposition that Baudry created this scribble himself. (See appendix A below.)

Narrative E (Henry Michaux, 1893)

At Bar-le-Duc, Pierre Michaux's birthplace, a committee planned a monument for him and his son that was dedicated in 1893. As was mentioned above, this was a reaction to the Drais

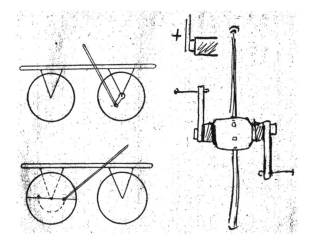

Figure 2.7 Scribble allegedly "attributed to Michaux, after *Revue allemande*" (Baudry 1891).

tomb and monument in Karlsruhe. The Michaux family, represented by Henry Michaux, was asked to publish a statement on the invention, which Henry did in a journal after coordinating his story with the committee, obviously without knowledge of narrative C:

> In March 1861 (and not in 1855), a hatmaker from Rue de Verneuil, Monsieur Brunel, brought his velocifer [draisine] to my father requesting the front wheel to be repaired by my father. The same evening my brother Ernest, aged 19 (and not 14), took the machine and tried it on Avenue Montaigne. On return he told my father in my presence: "I keep myself well in equilibrium, but it is just as tiring to keep the legs lifted as to push on the ground with the feet." My father remarked to him: "Just put two small footrests onto the front wheel, and once started, until you can keep equilibrium, you'll have the legs resting. Or better still: to place the feet, fit a cranked axle into the wheel hub and let it be turned like you turn a grindstone." (translated from *L'Eclair* of March 23, 1893)

So not a tricycle, but a draisine-like two-wheeler is said to have been equipped with cranks. (Henry Michaux was 16 years old in the presumed year, 1861.) Footrests were already known from the Johnson velocipede of 1819. Perhaps Michaux had indeed begun to build draisine-like two-wheelers around 1855, and the example coming in for repair was just one of those. The more realistic year 1861 was also reported in the first edition of *Le Vélocipède Illustré*, dated April 1, 1869.

Narrative F (Raymond Radisson, 1900?)

A 1975 typewritten copy of a presumed prewar manuscript of a family history was found and published in 2010. It contained a section titled "Memories of Raymond Radisson" (Reynaud 2012). Its author was an assayer of gold and silver in Lyon. The text reads as follows:

> In 1854, having traveled to Switzerland to buy scrap gold, I saw a fête at Carrouges. One of the attractions was a race for children above twelve years of age, on little ma-chines made of wood, consisting of a cross-beam to which two wheels were attached, one of which, the front one, could be steered by use of a 'T'. With their feet touching the ground, the children gave a scoot to their machines and arriving at a slope, when they let them go by raising their legs . . . just two steered their mount sufficiently well to make it to the finish. I immediately understood what use could be gained from this apparatus, if one were able to drive one of the wheels so as to keep it turning, even without the slope. And on returning home I started to construct what I believe to have been the first velocipede which had ever existed.

The writer goes on to report that he had presented the machine in a school courtyard in Lyon without yet having mastered it, and had gotten scientifically based comments the next day that he had tried something impossible. But he had persisted, and eventually he had been able to convince the skeptics. He then showed his second prototype to an uncle named Michel Perret, at Tullins, who asked him to make one for his nephew Marius Olivier:

> Briefly, Marius Olivier and his brother André [he means Aimé] set up a factory in Paris to make and sell them, but the business, badly managed, was not a success. An enthusiast changed the system of applying the force and transmitted this to the rear wheel (in my system, I power the front wheel) and gave the name bicyclette to the new machine which has become generally used. But it is the daughter of my bicycle.

This all-French panorama gets by without any foreign pioneers such as Karl Drais or John Kemp Starley, both of whom were well known among cyclists by then. To exclude archival intervention by a later chauvinist, the handwritten original, supposedly from 1900, should be found and compared with Radisson's handwriting. The Olivier brothers, Marius, Aimé, and René, would have been 15, 14, and 11 years old in 1854. That date coincides with narrative C and happens to be just one year ahead of the presumed Fischer-velocipede claim raised meanwhile in Germany in response to the Michaux monument of 1893. (See appendix A.)

Comparing these seven narratives about the application of the crank, we can't help but think that none of the narrators had first-hand knowledge of how the invention really happened. Most of them substituted plausible processes of how it could have come about. More circumstantial evidence will be required even to specify the most likely candidate among the narratives. Our impression is that Georges de la Bouglise deserves more attention as the technical mastermind of the initial project who left—or had to leave—when he was required to invest money that he may not have had (Olivier 1869).

Future research should focus on the other pioneers, including Charles Sargent, a coach maker in Paris. "Around the year 1864," René Olivier wrote in the report for his lawyer, "one of those velocipedes was sent by me to Lyon; one [meaning I] began to copy this model for which Monsieur Michaux had no patent at all (Messieurs Sargent et Maybou on Champs Élysées built these)." (translated from Olivier 1869) Sargent also patented a tandem (French patent 80,091 of 1868) and, in an addendum, a chain between the front crank and the front sprocket (Reynaud 2008, 206). One Sargent velocipede is kept at the Musée Vélo-Moto.

THE FRENCH VELOCIPEDE AND ITS SERIES PRODUCTION

After 1867, there were about 150 makers of vélocipèdes, most of them artisans, in France alone (Reynaud 2008). Most of them copied the leading manufacturer in Paris, who changed identities as follows:

Michaux (?–April 1868) (first-generation velocipedes)

Michaux & Cie. (May 1868–March 1869) (1,860 first- and second-generation velocipedes)

Compagnie Parisienne (April 1869–1874) (2,940 second-generation velocipedes).

These should not be mistaken for other short-lived companies operated by Michaux family members and by Pierre Lallement, including the following:

E. Michaux fils & Cie. (?–April 1868) (four-wheeled velocipedes)

Michaux père & Cie. (June 1869–March 1870) (324 second-generation velocipedes)

The Patent Velocipede Manufactory P. Lallement (Paris, 1869) (second-generation velocipedes)

Cycles H. Michaux & Cie. (Saint Cloud, 1894) (safety bicycles)

The Cycles & Automobiles Michaux Ltd. (Paris, 1894) (safety bicycles).

(In the lists above, the numbers of velocipedes produced are from Kobayashi 2008.)

The first-generation Michaux Vélocipède

The Michaux machine of 1867 was similar to a draisine, but had pedals and a crank attached to the front axle. The frame or perch was serpentine in profile. Because of the larger size of the wheels, its "dent" had to be much deeper than that of the old Johnson velocipede so the rider would be able to reach the ground with his feet. Thus, the rider could learn to balance easily, as on a draisine. Treading the pedals from such a low position was certainly harder than on later models. Pierre Michaux made the frame from D-section malleable cast iron (fonte malléable), the same material he used for his carriage fittings. It was stronger than wood or cast iron, but not as strong as forged steel. Castings were heated in boxes packed with hematite for five to twelve days, which reduced the carbon content to the equivalent of that of wrought iron. The wheels were made of wood. The twisting handlebar operated, by means of a leather strap, a metallic lever, hinged near the center of the frame, that squeezed a brake block onto the rear wheel's iron tire. The earliest machines had a leg rest above the front wheel to keep the legs above the whirling pedals when riding downhill. (See figure 2.10.)

The period designation of the machine has been "vélocipède Michaux." (Present-day collectors use the false neologism "Michauline," erroneously created in analogy to the name "Micheline" for a pneumatic-wheeled railcar built by Michelin & Compagnie in the 1920s; see *The Boneshaker* 168.) An example of such a machine kept at the Compiègne museum weighs 48½ pounds, only 3½ pounds more than a standard draisine. The second-generation models weighed at least 64 pounds, and those of competitors weighed as much as 88 pounds.

The Oliviers' second-generation velocipede

In April of 1868, the Michaux Company was awarded French patent 86,037 for a velocipede design that incorporated the ideas of the Olivier brothers. In an 1869 manuscript titled "Note pour MM. Olivier frères contre M. Michaux," René Olivier credited his brother with some of those ideas and claimed credit for others:

lighter, cord-operated brake with block and tackle (Aimé Olivier)

forged iron instead of malleable cast iron (Aimé Olivier)

diagonal frame that incorporated the rear forks (Aimé Olivier)

slotted cranks for length adjustment (René Olivier)

self-lubricating axle (René Olivier)

self-righting pedals with built-in oil reservoir (Georges de la Bouglise and Aimé Olivier)

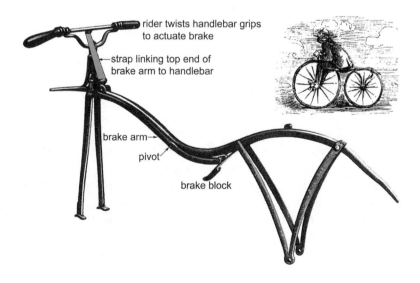

Figure 2.8 Michaux's first-generation serpentine frame (shown here in a drawing by Tony Hadland) let the rider's feet reach the ground. (Original source: *La Vie Parisienne*, March 28, 1867.)

Figure 2.9 One had to use its footboard to mount this second-generation cranked velocipede, made by Michaux & Cie. in 1868 (Alan Osbahr).

Actually, the diagonal frame was used earlier on Cadot velocipedes and Sargent velocipedes. (See above.) The new frame design was suited to the process of wrought iron forging (fer forgé), and the Pastré family, into which both René and Aimé Olivier had recently married, owned large forges in Marseilles. Pierre Michaux was now 55 years old. Although the Oliviers respected him, they considered his marketing and manufacturing methods old-fashioned, and they argued with him over his persisting in the use of fonte malléable and of the serpentine frame geometry. This was just one of the reasons they decided to sever the partnership.

The new frame geometry of the second-generation velocipedes made a decisive change in the machine's handling. Whereas a buyer of a first-generation machine from Michaux was able to learn balancing and riding as on a draisine, a buyer of the new version needed some help at first. The rider sat so high that he could no longer reach the ground with his feet.

Figure 2.10 Various ways of mounting and riding second-generation velocipedes (Steinmann 1870).

Treading the pedals from that higher position was indeed easier ergonomically, but a helper or teacher had to hold the machine for the rider to mount it. There are reports that street boys did this job for a small price. Most velocipede schools let beginners start on low-seat training machines.

Starting and mounting were especially fraught. On stopping, the rider let the machine tilt sideways until he could plant one foot on the ground, as is done by bicyclists today. Reversing this for mounting didn't work, because the inertia of the heavy machine was hard to overcome by mere pressure on the pedals. In turns, the front wheel chafed against the velocipedist's shanks; that required riders to wear high boots. Riding schools sprang up in cities across Europe and the United States, and smaller towns were served by traveling schools.

Daring velocipedists preferred a sometimes painful procedure, explained in these two quotations:

Vault in the saddle while the velocipede is going: Take hold of the cross bar guide handle, and run alongside of the machine till you have a moderate speed, and then spring into the saddle, placing your feet in the treadle and then propelling yourself as before described. When the rider is very proficient, and can vault in the saddle, he can use a larger velocipede, although his feet do not touch the ground, but there is always a little danger in so doing. (Muir 1869)

When the rider comes better to understand his machine, he will mount it by running alongside for three or four yards and vaulting into the saddle, but of course for a tyro to attempt such a method of ascent would be suicidal, and almost certain to end in discomfiture. (Firth 1869)

Well aware of the new problem, Michaux & Cie. supplied overseas customers with a "spring blade" that enabled a novice rider to sit as low as on a first-generation velocipede. The company's brochure *Note sur le vélocipède* quoted a letter to a customer in Indochina:

Because you will have neither teacher nor training machine down there, I have requested that you be sent two demountable spring blades for the seat: one low enough to let your feet arrive on ground before yourself does, if you lack equilibrium. The other less curved one is destined for the practitioner. (translated from Bouglise 1868)

In November of 1868, Alfred Berruyer, a manufacturer in Grenoble, applied for a patent for a spring-loaded side stay and mounting step that would retract when a velocipede began to roll (French patent 83,303 of 1869). Berruyer described it in his *Manuel du Véloceman* (Berruyer 1869). Eighteen patents were granted for start-assist devices in France—eight with the stay fixed below the seat, three with the stay on the front fork, and two with stay on the rear axle. Of the five patents for stabilizer wheels, four put them near the center of the frame and one put them near the front axle (Kobayashi 1993, 150). A mounting step that could be fixed to the rear fork or the rear axle was introduced around the end of 1869. The idea of the foot step, first illustrated in *Le Vélocipède Illustré* of March 17, 1870, has been credited to James Starley of the Coventry Machinists Company Ltd., although the French manufacturer Cadot offered a step a year earlier. The Compagnie Parisienne then offered a footboard that could be installed near the center of the frame on the left side.

The most comfortable way to learn to ride on one's own was to use a front-wheel-cranked tricycle that could be converted into a two-wheeled velocipede when the rider had developed enough confidence. A price list published by the Compagnie Parisienne tells potential buyers that one can convert a CP tricycle oneself into a two-wheeler simply by taking both rear wheels off, exchanging the long rear axle for a short axle, and installing a single wheel within the rear fork (Reynaud 2008, 107). In 1869 the prices of tricycles offered by Michaux & Cie. started at 350 francs; the prices of two-wheeled velocipedes started at 270 francs. It is conceivable that narrative C originated in this method of learning.

A freewheel between the pedal crank and the front-wheel hub would have solved many of the problems mentioned above. Indeed, the second freewheel for a two-wheeler was patented in provincial France. A. Boeuf, a manufacturer in Tarare, advertised some of its advantages: "No more dangerous learning. No more useless movements on descents. Discontinuation of leg rests." Although the Parisian manufacturer Jules-Pierre Suriray won races with a velocipede equipped with a freewheel and bearings, it took three decades for the freewheel to be adopted universally. Presumably to avoid paying royalties and more manufacturing problems, the price list of the Compagnie Parisienne didn't offer a freewheel.

As on today's bicycles, there was no real provision for a passenger. Sitting on the narrow seat spring behind the rider was impracticable. An optional portmanteau could be strapped onto the spring blade and could also serve as a provisional seat. Tandems were offered, but they weighed as much as 150 pounds.

The front-wheel bearings of a velocipede had to be easy running yet tight enough to resist the twisting pressure of the pedals. At first Michaux used plain bushes held by bearing caps. The second-generation model, which became the archetype for copyists, had cast bronze shell bearings held in the ends of the fork by a wedge-shaped key. This enabled the rider to take up play in the shells resulting from wear. The rear wheel ran loose on a bushed fixed axle.

Early road races in France led to experiments with ball bearings. At first the balls were ground by hand. James Moore won the Paris-Rouen race in November of 1869 on a machine whose front wheel was equipped with ball bearings manufactured by Jules-Pierre Suriray (Duncan 1928), the holder of the second French patent on ball bearings (French patent 86,680 of 1869). But the early ball bearings couldn't be easily adjusted for wear.

Velocipedes had wooden wheels with iron hoop tires, in the tradition of carriage wheels. This meant a velocipede was noisy on paved roads and occasionally subject to sideslip. By 1869, makers were offering rubber or leather coverings (already in use on garden phaetons) for the iron rims, some even providing the felloes (rims) with a channel to hold a solid rubber tire. The future aviation pioneer Clément Ader was the first to get "roues caoutchouées" (rubberized wheels) patented (French patent 83,112 of 1868). The Compagnie Parisienne followed suit with rubberized wheels in the addendum of Sept. 6, 1869 to its patent 86,016. Its additional price for such wheels was 20 francs.

Michaux's first brake design used a long double lever, hinged midway on the frame, that was pulled by means of a strap fixed to a revolving handlebar. The 1868 French patent 86,037 had introduced Aimé Olivier's idea for a smaller, weight-saving lever operated from the handle by a cord via a block and tackle. Nearly all manufacturers adopted that arrangement, apparently without paying royalties. The brakes on velocipedes of this era were generally suitable for their purpose, and we find few reports of accidents caused by failure to stop.

French innovations before 1870

Who were the 150 velocipede makers in France? Today many of them are known only from their advertisements in the trade journal *Le Vélocipède Illustré*. Most of them seem to have been associated with the carriage-making trade; others were small ironworkers; others were young enthusiasts, like the Oliviers, who enjoyed the sport and could buy the necessary parts from subcontractors. Typically, production was small—even the Compagnie Parisienne at its peak managed only fifteen machines a day. Manufacture was on the European system, even in America—that is to say, all parts required filing, fitting, and usually numbering before being disassembled for painting and then reassembled. There was no pretense to interchangeability of parts.

In France, 61 velocipede-related patents were granted in 1868, 128 in 1869, and 20 in 1870 (Kobayashi 1993, 149). The Compagnie Parisienne, under its new director Jean-Baptiste Gobert (a classmate of René Olivier), developed and patented many improvements in comfort (French patent 86,016 of 1869 and additions till 1870). Moreover, René Olivier patented "Improvement in Velocipedes" in the United States (US patent 97,683 of 1869); that patent covered essentially the same items as the French patent.

Three systems of suspension for the front wheel were proposed. The first was an auxiliary fork that slid within the outer fork and was damped by a coiled spring within the headset. The second was damped by leaf springs below (or, alternatively, above) the front axle. The third had lenticular rubber springs in the ends of the outer fork above the axle. In fact, the company's price list offers to upgrade existing velocipedes with springing in five variants (designated A to E) for an additional 100 to 230 francs. (See figure 6.18.) The cheapest variant, A, may have been represented by a drawing in a company catalog that shows a hairpin spring leaf placed between the headset and a simple front fork (Reynaud 2008, 124). Moreover, the handlebar was spring-mounted to protect against jolts. All these offers show an eagerness to make the velocipede more convenient for people who hadn't ridden any such vehicle in childhood.

....

Figure 2.11 Diagrams from Ravier and Schmit's undated "Tarif des Bicycles" (reproduced from Besse and Henry 2008).

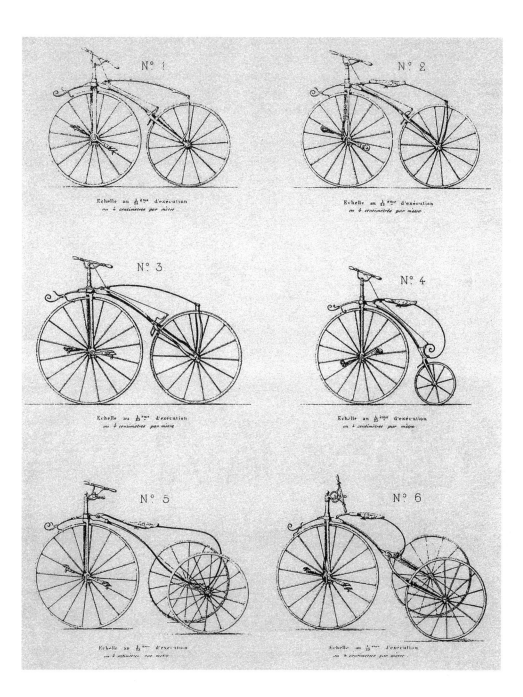

For easy riding on gradients, variation of crank length during riding was offered as an option for 100 francs. By means of a locking latch on the handlebar, the length of a 100-millimeter crank could be increased to as much as 200 millimeters so as to provide leverage for gradients while requiring more legwork. (See figure 7.10.) This was an alternative to a much heavier variable gearing system. No machine with such a crank is extant, but a photo of one exists (Reynaud 2008, 125).

The rear tires of the rubber-tired wheels offered in 1869 deteriorated rapidly under the action of the brake block. The Compagnie Parisienne filed an addendum to its patent 86,016 in September describing a kind of shoe brake pressing onto the ground and lifting the rear wheel instead when actuated by a lever near the handlebar. As might be expected, no machine

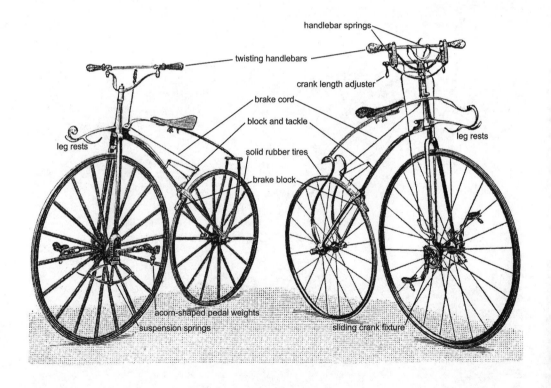

Figure 2.12 Two 1870 Compagnie Parisienne velocipedes, one with wooden spokes and one with wire spokes (Olivier 1892).

with such a device survives; it is well known that a two-wheeler with a blocked rear wheel is extremely hard to balance.

With its addendum of April 1870, the Compagnie Parisienne patented a wire-spoke wheel.

The Compagnie Parisienne stayed at the cutting edge of technology, catering mainly to well-heeled sportsmen and to racers. At the other end of the market, some firms were now producing machines that lower-class workers could afford; some were priced at only 150 francs. This was the end of the elitist era of the velocipede. By the end of 1869, enthusiasm was waning in France, and *Le Vélocipède Illustré* (the country's first cycling periodical), which had been in print for only a year, was suggesting that the future might lie with tricycles. In some place (for example, within Troyes in the summer of 1869) velocipede riding was prohibited by local ordinances. Roller-skating rinks, which held masked balls and other social events, stole the show from the velocipede. "Roller skating is the fashion," a booklet on the subject declared. "It has succeeded the velocipede advantageously." (Mouhot 1876) But in August of 1870, before the contest could be resolved, the Franco-Prussian War erupted. Bicycle racing ceased, the bicycle factories of Paris were requisitioned, and England (particularly Coventry) became the new center of cycle development.

DIFFUSION TO EUROPE AND AMERICA

International visitors to the 1867 exposition in Paris took reports (and a few velocipedes) back to their home countries, and velocipede mania rapidly spread around the world. It was a more substantial phenomenon than the draisine craze had been 50 years before, not least because populations and towns had become significantly larger.

Velocipedes in North America

New York was one of the first cities to be infected. In the spring and the summer of 1868, riding schools sprang up. Encouraged by the magazine *Scientific American*, local manufacturers applied for patents for fifty improvements within two years (Sanderson 2009). Henry Laurence of New Orleans was awarded a patent for retractable stabilizer wheels (US patent 92,462 of 1869). The New York carriage builder and entrepreneur Calvin Witty purchased the 1866 American patent of the French immigrant Pierre Lallement and applied a stranglehold on the trade, demanding royalties from manufacturers and even on private imports. Under different

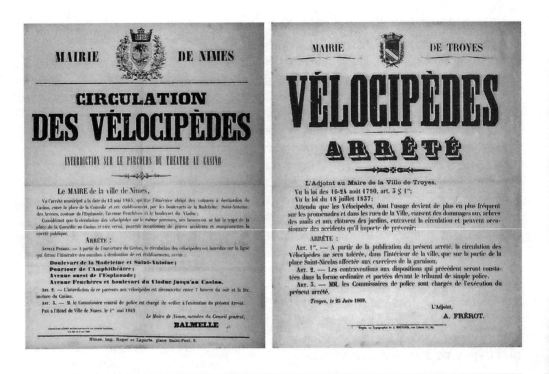

Figure 2.13 Two 1869 ordinances prohibiting velocipeding, one from Nîmes and one from Troyes. (Source: Musée Vélo-Moto Domazan. Photo by Claude Reynaud.)

Box 2.2   **THEORY OF THE VELOCIPEDE**

In August of 1869, *The Engineer* published the first in a series of articles on the theory of cycling by William John Macquorn Rankine, Professor of Engineering at Glasgow. The following year, Rankine's articles were published in French as *Théorie du Vélocipède* (Rankine 1870). Rankine arrived at a conclusion that Drais had already stated: that in order to maintain balance one has to steer into the side to which the velocipede begins to lean. Yet he added the

Box 2.2
(continued)

observation that this also serves to maneuver the line (connecting where the wheels contact the ground) underneath the center of gravity again. Moreover, he arrived at the conclusion that the velocipede doesn't roll in a straight line but in a wavy one. In another series of articles, Jean-Baptiste Gobert, director of the Compagnie Parisienne, expanded on this and arrived at the conclusion that a velocipede's suspension diminished its rolling resistance (Gobert 1870). In 1873, Alphonse Marchegay, a mining engineer, published his *Essai théorique et pratique sur le véhicule bicycle (vélocipède)* (Marchegay 1874); its three parts addressed the bicycle's dynamics (i.e., keeping balance), its applied mechanics (measurable resistances), and its human mechanics (rider requirements).

Since the days of Rankine, Gobert, and Marchegay, a considerable number of thinkers have tried to understand how a bicyclist maintains stability. (For a recent historical review, see Meijaard et al. 2011.) One American writer insisted that a bicycle was kept erect merely by keeping its point of support under it (Warring 1891). However, the 25-parameter model of the bicycle used by a research group in Delft (van Dijk 2007) predicts that at speeds greater than 0.7 kilometer (0.4 mile) per hour the centrifugal effect is always greater than the effect of shifting the support point. Warring strongly denied the importance of gyroscopic effects from the wheels in staying upright. This appears justified in light of the Delft researchers' model, which even stayed stable without a rider and with tiny wheels of inconsequential inert mass.

A true gem of the technical literature is Archibald Sharp's *Bicycles and Tricycles: An Elementary Treatise on Their Design and Construction* (1896, reprinted by the MIT Press in 1977). Sharp was an instructor in engineering design at the Central Technical College in South Kensington and also a patent expert with some inventions to his credit. A comparable book— *Bicycling Science*, by Frank Rowland Whitt (a British chemical engineer) and David Gordon Wilson (a professor of Mechanical Engineering at the Massachusetts Institute of Technology)—was published in 1974; it is now in its third edition (Wilson 2004).

The equation of motion of the bicycle for a simplified case, on a level road with the front wheel locked straight and ignoring the ever-present wind plus rolling resistance, can be solved without a computer (Liesegang and Lee 1978):

Box 2.2
(continued)

$$\text{Acceleration} = \frac{d^2x}{dt^2} = \frac{RFp(b\,/\,B)}{MR^2 + 2I} = \frac{F\,(p\,/\,R)(b\,/\,B)}{M + 2I\,/\,R^2} = \frac{\text{Effective thrust}}{\text{Effective mass}},$$

where

F = force on pedal,
p = length of effective pedal arm,
b = radius of sprocket,
B = radius of chainwheel,
R = radius of wheel,
M = mass of rider plus bicycle,

and

I = moment of inertia of wheel.

With Newton's law (force equals mass × acceleration) in mind, the above can be regarded as the division of an effective thrust $F(p/R)(b/B)$ by the effective inert mass $(M + 2I/R^2)$ of the bicycle and the rider.

If one subdivides mass M into $M^* + 2m$, where m is the mass of one rim plus tire and M^* is the total mass less rims and tires, and inserts for the wheel the moment of inertia of an annular mass,

$$I = mR^2,$$

one obtains for the total effective inert mass

$$\text{Effective mass} = M^* + 2m + \frac{2mR^2}{R^2} = M^* + 4m,$$

with the result that the mass of the rim plus the tire enters exactly four times (twice per wheel). Thus, lighter rims and tires require less power to accelerate.

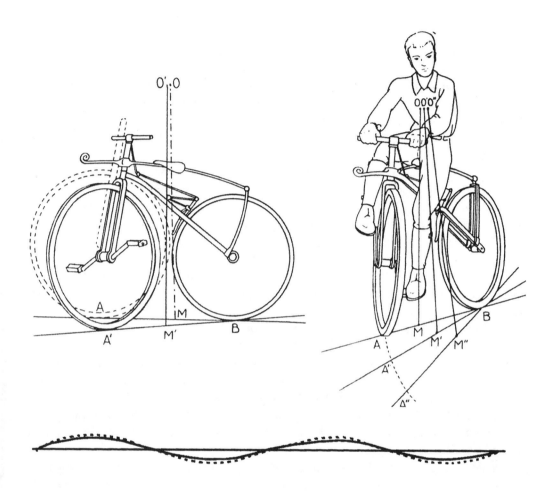

Figure 2.14 If center of gravity O topples to O' above M', steering in the same direction realigns the line A'B through M' again (Baudry 1925). Below: Resulting wiggly trace of both wheels (Rankine 1870).

ownerships, the Lallement patent controlled the American bicycle trade for more than ten years. (We know of no business conducted by Pierre Lallement and his partner James Carroll of New Haven after 1866.)

The Hanlon brothers, circus performers, raised interest with their stunts on French veloci-pedes and patented a very basic machine based on the first-generation Michaux velocipede (US patent 79,654 of 1868). Calvin Witty (who had acquired the Lallement patent) and some other New York carriage builders stepped into the new business and tried to improve on the French design.

US patent 86,235 of 1869, granted to Dr. William Laubach of Philadelphia, provided for a frame pivoted in the middle so that the rims of the front wheel wouldn't chafe the rider's legs during turns. Laubach claimed that his frame was perfectly stiff and that his machine weighed only 50 pounds when equipped with wheels 3 feet in diameter. The seat was suspended by a coil spring and was low enough to allow the rider to put his feet on the ground easily. Laubach sold the patent to the Pearsall brothers, operators of New York's first and most successful velocipede school. With $300,000 in capital, they formed a company to manufacture Laubach patent velocipedes. At least one machine is conserved at the Smithsonian Institution (Oliver 1974).

Thomas Pickering of Pickering & Davis, carriage builders in New York, introduced gas or steam tubing for the backbone and the wheel forks of an "improved velocipede" (US patent 88,507 of 1869). This saved weight, and the hollow spaces in the front fork served as oil res-ervoirs for continuous lubrication of the front axle. Production models offered under the trade name American Bicycle had a brake block fastened at the end of the seat's spring blade; the rider could actuate it by moving his weight backward. Pickering patented a triangular pedal three months earlier than the Olivier brothers. At least nine Pickering velocipedes still exist (Pickering 2009).

Joseph Irving, assignor to the carriage builder A. T. Demarest & Company of New York, provided a 45° steering column that made it practicable to mount a front wheel with a diameter as large as 50 inches (US patent 89,149 of 1869). A rider on a 45-inch Demarest achieved a speed of 33 miles per hour (Sanderson 2009). The front brake and the leg rest moved with the deflected front wheel. The seat was low enough to let the rider's feet reach the ground. This Improved American Velocipede showed the most sensible way to avoid the mounting and handling problems of the second-generation French velocipedes.

William Racey obtained a patent for an original way to ease mounting, and make riding more social, by bolting two velocipedes together in parallel (US patent 90,302 of 1869). This idea reappeared from time to time, but the ideal of a "bachelor machine" began to prevail.

The use of a freewheel within the front-wheel hub, patented by William van Anden (US patent 88,238 of 1869), allowed the rider to mount a velocipede by standing with one foot on

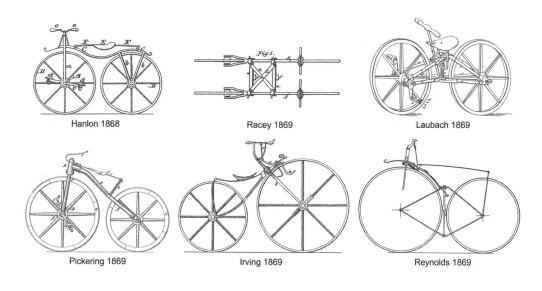

Hanlon 1868   Racey 1869   Laubach 1869

Pickering 1869   Irving 1869   Reynolds 1869

Figure 2.15 American and British patent drawings for velocipedes.

a pedal. (See figure 7.2.) This design was used on a machine made by Dexter, one example of which is held by the Smithsonian Institution.

In 1869 there were said to be 16,000 velocipedes in New York (*Galaxy Magazine*, April 1869). Yet, just as in 1820, city ordinances of 1869 forbade velociping on the sidewalks of New York and elsewhere on the East Coast (Dunham 1956, 111). Some artisans built cranked velocipedes in Canada, but no manufacturer produced them in numbers (Norcliffe 2001).

Velocipede mania ended in North America at the same time as in France: around 1870. However, in 1879 John Shire of Detroit was granted a patent on a wooden machine that was similar ergonomically to the Demarest machine (US patent 216,231 of 1879). At least two of these machines are extant.

Velocipedes in England

At the close of 1868, the cranked velocipede crossed the Channel to England. Perhaps the first the British public heard of it was a report in the *Times* of February 19, 1869 of a ride by three young men from London to Brighton—a story subsequently syndicated in 300 local papers. One of the three, Rowley Turner, was a nephew of Josiah Turner, manager of the Coventry Sewing Machine Company Ltd. and the Paris agent for that company's sewing machines. His proposals diverted the company into velocipede manufacture, effectively starting Coventry's long involvement with bicycles.

Rowley Turner, who had learned to ride at Pascaud's gymnasium in Paris, planned to use Coventry's idle engineering capacity to supply velocipedes for his new agency, Turner & Cie., and to market them as Vélocipèdes Américains. Demand blossomed in England, and new companies (listed in Clayton 1987b) entered the market. The second-generation C.P. model that Turner brought to England in November of 1868, which had a diagonal frame patented by the Oliviers, became the pattern for English copyists.

The first English velocipede patent of 1869 was registered on January 2. By September of that year, more than a hundred patent applications related to velocipedes had been filed. Surprisingly, none of the new ideas did much to make the velocipede more practical. It remained a recreational toy for young, athletic middle-class males. Weighing 80 pounds, it was hardly suitable for relaxation, for business, or for travel on the poorly surfaced roads of the day.

One improved velocipede, perhaps inspired by the American Laubach velocipede introduced three months earlier, was the Phantom, whose design was patented by Reynolds & Mays of London (British patent 1,216 of 1869, French patent 85,885 of 1869). The French cycle trade paper described it as follows:

> The axles of the two wheels are joined by an irregular rhomboid frame, the two obtuse angles of which are mobile horizontally around a vertical axle. This axle divides the rhombus into two parts or unequal triangles, which swivel on the common base and can fold onto one another so that the two wheels of the system can even come into parallel alignment. (translated from *Le Vélocipède Illustré* of July 26, 1869)

The Phantom was the first machine with wire-spoke wheels in the United Kingdom. (Beck & Candlish of New York produced Phantoms with wooden wheels until 1875.)

Although more than a hundred suppliers jumped into the marketplace, at the end of 1869 the new craze was already on the wane nationwide. The *Manchester Evening News* ran no velocipede advertisements in the spring of 1870; the previous spring it had run more than 200.

As in France, improvements stemming from racing eventually saved the day. England wasn't involved in the Franco-Prussian War. Moreover, this time English authorities did little to ban velocipede riding.

Velocipedes in Austria, Germany, and the Netherlands

In the Netherlands, several manufacturers began to produce copies of the Michaux veloci-pede, among them J. T. Scholte of Amsterdam in the autumn of 1868. Hendricus Burgers, a blacksmith from Deventer, with the help of a companion named van der Beld, began doing so in 1869 (Moed 2008). Forty cranked velocipedes have survived in the Netherlands.

Two officials responsible for the encouragement of trade, one from the Grand Duchy of Baden and one from the Kingdom of Württemberg, ordered velocipedes while in Paris for the International Exposition. These orders were reported in trade journals, and the velocipedes were exhibited in trade museums, encouraging local tradesmen to begin manufacturing them (Lessing 2010). In fact, the first of about thirty German manufacturers, Carl Friedrich Müller, started in 1868 in Stuttgart, the capital of Württemberg (Kielwein 2010). In Mannheim, on a velocipede made in Stuttgart, the automobile pioneer Karl Benz taught himself to ride within two weeks. In later interviews he stated that his exhilarating experience on the ve-locipede changed his plans: rather than a steam street locomotive for collective transport, he would build a light velocipede for motorized personal transport (Lessing 2010). Another known velocipede manufacturer, Heinrich Büssing in Braunschweig, also produced veloci-pede carousels in 1869.

In larger towns, velocipede clubs were formed to counter harassment by the authorities and outright bans on riding. (The city of Cologne forbade velocipeding altogether from 1870 until 1895.) Several velocipede tracks were built, not just for races but also simply to enable people to use their machines outdoors. Because of the harassment, the bans, and the compe-tition from roller skating, all the German manufacturers had closed down even before the onset of the Franco-Prussian War. In Vienna, Friedrich Maurer, who had promoted and sold Michaux velocipedes, switched to promoting roller skating (Norden 1999).

WHY NOT DRIVE THE REAR WHEEL? WHY NOT USE STEAM OR ELECTRIC POWER?

Patented concepts sometimes get way ahead of the practical possibilities of their realization. With velocipede mania fading rapidly, this happened with two ideas.

VÉLOCIPÈDES

für Erwachsene und Kinder
aus der Fabrik von
J. KOTTMANN
in
OEHRINGEN
WÜRTTEMBERG.

Geschwindigkeit 4 Stunden oder 15 Kilometer in einer Stunde.

Sämmtliche Vélocipèdes sind dauerhaft und solid gebaut, elegant lakirt, mit Bremse, elastischen gepolstertem Sattel und verstellbaren Fussstritten

Bei Bestellungen bitte ich das Längenmaass der Beine im Schritt gemessen anzugeben.

Bestellungen werden möglichst prompt effectuirt.

Vélocipède mit 2 Rädern, verstellbarem Sattel u. Patentfussritten in 6 Grössen. Fig 2.

Vélocipède mit 2 Rädern in 6 Grössen Fig. I.

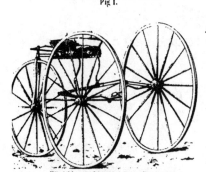

Vélocipède mit 3 Rädern in 4 Grössen, Kurbelbewegung, für 1 u.2 Personen. Fig.IV.

Vélocipède mit 3 Rädern in 6 Grössen für 1 Person. Fig. III.

Rear-wheel-drive velocipedes

With the pedaled front wheel chafing the rider's legs, and with the rider's feet slipping off the pedals on turns, it became obvious that driving the rear wheel rather than the front one was a good idea. The ubiquitous treadle sewing machine, especially the variant with two treadles turning a crankshaft by means of rods, served as a model (Merki 2009, 48).

An inventor named K. J. Winslow devised the first rear-wheel drive for a velocipede (British patent 258 of 1868). Treadles would unspool cords from drums on the rear wheel and would be pulled back by springs made of India rubber. (Here and below, except where we note otherwise, we presume that no such machines were built.) Another inventor, Claude Montagne of St. Étienne, put pivots on the frame so that double levers and rods could be used to drive the rear wheel (French patent 82,885 of 1868). The New York carriage manufacturer Calvin Witty, having acquired the Lallement patent, got a patent for a rod-operated velocipede half a year later (US patent 87,999 of 1869). The patent drawing would have required the rider to draw his knees up to his chin, but was declared to be merely schematic. Benjamin Lawson of New York put the linkage pivot on the steering column, which required reducing the size of the front wheel (US patent 90,563 of 1869). T. Bourne's patent was used by Peyton & Peyton to manufacture their Improved Bicycle in Birmingham (British patent 1,871 of 1869). Their advertisement in *The Ironmonger* of October 30, 1869 touted six advantages, but a surviving machine turned out to be much more awkward to ride than a Parisian velocipede (Radford 2010). Johann Friedrich Trefz of Stuttgart proposed pedal cranks in a hanger driving two cranks on the rear-wheel axle by means of rods (Württemberg patent, 1870). Trefz, who operated a private gymnasium for girls, allowed the patent to lapse when he emigrated to Chile (Lessing 1995). The patent drawing became widely known when it was published in the *Illustrirte Zeitung* of March 5, 1870.

In 1871, Émile Viarengo de Forville, the Italian consul to Nantes from Turin, obtained the following patents:

> French patent 87,869 of 1869, for "a new velocipede system, improving and perfecting the old system" (a spring-suspended velocipede with its rear wheel driven by means of a rod)

Figure 2.16 An undated flyer publicizing a German manufacturer of velocipedes (Technoseum Mannheim/Archiv).

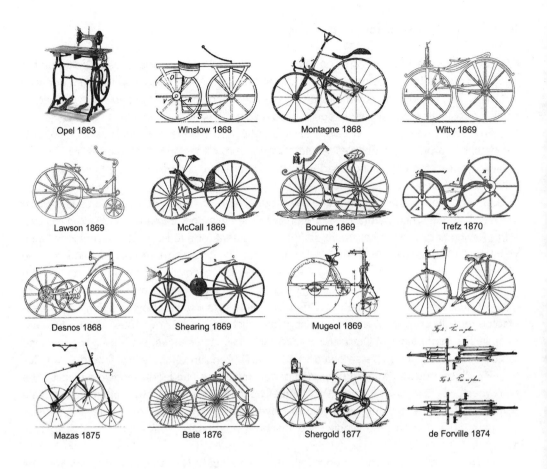

Opel 1863   Winslow 1868   Montagne 1868   Witty 1869

Lawson 1869   McCall 1869   Bourne 1869   Trefz 1870

Desnos 1868   Shearing 1869   Mugeol 1869

Mazas 1875   Bate 1876   Shergold 1877   de Forville 1874

Figure 2.17 Patent and magazine drawings illustrating rear-wheel-drive ideas for velocipedes, some with rod drive and some with chain drive, from 1868–1877 (photo © GM Corporation).

French patent 92,811 of 1871, for a "velocipede system called sprung bicycle with uniform movement and variable speed and perfection of the old system" (a drop-frame velocipede with a pedal-crank hanger, a rear wheel driven by means of rods, two gears, and suspension for both wheels)

French patent 101,848 of 1874, for different suspension, non-180° cranks to avoid a top-dead-center problem, and chain drive

British patent 23,313 of 1895, for an "Apparatus for Changing the Speed Gear of a Bicycle Driving Wheel" by alternately engaging the sprockets of two separate chains.

The French patent agency has, along with these patents, photos of six machines that were actually built—three gents' and three ladies' models. According to an interview published in the issue of *Rivista Velocipedistica* dated May 9, 1895, Forville allowed these machines to be built by a local manufacturer named Louis Gillet:

> News of the invention reached Paris. The son [Henry] of Monsieur Michaux . . . studied my invention and then offered to make it known in England. And indeed he did go to England, with six machines: three ladies' models and three gents' models. I heard no more of that trip. (translated in Reynaud 2010)

For reasons that aren't clear, there was little interest in Forville's bicycles. Perhaps chains good enough for the purpose of driving a wheel weren't available yet; perhaps race-oriented British enthusiasts of high-wheelers weren't interested in a more convenient machine.

There had been earlier rear-wheel-drive patents in France, starting with one for tricycles obtained by Charles Dubos of Bordeaux (French patent 80,106 of 1868). A chain-driven tricycle was proposed in a letter published in the *English Mechanic* of April 16, 1868. Charles Desnos-Gardissal, ingénieur de l'École Centrale of Paris, was granted a patent for a modern-looking rear-wheel drive "by belt or otherwise" using rather large pulleys (French patent 82,082 of 1868). Victor Mougeol's velocipede (French patent 86,676 of 1869) looked a bit like the later Star high-wheeler, with its huge rear wheel and small front wheel. The chain ran on sprockets nearly as large as the wheels. Retractable stabilizer wheels helped the rider to mount the saddle. The Norfolk bicycle presented by Frederick Shearing in the *English Mechanic* of July 30, 1869 already made use of pulleys of different sizes to increase the speed. A year after Forville's chain-drive patent, Louis Mazas, a tradesman in Montpellier, received a patent for a "variant of tricycular velocipede," a two-wheeler with the large pulley carrying the cranks counted as a third wheel (French patent 110,680 of 1875). The transmission of Mazas's machine consists of two cords, presumably of leather, as in most treadle sewing machines.

Mazas also thought of varying the gear by using pulleys of different diameters. A year later, an even bigger cranked pulley for a belt transmission was patented by Henry Bate (addition 1876 to French patent 114,717); it required the machine to be longer than a typical one and to have a small front wheel with bridle (rod linkage) steering from the handlebar. Though no existing belt-drive or chain-drive velocipedes are known, the Science Museum in London has a machine built by Thomas Shergold of Gloucester and dated 1877 on the basis of unillustrated advertisements in the *Gloucester Citizen*. Although it has rubber tires, the rest of the bicycle isn't up to the high-wheeler state of the art in England; it is more in keeping with Parisian velocipede technology (Roberts 1991).

Because their dating isn't substantiated by a period source, two other rear-wheel-drive machines haven't been mentioned. The rod-driven velocipede of the French immigrant Alexandre Lefebvre, kept in the California Bicycle Museum and claimed to predate Michaux, has a straight handlebar and other design elements associated with Michaux (Graber 2002; Ritchie 2002). A so-called Guilmet-Meyer velocipede with chain drive to the rear wheel is kept at the Arts et Métiers Museum in Paris (Clayton 1991; Reynaud 2008). It is crudely designed, quite untypical for the great Eugène Meyer. Because its frame connections are welded, it must have been built after 1892, when welding became known in France (Palmiéri 2007).

Early steam and electric velocipedes

British cartoons indicate that driving a steam-powered draisine was discussed in 1819. (Richard Trevithick had built a steam-powered road carriage 17 years earlier.)

In 1863, Sylvester Roper of Boston, Massachusetts, a budding inventor who would eventually accumulate fifteen patents, reportedly drove a four-wheeled steam carriage. The Smithsonian Institution has a two-wheeled steam velocipede built by Roper, dated circa 1869 (Oliver 1974); because an associate of Roper named Austin sometimes demonstrated it, it is sometimes called the Austin velocipede. The only period mention of a steam velocipede developed by Roper (this one with a single cylinder, whereas the one in the Smithsonian has two cylinders) is in the *American Artisan* of April 27, 1870 (Reynaud 2008, 378–379). The Roper velocipede had a long wheelbase to accommodate the fire-tube boiler with chimney behind the rider. The twisting handlebar not only actuated the brake but also controlled the throttle. The two cylinders pivoted on both sides of the chimney, and the piston rods worked directly on cranks at the rear wheel. (A Columbia safety bicycle in which Roper had installed a single-cylinder steam engine was reported to have achieved 40 miles per hour.)

Much better documented are the motorized velocipedes of Louis-Guillaume Perreaux (1816–1889) of Paris, a versatile inventor, a manufacturer of precision instruments, and the

Figure 2.18 Above: Roper's steam velocipede and Perreaux's electric velocipede. Below: Perreaux's steam bicycle and tricycle.

author of a two-volume work titled *Lois de l'univers—principe de la création* (Paris, 1877). He was awarded the following velocipede-related patents (Reynaud 2003, 59–74):

83,691 of 1869,for a flywheel that could be engaged from the handlebar with a gear-wheel on the front wheel to collect energy on descents and feed it back on gradients

addition of December 1869,f or use of aluminum and hollow parts, tubular spokes, and the freewheel now within the flywheel

addition of May 1870, for use of a battery-powered electric motor to drive the rear wheel by means of gearwheels, wire spokes, and oiling from two reservoirs addition of June 1871, for a high-speed steam velocipede with a brass-plated single-cylinder steam engine with an alcohol burner under the saddle, driving the rear wheel by means of twin belts

addition of March 1872, for better placement of the burner and the boiler, a new flywheel design, adding pedal cranks to the front wheel, treadle drive to the front wheel acting similar to a band brake, lighting the road by means of controlled openings in the chimney, and a tricycle with a steam engine that could be repositioned to warm the driver's feet

U.S. patent 124,621 of 1872, for a steam velocipede with flywheels and various improvements

addition of April 1873, for an improved heater

French patent 167,774 of 1885, for producing dry steam at low pressure.

Perreaux named his enterprise "Perreaux, vélocipèdes à grande vitesse à vapeur." He built several machines, one of them a 135-pound steam bicycle that reportedly achieved 9 miles per hour after warming up for 10 minutes. (One of his machines survives.)

Earlier French patents for electric velocipedes include patent 85,499 (granted to Joseph Marié of Paris in April of 1869 for a magneto-electric velocipede powered by horseshoe magnets surrounding a circular metal ring on the rear wheel) and patent 85,901 (granted to Delaurier and Maurin in June of 1869 for an "electrical velocipede" with the motor used for both acceleration and deceleration). Neither of these designs appears to have been practicable. Even the Compagnie Parisienne had tried the idea of electric power in vain: "An attempt to apply an electric motor to a velocipede has been tried by the Compagnie Parisienne. The project promised good results, but the half-built device had already an inadmissible weight. One had to give it up." (Deharme 1874, 271)

Box 2.3   **PERIOD NON-FICTION PUBLICATIONS UP TO 1872**

French

Bellencontre, Paracelse-Élie-Désiré. *L'Hygiène du vélocipède*. Paris: Le Petit Journal, 1869.

Benon. *Notice sur les vélocipèdes à deux et trois roues et moyens d'apprendre à s'en servir en quelques heures*. Sixth edition. Paris: Guérin, 1869.

Benon. *Origine du vélocipède, le vélocipède actuel*. Paris: Guérin, 1869.

Berruyer, Alfred. *Manuel du Véloceman ou notice, système, nomenclature, pratique, art et avenir des vélocipèdes*. Grenoble: Prudhomme, 1868.

Berruyer, Alfred. *Caducêtres ou jambes-étrières brevetées SGDG pour vélocipèdes*. Grenoble: F. Allier, 1869.

Desmartis, Télèphe Poytevin. *Sur l'hygiène du vélocipède*. Bordeaux, 1869.

Journal de la société pratique du vélocipède, statuts, notice, rapport, procès verbaux des séances. Paris: Brière, 1869–?.

Favre, Alexis-Georges. *Le Vélocipède, sa structure, ses accessoires indispensables, le moyen d'apprendre à s'en servir en une heure*. Marseille: Barlatier-Feissat & Demonchy, 1868.

Lamon, Rémy. *Théorie vélocipédique et pratique, ou manière d'apprendre le vélocipède sans professeur*. Paris: Lamon, 1872.

Le Grand Jacques (Richard Lesclides). *Manuel du Vélocipède*. Paris: Librairie du Petit Journal, 1869.

Le Vélocipède. Journal humoristique. Gazette des Sportsmen et des Velocemen (Grenoble), bi-weekly, no. 1 (March 1, 1869)–no. 6 (May 15, 1869)

Le Vélocipède Illustré. Moniteur de la vélocipédie. Journal bi-hebdomadaire de sciences et d'arts mécaniques (Paris). Editor: Richard Lesclides. Bi-weekly, then weekly, April 1, 1869–August 1871. Reappeared as *La Vitesse. Vélocipédie, sports, aviation* (July 16, 1871–August 13, 1871), then as *Le Vélocipède Illustré* (May 1872–October 1872).

Box 2.3
(continued)

NN (Georges de La Bouglise). *Note sur le vélocipède à pédales et à frein de M. Michaux, par un amateur*. Paris: Lainé/Hayard, 1868.

Rankine, W. J. Macquorn. *Théorie du vélocipède*. Paris: Gauthier-Villars, 1870 (translated from *The Engineer*).

American

Goddard, J. T. *The Velocipede, Its History, Varieties, and Practice. With Illustrations*. New York: Hurd & Houghton, 1869. (Reprinted as National Cycle Archive Publication 9.)

The Velocipedist (New York, monthly, February 1, 1869–?) (facsimile reprints available from La Vélocithèque, Pomeys).

German

de Wesez, Hippolyt (Friedrich Maurer). *Erste deutsche illustrirte Vélocipède Brochüre*. Vienna: Friedrich Maurer, 1869. Pirated translation of Lesclides' *Manuel du Vélocipède*. Facsimile reprint: Edition libri rari, Hannover, 1995.

Steinmann, Gustav. *Das Vélocipède. Seine Geschichte, Construction, Gebrauch und Verbreitung*. Leipzig: J. J. Weber, 1870. Reprint: Hyperion-Verlag, Neufahrn, 2008.

British

B.J.F. [Bottomley, Joseph Firth]. *How to Ride a Velocipede: Straddle a Saddle, Then Paddle and Skedaddle*. London: Simpkin Marshall, 1869. Second edition: *The Velocipede, Its Past, Its Present and Its Future*. Reprint: National Cycle Archive Publication 8.

Davis, Alexander. *The Velocipede and How to Use It*. London: A. Davis, 1868. Reprint: National Cycle Archive Publication 7.

Box 2.3
(continued)

Muir, Andrew. *The Velocipede: How to Learn and How to Use It, with Illustrations, Prices etc*. Salford: Andrew Muir, 1869. Reprint: National Cycle Archive Publication 5.

NN. *The Modern Velocipede: Its History and Construction, and Its Use on Land, Lake, River, and Ocean Practically Explained and Profusely Illustrated by Engravings of Elevations and Constructive Details. Compiled by a Working Mechanic*. London: George Maddick, 1869. Reprint: National Cycle Archive Publication 10.

NN. *The Velocipede: Its History and Practical Hints on How to Use It. By an Experienced Velocipedist*. London: J. Bruton, 1869. Reprint: Cyclists' Touring Club, Godalming, 1972.

NN. *The Velocipede, with Instructions How to Use It, and Descriptions of the Principal Velocipedes Invented Since 1779*. Glasgow: William Love, 1869. Reprint: National Cycle Archive Publication 6.

NN. *Bicycle, or the Wheel and the Way*. London: Phantom and Veloce Car Wheel Company, 1870. Facsimile reprint: Engaging Gear Ltd., Billericay, 2008.

Spencer, Charles. *The Bicycle, Its Use and Action. With Twelve Practical Illustrations*. London: Frederick Warne, 1870.

The Velocipede or *The Velocipede Rider's Magazine*, 1869–? (according to Bartleet 1931, 147; yet untraced)

Velox [Tom Burgess]. *Velocipedes Bicycles & Tricycles—How to Make and Use Them. With a Sketch of Their History and Progress*. London: Geo. Routledge & Sons, 1869. Reprint: Scholar Press, East Andsley, 1971.

Villepigue, M. *Velocipedes, how to learn without a master*. London: Auth 1869. Villepigue, F. F. *The Veloce*. London: The Veloce Company, 1869.

WIRE WHEELS

3

The invention of the lightweight wheel with tensioned wire spokes was crucial to the development of the bicycle. It took half a century for the new thinking that the wire-spoke bicycle represented to permeate other fields, such as architecture. (On "tensegrity," a design strategy that R. Buckminster Fuller began to develop and promote in the 1920s, see Krausse and Lichtenstein 1999.) Tension structures require less material than compression structures and therefore can be lighter.

THE EVOLUTION OF THE HIGH-WHEELER

Larger wheels had less rolling resistance and made it possible to achieve a higher speed with the optimal pedaling cadence. The Crampton locomotives of the 1850s, with their huge driving wheels, were a model.

Compression wheels

Building wooden wagon wheels was the art of local wheelwrights. Bent-timber wheels (also known as patent wheels), which had one-piece wooden rims, were preferred by builders of velocipedes. For cohesion, a bent-timber wheel relied entirely on perfect fit of the parts and on compression by the iron hoop—no glue was used. The weak spot was the hub or nave, ideally made of streaky elm wood to avoid splitting. Nevertheless, the nave had to be held together by small iron hoops. The holes for the spokes were bored precisely; an indexing plate was the preferred tool. The spokes of ash wood were turned a bit larger than the holes; the ends were then heated over fire and hammered into the holes. The heating drove out moisture and let the spoke ends shrink a bit. Once the spokes were in place, the moisture was reabsorbed from the air, swelling the ends again within the holes and providing a perfect press fit. The same procedure was used to fit the other end of the spokes into the wooden rim. The iron hoop was forged to a diameter a bit smaller then the wooden rim, heated in a fire to expand it, and then set around the wooden rim. When cooling, it shrank and pressed the wooden parts together, as well as forming the durable tire of the wheel. In addition, nails or screws through the outer face of the hoop, their heads countersunk into conical holes, prevented the hoop from sliding off the rim.

Since the humidity of the air is subject to daily variations, the parts of the wheel sooner or later worked loose by the jolts from the road. Repairing a wheel that had been loosened on a hot and dry day entailed disassembling the wheel, replacing the worn parts, and applying the hot iron hoop again. There was no way to readjust the parts without disassembly. Operators of the French express coaches called "vélocifères" regarded the wheels as consumable. After 3,000 miles or 42 hours they were exchanged for new ones, the old ones being used up on lighter carriages for local transportation (Ginzrot 1830, volume iv, 55).

The larger the wheels, the longer the spokes, and therefore the worse the lateral stability of the wheels because of the higher leverage exerted by the spokes onto their press fits. Wooden wheels buckled, too. More stability could be achieved with two rows of dished spokes, as in a modern bicycle wheel, but that required a larger hub that wouldn't be weakened by the additional bores. To achieve similar triangulation, for more lateral stability, spokes were staggered

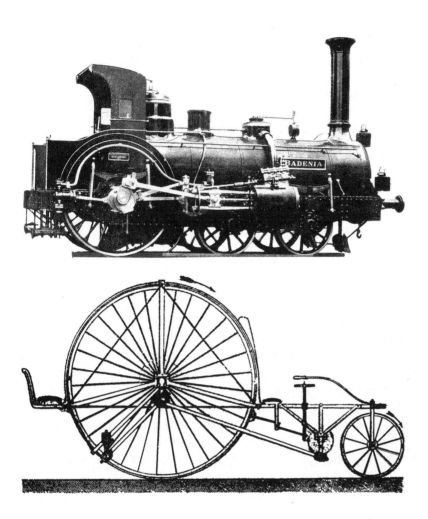

Figure 3.1   Above: a Crampton locomotive of the 1850s (Wikipedia Commons). Below: an 1869 Vélo Vitesse with a 100-inch wheel (Baudry 1891).

alternatively on the hub, as in the original draisine. Some of these problems could be avoided by using metallic hubs that didn't split and weren't deformed by humidity. Once metal hubs had been introduced, the adoption of metal compression spokes followed. Six French patents were granted in the 1860s (Kobayashi 1993, 161):

76,455 of April 29, 1867 to Louis Gonel & Cie. (carriage wheel)

81,584 of June 24, 1868 to Alexis-Georges Favre et al.

81,635 of July 14, 1868 to Louis Rives (bicycle with leaf spring)

82,178 of August 27, 1868 to Charles Desnos (improved velocipede)

83,700 of December 29, 1868 to Auguste-Adolphe Desruelles

84,464 of February 17, 1869 to Étienne Lagrange

addition to 76,455 of July 7, 1869 by Gonel.

Apparently, Gonel's original patent referred to carriages in general, and the other patentees had been quick to include metal spokes in their velocipede patents, so Gonel felt a need to expand his patent to velocipedes. Gonel's patent won some notoriety when it was bought by the Compagnie Parisienne; however, the C.P. then proceeded to pirate Meyer's patent instead of using Gonel's.

Gonel described spokes made of stiff tubes 10 millimeters in diameter that had to be cut to a precise length and provided with threads on both ends to screw them into hub and rim. He claimed these to be tension spokes, but owing to their stiffness they still worked in compression. Others tried to create a suspension wheel by making their spokes curved and resilient (Kobayashi 1993, 164); one machine with such a wheel still exists, and three patents are known:

84,369 of February 26, 1869 to Eugène Defeutrelle

85,202 of July 17, 1869 to Émile Roux

89,515 of April 2, 1870 to Pierre-Jacques Carmien.

An 1808 sketch by the aviation pioneer Sir George Cayley shows a wheel with cord spokes, instead of wooden ones, for more comfort. A similar idea, intended for carriages, was patented by Richard Edward Hodges (British patent 761 of 1854); it entailed using India rubber spokes in a state of tension to obtain elasticity between the rim and the hub.

Perhaps the most successful early attempt to build suspension wheels was that of the English cotton spinner William Strutt, who in 1814 fitted iron tension spokes to a pair of carts (Forbes 2013).

Meyer's suspension wheel

After several exhibitions in the provinces, Paris had a velocipede exhibition in the Pré Catelan area in November of 1869. *Le Vélocipède Illustré*, a semi-official organ of the Compagnie Parisienne, published an enthusiastic report:

> Monsieur Meyer showed steel wheels of extreme lightness and elegance, and veloci-
> pedes using these wheels. It is difficult to imagine anything more brilliant than these
> polished veloces. The spokes of these wheels are screwed inside the hub with brass
> nuts. These bicycles seem jewels rather than carriages. There was also a child's tri-
> cycle which was a marvel. Monsieur Meyer is so sure of his machines that he does
> not hesitate to use them himself in speed and distance races. He is one of the clever-
> est makers in France. (translated document quoted in Clayton 1992)

Eugène Meyer, a Paris mechanic born in Alsace, has long been overlooked as the inventor of the wired tension wheel and also of the high-wheeler (Clayton 1997). The reason was that for 120 years his name was misprinted as "Magee" and therefore could not be traced (Kobayashi 1993, 145). To reduce the weight of an all-metal wheel, Meyer relied on the tension of wires rather than on compression in massive spokes (French patent 86,705 of 1868). As a consequence, the metallic rim could be made lighter as well, since its structural stability was also provided by the tension spokes. Meyer described the principle in his patent application:

> As all the spokes of wire are stretched, they cannot be subject to any bending. The
> pressure is always exerted vertically and downward onto the hub, so that the wire
> spokes will be subject to it only when the rotation of the wheel brings them into the
> upper part above the horizontal line running through its center. Those spokes will
> therefore undergo no crushing. (translated)

In principle, the tension-spoke wheel can be regarded as hanging on the upward spoke from the rim, contrary to the compression-spoke wheel standing on the massive downward spoke. (See figure 3.2.) A light rim would bulge under that load, however, so horizontal spokes are needed. These are under tension, too. Still the rim would tend to flatten at its lower part. Additional downward spokes would restrain this bulging. Thus, by using a sufficient number of spokes capable of resisting tension, the load applied at the center of the wheel can be transmitted to the ground without appreciable distortion of the rim (Sharp 1896). Meyer's wheel fails immediately without sufficient tension.

Meyer's patent illustration shows a T-shaped iron rim with the spokes located in the web of the rim and bent at 90° close to the their heads. Their other ends, which are threaded, enter the hub's flanges by means of radial bores and are tightened by individual nuts. Thus, after removing the caps from the hub's ends, the spokes could be adjusted individually by turning their nuts. (Today it's the other way around: bent heads at the hubs and nipples at the rim.) Since Meyer's later machines had rubber tires, these used a U-shaped rim instead and spokes with straight heads well into the 1880s. (See figure 3.4.)

The Compagnie Parisienne jumps on the bandwagon

When the Meyer wheel became known, the Compagnie Parisienne bought a dozen wheel pairs from Meyer and wanted to adopt his design for use on C.P. machines. The C.P. offered to pay a commission for every pair of wheels it would make. Since 1869, Meyer had had a business associate who was in charge of the commercial side. This associate refused the deal, whereupon the C.P. did some research at the patent office and discovered that Gonel's patent preceded Meyer's by two months. So the C.P. acquired the rights to the Gonel patent. But the C.P. never used the patent to make wheels. In 1872 the patent expired, which ruined Gonel. Instead, the C.P. improved on the Meyer patent. According to a later report by a contemporary, the C.P.'s foreman Bock had the idea for the C.P. patent (Steinheil 1892). The outer headed end of the spoke was held by the V-shaped rim, and the inner end, having first passed through a threaded nipple, was also headed. This head held the tension applied by screwing the nipple into the hub flange (see figure 3.4) with no need to remove anything.

Meyer, busy building his high-wheelers, didn't sue the C.P. for violating his patent. But in 1878, when the C.P. no longer existed, he sued two Parisian manufacturers, Lefèvre and Poulet, for counterfeiting his wheels, having first ordered confiscation of their products. His adversaries insisted that tension wheels were long known and in the public domain, since the earlier Gonel patent (with its addition) had expired. Unfortunately, the judges didn't understand the difference between compression and tension wheels and condemned Meyer to pay 500 francs to both adversaries, plus the costs of the case (Reynaud 2011, 53).

Anglo-American wire wheels

Early ideas for wire wheels that seem not to have been taken up by manufacturers (Clayton 1997) include the following:

a notice by Edmund Tydeman in *The English Mechanic* of July 7, 1866 describing a simple plan for making a pair of "spider wheels" for a velocipede

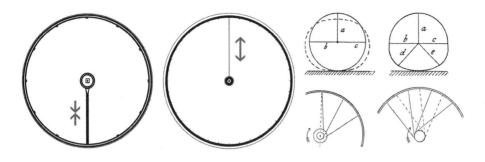

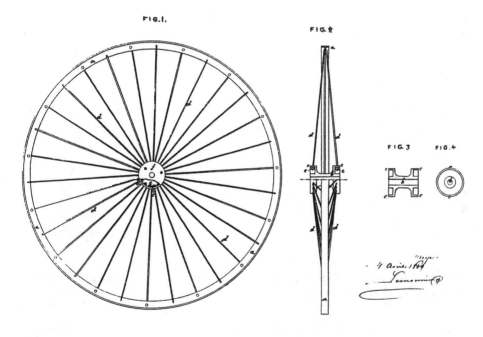

Figure 3.2 A wagon wheel relies on compression (left) and wire wheel on tension (center), but needs additional spokes to prevent the rim from bulging (top right). Radial spokes transmit the hub's rotation after deforming, tangential spokes (bottom right) do it better (Sharp 1896).

Figure 3.3 Meyer's French patent drawing of 1868 showing radial spokes. The number of the patent was 86,705.

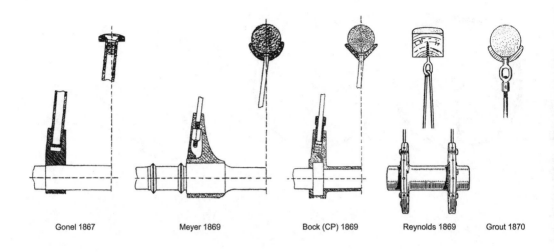

Gonel 1867   Meyer 1869   Bock (CP) 1869   Reynolds 1869   Grout 1870

Figure 3.4   Methods of fastening the metal spokes of a wire wheel (Steinheil 1892; Bartleet 1928).

British patent 3,886 of December 21, 1868, by E. A. Cowper (probably applied for on behalf of a French principal), for "wheels with a tyre of steel, iron, or brass of a hollow . . . section connected to the nave by spokes of drawn hard steel wire acting on the suspension principle"

a notice in *Scientific American* of April 17, 1869 describing a new style of velocipede with its wheels formed entirely of wire

British patent 1,463 of May 13, 1869, by Victor de Staines, for replacing spokes acting by "pression" with "a corresponding number of wires . . . acting by traction"

a notice in *Scientific American* of June 12, 1869 describing an improved bicycle with wire wheels invented by Virgil Price.

A successful patent application was filed by Reynolds & Mays of London for improvements of velocipedes and other wheeled vehicles (British patent 1,216 of April 21, 1869; French patent 85,885 of 1869). Their Phantom, a wire-wheeled cranked velocipede with a jointed frame, was produced until October of 1872. Their wheels still had a bent wooden rim with a metal tire shrunk on. These used doubled spokes, fed through staples at the rim with the ends clamped at the hub. The hub flanges were then forced apart, tensioning the spokes. For a year the Phantom was a favorite on the track. Its unthreaded spokes didn't break, but neither could they be tensioned individually to true the wheel. This, and the fact that the hinged frame of the Phantom made steering an art, gave it a unique but eventually terminal disadvantage (*The Field*, October 5, 1872).

William Henry James Grout, a builder of velocipedes in Shadwell, patented spokes that inverted the Compagnie Parisienne's geometry. They had an eyed nipple at the outer end of each spoke (British patent 3,152 of 1870). This is the way nipples are placed even today. Grout used this method on his high-wheelers, with minor modifications, for about ten years.

French beginnings of the high-wheeler

Contrary to widespread belief, the high-wheeler evolved in Paris before the Franco-Prussian War. Louis Rives, a manufacturer in Toulouse, was awarded French patent 81,635 for a machine with a 35-inch front wheel and a 16-inch rear wheel in 1868, when the wheels of a majority of the other cranked velocipedes differed in diameter by only 4 to 8 inches. Rives's wheels had metal spokes, but retained wooden rims. A similar velocipede by Ravier and Schmit, with the seat rather a long way back, is shown in figure 2.11 above. One advantage of the small rear wheel was less moment of inertia resisting rotational acceleration. This type of velocipede was among the winners of races in the summer of 1868 (Kobayashi 1993, 176).

At the important velocipede exhibition at Pré Catalan, a relatively unknown man was applauded for his "grand bicycle" by *Le Vélocipède Illustré* in its issue dated November 18, 1869:

> Monsieur Alexandre Moyon is well-intentioned, and we would be glad to say something positive about the Grand Bicycle he exposes, but for that we have to see it run. Monsieur Moyon, who is known for interesting inventions, may have good ideas, but this time by applying them he is wide off the mark. We doubt that one can reach on his apparatus the balance and speed one rightly expects from a véloce. (translated)

Though Eugène Meyer isn't mentioned for any "Grand-Bi" (as high-wheelers came to be called in France), he is mentioned for his beautifully engineered low velocipedes. Moyon is mentioned as an inventor of the high-wheeler. Alas, not much more is known about Moyon. His name cannot be found in the patent literature, Perhaps he shared the fate of many inventors who didn't survive commercially. The criticism in *Le Vélocipède Illustré* is understandable in view of that journal's battle against ever-larger front wheels. *Le Vélocipède Illustré* favored using a gear in the front hub to achieve higher speed. Transferred to technology, Sir William Osler's maxim that "in science the credit goes to the man who convinces the world, not to the man to whom

Figure 3.5 Left: Rives's bicycle, with wooden wheels circa 1869 (Robert Sterba). Right: Meyer's all-steel bicycle, circa 1869 (Keizo Kobayashi).

the idea first occurs" means, sadly, that an inventor must be competent both as an inventor and as an entrepreneur. In line with this, Eugène Meyer, rather than Rives or Moyon, gets the credit for making the high-wheeler feasible and making it known.

Eugène Meyer participated in races himself to make his machines known, so he must have been well aware of the need for lighter wheels and frames. For instance, he participated in the Paris-Rouen race of November 1869, placing tenth; the winner was James Moore (Kobayashi 1993, 380). Having obtained his spider-wheel patent of 1869, Meyer equipped all his machines with his light metal-spoke wheels; he also began to use smaller rear wheels. Unfortunately there is no brochure left describing his complete line of machines, if there ever was one. Thus the evolution of the high-wheeler in his workshop has to be reconstructed from small ads in *Le Vélocipède Illustré* and surviving machines in collections. (See figure 3.19 below.)

The move away from the standard second-generation velocipede to the high-wheeler can be dated to the end of 1869. The champion racer James Moore now used high-wheelers built by Meyer exclusively. In the August 1870 Champion Bicycle Contest at Molineux Park in Wolverhampton, Moore raced a Meyer bicycle with a 43-inch front wheel against England's finest on now-antiquated velocipedes. At the next race, six weeks later, his opponents had British high-wheelers too (Clayton 1997). By then, the Coventry Machinist Company Ltd. (CMC) had modeled its Coventry Bicycle and its Vélocipède Américain after the Rives and Ravier and Schmit's high-wheelers, though they still had wooden wheels. The vogue in France at the time is exemplified by a patent drawing by Barberon and Meunier (French patent 86,459, addition of 1870) showing a steel-wired high-wheeler with the seat close to the handlebar.

Meyer's workshop survived the Franco-Prussian War and the subsequent turmoil of the Commune. His high-end high-wheelers continued to be in demand. Gradually he switched to lighter tubes of round or oval cross-section for the frame spine. An undated publicity card (figure 3.6) shows a high-wheeler priced at 375 francs (polished) or 350 francs (painted), "with footrests, brake, crotch guard, steel bearings guaranteed under all conditions that leave nothing to be desired." Meyer continued to advertise his machines until 1883. Around 1891 he retired to Brunoy en Essonne, where he died at the age of 63. Here is an example of contemporary praise upon his retirement:

> A single mechanic, a man of rare talent, Monsieur Meyer, has retreated to his workshop. It is he who never built velocipedes of wood, even in 1869. His are of metal, and even on the metallic velocipede he has found these improvements: that the spine is no longer formed of an sharp-edged iron rod but rather of a cylindrical iron tube; and that spokes made of rod are superseded by spokes made of iron wire. He is a very skillful man, but also very fearful. He fears that the velocipede is merely a fashion like the crinoline. For his pretty, light and solid machines, that let the sun mirror itself in their polished iron, he awaits orders like a philosopher. (translated from Baudry 1891, 120)

James Starley and tangent spoking

Three days after James Moore's Wolverhampton victory on a machine with a Meyer spider wheel, James Starley and William Hillman applied for a patent on "Improvements in the construction of wheels applicable chiefly to velocipedes, and in the driving gear for such vehicles" (British patent 2,236 of 1870). Though no geared machine such as that described survives, the production model called the Ariel, without front gear, became well known. The Ariel, which had the first commercially available suspension wheel with tangent spokes, was in production for nine years. As it turned out, Starley became the most active wheel improver of the 1870s.

Both the Meyer system and the C.P. system remained in use for more than ten years, but they had the disadvantage that the spokes were arranged radially. In the case of a driving wheel, this means that a spoke is flexed and unflexed with every stroke of the pedal. (See

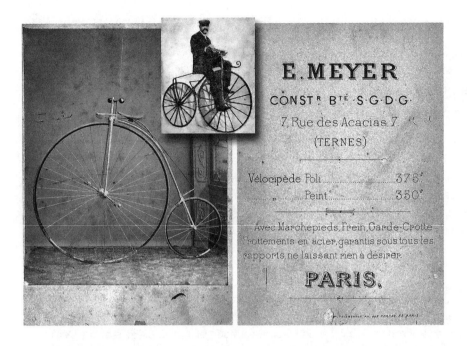

Figure 3.6 Meyer's bicycle and his advertising card 1872 (Helge Schultz) and only known photo of him (Gardellin 1941).

figure 3.2.) The flexing resulted in a high incidence of broken spokes. In contrast, tangential spokes were oriented parallel to the actual forces.

The Ariel's wheel had two serious faults. First, the spokes couldn't be tensioned individually, so a wheel couldn't be trued. Second, although the spokes resisted perfectly when the rider was pedaling forward, when the rider was back-pedaling while descending a hill the spokes came under compression and the wheel could become slack. This could be unnerving. If the wheel had been put into the forks the wrong way, with the tension rods trailing, the wheel could even collapse. Starley and Hillman soon left CMC to start their own firms.

Starley's next wheel patent was for the Tangent (British patent 3,959 of 1874). Screwing threaded spokes into either end of small steel studs passing transversely through the hub flanges produced a tangent-spoke wheel that was rigid in both directions, but the hub could accommodate only a limited number of studs. Starley's patent also covered two more bicycle

Figure 3.7 Left: An 1872 patent drawing of an Ariel. Right: a photo of James Starley. (National Cycle Library.)

designs using this wheel. The Lady's Ariel was produced to allow a sidesaddle position. To this end, the saddle and the small rear wheel were moved to the left side, out of the front wheel's plane, and the two treadles both worked on the left side of the front hub, as shown in figure 3.8. (This had been proposed earlier by Samuel Webb Thomas, though with a small third "stabilizer" wheel.) The prospect of a fall to the wrong side was so daunting as to make the design quite impractical. Another design (presumably not manufactured) was intended for two riders on two saddles side by side, with a pair of cranks on either side of the front hub.

In an agreement dated 1876 and signed by James Starley, Joseph Jefferis, and the Haynes brothers, Starley agreed to license the patent to them exclusively and to make tangent wheels for five shillings a pair. He would receive ten shillings for every complete velocipede they made, payable monthly, and he would not undertake to manufacture velocipedes himself. Starley thus terminated his cycle-making career early, but continued to come up with new ideas and

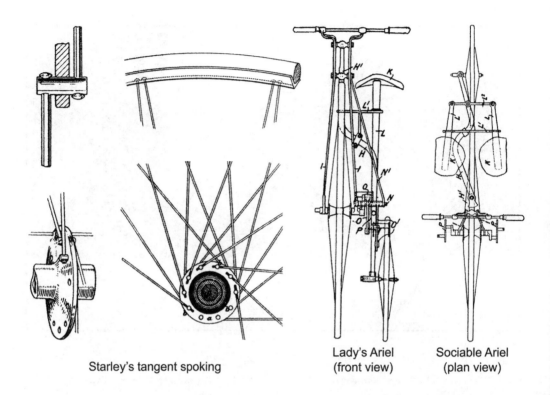

Starley's tangent spoking

Lady's Ariel
(front view)

Sociable Ariel
(plan view)

Figure 3.8 Starley's second spoke-wheel patent and bicycle designs for non-racers (patent drawings reproduced from Bartleet 1928).

inventions. When Haynes & Jefferis merged with Rudge in 1880, the tangent-wheeled bicycle was dropped, yet its front wheel was incorporated into the popular Rudge Coventry tricycle.

A plethora of spoking systems provided selling features for both large and small makers during the 1870s, when discussions focused on the practically and the aesthetically optimal number of spokes for a given size wheel. The year 1878 saw an explosion in the number of spokes per wheel that culminated in the Surrey Machinists' Invincible model, which had 300. Riders quickly discovered that such a wheel was difficult to clean, and that it was impossible to pass a hub lamp between the spokes or to light it when it was in place. By 1880, most makers had settled on direct spokes screwed into the hub, with the screwed end butted to avoid breakage, and were using "spokes for inches"—for example, a 54-inch machine would have 54 spokes.

The scramble for improvement and weight reduction abated somewhat in the 1880s, but laced piano-wire spokes had a brief run of popularity in 1883. The final arrangement appeared at the 1885 Stanley Show in the form of the New Rapid true tangent wheel, manufactured by the St. George's Engineering Company Ltd. (C. A. Palmer's British patent 15,451 of 1885). Headed spokes were held in light hub flanges, spanning at 90°, with five crossings, to spoke nipples at the rim. (Singer and others brought out copies; Humber resolutely refused to go the tangent route.) It was all of little consequence. At the same 1885 show, John Kemp Starley unveiled his first Rover safety bicycle, and large spider wheels were no longer needed.

THE HIGH-WHEELER

After the advent of the large front wheel, bicycling in Britain recovered from its temporary slowdown and enjoyed steady growth in popularity for the next 30 years. Fewer than 10 percent of the velocipede makers remained in the bicycle trade, which now required the skills of a machinist or a gunsmith rather than those of a carriage maker or an iron founder. Companies became more specialized. Many of the new factory owners were themselves bicyclists, so the step from testing prototypes to launching production could be short.

The term "ordinary bicycle" was used early in the era of the high bicycle to distinguish it from other types. By 1891, however, the word "ordinary" was being used nostalgically, as in "grand old ordinary." The popular nickname in the UK was "penny-farthing," derived from the relative sizes of two British coins.

Bicycle clubs began to form, first in London and then at universities and in the provinces. By 1875 the movement had achieved critical mass. *Bicycling News*, *The Bicycle Journal*, and a relaunched *Bicycle* appeared in 1876, enabling subscribers to exchange opinions on cycling matters and to learn of the merits and demerits of various makes. The second half of the 1870s saw the high-wheeler refined into a beautiful, lightweight, practical recreational mount.

The bicycle of 1871 had been completely transformed by 1874, and it was transformed again by 1878. It can be argued that the high-wheeler was perfected by 1880. "Last Season," Henry Sturmey wrote in his "Introductory Notes on Progress" to *The Indispensable Bicyclist's Handbook 1879*, "one would almost have thought the bicycle a perfect article, so strong, swift, handsome and almost lifelike it had become; and that few, if any, improvements or alterations would be made for many years to come."

Figure 3.9   An 1879 Bayliss & Thomas 55-inch Duplex Excelsior (Alan Osbahr).

In 1883, Harry Griffin, in his book *Bicycles of the Year*, speculated that "roadsters have reached so great a pitch of structural perfection, that it is difficult to find room for further improvement." Hundreds of patent applications had been filed during the 1870s. Among the many trivia were some groundbreaking designs, techniques, and principles that were to become standard in the bicycle and motor trades for years to come, including roller bearings (1871, John Keen), tubular frames (1872), hollow forks (1874, Jules Truffault), detachable cranks (1876, John Kemp Starley), rat-trap pedals (1876, John Keen), adjustable ball bearings (1877, Daniel Rudge and William Bown), hollow rims (1878, Coventry Machinists' Company), detachable handlebars (1878), and drop handlebars (1879).

The bicycle of 1880 was indeed King of the Road, and those lucky to be young and fit enough to ride one and wealthy enough to buy one were indeed blessed. The motion of the highwheeler was more exhilarating than that of the later safety bicycle. One writer put it this way:

> The position, so nicely balanced, nearly on one wheel; the absence of a wheel to be pushed in front, wheelbarrow fashion; the free, billowy, rolling motion that ensued, gave to riding and coasting on it a peculiar charm that was wholly its own, and afforded sensations which those who have enjoyed them count as among the most beautiful of their lives. (Porter 1898)

One particular joy was coasting. The approved method for enjoying a descent, where the road to the bottom could be seen to be clear, was to hang the legs over the handlebars. Barring mechanical failure or unforeseen misadventure, such as the tire leaving the rim, the practice was less dangerous than it might seem. In the event of misfortune the rider was at least propelled clear of the bicycle, rather than being centrifugally smashed into the roadway.

Riders were not unaware that speed had been bought at the price of danger, and for ten years a "safety bicycle" was talked about. But the danger added piquancy to the sport, and cycling publications were happy to receive and print letters from enthusiasts who had survived falls.

The problem of "headers," "croppers," or "imperial crowners," as the cognoscenti called over-the-handlebar falls, was intimately tied up with the development of satisfactory brakes. For more on this, see box 3.1 and chapter 8.

Anti-croppering measures

While some inventors were busying themselves with new brake designs, others attempted to overcome the consequence of the overenthusiastic use of the existing brakes. There were many applications for patents on anti-croppering devices.

Figure 3.10 Mounting a high wheeler using a footrest (National Cycle Library.). Left: anti-cropper device in action (*Der Radfahrer* of October 1, 1887).

Several devices attempted to alter the rider's situation quickly when danger struck. A rider who went over the front wheel could be trapped by the handlebar and entangled in the wreckage. Potential victims reasoned that the outcome would be less dire if the handlebar weren't there, or if the forks could be prevented from overriding the wheel when it was stopped by an obstruction. These individuals resembled those who pondered perpetual motion—a popular notion of the day. Someone even speculated that if a rider could nearly fall over the handlebars but never quite do so, it would give added forward propulsion.

In 1879, several devices for quickly moving the saddle a few inches rearward before commencing a descent were patented (Sturmey 1879). Because these added weight and complication and were difficult to engage quickly, they were not widely adopted.

As an alternative to adjusting the saddle position, other devices changed the rake of the front forks while in use, either by hinging the rear forks to allow the rear wheel to move upward and backward or by using an eccentric under the steering head to increase the front fork rake. Both maneuvers proved difficult to perform while in motion. Charles Antoine Fournier's British patent (2,720 of 1876) was the first patent for such a device.

The purpose of removable or rear-facing handlebars was not to make croppers avoidable, but to make them more survivable. J. S. Whatton ("The Flying Cantab"), a member of the Cambridge University Bicycle Club, devised bars that passed under and around the rider's thighs. A bike with such bars could be mounted only when stationary, and the idea didn't catch on, although some later tricycles had "Whatton Bars." Similar arrangements were patented by C. W. Francis (British patent 141 of 1882) and by R. C. Thompson and W. Spence (British patent 5,199 of 1883). Another optimistic patentee, R. J. Johnson (British patent 3,272 of 1881), proposed that "in order to prevent headers, the steering-handle is removably fixed to the steering-fork, so that the rider, when he feels himself being thrown from his seat, can detach the handle and spring forward on to the ground."

Foote's Anti-header of 1886 (British patent 843 of 1886) and Fisher's Non-cropper 1887 (Sturmey 1887) came too late. The first jammed a roller between the front wheel and the forks as soon as the forks threatened to overrun the wheel; the second did the same job at the hub with a ratchet and a pawl. (The patent hasn't been traced, but J. W. Smallman's patent 3,596 of 1885 covers a similar idea.) A demonstrator who rode a machine fitted with a so-called Non-Cropper safely up and down several eight-inch curbs impressed a representative of *Bicycling News* (see reprint in *The Boneshaker* 15, 1959), but one suspects that the device would have been of little help to a rider of a runaway roadster in hilly country.

At the 1886 Stanley Show, a London maker named J. Dearlove introduced a "rational" bicycle. "Constructed with a view of giving increased comfort and safety without sacrificing speed," it had thicker rubber tires, a larger rear wheel, a narrower tread, and more rake than the standard high-wheeler. Two years later, most makers had "rational" models in their catalogs.

Cockeyed proposals were inevitable in a heated market of quickly changing technology and fashion, but new ideas for spoking systems, for bearings, and for tubing led to lasting progress.

Before 1889, steel tubing was an expensive commodity. Fire-welded steel tubes had been manufactured in England since 1825, had been cold-drawn from hollow blocks since 1854, and had been used mainly for gas or water piping. By the time of the bicycle boom of the mid 1890s, manufacturing cold-drawn tube had, like manufacturing ball bearings, become a huge industry that owed its success mainly to the demand from the bicycle industry. (For more on this, see chapter 5.)

Ball bearings

The draisines of 1817 had mainly used plain brass bushings in the wheels, yet in his 1837 lecture "On the Velocipede" Thomas Stephens Davies recalled that "the friction caused by making the wheels of wood, with the axis working in a box, impeded the motion very much though this evil was sometimes lessened by employing friction rollers."

The cranked velocipede presented a new problem, as the driven front wheel also required sideways restraint. Flanged bronze shell bearings were generally used on the front wheel, held in the ends of the forks by a tapered pin that allowed adjustment for wear. These continued to be used on early high-wheelers, but the larger wheel had greater side torque and demanded freer running and firmer restraint.

In 1869, James Moore won the Paris-Rouen road race on a velocipede with specially made ball bearings (Duncan 1928). On English high-wheelers, roller bearings rather than ball bearings were favored for a while. Many designs were in use by 1878, as were cone bearings of various kinds. In that year, Daniel Rudge and Joseph Henry Hughes were granted British patents for single-row ball bearings that were easy to adjust for wear. (Rudge received patent 526, Hughes patent 4,709.) When the Rudge patent was later sold, there was scope for a legal challenge, but the principle of a single row of balls in a threaded, coned case remained the basis of cycle bearings until relatively recently, when sealed bearings came into use. The bicycle industry fathered a huge new industry: the manufacturing of steel balls, facilitated by an advance in the manufacturing process. At first the balls were turned individually on automatic lathes, but in the mid 1880s the Simonds rolling machine made it possible to produce precise spheres at a rate of about 18,000 a day (Kanigel 1997). Simonds machines (made in the United States under US patent 466,444) were soon installed in British and Continental bearing factories.

A crucial design element of the high-wheeler was the "head" at the top of the backbone, where the front fork was mounted on a pivot. The unpatented Stanley head (named after the Stanley ordinary, manufactured by Hydes & Wigfull of Sheffield) was copied everywhere. The backbone ended in a vertical hull containing a spindle with conical apexes running in cone bearings, the upper one held in place by a set screw. This type of pivot had to be oiled often so it wouldn't bind after a shock. When mass-produced bearing balls became available, the conical spindle tips were placed into two rings of balls; that design, called the Regent Ball-Bearing Head (figure 3.11), was soon followed by more ball-bearing-specific variants.

The step

A small step was used in mounting a high-wheeler. The standard procedure was to place one foot on the step, take a few hops, stand up, and slide neatly into the saddle. The Compagnie Parisienne velocipede that James Starley copied at the end of 1868 had no step, and throughout 1869 velocipedes continued to lack them. In late 1869 or early 1870, supposedly to overcome his own difficulties in mounting (Street 2000), Starley designed his Coventry model, which had a C spring and a mounting step. That design was patented by CMC's Paris agent Rowley Turner in France in 1869 (*Cycling*, July 22, 1915).

Other names have been proposed for the step's inventor; however, Starley was credited with it early on, and CMC was England's best-known maker of bicycles at the time. From early 1870 on, most bicycles were fitted with steps, and they remained a requirement on ordinaries and safeties until freewheels became the norm at the end of the century. In its later form, the step became an axle extension, usually on one side of the rear wheel but sometimes on the

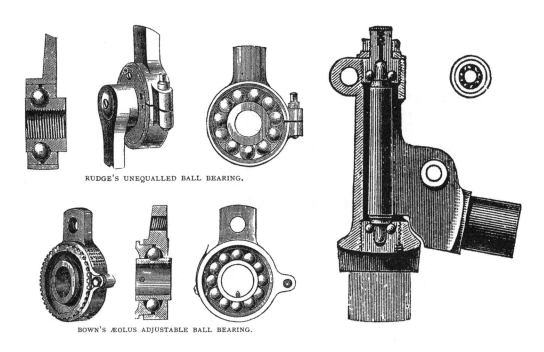

RUDGE'S UNEQUALLED BALL BEARING.

BOWN'S ÆOLUS ADJUSTABLE BALL BEARING.

Figure 3.11   Left: two leading front-wheel bearings (Sturmey 1885). Right: The Regent Ball Bearing Head (Griffin 1886).

front wheel. In the last quarter of the twentieth century, axle-extension steps reappeared when BMX stunt riders adopted them, sometimes on both sides of both wheels.

During the years of the high-wheeler, there were mushroom steps, saw-tooth steps, rubber-clothed steps, safety steps, skeleton steps, and many patented adjustable steps. By 1887, Henry Sturmey saw the saw-tooth step as the "most universal"; nevertheless, he described eight other styles (Sturmey 1887).

The high-wheeler abroad

In the United States, cranked velocipedes had been so completely legislated off the sidewalks (the only places they could be ridden) that their manufacture ceased altogether after 1870. In

1876, at the Philadelphia World's Fair, the high-wheeler was introduced to the United States. Five Ariels made by Haynes & Jefferis of Coventry were imported and exhibited by a Baltimore company. They found one particularly interested observer: Colonel Albert Pope of Boston, a manufacturer of shoe buckles and air pistols. He decided to import the new plaything for the elite, learned to ride it himself, then traveled to England to find a model that he could use as a prototype. He settled on the Duplex Excelsior, made in Coventry by Bayliss, Thomas & Company, England's fourth-ranking manufacturer after the Coventry Machinists' Company, Singer, and Haynes & Jefferis. Pope then had the Weed Sewing Machine Company in Hartford build high-wheelers copied from that model. Manufacturing turned out to be more difficult than had been expected. The rake of the fork of a Duplex Excelsior could be adjusted. The fork could be made perfectly upright or even leaned forward for the purpose of ascending a hill, then leaned back for a descent. Building the head required five forging dies, the largest and most elaborate of them costing more than $500 to make. The finishing die broke on the eleventh stroke and had to be rebuilt (Epperson 2010, 31). In the next ten years, Pope bought the Weed Sewing Machine Company and turned Hartford into the manufacturing center for his Columbia brand, with added factories for tubes and tires. The Columbia high-wheelers now had simplified heads. After a patent war over the Lallement patent, Pope acquired that patent and many others in an attempt to monopolize the American bicycle market. Competitors then had to pay Pope a license fee of $10 for each ordinary they manufactured.

Pope introduced marketing innovations that will sound familiar to present-day automobile buyers. He created a national network of agencies to sell his bicycles at fixed retail prices. He set a standard freight rate for the nation as a whole, offered guarantees for the machines, and established an extensive sales force.

Moreover, Pope applied his marketing talents to bicycles in general. He founded the League of American Wheelmen, which lobbied for better roads in Washington and the state capitals, drawing opposition from tax-paying farmers who could not see any benefit to them. Pamphlets for the Good Roads Movement were printed and sent to politicians. Pope launched a magazine, *The Wheelman Illustrated*, which he later merged with his other magazine, *Outing*. Pope spent considerable sums on his Good Roads Movement and fought against anti-cycling ordinances. He donated $6,000 to encourage the Massachusetts Institute of Technology to develop a department of highway engineering, the first full department of its kind in the United States. The emphasis on cycling on public roads distanced the League of American Wheelmen from racing. "There is no more sense in the LAW running bicycle races," the chief consul of Michigan's LAW division opined, "than the poultry association staging cock fights or the dairy association, bull fights." (Epperson 2010, 93)

After the expiration of the Lallement patent, seven companies produced high-wheelers in the United States, but only one responded early to the urge for more safety: the H. R. Smith

Figure 3.12   The 50-inch Expert Columbia on which Thomas Stevens circled the globe in 1884–1886 (manufacturer's catalog).

Manufacturing Company of New Jersey. It manufactured the American Star, which looked like a high-wheeler turned backward. Riders noted that it was superior for coasting downhill, but had to be carefully ridden uphill because it tended to do a "backward header," lifting the front wheel off the ground if pedaled too hard (Kron 1887, 370). The American Star was manufactured under license in Germany by Erste Deutsche Star Bicycle E. Kretzschmar Company of Dresden until well into the 1890s.

Heinrich Kleyer, a mechanic's son who had studied engineering at the Darmstadt Polytechnic Institute, had a career similar to Pope's. Having discovered high-wheelers in Boston, he began to manufacture them in Frankfurt under the brand name Adler (German for "eagle"). He founded a bicycle club in Frankfurt; he also built a velodrome there and raced on it, and on other tracks, to promote the new activity. Later, his huge Adlerwerke also produced typewriters, motorcycles, and then automobiles. (It continued to manufacture bicycles until 1958.) The earliest of 26 German manufacturers of high-wheelers was Dissel & Proll of Dortmund; two later large ones were Opel and NSU (Seyfert 1912).

In France, Adolphe Clément's broad range of machines included some imported from Britain. Les Fils de Peugeot Frères at Valentigney, who previously had manufactured steel hoops for crinolines and other goods, decided to begin manufacturing high-wheelers in 1885 (Reynaud 2011, 156). The similarity between Continental and British high-wheelers and tricycles can be explained by the fact that in Europe bicycle parts could be ordered from the United Kingdom easily and economically.

HIGH-WHEEL TRICYCLES

The high-wheeler was considered unsafe because of the difficulty of mounting and dismounting, especially in town traffic, and because of the ease with which the rider could be thrown over the handlebars. There were two main ways of "designing out" these problems. One was to build "rational ordinaries." (The seat of a "rational ordinary" was lower and was farther behind the front wheel's axle.) The other was to add a third wheel.

From the very beginning of bicycling, most people feared balancing on two wheels and preferred the stability of three wheels. From 1817 on, tricycles and bicycles developed symbiotically. In 1870 and then again around 1880, it appeared to the cycling press that the tricycle, rather than the bicycle, might be the vehicle of the future.

Before 1860, quadricycles were even more popular than tricycles (see chapter 1), but both designs suffered the drawback that two driven wheels on one axle resulted in scrubbing of the tires during cornering and any time one rode on rough surface. One solution was to have one wheel free on the axle and the other one driving, although that reduced traction and could make the steering jumpy. Some makers (for example, Sawyer) preferred to keep the two wheels fixed and let the metal tires slip on a loose road surface.

Three-wheeled Parisian velocipedes took center stage in 1870 when a race from Paris to Saint-Germain was restricted to three-wheeled and four-wheeled machines. One competitor, William Jackson, an Englishman living in Paris, was praised for a tricycle that "shone in the sun like a steel jewel" as "everyone admired its easy, elegant progress" (*Le Vélocipède Illustré*, July 7, 1870). A Jackson machine, very advanced for its time, is in the Velorama collection in Nijmegen. This lightweight three-wheeler, furnished with Meyer wire wheels, looks scarcely inferior to the Monarch tricycle, launched in Birmingham by William Thomas Eades more than 12 years later (Clayton 1999). The only difference is that the Monarch had double ratchet drive, whereas Jackson's was driven by only one wheel.

The hiatus in French production after August of 1870, caused by the Franco-Prussian War, destabilized the balance between tricycles and bicycles. Tricycle fever, so evident in the pages of *Le Vélocipède Illustré*, failed to cross the Channel when the center of the trade moved to Coventry. In Britain, only a few tricycles were being made, all with wooden wheels. Tricycles with steel-spoke wheels and tube frames got a rather late start in the British Isles, in 1876, with the front-steering Dublin tricycle and the side-steering Coventry tricycle. The Dublin was patented only 14 days ahead of the Coventry.

Front-steering rear-drive machines

With two front wheels steering, the inner wheel travels a shorter distance than the outer, following a tighter radius. Ideally, therefore, the inner wheel has to be pointed more sharply into the turn. Erasmus Darwin, grandfather of Charles, identified the problem and the solution in the 1760s; it was also identified and effectively resolved through the use of stub axles by Georg Lankensperger, a Munich carriage maker (Bavarian privilege of 1816). Rudolph Ackermann of London—a former German saddler turned coach designer—obtained a patent with Lankensperger (British patent 1,412 of 1818) specifying that a theoretical line taken through each front wheel's axle should intersect near the inner rear wheel's center (Lankensperger 1818). However, "A-steering" (the A standing for Ackermann) wasn't generally adopted on iron-tired carriages (Eckermann 1998), or on early iron-tired quadricycles or tricycles. A tricycle with a single front steering wheel and one loose wheel on the driving axle was a reasonable compromise.

William Bindon Blood, a velocipedist who was a professor of engineering at Queen's College in Galway, designed a "Dublin tricycle" with a central rear driving wheel. Its steering achieved

Ackermann angles with the front wheels within forks rather than on stub axles (British patent 4,250 of 1876). This system wasn't identical to Ackermann's patent of 1818, but followed the same original thought. Henry Sturmey described it in detail:

> It is very simple and consists of a rod running straight back from each fork some 12in to 18in, and then united by a third rod bent to a curve at each end. These rods connect the forks of the two wheels, and when one is turned by means of a rack and pinion, or a direct handle, the other is also turned, and not only so, but the angle of each is such, that both describe arcs of different sized circles, according as they are in or outside in turning, thus avoiding any jumps, scrape, or tyre tearing. (Sturmey 1881)

Now, for the first time, A-steering became a standard feature of some tricycles. Linley & Biggs used it with stub axles on the Whippet Double Steerer of 1888. The Olympia, a double-steering tandem tricycle made by Marriott & Cooper, was said to be one of the most successful of modern tricycles; it also featured A-steering with stub axles (Sharp 1896). In the United States, the Pope Manufacturing Company produced a single-seater with stub-axle A-steering, the Surprise Columbia Tricycle; it had double steering and allowed the operator to reduce its track from 34 inches to 30 inches while riding, apparently to make it easier to negotiate narrow tracks. A great variety of "compressible" tricycles of various types were manufactured in the UK, the aim in these cases being to enable the machines to pass through a standard doorway (Hadland and Pinkerton 1996, 3–7). Another stub-axle application was the patented Rudge Quadricycle single of 1889. The claim was that "one has to overcome rolling resistance only in two tracks instead of three." Rudge's Quadricycle for Three Riders, built on the same plan, achieved a record speed of 26 miles per hour. Thus, the A-steering plan was already in use and well known before it was widely adopted by makers of automobiles.

Side-steering and rear-steering machines

Coventry was the center of the British cycle industry, as has already been noted, and it was there that James Starley produced the most successful series-produced tricycles. His break-through design, the lever-drive Coventry of 1876 (later known as the Coventry Lever Tricycle), was patented under the names of his son James and his nephew John Kemp Starley (British patent 4,478 of 1876). Reportedly it was derived from the Ariel. Its original tiller steering was soon altered to a single spade-style handle that turned both small wheels by means of a rack and a pinion.

Figure 3.13 Above left: Lankensperger's stub axle and Ackermann's patent drawing (Eckermann 1998). Above right: Blood's Dublin tricycle of 1876. (Science Museum Creative Commons.) Below left: Pope's Surprise Columbia Tricycle of 1889 (manufacturers' catalog). Below right: the Rudge Quadricycle of 1889 (manufacturers' catalog).

A chain-driven version introduced in late 1879 or early 1880 was called the Coventry Rotary Tricycle. Although originally sold by Starley Brothers, the Starley tricycles were later marketed by the Tangent & Coventry Tricycle Company, which was acquired by Rudge in 1880 (Roberts 1991, 41).

Starley's Coventry Lever and Rotary tricycles borrowed some technological features from the ordinary, including wire-spoke wheels and hollow tubing. A Coventry Lever or a Coventry

Rotary tricycle had one large wheel on the left side and a pair of smaller, steered wheels on the right of the rider's seat, one fore and one aft. In 1877, Starley made a two-seater version, with the riders seated side by side and a second large wheel to the right of the right-hand rider. That four-wheel "sociable" was marketed as the Salvo Quadricycle. Its particular significance was that what was variously known as a balance, double-driving, or differential gear was used to enable both of the driving wheels to be driven from a single power input when turning corners. Previous attempts had involved either each rider driving a separate wheel (which required almost unattainable coordination) or driving a single wheel (which resulted in poorer traction, different handling in left and right turns, and a tendency to pull to one side).

The idea of a differential gear wasn't new. Centuries earlier, in China, there was a military chariot with an indicator that always pointed the same way; presumably it was useful in dusty combat situations and in the absence of easily visible landmarks. At its heart was a differential mechanism. Old Meccano enthusiasts may recall building a "Pharaoh's Chariot" that worked on the same principle. The first inventor to patent a differential gear appears to have been Onésiphore Pecqueur (French patent 6,840 of 1828). An Englishman named Richard Roberts soon patented one too.

Differential gears can take various forms, but here is an explanation of how a simple differential gear works: The two driven wheels are on separate drive axles that meet in a differential gear casing. Within that casing, the inboard end of each wheel's shaft has a bevel gear on it; we will call them the left-wheel bevel and the right-wheel bevel. Each of the two bevels meshes at a 90° angle with a drive bevel, which is held in a rotating frame within, or integral with, the differential casing, and is driven by the power source (e.g., a chain). When the vehicle is traveling in a straight line, the bevel gear in the drive frame will pull both of the bevel gears around equally. If the vehicle turns right, the right-hand drive wheel is retarded by being on the inside of the turning circle and the left wheel is accelerated by being on the outside of the circle. The drive bevel automatically allows the rotation and the torque to be shared proportionally, according to the sharpness of the turn. If one wheel is stationary, and the vehicle is "turning on the spot," that wheel's bevel will be static. The drive bevel, reacting against it, will automatically distribute all the rotation and torque to the other wheel. (For smooth running, it was customary to use more than one drive bevel.)

Figure 3.14   Above: an 1884 Humber Cripper tricycle (R. John Way). Below: an 1877 Coventry Lever Tricycle (Alan Osbahr).

A simpler system used on some tricycles with two-wheel drive had the two driven wheels fitted with freewheels and mounted on the same driven axle. This made it possible to drive both wheels when the tricycle was going straight ahead. In a turn, no drive was delivered to the wheel that was on the inside of the turn, as it was rotating more slowly than the drive axle. This system was less satisfactory than using a differential, as only one wheel was driven in a turn. It was, however, better than driving only one wheel, which delivered poor performance when the driven wheel was on the inside of a turn.

James Starley seems to have evolved his own "balance gear" (British patent 3,388 of 1877) from scratch. Its significance derives from the subsequent universal adoption of differentials in almost all automobiles and trucks. Starley went on to produce a successful range of technically advanced Salvo tricycles with front steering, chain drive, and the "balance gear."

By the late 1880s, when the safety bicycle had begun to persuade the more timid riders to return to two wheels, about 80 percent of tricycles being produced were of the direct-steering type, a design pioneered by the unpatented Humber Cripper (figure 3.14). The name was derived from Robert Cripps, who won many races on machines of that design. Whereas early tricycles had had rack-and-pinion steering, the Cripper had an inclined steering head and a direct connection between the front forks and the rearward-curving handlebars. After 1887, all three wheels were about 28 to 30 inches in diameter. This convergence in design allowed dealers to keep their inventories smaller, though by that time the whole tricycle market was shrinking and dealers were having to stock a growing array of safety bicycles.

The Otto bicycle and the Welch Dicycle

Among the velocipedes having only two tracks, like the Coventry tricycle, a two-wheeled design with the wheels side by side appeared in 1879. The idea of supporting a running man by two side wheels, instead of two wheels in line, arose as early as 1819, as Howell's Pedestrian Chariot from Bristol and Siviers's Patent Pedestrian Carriage attest (Street 2011). The idea surfaced again in 1869 with J. J. White's US patent 88,930. And in 1879, Eduard Carl Friedrich Otto, a brother of Nikolaus Otto of gasoline-engine fame (Boys 1884), resurrected it once more (British patent 1,274).

In Otto's design, a crankshaft drove the two wheels independently by means of two rubberized Italian hemp belts (later superseded by steel bands). Steering was by means of spade handles that compressed a spring tensioner and thus slackened one belt or the other and slowed the wheel that was connected to that belt. Braking the wheel by means of a finger grip within the spade handle would cause the machine to turn more smartly around the blocked wheel, if necessary within a five-foot circle. The art of balancing without overturning had to be learned.

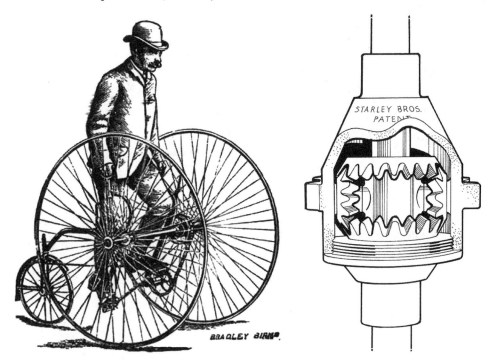

Figure 3.15 Left: The 1884 Starley & Sutton Rover tricycle (National Cycle Library). Right: Starley's differential or "balance gear" (R. John Way).

Figure 3.16   Left and center: two-track bicycles of 1879 and 1886. Right: the Otto Safety Bicycle Company's spoke pattern (brochure and patent drawings).

Tilting backward was prevented by a small-wheeled tail skid; falling forward was controlled by accelerating or, as a last resort, putting one's feet down. Otto persuaded the Birmingham Small Arms Company to manufacture the machines for him after demonstrating one on the table of the boardroom, and Birmingham Small Arms (BSA) built 953 machines of the highest quality.

In 1886, the Coventry Machinists' Company offered the Kingston Club Dicycle, a competing chain-driven design by Kingston Welch. (A dicycle has two wheels on the same axis, rather than one in front of the other.) Because it infringed Otto's patents, it was withdrawn. Otto then switched his machine to central chain drive, using a differential to take care of steering. Now called the Otto Dicycle, it faced competition from the new safety bicycles, which cost half as much. The Otto Safety Bicycle Company soon failed. The 1887 Stanley Show saw the final appearance of the Dicycle, now equipped with corrugated wavy spokes and "tyres wired in by Otto's patent process, which has been largely taken up by the trade, including Singer, who applies it to all his machines" (Sturmey 1887).

The Lady's Otto figured prominently in a lecture given by Charles Vernon Boys at the Royal Institution (Boys 1884); it was also mentioned in a fashion magazine:

> The Lady's Otto.—The same in all technical details, save that 50-inch wheels are used, and the whole is made lighter; dress guards, etc., are also provided. The Otto is the very *beau idéal* of a lady's cycle, safe, handy, and speedy—I was about to write fast, but the word might be mis-interpreted, as cycling on the Otto is a delightful exercise for the fair sex, less showy even than the most demure looking tricycle, whilst no more of the boot tops are shown than in walking. (*The Bazaar*, February 15, 1882)

Tricycle typology

In October of 1880 the Tricycle Union was formed as a breakaway from the Bicycle Union. A magazine titled *The Tricyclist* was launched in 1882. As development of the ordinary bicycle neared its end, tricycles were rapidly changing and advancing with every season. Once again it seemed as though the tricycle might become the personal mobility vehicle of the future. At the 1883 Stanley Show, tricycle models outnumbered bicycles. "The wonderful improvements in the construction of tricycles and the enormously increased demand for them," the cycling writer Harry Hewitt Griffin commented (1884), "has quite cast bicycles into the shade, both in manufacturing and popularity."

Archibald Sharp, a patent lawyer and a lecturer on engineering design, later published a classification table to characterize the highly diversified range of machines. (See figure 3.20.) He differentiated front steerers, side steerers, and rear steerers, then front-drive and rear-drive machines, with an additional category for the side-drive Coventry. Moreover, he differentiated between geared and ungeared machines—that is, between those that were chain driven and those that were pedaled directly or propelled by means of levers. "Single drivers" and "double drivers" referred to the number of wheels driven.

The Salvo was the first tricycle to be equipped with chain drive. Thereafter tricycles no longer demanded large wheels but could simply be geared up (Starley 1898).

M. Doubleday and Thomas Humber patented a tricycle driven and steered by the two front wheels, with the rider seated on a trailing backbone as on a high-wheeler (British patent 3,126 of 1878). Although The Humber was prone to "headers" (as high-wheelers also were), it proved very fast, and it became a favorite with racers. In the 1890s, the Cripper configuration, with three 28-inch wheels, became the standard tricycle of all safety manufacturers, and was motorized by Count de Dion as the Voiturette. Ingenious fold-away steering columns eased access to the saddles of front-steerers, especially for women; other types were steered by a spade handle placed to the side of the rider.

The majority of early tricycles began as single-drive rear-steerers with one of the large wheels loose on the driving axle. They were soon improved by making both front wheels drive, allowing for the overrunning of one wheel or the other by a clutch using rollers and cams (an anticipation of the later freewheel). T. Butler of Wokingham provided his three-wheel Omnicycle (British patent 1,909 of 1879), later produced by Singer, with three speeds for hill climbing. Its driving levers were fitted with leather straps that passed over segments fixed to the axle and worked by ratchet action. The metal tops of these segments could be altered to form arcs of three different circles, the smallest giving the lowest gear. Sturmey (1881) saw it as "really well made, being constructed throughout by machinery on the interchangeable system."

The Dual tricycle, built by a watchmaker named William Jeans in the English town of Christchurch in 1882, had two speeds. By means of gearwheels, either the left or the right wheel was driven while the other was freewheeling (Street 1979).

Though tricycles were seen from the start as safer than bicycles, horrendous accidents did occur. Some braking control was achieved, as in the bicycle, by backpedaling against a fixed drive. Spoon brakes, pressing onto the tires of the large wheels and operated by a brake lever, were succeeded by mechanisms that acted on the differential casing or the bottom bracket and could be applied without releasing one's grip on the handlebar.

The Rudge Tandem Tricycle No. 1 of 1889 had a band brake on the crankshaft and a handlebar-mounted "brake holder" for parking.

Commercial uses of tricycles should not be overlooked. Singer reportedly offered twenty different models of trade cycles in 1886, and Rover offered the Despatch, a variant of the Coventry Chair that was meant to carry goods. A tricycle was stable and could be designed to carry a considerable load. The Commissionaire Carrier Roadster of 1886 held a 19 × 19 × 14-inch box. Warwick later made carrier tricycles for many years.

One cargo cycle, Edward Burstow's Centre Cycle (British patent 4,707 of 1880), was designed to combine the best characteristics of the bicycle and the tricycle. It had one 52-inch wheel and four 18-inch wheels (one at each corner) held in a framework that allowed them to lift or tilt. A batch of Centre Cycles was built in 1882 by Martin Rücker, a colorful character who two years later launched an equally unlikely tandem with two 56-inch wheels in line. The Horsham Post Office operated a small fleet of Centre Cycles fitted with mail bags on either side, but Rücker's business failed in 1885 and the machine wasn't adopted for general commerce.

Many manufacturers produced tricycles: Coventry alone had twenty makers by 1879. Through the 1880s, tricycles were popular alternatives to the high-wheeler for those who wanted a safer means of human-powered travel. But despite their popularity and their mechanical refinement, tricycles were soon pushed to the sidelines by the development of safer

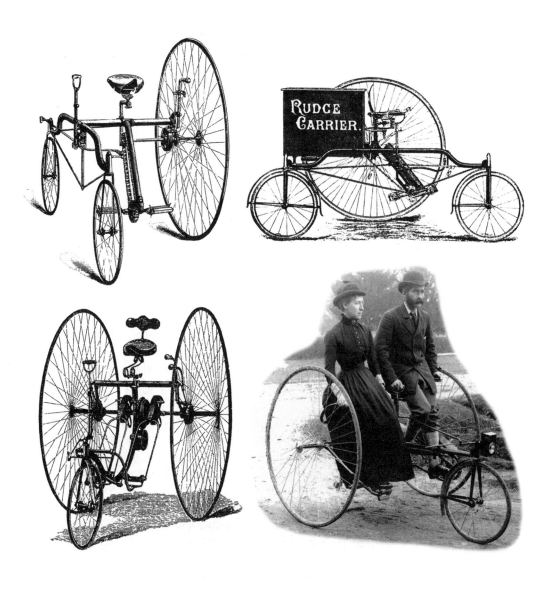

Figure 3.17 Above: Rudge's Coventry Rotary and Carrier tricycle (from manufacturer's brochures). Below: Singer's Omnicycle (from manufacturer's brochure) and Starley & Sutton's Meteor of 1883 (photo by Roger Street).

bicycles. A tricycle was, in any case, inherently heavier, more costly, and more cumbersome than a comparable bicycle, and the third wheel gave it somewhat higher rolling resistance.

Motorized velocipedes

By 1881, Karl Benz, who had experienced the exhilaration of speed on a cranked veloci-pede, was manufacturing stationary gas engines in Mannheim. There he developed a compact ¾-horsepower gasoline engine for his Patentmotorwagen of 1886, a front-steering tricycle sociable with a bench seat (figure 3.18). The wire wheels and presumably the tubular chassis were built by Heinrich Kleyer's Adler firm in Frankfurt. (Benz's associate Max Rose operated Kleyer's Mannheim dealership.) It can reasonably be argued that this was the earliest suc-cessful gasoline-fueled motorcar (German patent 37,435 and British patent 5,789 of 1886, American patent 386,798 of 1888). Karl Benz thus is the chief witness that the automobile evolved from bicycle technology and bicycle culture. The automobile historian James Flink puts it this way:

> No preceding innovation—not even the internal combustion engine—was as import-ant to the development of the automobile as the bicycle. Key elements of automo-tive technology that were first employed in the bicycle industry included steel-tube framing, ball bearings, chain drive, and differential gearing. An innovation of particular note is the pneumatic bicycle tire. . . . The bicycle industry also developed tech-niques of quantity production utilizing special machine tools, sheet metal stamping, and electric resistance welding that would become essential elements in the volume production of motor vehicles. A number of the more important early automobile man-ufacturers were first bicycle manufacturers. . . . A substantial proportion of engineer-ing talent as well in the early automobile industry was provided by former bicycle mechanics. . . . The greatest contribution of the bicycle, however, was that it created an enormous demand for individualized, long-distance transportation that could only be satisfied by the mass adoption of motor vehicles. (1988, 5)

Nazi propaganda denied the Benz gasoline tricycle's descent from British cycle technol-ogy (Lessing 2010) and hailed it as the quintessential automobile design: "Vehicles of various kinds were indeed available, but these were unsuitable for any mechanical propulsion. There-fore they had to be shaped anew: chassis and power source had to become an integrated whole." (Rauck 1943) According to that, there were no pedal tricycles to motorize.

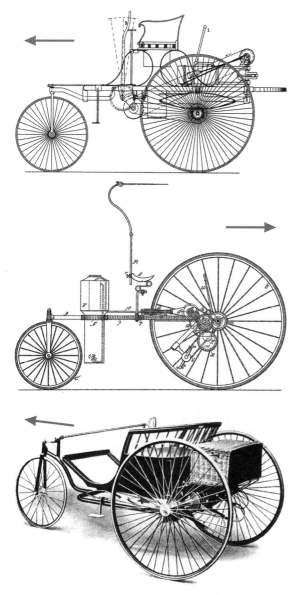

Figure 3.18 Above: Benz's gasoline motor velocipede (Patentmotorwagen) of 1886 (patent drawing). Center: Copeland's steamer Phaeton Moto-Cycle of 1887 (patent drawing). Below: Starley's electrified Despatch tricycle of 1888 (Heritage Trust).

In 1884 or 1885, in Phoenix, Arizona, Lucius Day Copeland equipped a Star high wheeler with a small steam engine and a boiler and operated the machine successfully. In 1886 he applied for a patent for a steam-powered automobile (US patent 360,760 of 1887). That patent was the basis of a prototype tricycle that the Northrop Manufacturing Company of Camden, New Jersey built for Copeland. The Moto-Cycle Manufacturing Company, formed in 1890 in Philadelphia, bought Copeland's patent and produced a steam automobile with a 4-horsepower engine under the name Phaeton Moto-Cycle until 1891 (Oliver 1974). After building up steam for 5 minutes, it could attain a speed of 10 miles per hour. According to an unsubstantiated source, 200 units were built.

Earlier still, a three-wheeled gasoline-fueled steam automobile was patented by George Long of Northfield, Massachusetts (US patent 281,091 of 1883). That machine was eventually reassembled by the Smithsonian Institution.

An electric automobile based on a Coventry Chair converted to a Despatch carrier was tested by John Kemp Starley of Starley & Sutton in 1888. A storage battery filled the wicker basket on the rear axle. This tricycle was taken to Boulogne for testing, since the Red-Flag Act imposed a speed limit of 4 miles per hour in the UK (Pinkerton and Roberts 1998).

Many more automotive pioneers were working in isolation, unaware of the accomplishments of others. In his autobiography, Hiram Percy Maxim, an automobile developer in Pope's Motor Carriage Division, expressed "amaze[ment] that so many of us began to work so nearly at the same time, and without the slightest notion that others were working at the same problem" (Flink 1988, 7).

Box 3.1   **HEADER LETTERS**

A rider was thrown on to some iron spikes, one of which ran through his jaw, cheek and eye. He happily recovered. *(Icycles Christmas Annual*, 1880)

Mr. H.A. Venables sustained frightful injuries from a fall, whilst racing down Handcross Hill; he fractured his skull and dislocated his jaw, which together with concussion of the brain, served to make his an almost hopeless case. He was taken to Guy's Hospital, and, with the vigorous vitality of a bicyclist, came round, and is, we are glad to say, happily recovered. *(Icycles Christmas Annual*, 1880)

A younger brother of the well-known P.G. Hebblethwaite, of Dewsbury and the L.A.C., met with a tremendous cropper down Garrowby Hill, in Yorkshire, through attempting to descend it on a brakeless 64-inch Carver; he sustained serious injuries, but is progressing favourably. *(Icycles Christmas Annual*, 1880)

Fred Crampton had a serious smash, through the breaking of a hub lamp. Harry Swindley had a bad fall over a gutter riding up from Ripley; T. Cowell Barrington, a cropper over a dog, with as result a very serious injury to the muscles of his arm; and many more minor injuries might be chronicled. (*Icycles Christmas Annual*, 1880)

A word or two respecting the Ariel lever machine that a friend of mine has, much to his regret. The result of his first trip was this; he was going at a good pace along a country road when the rubber tyre of his front wheel came suddenly off, and getting between the spokes and the frame, caused the machine to turn a complete somersault, landing the driver in the ditch at the roadside, cutting his hands and face, tearing his dress, and so injuring the machine that he could not ride it home. (*The Field*, November 22, 1871)

As Jones flew down hill admiring the light of his new lamp with his happy legs over the handles of his bicycle, in a sudden the lamp disappeared only to reappear quickly sideways between one of the spokes and the fork of the machine; it was not a log of wood that struck the earth but merely the top of Jones's skull. (Card 2008)

Frame style	Details & addresses	Frame x-section	Approximate date
	Meyer Classic vélocipède (with footrests) 35 Avenue de Wagram, Paris	◆	Before September 30, 1869
	Meyer et Cie Classic vélocipède (with footrests) 35 Avenue de Wagram, Paris	◆	From September 30, 1869 onward
	E. Meyer transitional vélocipède Rear wheel a little smaller (no footrests)	◆	1869–1870
	Grand bi Solid diamond-section frame spine (no name plate)	◆	1870–1872 (?)
	E. Meyer Grand bi, solid round-section frame spine 7 rue des Acacias Ternes, Paris	●	1873–1881 (*from street directory*)
	E. Meyer Transitional vélocipède 7 rue des Acacias Ternes, Paris	◆	From January 10, 1874 onward
	E. Meyer Grand bi, round-section tubular frame spine 7 rue des Acacias Ternes, Paris & 33 Avenue Rapp, Paris	◯	1872–1883 Avenue Rapp from 1882 onward (*Le Sport Vélocipédique* 9/27/1882)
	E. Meyer Grand bi, oval-section tubular frame spine 33 Avenue Rapp, Paris	⬭	1882 to the end

Figure 3.19 Meyer's production of 1869–1890, as reconstructed from collected machines (Reynaud 2011).

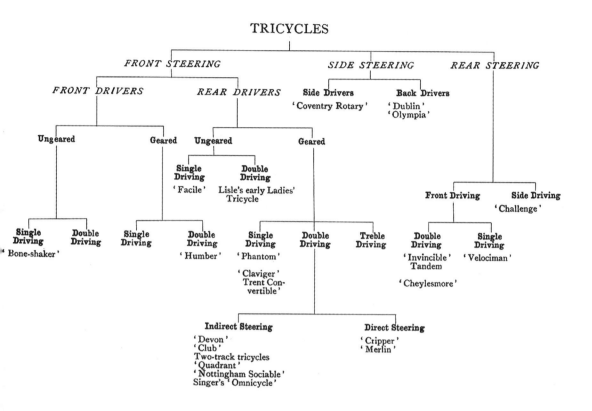

Figure 3.20 Archibald Sharp's typology of tricycles (Sharp 1896).

INDIRECT DRIVE

4

As bicycle technology advanced and roads improved, it became apparent that a bicycle should travel about 16 feet on level ground for each propulsive thrust of the rider's left and right legs. Achieving that with cranks fixed directly to the driving wheel required a front wheel about 60 inches in diameter. Riding a bicycle with so large a wheel was difficult. A primary drive system that allowed a smaller, more manageable driving wheel was therefore desirable.

Various systems were tried, some employing levers and cranks, some belts and pulleys, some rotary driveshafts, some meshing spur wheels, and some chains and sprockets. In this chapter, we review these alternatives and show how the chain achieved dominance as the means of indirect primary drive. The related topic of variable gearing is covered in chapter 7.

LEVER-AND-CRANK DRIVES

Riding a draisine was more efficient than walking, because the rider's legs didn't have to support the body's weight. However, even when rider's weight is supported, energy is needed to accelerate and decelerate the legs. That energy isn't efficiently recovered, because muscles must be used to slow down and to swing the legs. But a circular crank motion, or a treadle action, makes it possible to recover energy. When one leg slows down, the kinetic energy is transferred to the opposite leg, since the left and right drives are rigidly connected.

Mechanical drives have an even greater advantage: they make it possible to apply higher forces more efficiently at lower limb velocity, so the rider can travel faster. The relationship between force and velocity is optimized to achieve maximum power. In muscle motion, maximum force occurs at zero velocity, and zero effective force occurs at maximum velocity. Maximum power output is achieved somewhere between the extremes.

Lever-and-crank drives were well known to nineteenth-century engineers, having been used in steam engines, in industrial machinery, and in railway braking systems for many decades. Such drives were applied to derivatives of the high-wheeler to produce bicycles that were easier to mount and presented less risk that the rider would be sent over the handlebars. During the velocipede craze of 1869, US patent applications for lever-operated rear-drive bicycles were filed by John Smith of Brooklyn (patent 89,695), Benjamin Lawson of New York (patent 90,563), Thomas Morse of Fairhaven, Massachusetts (patent 92,991), and Charles Dayton of Meriden, Connecticut (patent 96,208).

Most lever-drive systems were what Archibald Sharp described as "four-link kinematic chains." The four links were the crank fixed to the wheel hub, a lever oscillating around a fixed center, a coupling rod connecting the end of the crank to a point on the oscillating lever, and a fixed link formed by the frame of the bicycle. The rider pushed a pedal fixed to the oscillating lever, causing it to rotate the wheel.

The Singer Xtraordinary, which had a lever and a crank, had slightly smaller wheels than comparable machines and a riding position that was lower and farther back. The crank, connected directly to the hub of the front wheel, was also connected to a nearly vertical lever. The top of the lever was connected to the upper part of the fork by a short pivoting link. The lower end of the lever curved down below and behind the hub to support the pedal. The Xtraordinary was designed by George Singer (British patent 4,265 of 1879) and made by Singer & Company Ltd. of Coventry.

The Facile was another high-wheeler derivative with lever-and-crank drive. On each side of the machine, the fork was extended downward and forward from the hub to provide a fulcrum for a drive lever, which was approximately horizontal. A coupling rod connected the wheel crank to the middle of the drive lever. To maximize leverage, the pedal was attached to the rear end of the lever. The Facile's lever-drive system was later used on a rear-drive bicycle. Front-drive and rear-drive versions of the Facile were available with an epicyclic gear in the hub to turn the drive wheel faster for each pedal thrust. The Facile was designed by John Beale (British patent 33,225 of 1878). Ellis & Company made Faciles in the first half of the 1880s, and Beale & Straw produced them until 1892 (Clayton 2012b).

Another rear-driver with lever-and-crank drive was the Claviger. On each side of the hub of the rear wheel was a crank linked to a curved lever. The pedal was at the forward end of the lever, midway between the wheels. A long coupling rod connected the middle of the lever to the down tube of the bicycle, below the saddle.

The Claviger range of cycles was launched in 1887. William Golding's 212-page patent (British patent 11,990) was for an "Improved Method for the Conversion, Modification, Regulation and Transmission of Motion." The patent mentioned cycles only briefly, but between 1886 and 1887 Golding was awarded four British patents specific to cycles, and other patents in Belgium, France, and Germany. In 1887, in the United States, he applied for a consolidated patent, specific to cycles, that incorporated elements of the earlier patents (US patent 400,204 of 1889). By 1889 it was clear that the design had no commercial future (Clayton 2001).

SWINGING-LEVER AND LINEAR DRIVES

Each of the drive systems mentioned above required a rotary or oval motion of the pedals. Some lever drives required a more linear, treadling action. This had the disadvantage that the rider's legs and feet had to be repeatedly accelerated and decelerated in a jerky action.

By 1869, one J. Cox had applied for a patent for a swinging-lever drive specifically for a bicycle (British patent 834 of 1869). In a typical swinging-lever or treadle drive, a lever on either side of the bicycle was suspended from a point on the frame and had a pedal at its lower end. Thus the pedal could only move back and forth along an arc. In early designs, such as Cox's and those alleged to have been built in the middle of the nineteenth century by Johann Trefz, Thomas McCall, and Viarengo de Forville, the swinging levers drove a crank on the rear wheel's axle by means of connecting rods. (In Cox's design, there was an optional ancillary vertical lever that could be strapped to the rider's body to enable him to sway his body back and forth to input more energy—an idea that, not surprisingly, failed to catch on.)

Some later treadle systems worked differently. Attached to the swinging lever or treadle was a length of drive chain, which wrapped around a freewheel sprocket on the rear wheel.

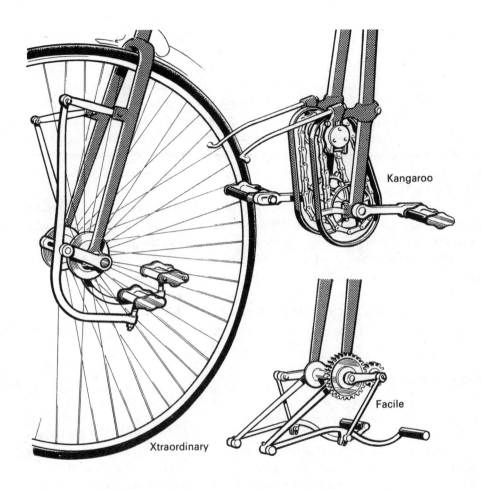

Figure 4.1 Three early ways of lowering the riding position of a front-drive bicycle (R. John Way).

The end of the chain was held tight by a coil spring. When the rider pushed the treadle, the lever pulled the chain, thereby rotating the sprocket and the drive wheel. Having reached the limit of travel, the rider let the treadle return to the rest position under the action of the coil spring. The second version of the American Star, designed by William Kelley of Smithville, New York, had a particularly sophisticated treadle-drive system with leather straps instead of chains (US patent 321,819 of 1885).

Several later designs had a variety of attachment points for the drive chains, sometimes on bell cranks. The variable leverage gave the effect of variable gearing. The 1892 Svea, conceived by the brothers Fredrik and Birger Ljungström of Stockholm and financed by Alfred Nobel (Hult 1992), had a drive system of this kind. Between 1894 and 1896, Birger Ljungström applied for three British patents relating to treadle drive. (The subsequent US patents were 556,545 of 1896, 571,197 of 1896, and 631,219 of 1899.) The machines were made in Sweden, in England, and in France. The Svea seems to have inspired a similar and contemporary British machine, the Alert, which used steel cables where the Svea used chains (Street 2010).

Lever-drive bicycles enjoyed a late flourishing in France in the period 1895–1905. The Terrot Lévocyclette of 1905, a license-built Svea, provided a 10-to-1 gear range by means of a dozen notches for the drive chains.

Lever-and-crank systems have been reinvented from time to time but have never been commercially successful on a large scale. The J-Rad, a recumbent of the early 1920s, had a treadle drive. In 1937, Eugen Woerner, whose factory in Feuerbach (a suburb of Stuttgart) manufactured lubrication pumps, obtained patents for a bicycle lever-drive system in most of the Western world (German patent 675,648 of 1939, British patent 499,002 of 1939, US patent 2,168,110 of 1939). Woerner also wanted to build an add-on lever drive for bicycles with coaster-brake hubs (German patent 654,364 of 1937), but World War II curtailed his plans (Grützner 2009).

A more recent example was the 1985 Alenax Transbar bicycle, invented by Marn Seol of Rochester, New York and produced by the Alenax Corporation for about three years (US patent 4,630,839 of 1986). It had a drive system very similar to that of the 1892 Svea.

An interesting linear cable drive, developed in the late 1990s, was invented by Dutch brothers Lambert and Derk Thijs (world patent 00/12378 of 2000). Instead of a length of bicycle chain, it had a steel cable wrapped around a grooved cone (a technology known to clockmakers as a fusée) on the rear wheel. The fusée, which the inventors called a Snek, contained a clock spring to enable it to rewind automatically after each pull of the cable. The cable was pulled partly by a sliding carriage pushed by the pedals and partly by pulling on pivoting handlebars. Because the rider's propulsive action was similar to rowing, the recumbent bicycle built around the Snek was called the Rowbike.

Figure 4.2 Left: A 1936 brochure for Woerner lever-drive bicycles. Right: detail of the hub internals of a Woerner bicycle, from an undated brochure.

An innovative aspect of the Snek cable drive was that a derailleur shifter allowed the cable's stroke to begin on different parts of the fusée cone, which gave the effect of a higher or a lower gear. This drive system achieved some success in recumbent races and record attempts (Wilson 2004, 335).

BELTS AND PULLEYS

Belt drives were widely used in industrial machinery by the early nineteenth century and later came into use in agricultural machinery. Industrial use of belt drives continued well into the twentieth century. Many of the belts were made of balata (a non-elastic rubber from a South American tree), although leather and rope were also used.

B. Smythe's British Facilitator tricycle design of 1819 called for a two-speed belt drive. (Whether such a machine was actually built isn't known with certainty.) In 1869, Frederick Shearing of Norfolk designed a bicycle with belt drive to the rear wheel. He claimed to have built three machines (Ritchie 1975, 122–123). Also in 1869, Alphonse Barberon and Joseph Meunier of France patented a three-speed belt-drive system. Similar in principle to stepped pulley systems that had been used for decades in factories, it was a precursor of derailleur gearing. Whether Barberon and Meunier marketed their belt-drive system (for which they received British patent 2,626 of 1869) is not known.

A rare early instance of use of a flexible drive belt on a commercially made cycle was the BSA-manufactured Otto dicycle, discussed in the preceding chapter. Eduard Carl Friedrich Otto, a British subject living in Surrey, patented his belt-drive system in the UK and the US (British patent 1,673 of 1880). Most drive belts of that time were canvas or leather, but Otto's was steel. It ran on pulleys covered with India rubber, vulcanite, or leather for better grip. As recently as 2011, David Gordon Wilson experimented with a modern stainless steel belt and found that the high tension it required caused the cycle's frame to break (Wilson 2004, 326).

With belt drives, as Archibald Sharp pointed out (1896, 396), "the effort transmitted is the difference of the tensions of the tight and slack sides of the band; the maximum effort that can be transmitted is therefore dependent on the initial tightness." "If the speed . . . be low," Sharp added, "the tension necessary to transmit a certain amount of power is relatively high. In such cases the available friction of a belt on a smooth pulley is too low. . . ." Because the flat belts of the time depended on friction, belt drive made little progress in the early days of cycling.

In the 1970s, interest in belt drive revived. At the Massachusetts Institute of Technology, David Gordon Wilson converted a 1960s Moulton bicycle to belt drive, using an ordinary industrial toothed belt (Whitt 1978, 131). Since the 1960s, toothed belts had become more durable and more efficient, owing to the use of materials such as urethane for the belt and teeth and aramid fibers for tensile reinforcement. But because of the bending that occurred as the belt passed over its sprockets, toothed belts were generally not quite as efficient as well-lubricated roller chains. There was also the possibility of a slight loss of efficiency caused by stretching of the belt under extreme tension. Furthermore, a drive belt on a bicycle sometimes jumped a tooth, even when the tension was correctly adjusted—for example, when a heavy rider accelerated energetically after a stop. On the other hand, a toothed belt required no lubrication and was more efficient than a poorly lubricated chain.

By 1985, Bridgestone had launched its Picnica, a folding model that Bridgestone claimed was the world's first series-produced belt-drive bicycle. Bridgestone also produced belt drives for bicycles made by other companies, such as those used on the 2012 Corratec B-Drive city bikes.

From time to time, other belt-drive bicycles appeared on the market, mostly short-range folding or commuter models. One of the best-known and most enduring was the Strida, a folding small-wheeler. Conceived by the British designer Mark Sanders, it has been in and out of production since 1987.

The Gates Corporation of Denver, founded in 1911, became a market leader in drive belts for many different applications. Gates designed and made the belt drives used on the Strida from the 1980s on. These belt drives were specifically refined for bicycle use. Gates had to overcome problems with thermal expansion of aramid tensile reinforcement, and also

Figure 4.3 A Gates Carbon Drive system. Note the provision for separating the seat stay from the wheel dropout for replacement of the belt (Gates Corporation, photo by Robert Gebler).

redesigned the belt teeth to minimize tooth jumping. Gates's lightweight Carbon Drive belt-and-sprocket system, introduced in the early twenty-first century specifically for bicycle use, had strands of carbon fiber and teeth of nylon-jacketed polyurethane. The back of the belt was ribbed at an angle of 90° to the length of the chain to reduce bending resistance. The Carbon Drive achieved some success in racing and was used in 2009 by the British rider James Bowthorpe on what was then the fastest around-the-world bicycle ride. Moreover, in an independent third-party test conducted in September of 2007 the Carbon Drive was found to be as efficient as a chain drive (Microbac 2007).

The German Thun system of the late 1990s used a toothed V-section belt and an over-sized plastic rear sprocket that was also an internally toothed ring. The ring engaged with a plastic spur wheel on the rear hub. As the belt pulled the "floating" rear sprocket around, the engagement of its inner teeth with the spur wheel turned the rear hub. The Thun system, used on the special edition Alex Moulton Bentley bicycle, proved troublesome (typically the rear sprocket failed) and soon went out of production.

The Speed E flexible drive, created in the 1970s by Winfred Berg of East Rockaway, New York, had a belt that resembled a chain and a pair of stranded steel tension cables bridged by polyurethane buttons that engaged with the sprocket's teeth. This lightweight system was extremely efficient when used on human-powered aircraft, such as the *Gossamer Albatross*, but it wasn't sufficiently robust for use on bicycles (Wilson 2004, 324).

One problem with applying belt drive to most bicycle designs was the need to make a part of the frame removable. A drive belt couldn't be split, as a chain could, so unless the bike had a cantilevered rear fork it was usually necessary to "break" the rear triangle to install or replace a belt, or even to change a tire or an inner tube. Typically a section of the seat stay had to be removed. Alternatively, a modified dropout, with a break between the chain stay and the seat stay, could be used. Such adaptations increased a bike's cost and could result in weakness. And despite many attempts by inventors (among them Barberon & Meunier) as early as 1869, no successful derailleur-style gear was marketed for a belt drive. Thus, the user was generally limited to a single-speed transmission, hub gears, bracket or chainwheel gears, or a combination of these. In addition, doubts remained about the durability of belt drives in stop-and-go city traffic—anecdotal evidence suggested that premature belt failure could occur. Thus, for the most part, belt drive remained a niche option offered by a few makers of portable and commuter bicycles.

In a recumbent with two-stage drive, a belt and a chain could be used together. About 40 years after he converted a Moulton to belt drive, David Gordon Wilson built a recumbent with belt drive from the cranks to the bottom bracket and a conventional final drive with a chain and a derailleur. There was no cycle-specific belt long enough, so he again used a standard industrial belt (a Browning Gearbelt 2400–8M.20).

Figure 4.4 Wilson's recumbent, with Browning belt and conventional chain drive (David Gordon Wilson).

SHAFT DRIVE

Using a shaft and bevel gears to transmit drive from the pedals to the rear wheel is a visually and technically elegant approach. In 1881, Ephraim Shay of Michigan patented a novel concept (US patent 242,992) for a shaft-drive locomotive to be used on lightly constructed lumber railroads with log ties, where it was beneficial for the locomotive's tractive effort to be spread over many lightly loaded wheels. This undoubtedly helped to popularize the general concept of shaft drive with bevel gears.

Shaft drive was used in Thomas Moore's Orbicycle tricycle in the same year Shay was granted his patent, by which time the Lima Locomotive Works in Ohio had been delivering shaft-drive locomotives for several years. The Orbicycle used bevel gears in an oil-filled orb

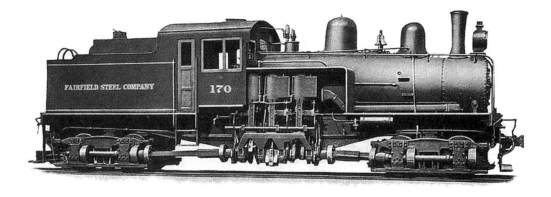

Figure 4.5   A Shay shaft-drive locomotive (Wikipedia Commons).

at each end of the driveshaft. This meant that the driving mechanism was well lubricated and safe from water, dust, and grit, especially in comparison with the chain drives then being widely adopted. Moore's shaft drive was said to have been patented, but no such patent has been traced. It may not have progressed beyond the provisional or pending stage.

By 1891, the Partington Cycle Company Ltd. of Middleton, near Manchester, was making bicycles and tricycles with Richard Kent Hartley's hand-rotary power attachment, using either shaft or chain drive (British patent 14,045 of 1889). The first commercially available application of shaft drive to a bicycle (as distinct from a tricycle) was made possible by this unusual auxiliary front-wheel-drive system.

The Start Cycle Company of London showed a chainless safety bicycle at the Stanley Show in 1890, but it was never patented. A Mr. A. Fearnhead (whose business was registered at Little James Street, Gray's Inn Road, Holborn, London) is said to have applied for a patent

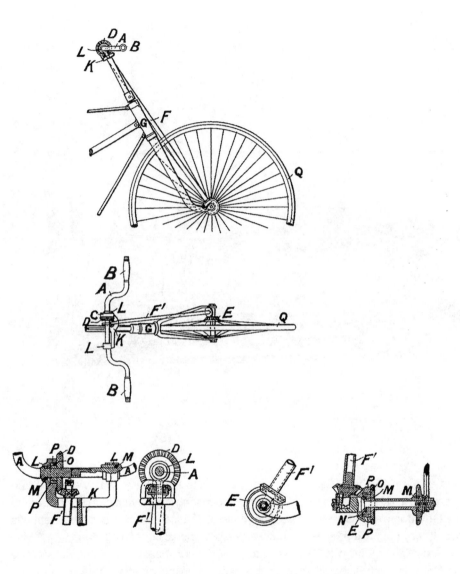

Figure 4.6 Hartley's design for a hand-driven front-wheel shaft drive (patent drawing).

for a bicycle shaft drive the same year, but we have found no reliable evidence. However, the magazine *Cycling* reported in its issue of October 3, 1891 that Fearnhead displayed a shaft-drive bicycle that autumn. "The chainless-safety has no charms for me," a reporter for the *CTC Monthly Gazette* opined in the January 1892, "and I do not think it will ever become very popular."

In 1896, Archibald Sharp, Britain's most eminent technical writer on cycle design at the time, wrote:

> The Fearnhead Gear was a bevel-wheel gear, bevel-wheels being fixed on the crank-axle and hub respectively and geared together by a shaft enclosed in the lower frame tube [chain stay]. If bevel-wheels could be accurately and cheaply cut by machinery, it is possible that gears of this description might supplant, to a considerable extent, the chain-driving gear; but the fact that the teeth of bevel-wheels cannot be accurately milled is a serious obstacle to their practical success. (461–462)

Around the time Fearnhead invented his shaft drive, Walter Stillman Jr. of Closter, New Jersey applied for a patent for a similar system (US patent 456,387 of 1891). Stillman's drive-shaft ran below the chain stay. Another American design, by Sidney Grant of Springfield, Massachusetts, had the shaft in the chain stay, as Fearnhead's did. Although Grant's design (US patent 509,079 of 1893) called for conventional bevel gears on the crankshaft and the rear hub, the gears on each end of the driveshaft had spin rollers instead of cut teeth. An 1899 shaft-drive design by Frederick Schoenthal of Buffalo (US patent 653,968 of 1900) used a similar approach, as did the Overman Victor Chainless bicycles of 1899.

The Orient shaft-drive bicycles made by the Waltham Manufacturing Company of Massachusetts had spin rollers throughout the drive train, rather than bevel gears or a mix of bevel gears and spin rollers. The transmission design used by the Waltham company had been devised by James Henry Sager of Rochester, New York (German patent 100,180 of 1898 and probably Canadian patent 60,484 of 1898). The great racing cyclist Major Taylor broke many records on Waltham Orient shaft-drive machines (Wilson 2004, 333). In Britain, Walter John Lloyd of Birmingham patented his Cross Roller shaft drive, which similarly used spin rollers throughout the drive system (British patent 6,345 of 1897). The British Quadrant shaft-drive bicycle used Lloyd's Cross Roller system.

Shaft drive was adopted more eagerly in the United States and in France than in Britain. The League Cycle Company of Hartford began producing shaft-drive machines in 1892; later it was absorbed into Colonel Pope's company. In 1897, trying to breathe life into the dying American cycle boom, Pope launched a new range of shaft-drive Columbia machines.

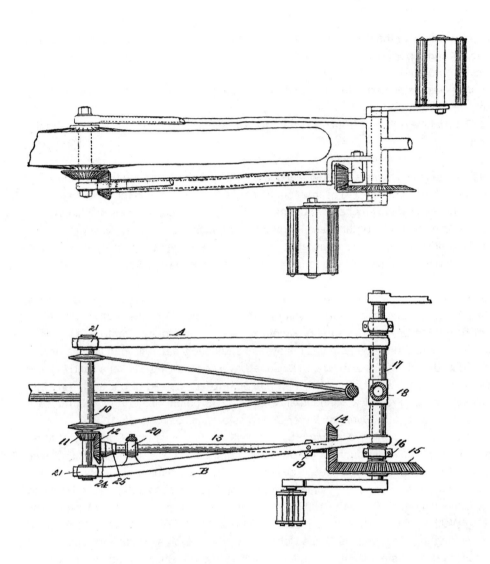

Figure 4.7 Above: Fearnhead's shaft drive (National Cycle Library). Below: Stillman's shaft drive (patent drawing).

Figure 4.8   Above: Patent drawings of Sager's spin-roller shaft drive (left) and Lloyd's cross-roller gear (right).
Below: 1897 Quadrant shaft-drive bicycle (National Cycle Library).

Columbia continued to offer shaft-drive models until 1920. The first of these were expensive, costing almost twice as much as a comparable chain-drive bike (Herlihy 2004, 286–290). Most other American manufacturers also produced shaft-drive machines in the late 1890s.

An interesting American refinement to bevel-gear shaft drive, designed in 1897 by William Cowan of Los Angeles, put a universal joint at each end of the shaft (US patent 633,753 of 1899). Cowan's aim was to make the alignment of the shaft less critical and thus allow lighter and cheaper frame construction.

Universal joints (also known as universal couplings, U-joints, Cardan joints, or Hooke's joints) were used in some tricycle drive systems, such as the Eclectic of the early 1880s. Whereas a single universal joint has a jerky action, a pair of joints 90° out of phase on the same shaft can achieve nearly constant velocity.

Métropole, the leading French maker of shaft-drive bicycles, offered its Acatène (French for "chainless") range from 1895 until at least 1907. Acatène cycles had a bevel-gear shaft drive of a design patented by Paul Malicet and Eugéne Blin of Aubervilliers, France (British patent 18,122 of 1894). As in many other shaft-drive systems, the shaft was within the chain stay.

By 1897, Humber was building Métropole Acatènes under license in England. However, shaft drive made relatively little impact there, even though the Wilkinson Sword Company (in or around 1898) offered bicycle manufacturers a "packaged" shaft-drive system.

An interesting bevel-gear shaft drive was developed by a former French artillery captain name Octave Robert. Patented in France early in 1899, it was the subject of two subsequent modification certificates. Robert sought to improve existing shaft-drive systems, such as that used on the Acatène, by providing an easily removable and adjustable bevel pinion and by adding a spring-loaded link between the crankshaft and the large bevel wheel. A spring-steel link between the crank and the bevel acted provided elasticity during acceleration. Whether this was of any real advantage is debatable, but the design was relatively successful. It was used on La Percutante, a chainless bicycle launched by the Saint-Étienne maker Jussy at the Paris Salon du Cycle in 1901 and was subsequently marketed by Peugeot from 1903 until 1912 (Chaussinand 2010).

Makers of shaft-drive bicycles in other countries around this time included Bratří Potůčkové in Czechoslovakia, Fabrique Nationale in Belgium, and Graziosa and Noricum in Austria. In Germany there was a craze for chainless bicycles around 1900 (Grützner 2008.) German shaft-drive brands included Adler of Frankfurt (which used Sager's spin-roller system), Brennabor of Brandenburg, Dürkopp of Bielefeld, Gritzner of Durlach, Presto of Chemnitz, and Wanderer of Dresden (Grützner 2009).

Figure 4.9 The Eclectic drive system, with three universal joints (Henry Sturmey, *The Tricyclists' Indispensable Annual and Handbook*, ca. 1882).

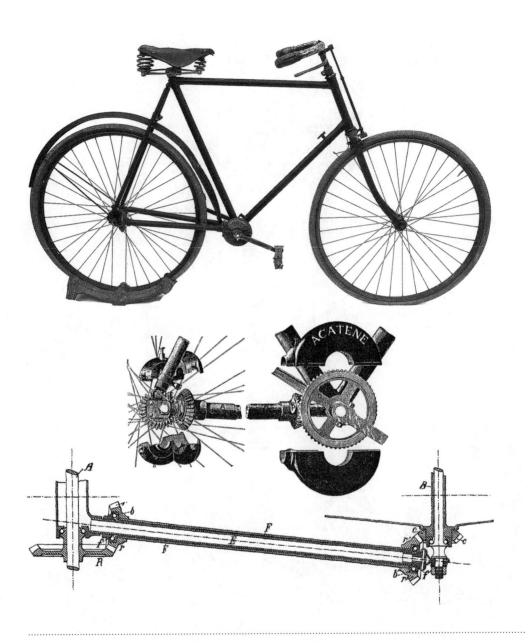

Figure 4.10   Above: A Métropole Acatène, circa 1897–98 (Helge Schultz). Center: The Acatène's drive system, from an 1897 UK catalog (National Cycle Library). Below: Malicet and Blin's shaft drive (patent drawing).

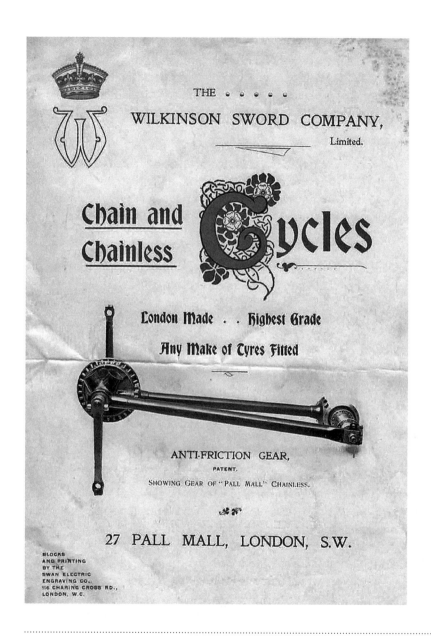

Figure 4.11 A Wilkinson Sword Company brochure offering shaft-drive kits (National Cycle Library).

A so-called shaft drive patented by the British engineer Arthur John Battersby (Canadian patent 41,259 of 1892) was something of an oddity. Shafts on both sides of the rear wheel were connected to a short crank on the rear hub. The front end of each shaft was connected to a crankshaft driven by a spur gear that meshed with an internally toothed gear ring on the axle of the pedal crank. Thus, the shafts were reciprocating connecting rods, not rotating driveshafts.

In more recent times, shaft drive has been reintroduced periodically but has achieved little commercial success. The Kariz system was marketed from 1995 to 1997. The Korean Tara No Chain bike, launched in 2005, soon disappeared. As of 2012, a Danish cycle maker called Biomega was producing two shaft-drive machines, the Amsterdam and the Copenhagen.

Early shaft-drive bicycles were typically single-speed machines. Later ones sometimes combined shaft drive with a multi-speed hub gear. Shaft drive could not be used with a derailleur in any practicable configuration.

There were two principal problems with typical shaft drives. First, to work efficiently, the bevel gears had to be made very accurately and aligned precisely, and even when that was done shaft drive usually was less efficient than chain drive. Second, owing to their small radius, the bevel gears on the driveshaft were subjected to much more stress than the corresponding components in chain drives. In addition, torsional forces in the driveshaft could reduce efficiency. Beyond that, a durable and efficient shaft drive was expensive to make, and it required a bicycle to have a non-standard frame.

SPUR-GEAR DRIVE

Another way of transmitting power from the cranks to the rear wheel was by means of spur gears. The chainwheel and the sprocket were replaced by spur gears (pinions), and a third pinion meshing with them completed the drive train. In 1897 the Carroll Chainless Bicycle Company of Philadelphia introduced a machine with such a drive. This bicycle was called, accurately enough, the Gear-to-Gear (Canadian patent 59,038 of 1898). Another example, very similar to Carroll's, was the George Machtler bicycle (circa 1900). Neither of these machines gained much of a following.

In the 1890s, a few rear-guard manufacturers of front-drive bicycles adopted spur gearing. These descendants of the high-wheeler retained rotary cranks on the front wheel but used spur gearing to make a smaller front wheel rotate farther for each turn of the cranks. The most successful and neatest designs used a single-speed epicyclic gear at the hub. The Crypto

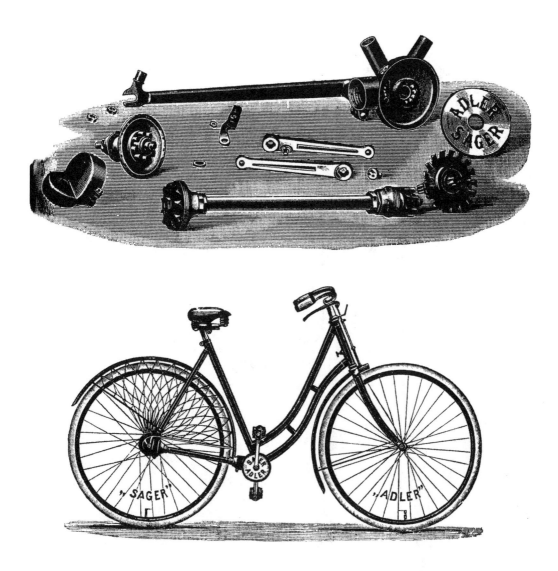

Figure 4.12 The German Adler bicycle had Sager's patent shaft drive (Schiefferdecker 1900).

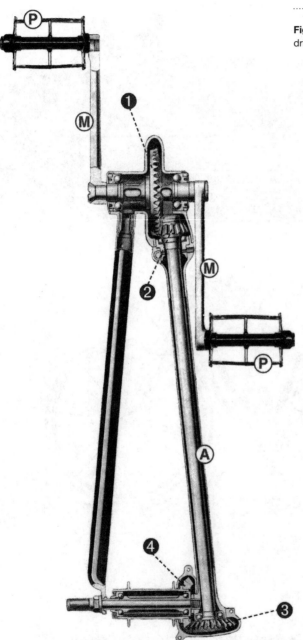

Figure 4.13 Fabrique Nationale (F.N.) shaft drive (© Ars Mechanica Foundation).

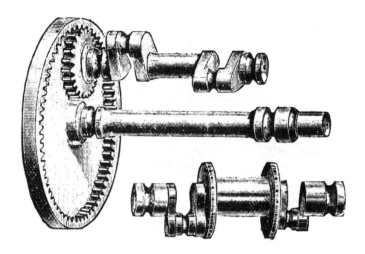

Figure 4.14 Arthur John Battersby's "shaft drive" (National Cycle Library).

Bantamette, shown in chapter 15, is a classic example. Spur gearing was also used on some tricycles, such as the 1882 Duals.

Electrical and hydrostatic drive were suggested for use on bicycles, but neither proved practicable. It was, of course, chain drive that proved supreme.

CHAIN DRIVE

Under ideal conditions, chain drive was very efficient, didn't require high tension, didn't slip in the wet, and was cheaper than shaft drive. And chain drive was, to an extent, a known art—as early as 1843, Isambard Kingdom Brunel had used four huge inverted-tooth chains to transmit up to 1,000 horsepower from the four-cylinder steam engine of the steamship *Great Britain* to the propeller shaft.

The idea of using a chain to transmit one manpower to the drive wheel of a bicycle was being discussed in the British technical press by the mid 1860s. In 1869, Newton Wilson secured a British provisional patent (number 1,248) (Roberts 1991, 62). In France, before the bicycle industry closed down in 1870 for the duration of the Franco-Prussian War, at least three inventors applied for patents for chain-driven bicycles: Dubos (French patent 80,106 of 1868), Desnos-Gardissal (82,082 of 1868), and Mougeol (86,676 of 1869). A French machine devised in 1870 by Sargent had a large front wheel (about 55 inches in diameter) driven by a chain.

Despite competition from the other drive systems, chain drive became commonplace with the move from direct front-wheel drive to indirect rear-wheel drive and the coming of the safety bicycle. Chain drive was also used on some late front-drivers, such as the Kangaroo (Clayton 2012), to achieve a lower riding position. (See figure 4.1 above.)

After about 1885, simple block chain (often called Humber chain) became the most popular type. Block chain had solid blocks of hardened steel alternating with pairs of side plates. Each pair of side plates was riveted together by pins passing through holes in the blocks. The rivet pins were shouldered to ensure correct spacing of the side plates. The teeth of the sprockets could engage with the chain only by means of the spaces between the side plates on every other link. Thus, the sprockets and chainwheels had large gaps between the teeth. These chains were, however, cheap to make, and they were robust.

Although track racers used block chain for at least 60 years, bush-roller chain was used on virtually all non-racing cycles. Hans Renold invented block chain in 1885 but failed to patent it. However, he had already patented bush-roller chain five years earlier. In bush-roller

"THE DUAL."
THE ZEPHYR TRICYCLE CO., LOWER FORD STREET, COVENTRY.

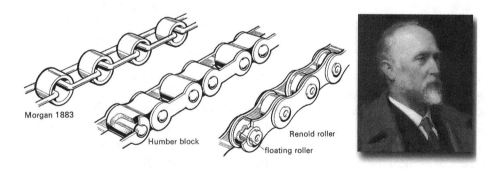

Figure 4.15 A 1882 Dual tricycle with spur gearing (*The Tricyclist* 1, 1882–83, 24).
Figure 4.16 Left: Three chain types of the late nineteenth century (R. John Way). Right: A portrait of Hans Renold (copyright Renold plc 2012).

chain, the block was dispensed with and replaced by a pair of inner side plates. The inner plates could rotate on the rivet pins and had bushings (hollow rivets) on which ran loose rollers. Thus a large, freely rotating bearing surface was provided for the teeth of the sprocket and the chainwheel.

Hans Renold was born in Switzerland on July 31, 1852, the son of a baker. At the age of 18 he entered the Polytechnic School in Zurich to study engineering; he then served in the army (Tripp 1956). In 1871 he was in Paris, engaged in reconstruction work. In 1873 he took a job with the machine exporters Felber-Jucker in Manchester. A brief but unsuccessful partnership in the same trade with a Mr. Calvert followed. In 1879 Renold bought a small bankrupt business in Salford. This was the business of James Slater (previously Slater & Steele), which made various kinds of chains for mills and quarries. Slater had a patent for both bowl chain and bush chain dating from 1864 (Clayton 1993).

Renold could hardly have foreseen the coming cycle boom, but his timing proved impeccable. Early tricycles had been lever-driven, with a cranked axle. James Starley's Salvo tricycle of 1878 was the first to have a chain drive. One advantage of chain drive was that the drive ratio could be changed easily to suit the customer. John Starley later said his uncle James, not knowing where suitable chain could be obtained, had made the first few chains himself before buying plain roller chain (based on Slater's patent) from Renold's Manchester firm. John Starley claimed to have suggested the idea of the bush-roller chain around the time that Hans Renold brought such a chain to Coventry for Starley to see. According to Starley (1898), Renold later paid him royalties on all the chains he used. Whatever the chain of events, Renold received his basic patent (British patent 1,219) in March of 1880.

Although patent chain (as it became known) solved the problem of wear between the inner link plates and the pins, wear to the sprocket teeth—which could cause a worn chain to jump teeth—remained problematic. Aware that his product depended on the correct design of sprocket teeth, Renold supplied users with technical drawings and even correct milling cutters. His steel strip was obtained from Arthur Lee in Sheffield, and he invented special-purpose machines for chain production. His son, Sir Charles Renold, eventually took control of the company, which is still active today.

Though most solid-tired safety bicycles were fitted with block chain, Renold's one-inch-pitch patent chain was usually preferred for the large sprockets used on tricycles. (A chain's pitch is the distance between the centers of any two adjoining pins.) For a while, Renold maintained that his patent chain could not be made satisfactorily with a shorter pitch. It remained for competitors, upon the expiration of the patent in 1894, to prove him wrong. Perry & Company began producing half-inch chain, and Renold eventually followed suit in 1899. Soon half-inch-pitch bush-roller chains were a world standard.

But whereas the pitch became standard, narrower and narrower chains were introduced. A narrower chain could accommodate thinner and more closely spaced sprockets as the number of cogs on derailleur freewheels increased from two or three to twelve. In the early 1980s, chains without bushings were introduced; these were more flexible. (For more on developments in chain technology, see chapter 7.)

Mud and dust from roads caused chains to clog and wear. This was one of the major reasons why there was so much interest in shaft drive in the 1890s. Since the days of Starley's Salvo tricycle, riders had been encouraged to keep their chains well oiled and to clean them after riding in foul weather. That was never easy, and a well-oiled chain tended to transfer its oil to the rider's clothes. One solution, first proposed in 1886, was J. Harrison Carter's patented Oil-tight Chain Lubricator and Gear Cover (British patent 9,283 of 1886, improved by patent 9,157 of 1888), forerunner of the famous Little Oil Bath Gearcase. Carter was a manufacturer of lubrication cases for milling machines. His designs for cycles began the use of an accessory that is still with us today. In the 1890s most major manufacturers offered chain cases on their better roadsters, and the merits of different styles were much discussed in the cycling press. "If a chain safety is used fail not to have Harrison Carter's case fitted," Harry Griffin advised (1892); "the initial cost will be repaid times over in extra comfort and ease of running." Chain cases were particularly popular on ladies' models.

ASYMMETRIC CHAINWHEELS

Chain drive enabled designers to reconsider the problem of pedaling through "dead center," when the cranks are at the top and bottom of their stroke and there is no effective tangential force from the rider's feet. By the early 1890s, some inventors thought that a non-circular chainwheel might help. (See, e.g., US patents 513,589 and 515,449 of 1894.) From then until the present day, various attempts have been made to use asymmetric chainwheels—oval, elliptical, or in a more complex non-circular shape. The idea came and went many times for more than 100 years. For example, Roger Durham's elliptical chainwheels, introduced in the early 1970s, enjoyed brief popularity in the United States for racing and touring. (Durham's US patent, number 3,899,932 of 1975, concerned improving chain retention by using longer teeth on the shorter diameter.) Usually the idea was to have a larger diameter where the cranks were horizontal and offering maximum leverage, and a smaller diameter around the dead spot so it could be got over quicker. Hence, the effective gear was constantly fluctuating as the crank rotated.

The objection to asymmetric chainwheels was that the extra leverage in the power phase of the stroke encouraged riders to over-exert themselves to the point of suffering knee damage. Shimano's Biopace chainwheel, invented by Masashi Nagano (US patent 4,522,610 of 1985) and introduced in 1983, aimed to reduce the load on the knees to less than that experienced with a conventional circular chainwheel. It did this by having a smaller diameter when the cranks were horizontal and a larger one when they were vertical. The idea was that the lower gear during maximum leverage (with the cranks horizontal) enabled faster acceleration of the legs, the momentum thus gained carrying the pedals through the dead-center position. This idea resulted from extensive study and analysis of the motion and momentum of legs and cranks. Biopace chainwheels, not simply elliptical but more complex in shape, worked best with slower cadences. After a heavy promotion in the years 1983–1992, during which rival makers produced licensed copies or similarly oriented elliptical rings, they were quietly discontinued.

Asymmetric chainwheels were revived from time to time. For more than 20 years, beginning in 1988, Chris Bell produced custom-made elliptical EGGrings, with ovalities ranging from 10 percent to 30 percent, in his workshop in Wales. In 1994, two French engineers, Michel Sassi and Jean-Louis Talo, designed their first O.Symetric chainrings, which had two curves that were symmetrical about a single point (US patent 5,549,314 of 1996). Using O.Symetric chainrings, Bradley Wiggins won both individual time trials of the 2012 Tour de France.

An alternative approach to the perceived dead-center problem involved linking the cranks to a circular chainwheel with levers. This was done to achieve a result similar to that achieved with an asymmetric chainwheel, by varying the circular ring's rotational speed relative to that of the crank. Various patents were granted for devices of this type (e.g., Swiss patent 359,050 of 1957). A design created by Pablo Carrasco Vergara in 2000 probably led to the most successful of these devices, those made by the Spanish company Rotor (world patent 02/28680 and later patents). Vergara later patented an asymmetric chainwheel with adjustable settings to enable fine tuning between the traditional and Biopace orientations (US patent 7,749,117 B2 of 2010).

Whatever their advantages, most of the various alternative drives fail for various reasons. Providing a wide range of gears can be difficult, expensive, or impossible. Crucially, most alternative systems cannot be retrofitted to a standard bicycle. And chain drive, which has been evolving for more than 100 years, is difficult to displace.

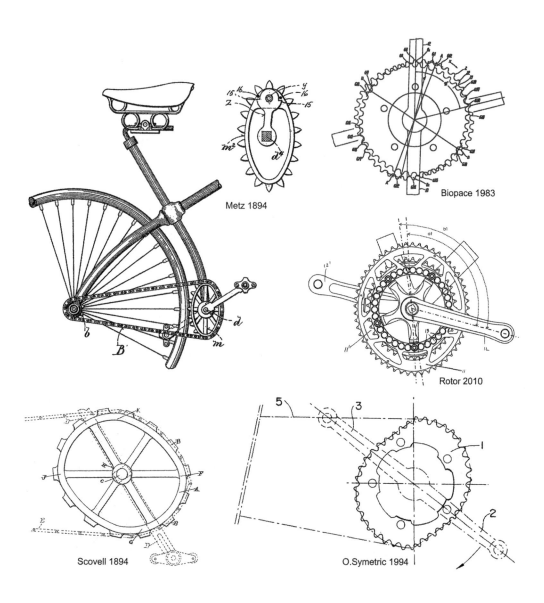

Metz 1894

Biopace 1983

Rotor 2010

Scovell 1894

O.Symetric 1994

Figure 4.17 Asymmetric chainwheels old and new (patent drawings).

THE SAFETY
BICYCLE

The high-wheeler was simple, efficient, and elegant, but it was an evolutionary dead end. By about 1880 it had reached its peak. The name "ordinary," rapidly adopted in the UK to differentiate the high-wheeler from the newer safety bicycle, testified to how well established it had become. The name by which it is perhaps best known to today's general public, "penny-farthing," was British slang; as was mentioned in chapter 3, it referred to the difference in proportion between the machine's front and rear wheels, analogizing them to the penny and farthing (quarter-penny) coins of the day.

A number of technological developments contributed to the evolution of the safety bicycle. Not least of these were indirect drive systems, which we considered in chapter 4. In that chapter we also noted several attempts to make the high-wheeler safer by lowering the saddle and moving it back toward the middle of the wheelbase. In the Facile and the Xtraordinary, lever drive was applied to facilitate this; in the Kangaroo, chain drive was used. In this chapter, we examine the early evolution of the safety bicycle's frame as the search for safety continued. Then, having seen how the classic steel-tube diamond frame evolved, we continue tracking development of frames for mainstream cycles, including attempts to break away from the classic solution.

EARLY ATTEMPTS TO PRODUCE A SAFER BICYCLE

One important idea in the development of the safety bicycle was applying drive to one wheel and steering the other, rather than trying (as in the Michaux-style velocipede and the high-wheeler) to drive and steer the same wheel. An early example was Thomas Wiseman's 1869 front-driver, which had a smaller rear wheel steered by a rod linkage under the seat. This arrangement allowed a lower riding position near the middle of the wheelbase. Riding lower was more comfortable, and there was much less danger of being thrown over the front wheel, but it still allowed the use of a relatively large driving wheel (Ritchie 1975, 122).

By the time Wiseman publicized his machine, another Englishman, Frederick Shearing, had come up with his "Norfolk" bicycle. Although it wasn't mass produced, Shearing later claimed to have built three examples. Like Wiseman, Shearing separated driving and steering, but he did it in a way that was eventually to become a world standard, with the rear wheel rather than the front one driven. Moreover, as was noted in the preceding chapter, he used belt drive. In 1868 and 1869, other designers, among them Mougeol, Dubos, and Desnos-Gardissal, were proposing rear-wheel chain drive. As was mentioned in chapter 4, in 1870 a French inventor named Sargent produced a bicycle with a large chain-driven front wheel and a smaller steerable rear wheel (Roberts 1991, 63).

The established high-wheeler was the starting point for many designers' attempts to make bicycles safer. For example, Henry John Lawson and James Likeman's 1876 design appeared to be a back-to-front high-wheeler. The small wheel was now at the front, and was steerable. The rider sat low, between the wheels, driving the large rear wheel (84 inches in diameter in early examples) by means of a treadle-operated lever-and-crank system. In an early version, the support of the rear wheel slavishly followed the high-wheeler pattern, to no great advantage. The frame's "backbone" formed a quarter-circle and terminated directly above the rear axle (British patent 2,649 of 1876). By early 1877, such bikes were in production. Later in 1877, Lawson advertised a semi-racer version with a more practical frame, which his own works made in Brighton. (He subsequently became manager of the Tangent & Coventry

Tricycle Company and later of Rudge.) By that time, Lawson claimed to be the sole patentee and inventor. James Likeman's role remains obscure, but he was probably an investor, not an engineer. Interestingly, the registered name for this machine was Safety (Roberts 1991, 58).

Lawson's second design (British patent 3,934 of 1879), nicknamed "the Crocodile," was a far superior machine. The legacy and the influence of the high-wheeler were still clear, the 40-inch front wheel being unnecessarily large. But the frame was much more practical, having a single main beam from the steering head to the crown of the rear fork, which held the 24-inch rear wheel. A vertical seat tube extended down to a yoke holding the pedal-crank assembly. The yoke was braced to the ends of the rear fork by thin chain stays, forming a triangle. Steering was indirect, by means of a bridle-rod linkage.

Lawson opened a distribution center in Paris. Finding that the word "safety" had little cachet among the French, he renamed his product the Bicyclette, which eventually became the generic French word for "bicycle." By the spring of 1886, he had introduced a revised diamond-frame version, which was much more like a modern bicycle. An illustration of the revised version was included in Lawson's application for a US patent, which was not filed until March 1886, more than six years after the corresponding British patent. (He was granted US patent 345,851 in 1886.)

The influence of the high-wheeler continued to be felt in some of the newer, safer designs. The American Star, for example, was essentially a back-to-front high-wheeler with direct steering of the small front wheel and with lever drive to the large rear wheel. Its inventor was George Pressey of Hammonton, New Jersey (US patent 233,640 of 1880).

Humber considered manufacturing the Star but decided against it. Indeed, Pressey's original design was relatively unsuccessful. Five years later, however, William Kelley of Smithville, New Jersey patented an improved version (US patent 321,819 of 1885) that maintained Pressey's original layout but had much more refined engineering. (Kelley's patent was eleven pages longer than Pressey's.) The second version of the Star, manufactured by the H. B. Smith Company of Burlington, New Jersey, was a success. Stars were ridden by the great American racing cyclist A. A. Zimmerman and by the trick riders Kaufman and MacAnney (Bartleet 1931, 42–43).

The 1884 McCammon Safety was another design that clearly showed the influence of the high-wheeler. Because the inherited "spine" served as the seat tube, there was no need for a separate down tube or head tube, and thus the machine was suitable for riders in skirts (Clayton 2010a).

Figure 5.1 Above: Lawson's 1876 safety (Alan Osbahr). Below: Lawson's 1879 Bicyclette (Alan Osbahr).

Figure 5.2   Left: The first version of the American Star (patent drawing). Right: The much-improved later version (R. John Way).
Figure 5.3   A McCammon safety of 1884 (Alan Osbahr).

DIAMOND-FRAME REAR-DRIVE SAFETIES

The year 1885 was the first in which all the major British cycle makers produced rear-drive safety bicycles. Their products were displayed in late January and early February at the annual Stanley Show, held in a tent on the Thames Embankment near Blackfriars Bridge in London. Machines with various kinds of frames—principally cross and diamond designs—were shown. Most of the new designs probably were developed during 1884, but they are commonly dated to 1885, the year in which they were first shown to the public.

The name "diamond frame" is slightly misleading. Very few bicycles have had a frame that, viewed on elevation, is a true "diamond" or rhombus—that is, a quadrilateral with four equal sides. For present purposes, "diamond" can usefully be defined as describing a frame with the following features:

a top tube linking the steering head to the seat mount

a down tube linking the steering head to the bottom bracket (crank-axle housing)

chain stays linking the bottom bracket to the rear-wheel dropouts

seat stays (sometimes called back stays) linking the seat mount to the rear-wheel dropouts.

There has been much argument about who introduced the first diamond frame. If we refine the above definition to include only machines in which the elements listed above were all straight, it appears that G. L. Morris's Referee was the first, and the Starley Brothers' Psycho a close second. But the earliest so-called diamond frames generally had at least some curved tubes. We should bear in mind that the term "diamond frame" or "diamond-shaped frame" didn't come into common use until the late 1880s, when it was used to differentiate the frames in question from cross frames and other designs used on safety bicycles.

One important early diamond-frame model was Humber's 1884 "dwarf roadster." This had a relatively large chain-driven rear wheel and a very small directly steered front wheel with suspension. The steerer tube sloped considerably. Like many early diamond-frame machines, the 1884 Humber lacked a seat tube running from the bottom bracket to the seat mounting. In other words, its-frame was an "open diamond." (A diamond frame with a full-length seat tube is called a "closed diamond.")

The most famous of the rear-drive safeties introduced in 1885 was the Rover, produced in Coventry by John Kemp Starley (a nephew of James Starley Sr.) and William Sutton. This was the first of a successful series of Rover bicycles—so successful that the Polish word for

Figure 5.4   A 1884 Humber safety (National Cycle Library) and a portrait of Thomas Humber (John Tarring).

bicycle is "rower," with the "w" pronounced like an English "v." Writing only eleven years after its introduction, Archibald Sharp described the early Rover as "the first rear-driving bicycle that attained popular favour" (1896, 153). But the very first (and short-lived) Rover still seemed to be in awe of the recent past. The front end essentially consisted of the front wheel and backbone of a high-wheeler, though somewhat reduced in size. Onto this was grafted a much smaller chain-driven rear wheel and a saddle supported on a spindly framework. Steering was done by means of a bridle-rod linkage. Thus the first Rover was rather like an untidy version of Lawson's Bicyclette.

Later in 1885, a superior second version of the Rover was introduced. Although the front wheel was still larger than the rear, the difference in diameter between the wheels was less pronounced. Steering was now direct, Starley and Sutton having copied the Humber's inclined steerer. Because the handlebars now were closer to the rider, there was no need for steering linkage. This design, which gave a caster effect to the steering, eventually became the world standard (Clayton 2010b).

In the autumn of 1886, George Smith broke the world 100-mile speed record on a second-generation Rover (Ritchie 1975, 130). Although the new record stood for only a month, it demonstrated that the new design was no slouch. It was another nail in the coffin of the high-wheeler.

Other manufacturers were quick to see the advantages of the diamond frame. For example, Harry Lawson adopted it in his 1886 design, which also featured equal-sized wheels (US patent 345,851 of 1886). In the next two years, frames resembling the "closed diamond" began to appear. Humber, G. L. Morris, and Woodhead & Angois (precursor of Raleigh) were among the first manufacturers to insert a seat tube extending down to the bottom bracket and thus making the frame more rigid in the vertical plane. At the 1886 Leicester Show, Woodhead & Angois exhibited a Raleigh safety bicycle whose crank-axle casing was an integral part of the frame rather than bolted on. This was another feature that was to become a world standard (Hadland 2012, 13).

One thing that militated against the adoption of a straight down tube and an integral bottom bracket was the short wheelbase of early diamond-frame safeties. Most had the crankcase just ahead of the rear wheel. Thus a seat tube had to either curve around the wheel (as in Morris's Referee) or intersect with the top tube somewhere forward of the seat post (as in the 1888 Woodhead, Angois & Ellis Raleigh). Around 1890, the move to a slightly longer wheelbase, with a clearance of several inches between the rear wheel and the bottom bracket, resolved this problem. Humber was a leader in this development (Sharp 1896, 157–158).

The top tube prevented women in skirts from riding diamond-frame bicycles. Many manufacturers adopted the obvious solution of sloping the top tube down from the top of the head tube to a point on the seat tube a few inches above the bottom bracket. This made the frame less triangulated and weaker in torsion. In many cases, the sloping top tube was nearly parallel to the downtube. Some designers, however, made the top tube's junction with the seat tube lower or higher. A lower junction made it easier for a skirted rider to step through but made the frame even weaker in torsion. A higher junction made the frame stiffer but made mounting more difficult.

A more expensive way of producing a strong ladies' frame with a deep step-through was to use a loop frame with a curved top tube, which allowed a relatively high junction of the top and seat tubes. At their closest point, the curved top tube and the straight down tube would almost touch, and they were often brazed together at this point to increase rigidity.

Figure 5.5   The first Starley Rover bicycle (1885) and an 1886 portrait of John Kemp Starley from a Rover catalog (*CTC Monthly Gazette*, May 1885; John Tarring).

Some designers merely used a single down tube. This gave a very low step-over height but poor torsional rigidity. An example of this type is the 1889 Lady's Rover safety. Machines of this design continued to be produced in the twentieth century and beyond.

A more complicated approach to designing a ladies' frame was taken by Charles William Brown of North Finchley, London. His 1894 design, patented in the United Kingdom and also in the United States (US patent 538,232 of 1895), provided additional triangulation around the bottom bracket. Brown's patent also covered a tandem that put the lady in front. The patent was assigned to Humber. Triangulated frames based on Brown's designs also were made by Centaur and by Cogswell & Harrison. Although the Brown design gave great vertical and lateral strength, the bottom bracket was not as well supported as in a more conventional frame (Bartleet 1931, 90). It was also complicated and expensive to make.

Figure 5.6 An advertisement for the "breakthrough machine" of 1885: the second-generation Rover.

Figure 5.7 Above: Lawson's 1886 safety bicycle (patent drawing). Middle: The Rover safety of 1888 (Alan Osbahr). Below: An 1889 Lady's Rover (catalog picture).

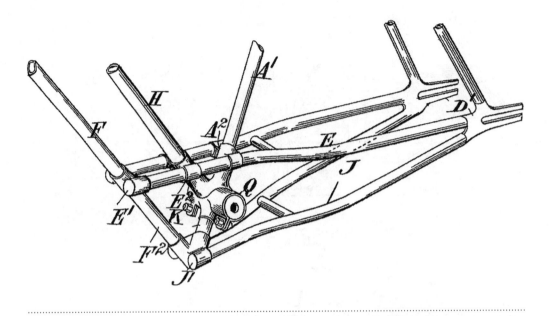

Figure 5.8   The lower portion of Brown's 1894 triangulated frame for a ladies' bicycle (patent drawing).

CROSS-FRAME REAR-DRIVE SAFETIES

The diamond frame was not without rivals in the early days of the safety bicycle. Its principal competitor was the cross frame, which got its name because it typically had a main beam (linking the steering head to the rear wheel) intersecting at approximately 90° with the seat tube (which extended downward to the crankcase). Because of its open design, manufacturers of cross frames didn't have to make separate models for men and women. However, the height of the main beam was more of an impediment to a skirted rider than most ladies' derivatives of the diamond frame.

Lawson's Bicyclette of 1879 had a cross frame of a sort. More cross-frame machines began to appear about four years later: the Marvel in 1883, the Pioneer in 1884, the BSA safety bicycle in 1885. The Premier, introduced by the Coventry firm of Hillman, Herbert & Cooper's in 1886, was more sophisticated, and elements of its design were patented (British patent

1,775 of 1886). The steering was self-centered by a spring and chain slack was adjusted by tensioning a stay linking the bottom bracket to the main beam. The Premier was popular for several years.

Dan Albone's Ivel cross-frame machine, introduced shortly after the Premier, was, in contrast with most other early safety bicycles, fairly easy to ride in the "no hands" style. In 1886, George Pilkington Mills, an engineer as well as an athlete, broke the 50-mile and 24-hour records on an Ivel. Mills worked for Albone before joining Humber and later Raleigh.

In 1888, Starley & Sutton briefly made a cross-frame machine; it was not commercially successful. The following year, M. A. Holbein, riding a Hillman, Herbert & Cooper cross-frame bike, broke the 24-hour record, covering 324 miles (RRA 1965, 40). But by that time, William Hillman had already patented his own "diamond-shaped frame" (British patent 16,736 of 1888). The stronger, more fully triangulated diamond frame had already made its mark, and cross-frame bikes began to disappear from manufacturers' catalogs.

Some "semi-diamond" designs combined elements of the cross frame and the diamond. One such was the 1889 Starley & Sutton Universal Rover, a safety bicycle that was relatively cheap by that company's standards. Like a closed diamond, its frame had a rear triangle formed by the seat tube, the chain stays, and the seat stays. But like a cross frame, it had a main beam between the seat tube and the steering head. In common with the Ivel, it had a thin tie between the front of the main beam and the bottom bracket.

From time to time, cross frames made a comeback. The American Compax, designed in 1937 by Albert Rippenbein of New York (US patent 2,211,164 of 1940), had a cross frame, as did several designs of the late 1940s and the early 1950s, including one produced by Dilecta of France, two prototypes built by the British cycle mechanic Jack Lauterwasser (prompted by the postwar steel shortage), and a widely publicized prototype built by Sir Alliott Verdon Roe, the aeronautical engineer who founded the Avro and Saunders-Roe aircraft companies. The German Hercules HK, introduced around 1958, had a cast aluminum cross frame. All these machines had wheels of conventional size. However, from the 1960s on, cross frames and other open frame designs were more commercially successful when used on small-wheeled bicycles than when used on larger ones. Some open designs (such as the H frame used on Raleigh's 20 series) had a standard rear triangle, with seat stays and chain stays. The lazy F, typified by the early Moultons, had a main beam so low that the bottom bracket was directly mounted on its underside. In both of these cases the name "cross frame" is inappropriate, as the seat tube and main beam don't cross to any great extent. There were also many U frames, with a single curved tube forming the seat tube and the main beam. (U-frame bicycles for women had been produced in 1895 by Reichstein Brothers in Germany and by Humber in England.) Many of these open frame designs—cross frames, H frames, U frames, lazy Fs— used gussets, struts, or stays to brace the main beam to the head tube or the seat tube.

Figure 5.9 Above: An 1887 cross-frame Rudge with bridle-rod steering (Alan Osbahr). Middle: A cross-frame Ivel (R. John Way). Below: An 1889 Universal Rover (catalog picture).

Simple cross frames of the 1880s, such as those of the Ivel and the Premier, should not be confused with more complex later designs—also called cross frames—that were more like reinforced diamond frames. The best-known example of the latter was the Raleigh X frame, created by George Pilkington Mills after he left Humber to join Raleigh. Although Raleigh had produced something similar a few years earlier, the X frame featured prominently in the company's advertising from 1901 until the 1920s. Mills observed that a large men's diamond frame wasn't fully triangulated, owing to the length of the head tube. His X-frame design remedied this by sloping the top tube forward and down to the point where the down tube and the head tube met, introducing an additional tube linking the bottom bracket to the top of the head tube, and making the additional tube intersect the sloping top tube.

Raleigh used the name Modèle Superbe for most of its X-frame bikes. Various other makers copied the design. There was also a ladies' version; it maintained the step-through feature of the ladies' diamond frame, but instead of the normal sloping top tube above the down tube it had two intersecting tubes. X frames were, according to Professor Sharp, "appreciably more rigid than the usual diamond frame." But they were also heavier and much more expensive.

DWARF FRONT-DRIVERS

As was noted in chapter 4, epicyclic ("sun and planet") gearing was used in some later front-drive bicycles to allow the use of a smaller and more manageable front wheel. The gearing was sometimes used in conjunction with lever drive, as in the Geared Facile. Machines on which it was used with ordinary cranks were classed as "geared ordinaries."

In the 1890s, there was a rear-guard action by proponents of front drive. For example, in 1893 Raleigh offered a "Geared Front Driver," which was a straightforward, pneumatic-tired geared ordinary. At the Stanley Show in London that November, Shaw & Sydenham demonstrated a more radical approach. Their Crypto F.D. Safety No.1 ("F.D." stood for front-drive) was a compact machine with a choice of wheel sizes from 22 to 24 inches, geared up to the equivalent of 60 to 66 inches. The following year, the machine was advertised as the Bantam. It had a horizontal main beam and an almost vertical rear fork, braced to the underside of the main beam by thin ties. The best-known version of the Bantam was the No. 2 model, launched in 1894. It had a smaller rear wheel and a curved spine, both features reminiscent of a high-wheeler, but it was considerably more compact than Raleigh's geared high-wheelers. In 1895, a ladies' version, the Bantamette, was introduced. Two years later, the Alpha Bantam was launched; it had wheels of equal size, parallel top and down tubes, and a cantilever rear fork. But by 1898 the days of the dwarf front-driver were coming to an end.

Figure 5.10   A 1903 Modèle Superbe (Raleigh).

THE TRIUMPH OF THE DIAMOND FRAME

By the late 1890s, the diamond frame had evolved into a form recognizably similar in almost all respects to the design that now has been dominant for more than a century. It consisted mostly of straight steel tubes, brazed or welded with modern techniques. A longer wheelbase permitted a straight seat tube. An integral bottom bracket housed the crankcase. A roller chain drove the rear wheel. Steering was direct, with caster action. The wheels were equal in size, and the tires were pneumatic.

Cross frames were, for the most part, consigned to history. The dwarf front-drivers, too, soon disappeared.

Occasionally a new frame design with some merit would appear. One meritorious new design was patented by Mikael Pedersen in 1893 a few weeks before the launch of the Crypto Bantam. Unlike the dwarf front-drivers, it was one of a handful of non-diamond-frame designs that, while never achieving widespread popularity, had sufficient merit to attract an enduring following. Cycles of this design were manufactured in small numbers at various times and in various places during the twentieth century and later.

STEEL AS A FRAME MATERIAL

Nineteenth-century improvements in materials manufacture led to parallel improvements in bicycle design and manufacture. According to Andrew Millward, instigator of Britain's National Cycle Archive,

> One of the striking features in the development of the bicycle by UK manufactur-
> ers from the late 1860s was the drive to lighten the machine without compromising
> strength, particularly using steel in construction as opposed to iron and wood. While
> experimentation with new materials took place on specialized competition machines
> from the early days, cost reductions in the manufacture of steel throughout the 1870s
> and 1880s encouraged it to be used more widely on cycles, and the general improve-
> ment in the performance of machines encouraged further interest in cycling. (Millward
> 1999, 87)

Pierre Michaux's 1868 patent (French patent 80,637) included a claim for a tubular steel frame, although it is not thought that any such frames were made by Michaux. The New York firm of Pickering & Davis, however, used hydraulic tube around the same date for both frame and forks, brazing the tube into brass lugs. Two years later, English makers of high-wheelers began to use hollow backbones to make their machines lighter. As early as 1872, the Meyer high-wheeler and the Ariel bicycle had tubular backbones (*The Field*, April 20, 1872). Hollow tube became associated with lightness and strength. The first attempts to use tubing for front forks were made by Jules Truffault of Tours (who used scabbards) and by S. Tolman of Wolver-hampton in 1874 (CMC catalog 1880). J. C. Garrood of East Anglia obtained a patent for a hol-low-fork bicycle in 1876 (British patent 3,875 of 1876), and the Coventry Machinists' Company Ltd. and other large firms were making hollow forks by 1878. The use of hollow tubing then spread to rear forks, handlebars, axles, and wheel rims. James Carver of Nottingham took it to the ultimate with his New Hollow Spoke bicycle (British patent 616 of 1877).

These developments were made possible by recent major advances in steel production. The similar pneumatic smelting processes created by the American William Kelly and the

Figure 5.11 An 1894 Crypto Bantam No. 2 (National Cycle Library).

Englishman Sir Henry Bessemer for mass production of low-carbon steel from high-carbon pig iron were made commercially viable by the British metallurgist Robert Forester Mushet, who improved on Kelly's and Bessemer's techniques by first burning off impurities and carbon, then adding spiegeleisen ("mirror-iron," a ferromanganese alloy) to reintroduce manganese and carbon in a carefully controlled manner (US patent 17,389 of 1857). The Bessemer and Kelly processes, enhanced by Mushet's technique, reduced the price of steel relative to that of wrought iron. However, much of the steel used in early British bicycle frames was low-carbon steel imported from Sweden (Millward 1999, 88).

The arms industry led the way in devising new ways to make better steel tubing. J. D. M. Stirling's 1854 patent (number 472) for forming seamless steel tubing from hollow steel castings by cold drawing was a significant early development. Other developments followed,

Figure 5.12 An example of the perfected diamond frame: a 1907 Golden Sunbeam (Alan Osbahr).

and the improved tube-making technology crossed over into the cycle industry. One important early manufacturer was the Credenda Cold Drawn Seamless Steel Tube Company Ltd., founded in Birmingham in 1882 (Millward 1999, 90).

In the mid 1880s, in Remscheid (south of Düsseldorf), the brothers Reinhard and Max Mannesmann were working on improving the hardening of cotter pins by using a three-roll oblique rolling machine. In the course of their research, they discovered that the process could produce a central void in the steel. "It is like a fox which had the hide pulled over his ears," explained their consultant, Professor Franz Reuleaux. The Mannesmanns were granted US patents 361,954 of 1887 and 389,585 of 1888. In 1892 they added the "Pilger" or "step" process, a known idea that had been patented in England in 1841. The word "Pilger" means "pilgrim" and stems from the similarity between the action of the mill and a type of procession

Figure 5.13   A Pedersen bicycle, patented in 1893 (Alan Osbahr).

involving two steps forward and one back. For the first time, a solid steel bar could be converted into a seamless tube in a few seconds. By 1887, Mannesmann techniques were in use
at the Landore Siemens steelworks near Swansea in Wales. The Mannesmann brothers soon
bought the Landore works and started what was to become a huge industrial corporation,
with headquarters in Düsseldorf (Boore 1951). The Mannesmanns lost the American market
when a former employee, a Swiss engineer named Ralph Stiefel, went to the United States.
He became a major shareholder and the general manager of a plant making seamless tubes
in the new town of Ellwood City, Pennsylvania; later it became a part of the Shelby Steel Tube

Company. Stiefel's variant of the process (US patent 551,340 of 1895) circumvented the Mannesmann brothers' patents.

Production of seamless steel tube in the United States didn't begin in earnest until the early 1890s. Before then, the US imported most of its bicycle tubing from the UK. Although at times this resulted in shortages of tubing in the UK, it stimulated the growth of the UK's seamless steel tubing industry; by 1896, more than a dozen firms were making steel tubes in Britain. But by then, companies making general-purpose seamless tubing, such as the Shelby Steel Tube Company of Ohio, had become established in the US, and the US became largely self-sufficient (Millward 1999, 92–93). Albert Pope built his own tube works in 1896; originally it was to be a joint venture called the Pope-Mannesmann Company (Epperson 2010, 113–117).

In the 1890s, numerous patents relating to steel tubing were granted. These included about 140 for seamless tubing and others for brazed, welded, butted, oval, and D-section tubing (Marks 1903, 134–153).

The development of better, lighter, and cheaper steel tubing was paralleled by the evolution of increasingly sophisticated stamped steel components. Flat steel sheet was passed through a series of pressing operations to create complex three-dimensional components, including bottom brackets, fork crowns, frame lugs, chainwheels, sprockets, and pedals for bicycles. Previously such items had typically been made from iron castings or forged stampings, which had had to be machined to achieve the required precision and appearance. Pressed steel eliminated many of these processes and produced lighter, cheaper, and neater components. The technology was in use in Germany by the 1880s. In the 1890s, American industrialists developed it further. The Western Wheel Works of Chicago, founded by an immigrant named Adolph Schoeninger, became the dominant manufacturer (Hounshell 1984; Lessing 2008). By 1900, British cycle makers, led by Raleigh, were adopting the technology and importing American expertise and tooling. Raleigh's long-running slogan "The All Steel Bicycle" originated from its adoption of pressed steel parts in place of iron or non-ferrous components (Millward 1999, 140–141).

With the development of seamless steel tubing and stamped steel frame components came new ways of joining these parts to form the frame. Liquid brazing, whereby the assembled frame was dipped in molten braze, saved labor, reduced wastage of materials, and helped eliminate weak joints. The technique was pioneered in the US and widely adopted in the UK. Another American innovation was electrical welding; it became popular with American cycle makers, who tended to use heavier-grade tubing (more suitable for this technique) than their British counterparts. In the UK, lugged and brazed construction was the norm. However, by the end of the nineteenth century electrical welding was being used in Britain to join steel pressings (Millward 1999, 141–142).

On the later development of steel frames, see chapter 2.

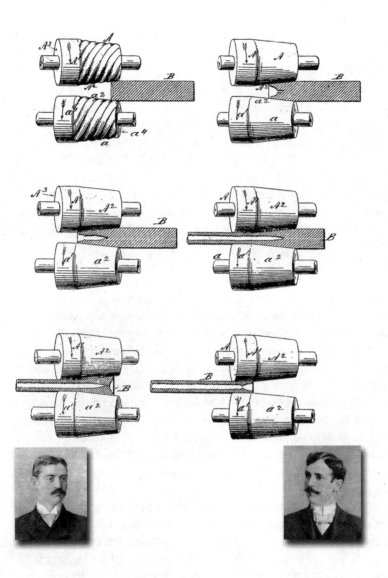

Figure 5.14 Above: Stages in production of Mannesmann tubes (Salzgitter AG-Konzernarchiv/Mannesmann-Archiv, Mülheim an der Ruhr). Below: Reinhard (left) and Max Mannesmann.

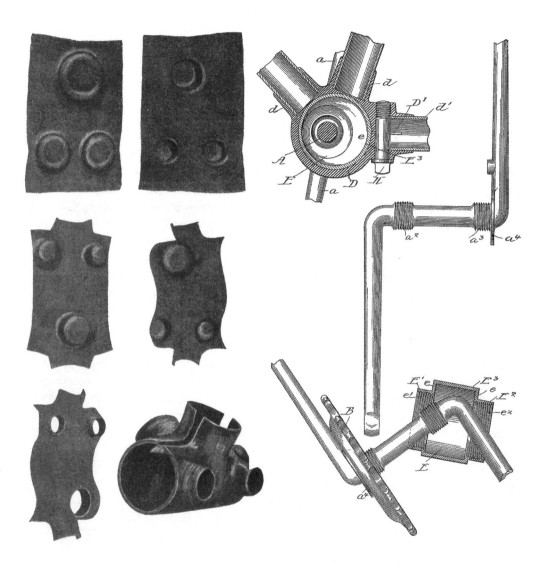

Figure 5.15   Left: Stages in forming a bottom bracket by pressing a flat sheet of steel (*Polytechnisches Journal* 304, 1897, 269). Right: William Fauber's one-piece crank set, designed in 1897 (US patent 624,636).

OTHER FRAME MATERIALS

Timber was, of course, used in the very first cycle frames. In the mid 1890s, when the development of new steel frame technology was at its peak, an organic frame material reappeared on the scene: bamboo (a grass). A patent application for a diamond-frame bamboo bicycle was filed in 1895 by August Oberg and Andrew Gustafson of Waterloo, Nebraska (US patent 565,783 of 1896). They put hardwood plugs in the ends of a bamboo tube, then carefully tapered the outsides of the tube to make it fit tightly into a steel lug. A steel pin was then passed through the lug, the bamboo, and hardwood to keep the joint from working loose.

The Bamboo Cycle Company Ltd. of London sold bamboo bicycles for several years during the mid 1890s. According to an 1895 advertisement, the Bamboo Cycle Company's products were "Better than steel" and "Patronised by the Nobility." Lord Edward Spencer Churchill reported having ridden 1,500 miles on his bamboo bicycle, which he stated was "quite the best for hill climbing I have had." Reflecting the parallel developments in steel brazed frames, the Bamboo Cycle Company's 1897 brochure claimed that the "improved and patented method by which the Joints are made" rendered them "far more reliable than the brazed Joints of Steel Machines."

From time to time, interest in bicycles built of bamboo or timber revived, often in response to changes in the availability and cost of metals. One example is the Vianzone wooden bicycle, produced by the Italian company Fratelli Vianzone, which made skis and various other products of bent wood. After Italy's invasion of Abyssinia in the autumn of 1935, the League of Nations applied economic sanctions, which resulted in a shortage of steel in Italy. Vianzone devised an elegant bicycle built primarily of timber and aluminum, both of which were readily available. Between 1938 and 1956, about 250 to 300 of these machines were made, including an open-framed ladies' version. The diamond frame consisted mainly of steamed laminates of various woods, with aluminum fittings. Even the seat post and the pedal tread blocks were of wood (Lawrence 2005a).

Figure 5.16   Oberg and Gustafson's bamboo frame (patent drawing).
Figure 5.17   A Vianzone wooden bicycle (Tony Hadland).

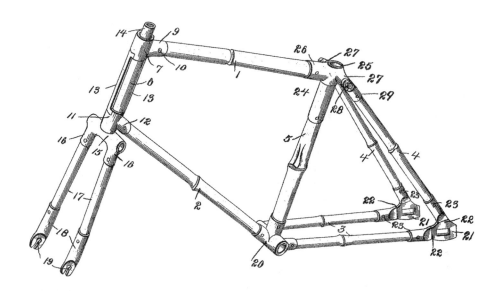

In the first decade of the twenty-first century, a significant number of patent applications relating to bamboo bicycles were filed, many of them in the Far East. The B2O, a bicycle with a laminated cross frame and fork designed by Antoine Fritsch and Vivien Durisotti, won a prize in the Prix GEO 2009 environmental design competition. Two years later, at Oxford Brookes University, a team of students led by Shpend Gerguri and James Broughton designed and built a concept frame that complied with European safety standards. The two academics success-fully rode mountain bikes with frames of this design in an eight-day 400-mile Alpine race that entailed 21,000 meters of climbing.

A major drawback of timber and bamboo is that their grain gives them considerable strength in one direction but very little in any other. Laminating timber in alternate directions (as in plywood) gives good strength in two directions but very little in the third. Another drawback is the difficulty of joining frame members made of timber or bamboo. Even if lugs or sockets are used, it can be difficult to produce a durable purely mechanical joint. Gluing tends to bond only the outer layers of the wood or bamboo. And bottom-bracket stresses pose particular problems for designers of timber or bamboo frames (Burrows 2000, 54).

In Africa, home-made wooden bicycles, with simple triangular frames and small solid tim-ber wheels, have long been used by children. A bike of this kind typically lacks a drive system; the rider scoots along as on a draisine.

Interest in the use of glass-reinforced polyester (GRP) and other molded plastics as ma-terials for bicycle frames increased after World War II. The best-known example is a frame designed by the automotive engineer Benjamin Bowden of Leamington Spa. Bowden applied for a British patent for his bicycle frame in the autumn of 1946 and for a US patent two years later. His US patent (2,537,325 of 1951) covered a hollow monocoque frame made up of complementary metal pressings or plastic moldings "secured to one another, along the central plane of the frame." An aluminum shaft-drive prototype was built for an exhibition held in the autumn of 1946 at London's Victoria and Albert Museum. The show, organized by the Council of Industrial Design to promote the UK's productive capabilities, was called "Britain Can Make It." But financially crippled postwar Britain didn't make Ben Bowden's bicycle.

Bowden later moved to the United States, and in 1960 he managed to put his machine into production. The production model, with a frame made of GRP, was called the Space-lander. Only 522 were produced, and some unauthorized copies were made after produc-tion ceased (Dixon 2007). In 1965, Bowden obtained a design patent for another monocoque frame (US patent Des. 201,605 of 1965). Three years later, plainly influenced by the Moulton bicycle but applying his own GRP monocoque approach, Bowden designed a full-suspension small-wheeler (US patent 3,375,024 of 1968); it was never produced commercially.

Bowden's Spacelander is sometimes confused with the Elswick-Hopper Scoo-ped, which came on the market in the UK in 1959. Designed by Maurice Moss, it resembled a motor

Figure 5.18 Ben Bowden's 1965 monocoque (patent drawing).

scooter and was pitched at people who normally didn't ride bikes. Although clad in GRP, it had a conventional steel frame (unlike the Spacelander). But the Scoo-ped was even less commercially successful than the Spacelander; only 36 were made (Land 2010, 142–143).

Other bicycle companies experimented intermittently with GRP. Around 1970, Raleigh tried it for children's bikes, building a prototype (a derivative of the RSW11 small-wheeler). The central section of the frame, made of GRP, was, like that of the Spacelander, made up of two molded halves. Later, Raleigh built a prototype of a part-GRP version of the Chopper high-rise bicycle. But productionizing dough molding with chopped GRP fibers was more difficult than constructing a bike by the traditional labor-intensive method of manually laying down sheets of GRP and applying resin to each layer. The process proved far too expensive, and Raleigh never mass produced a bicycle that made structural use of GRP. Carbon fiber was similarly labor intensive, but that material eventually came to be used in expensive upscale sports and racing machines, whose profit margins were higher than those of mass-market bikes.

From time to time, especially during the 1970s, plastic bicycles of various kinds were proposed. Le Speelo, demonstrated at the Paris Salon du Cycle in 1979, was nearly put into production. The diamond frame, the rims, and the brakes were made of glass-filled polyamide (GFPA). An integrated partial rear mudguard replaced the conventional seat tube. A separable front fork facilitated stowage in the trunk of an automobile. Cycles France-Loire wanted to produce a version, but Le Speelo never was mass produced.

More successful at capturing the attention of the media and the public was the Itera bicycle, developed in 1978–1980 by a design team from the Swedish carmaker Volvo. The components of the unisex open frame were molded from acrylonitrile butadiene styrene (ABS). Whereas Le Speelo had had GFPA wheel rims and conventional steel spokes, the Itera's wheels were molded from GFPA; each had eight integral spokes and a hub shell. And whereas Le Speelo had been a sports model, the Itera was aimed at commuters: it had integral lighting, a built-in lock, and a luggage rack. But the design and the materials weren't adequate for the intended use. The frame's lack of rigidity sapped the rider's energy and fatigued certain components, particularly the plastic handlebars that were used on early production models. Later Iteras had steel handlebars (Lawrence 2005b). The Itera went on sale, with enormous publicity, in 1982, but production ended after only three years; in all, about 30,000 units were made. There were rumors of sabotage by the unions. For a few years thereafter, Iteras were a familiar sight on the streets of Oxford, where a rental company had obtained a stock of

....

Figure 5.19   An Elswick-Hopper Scoo-ped (Nigel Land).
Figure 5.20   A plastic Speelo pre-production model of 1979 (Renate B. Lessing).

Figure 5.21   A 1982 Itera commuter bicycle (Lars Samuelsson).

them—presumably at a huge discount. After that, the Itera became a curiosity, rarely seen outside a museum. The goal of a good cheap plastic bicycle, "molded for the masses," seemingly remained unachievable.

Aluminum, magnesium, and titanium frames are discussed in chapter 12. Other metals, including nickel alloy, stainless steel, and beryllium, have occasionally been used.

CYCLING SPAWNS THE AIRPLANE

Bicycle posters of the 1890s often featured birds in flight. In Germany, six-day racers called themselves "Flieger" ("flyers"). Most of the first pilots in the United States, in France, and in

Bicycle Parts Used On Wright Aeroplanes

Oversized bicycle chains and sprocket used to turn the propellers. Regular and oversized bicycle tubular steel was used in the propeller shaft supports.

Double Bicycle-type sprockets on the back of the engine turned the propeller chains. They purchased the chains from the Diamond Chain Co., Indianapolis, Indiana.

Bicycle chain and sprockets turned engine camshaft at the front of engine. Idler pulley had ball bearings, center under the chain.

A mannequin of Orville Wright with left hand on the front elevator control. Section of bicycle chain connected to control (spoke) wires.

Section of bicycle chain over pulley (in 4 places) inserted in wing warping (spoke) wires to prevent metal fatigue. Bicycle spoke wire used to brace the wings.

Bicycle to Biplane over sized double triangle shaped like a bicycle frame on both sides of the 1905 Wright Flyer above, and on some other models of Wright Flyers. See page 31.

Section of bicycle chain in front elevator control (spoke) wires. Pivot shaft of bicycle tubular steel.

During take off, aeroplane rolled on oversized bicycle wheel hubs (in 2 places). Later aeroplanes used bicycle type wheels. Ball bearings first used on bicycles were used on the Wright Flyer.

An interesting note, the tubing hose leading from the gas tank to the engine is a bicycle foot pump hose.

Figure 5.22 Bicycle parts used on the 1905 Wright airplane: an illustration originally published in Fisk and Todd 2000 (Fred C. Fisk).

Germany were former racing cyclists (Kyle 2007). Otto Lilienthal, who pioneered what today is called hang gliding (German patent 77,916 of 1893), was a keen cyclist, and in an address to an 1894 convention of engineers in Berlin he compared gliding to cycling:

> Gradually one achieves a great security, just like a trained cyclist, but the exercises are still somewhat more difficult than those required for guiding a two-wheeler. This apparatus needs to be steered not only to the right or left, as achieved by shifting one's point of gravity, but also to the fore and aft. Because of this one could compare flying rather to riding a unicycle. (translated from Lilienthal 1894)

Lilienthal died as a result of a gust of wind, but cyclists still believed that muscle-powered flight was just around the corner. Inventors were testing prototypes of muscle-powered flying cycles and competing in contests sponsored by Peugeot, Dubois, and Michelin. But the initial requirement of flying a distance of 33 feet to and fro had to be reduced if there were to be any contestants at all (Schulze 1936).

In the 1890s, Orville and Wilbur Wright ran a printing shop in Dayton, Ohio. In 1892 Orville bought a new safety bicycle (a pneumatic-tired Columbia) and Wilbur bought an Eagle safety bicycle at an auction. That same year, they opened a bicycle shop. Orville took part in races at the YMCA Athletic Park, with Wilbur acting as the starter, and won several medals. After a trip to the World's Columbian Exposition in Chicago, they began building bicycles under two brand names, Van Cleve and St. Clair. An illustrated article on the flying machines of Otto Lilienthal and Octave Chanute in an 1894 issue of *McClure's Magazine* turned their minds toward flying (Fisk 2000).

The Wright brothers, of course, went on to earn worldwide fame with their gasoline-motor flying machine (US patent 821,393 of 1903). What has been said about the bicycle's technological influence on early automobiles also holds for early motorized airplanes: railroad technology would have been much too heavy.

COMFORT

6

In this chapter we examine technological developments in tires, in sprung supports for saddles, in sprung handlebars, and in wheel suspension.

TIRES

Developments in tire design eventually provided considerable improvements in ride comfort, quite apart from contributing to lower rolling resistance, improved road holding, better traction, and safer braking. Tires can add greatly to comfort, helping isolate rider and machine from vibration and shock caused by irregularities in the road surface. But the earliest tires contributed nothing to a rider's comfort.

Iron tires

Karl Drais's machine had traditional spoked wooden wheels. The wooden spokes, which radiated from a wooden hub, were attached to a circular rim formed by wooden segments called felloes. The whole ensemble was held together by an iron tire. This was formed from flat strip, which was welded into a ring, heated, fitted around the felloes, then shrunk to fit by cooling with water. The iron tire not only held the wheel together; it also provided a durable running surface for the wheel. But it offered no isolation from road shock.

On a smooth, hard road surface, such wheels rolled well. But smooth, hard road surfaces were far from the norm. The wheels cut grooves in soft and loose surfaces, dissipating the rider's energy and slowing the machine down. Energy was also lost through impact with irregularities in the road surface. As Archibald Sharp pointed out (1896, 487), "in the first bicycles made with wooden wheels and iron tires, and sometimes without even a spring to the seat, the mass [rigidly connected with the tire] included the whole of the wheel and a considerable proportion of the mass of the frame and rider; so that the energy lost in shock formed by far the greatest item in the work to be supplied by the rider."

Solid rubber tires

Natural rubber was hard when cold but sticky when warm. Vulcanization helped to overcome those properties. Processes for vulcanizing rubber by adding sulfur were developed from 1839 on, notably by Charles Goodyear in the United States and Thomas Hancock (who coined the word "vulcanize") in Britain. Hancock had examined some waterproof boots made by Goodyear, detected the presence of sulfur, and obtained his own patent. Stephen Moulton, great-grandfather of the bicycle designer Alex Moulton, introduced Goodyear's process to the UK and unsuccessfully fought Hancock's claim to priority (Dodds 2001, 105).

By the time of the Michaux-style velocipede, the rubber industry had established itself in the major industrial countries. Soon, solid rubber tires, typically about ¾ inch wide and circular in cross-section, were fitted to the wheels of velocipedes. Sharp commented:

> If the tyre of the wheel be made elastic so that it can change shape sufficiently during passage over an obstacle, the motion of the wheel center may not be perceptibly affected, and the mass subjected to impact may be reduced to that of a small portion of the tyre in the neighborhood of the point of contact. Thus, the use of rubber tyres on an ordinary road greatly reduces the amount of energy wasted in jar of the machine. Again, the rubber being elastic, instead of sinking into a moderately soft road,

is flattened out. The area of contact with the ground being much larger, the pressure per unit area is less, and the depth of groove made is smaller; the energy lost by the wheel sinking into the road is therefore greatly reduced by the use of the rubber tyre. (1896, 487).

Sharp pointed out that on a hypothetical perfectly smooth road the rolling resistance of a rubber tire was higher than that of an iron one. (That is why rubber tires were rarely used on railroad rolling stock.) For road vehicles in the real world, however, the neutralizing of minor irregularities of the road surface more than compensated.

An early example of a solid rubber bicycle tire was found on a Michaux velocipede built between September 1868 and April 1869 (Reynaud 2008, 91). Such tires were typically held in a channel-section wooden rim; some had a thin metallic outer running surface (Reynaud 2008, 279).

Cushion tires, introduced in an attempt to provide more comfort than a solid rubber tire offered, enjoyed some popularity in the 1880s. Such a tire typically had a carcass of vulcanized rubber containing voids filled with a compressible medium, such as air, cork, or gum rubber. Cushion tires enjoyed limited popularity in the 1880s but then went out of fashion. They reemerged a few years later in response to the difficulty of repairing punctures in early pneumatic tires. (Cushion tires are discussed in more detail in chapter 6.)

Pneumatic tires

A Scot named Robert William Thomson patented the pneumatic tire in the UK in 1845, principally for use on railroad cars (British patent 1,099a of 1845). Although used on some horse-drawn vehicles, Thomson's tire wasn't commercially successful and wasn't applied to velocipedes. Another Scot, John Boyd Dunlop, a veterinary surgeon living in Belfast, reinvented the pneumatic tire in 1887 and patented it the following year (British patent 10,607 of 1888). Dunlop's invention, first used on his son's tricycle, was rapidly adopted by cyclists. Its efficiency was demonstrated in racing from 1889 on.

John Boyd Dunlop wasn't a businessman, though for a while he served as the technical director of the company named after him. The entrepreneurial energy, however, was provided by a Dubliner, William Harvey du Cros, the sole executive director of the Dunlop Pneumatic Tyre Co. Ltd until 1896. Du Cros took the lead in organizing the new company to manufacture and promote the pneumatic tire. Dunlop's patent was voided in 1890, when the British Patent Office became aware that Thomson had already patented the concept. Du Cros, by then fully committed to the pneumatic tire, pursued a policy of buying up competing ones and compatible patents.

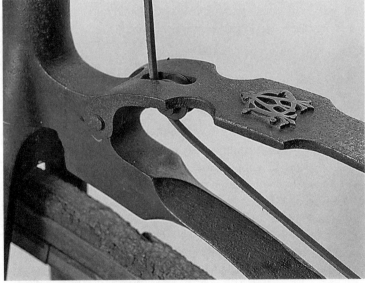

Figure 6.1 Above: A rubber-tired Michaux velocipede of 1868 or 1869 (Jean-Pierre Pradères). Below: A close-up showing a tire, a leather brake cord, and the owner's monogram (Musée d'Art et d'Industrie, Saint-Etienne).

Dunlop's earliest tires had to be fitted at the factory, but that soon changed as others copied and developed the pneumatic tire. C. K. Welch's revised British patent 14,563 of 1890 proved the answer to the vexing problem of removing a pneumatic tire in order to repair it. Bartlett's beaded-edge tire (British patent 16,783 of 1890), Woods's cycle valve, and West-wood's tubular-edged cycle rim (British patent 2,102 of 1890) had all been bought by the Dun-lop Pneumatic Tyre Co. Ltd by 1891. Through the rest of the decade, the company defended its intellectual property in the courts.

Edouard Michelin's removable tire (French patent 216,052 of 1891) was soon superseded by simpler designs.

As pneumatic tires improved, they were rapidly adopted. For example, most of the bicycles in the 1891 catalog of the British company Sunbeam were offered with a choice of solid or cushion tires, and only one with pneumatic tires as an option. The following year, all Sunbeam bicycles except one had pneumatic tires as an option. By 1898, only pneumatic tires were offered.

Tire design was settling down into several classes. Single-tube tires (the tire itself consisting of a single tube) soon went out of favor in the United Kingdom and in many other markets but remained in use for a long time in the United States, where US Rubber dominated the market. Frank Schwinn described US Rubber's nearly unrepairable product as "a glorified piece of endless garden hose with a valve in it" (Crown and Coleman 1996, 32).

Sew-ups or tubulars (with a thin outer cover wrapped around an inner tube and sewn up along its inside, then glued to a shallow rim) became the norm for serious racing.

Interlocking or beaded-edge tires, such as the Clincher, were held onto the rim by ridges in the edges of the outer cover, which were forced by air pressure into recesses in the hooked edges of the rim.

Then there was the wired-on tire, with a steel wire embedded in each edge of the outer cover. In some early examples this wire was adjustable, but that facility was soon abandoned. A wired-on tire was also held onto the rim by air pressure. Because the wire in its edges stopped the tire's circumference from increasing during inflation, it held onto the rim without needing ridged edges locking into recesses in the rim.

Although the beaded-edge tire remained in use for many decades, the simple non-adjustable wired-on tire, such as the Dunlop Detachable, was to become the world standard for normal use. The patent that Dunlop used for its wired-on tires was British patent 14,563 of 1890, developed by Charles Kingston Welch.

The wired-on tire became commonly known also as the "Clincher" regardless of the maker and despite the fact that the original Clincher wasn't a wired-on tire. The Clincher was, however, the first tire to depend primarily on air pressure to keep it on the rim. Unlike some other kinds of tires, which were held onto the rim principally by mechanical means, they could not slip relative to the rim during braking or under traction.

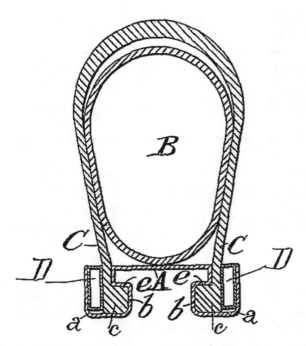

Figure 6.2
A patent drawing of Edouard Michelin's
removable tire, which required a special rim.
Figure 6.3
Left: John Boyd Dunlop (Wikipedia Commons).
Center: A Dunlop Roadster beaded-edge tire
of the early twentieth century (Dunlop Tyres
UK). Right: The wired-on version of same tire
(Dunlop Tyres UK).

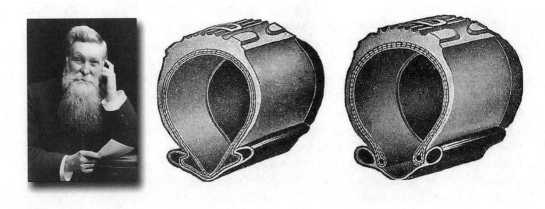

The hooked edge made a comeback in the late twentieth century. Most good rims of the early twenty-first century had a slightly hooked internal edge (which helped hold the bead of the wired-on tire better), and some wired-on tires had a hooked-bead. From the late 1970s on, the beads of some upscale tires had Kevlar cables rather than steel wires in them.

In 1896, Sharp observed that a pneumatic tire with a circular cross-section of about two inches, most of which was outside the shallow rim, could easily pass over a one-inch-high stone "without influencing the motion of the wheel to any great extent, provided the speed is great," and that "the provision against loss of energy by impact in moving over a rough road is more perfect in this case [than with a solid tire]." "Again," Sharp continued, "the tyre being of larger [cross-sectional] diameter, its surface of contact with the ground is greater, and the energy lost by sinking into a road of moderate hardness is practically *nil*." (488) Sharp pointed out that the rolling resistance of a pneumatic tire was very low:

> The work done in bending the forward part of the [tire] cover [as it rolls along] will be a little greater than that restored by the cover as it regains its original shape. Probably the only appreciable resistance of a pneumatic tyre is due to the difference between these two forces. The work expended in bending the tyre will be greater, the greater the angle through which it is bent. This angle is least when the tyre is pumped up hardest; and therefore on a smooth racing track pneumatic tyres should be pumped up as hard as possible. (489).

In 1913, Frank Bowden, chairman of Raleigh, wrote a little less scientifically:

> I think I may safely say that those [bicycles] of the present day, with pneumatic tyres, are propelled up a slight incline with at least three or four times the ease of those made in the eighties, with solid rubber tyres of from ½ to ⅞ of an inch in diameter. (1913, 5)

In the early years of pneumatic bicycle tires, there was a lot of experimentation with carcass construction. Then, as now, tires' carcasses were made up of bands of textile cords ("canvas") coated with rubber. Early pneumatic bicycle tires were of radial-ply design, the cords running transversely and circumferentially (Sharp 1896, 492). However, bias-ply or cross-ply designs, with crossed layers of cord running diagonally to the tread, were found to be better and became the norm. Radial-ply bicycle tires have been reintroduced from time to time—for example, by Panasonic in the 1980s, and by Maxxis in the Radiale, a tire available at the time of writing. But radial-ply tires are more prone to sideslip than bias-ply tires, and many cyclists dislike that (Wilson 2004, 298).

Tire sizes stabilized during the 1890s as 30-inch wheels fell out of use. Most bicycles now had 28-inch wheels front and rear. Bicycles made for smaller riders, and some sports machines, had 26-inch wheels. For commercial reasons, different territories devised their own series of tire sizes—North American, British, French, Dutch, Italian, and so on. Owing to the early dominance of the US and UK bicycle industries, all tire sizes were based on nominal wheel diameter expressed in inches. They often varied, however, in the crucial dimension: bead seat diameter. Confusing matters further, cross-sections progressively shrank. Today a nominal 28-inch tire, such as the widely used French metric format 700C (700 millimeters, a rounded conversion of 28 inches, was the original diameter; C denoted the original cross section), may have an actual outer diameter of as little as 26.3 inches; the cross-section has been reduced considerably, though the bead seat diameter hasn't changed.

Occasionally a manufacturer would create a new "out of series" tire. In the late 1930s, fearing that French 700C tires would be imported into the UK, Dunlop introduced a 27-inch tire with a bead seat diameter 8 millimeters larger than that of a 700C. It is noteworthy that one can interchange a 700C wheel with a wired-on tire with a 28-inch sprint wheel with a tubular (sew-up) tire without the having to adjust the brake calipers. In the 1960s, emulating this approach, Alex Moulton introduced an out-of-series wired-on tire and a matching rim so that users of 18-inch sprint wheels with tubular tires could easily switch to a wheel with a more durable wired-on tire.

During the first half of the twentieth century, especially in France and the United Kingdom, 28-inch wheels gradually lost ground to 26-inch ones. Frank Bowden (1913, 55) argued that "the lighter tyres and smaller wheels save pounds in weight in the place where it is felt the most, the periphery of the wheels." Bowden, like Vélocio, favored "open-sided" or "skin-wall" tires. Because they had very little rubber covering the canvas sidewalls, they rolled more easily, though they were more fragile. Vélocio went further and advocated wide-section tires of even smaller diameter. The practical effect of Vélocio's influence can be seen in the adoption by the French of the 650B demi-ballon tire, a medium-width tire in the 26-inch format. At the time of writing, 650B tires are enjoying a minor resurgence among riders of mountain bikes.

A return to wide-section tires came with the development of balloon tires by Continental in Hannover, Germany. (Balloon tires are defined as wide-section pneumatic tires designed for relatively low air pressure.) Continental began making balloon tires for automobiles in 1923, for motorcycles in 1925, and for the Brennabor and (German) Triumph bicycle companies in 1926. Early 1927 saw the first appearance of bicycle balloon tires on Continental's price list, in 28 × 1.75-inch and 28 × 2-inch sizes. Continental competitor Excelsior listed 26 × 2-inch balloon tires in its catalog for 1928 (Euhus 2003).

Continental devised a new valve for the balloon tire. The widely used Woods valve (sometimes known as the Dunlop or English valve), invented by Frederick Woods in 1891, had a

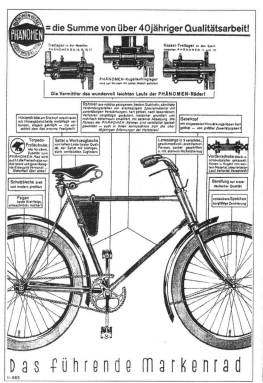

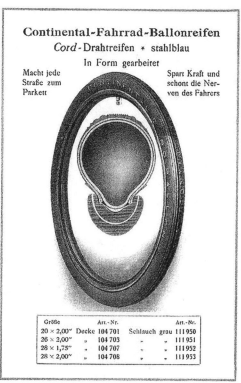

Figure 6.4 Left: A flyer for the 1930 Phänomen balloon-tired bicycle. The maker's advice was "Keep the air pressure only as high as is necessary to avoid the rims grounding." Right: A Continental balloon tire (company brochure).

rubber sheath over a tube, the end of which was sealed. There was a hole in the side of the tube, and air pressure from the pump entered the inner tube by being forced through the hole and lifting the rubber sheath away from the tube. If air at sufficient pressure wasn't passing through the hole, the sheath would snap shut, sealing the air into the inner tube. Applying enough pressure necessary to force air past the rubber sheath took a lot of effort. The new Continental valve did away with the valve rubber, substituting a freely moving rubber piston on a thin metal rod, and made it much easier to add air.

At about the same time, the German company Alligator, a subsidiary of Steiff, patented a somewhat similar but cosmetically different valve. The Alligaro Easypump valve went on the

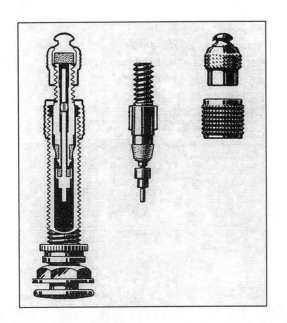

Figure 6.5 Left: Continental's improved tire valve, shown here with an adapter for use with automobile pumps and airlines (company brochure). Right: The rival Alligaro valve (company brochure).

market in 1930. In the 1960s, Dunlop also sold valves under the name Easypump; they resembled the Continental design more than the Alligaro, however. Today, valves that fit the 8.3-millimeter rim holes originally sized for Woods valves are becoming rare in many markets. However, they are still available in certain territories, and in some places one can still buy the original Woods-style valves with replaceable rubbers.

In 1932, Frank Schwinn, son of the founder of the Schwinn bicycle company, went to Germany to visit some relatives and bought some samples of balloon tires to take back to the United States. By threatening to import German tires, Schwinn coerced US Rubber into making balloon tires for him. In 1933, Schwinn launched the B10E "Super Balloon Tire Bicycle," which had low-pressure tires 2⅛ inches wide. In 1935, Schwinn made more than 100,000 balloon-tired bikes. The "fat tire" became an American standard (Crown and Coleman 1996, 32 and 33). Balloon tires, with flexible sidewalls and relatively smooth treads, are available today; Schwalbe's Big Apple tires, for example, are available in cross-sections as large as 2.125 inches.

Figure 6.6   A Schwinn Phantom of the 1950s (Bicycle Museum of America).

Early in the twenty-first century, several Alaskan frame builders made mountain bikes with ultra-wide tires for use in snowy conditions. In 2005, the Minnesota-based company Surly Bikes launched a mass-produced "fat bike" called the Pugsley. Another Minnesota company, Salsa, followed suit with similar products. At the time of writing, "fat bikes" with tires as wide as 4¼ inches are commercially available.

With the coming of the balloon tire, Schrader valves (first used on automobiles) became the norm for bicycles in North America. By the 1950s, British bicycles destined for the United States were fitted with Schrader valves. Gradually their use spread to Europe; they also became widely used elsewhere on most types of bicycles (except racing machines, on which Presta valves have long been preferred). The two main disadvantages of the Schrader valve are that it requires a 9-millimeter hole in the rim (which makes it unsuitable for narrow rims) and that, because the valve piston is spring loaded, it requires a little more effort than the Alligaro or the Presta.

The Presta valve (also known as the Sclaverand or French valve) and the Alligaro valve are similar in operation, each having an unsprung piston. However, the Presta is slightly smaller in diameter (requiring only a 6.8-millimeter hole in the rim), and it has the advantage that the air seal can be screwed tight by hand.

The craze for balloon tires didn't last long in Germany; it was all but over by 1937. Meanwhile, in the UK, tires had been getting narrower rather than wider. The standard widths of tires became 1⅜ inch for roadsters and 1¼ inch for racing bicycles.

The materials used in tires improved over time. Flexible and rot-resistant synthetic textile cords (such as Nylon) became common in the 1960s, and there were many advances in synthetic rubber technology and manufacture. Filling agents such as silica were often used as a compromise between good grip and low rolling resistance. Some tires incorporated several different rubber compounds, so that optimum characteristics could be provided for the tread, the sidewalls, and the "shoulders" (the transition from tread to sidewall, important in cornering).

Butyl rubber, which holds air better than pure latex, became the norm for inner tubes. Some racing cyclists preferred latex for its perceived low rolling resistance, and techniques evolved to line latex inner tubes with a microscopic coating to improve air retention. For example, in 1978 Raleigh patented a process for applying polyvinylidene chloride to latex inner tubes.

Some tires incorporated sophisticated modern versions of the anti-puncture layer (an old idea). Among the materials used were Kevlar, natural rubber, and a mix of the two.

By the 2000s, tubeless tires, which dispensed with the inner tube and instead made an airtight seal to the rim, were gaining some popularity among bicyclists. The best known of these, the UST (Universal System Tubeless), pioneered in France for mountain bikes by the tire makers Hutchinson and Michelin and the wheel maker Mavic, didn't require rim tape. A UST could be set to relatively low pressure for use on rough terrain without the risk that pinching of the inner tube would cause a puncture. Conventional wheels and tires could be converted for use with tubeless tires by sealing the nipple holes with a special tape and injecting a void-filling latex-based fluid into the tire before inflation to create an airtight seal. Tubeless systems for road bikes were also available.

Before we leave the subject of pneumatic tires, we wish to make a point concerning the standard wired-on tire without a hook-edge bead. For safety reasons, the fit between the tire's bead and the rim must be relatively tight and even. If it isn't, air pressure in the inner tube may lift the tire at some point on the circumference, producing a bulge that may cause the tire to jam in the frame, or to be punctured, or both, with potentially disastrous results. Reference lines are molded around the sidewalls of bicycle tires to facilitate correct fitting. These lines should be equally spaced from the rim, all the way around the inflated tire, on both sides of the wheel. Also, a puncture in a front tire that has a slack fit between its bead and the bead seat in the rim can result in dangerous instability. A tight fit may make fitting or repairing a tire difficult, but it makes a huge difference in a flat tire's stability (Wilson 2002, 13, 17–19).

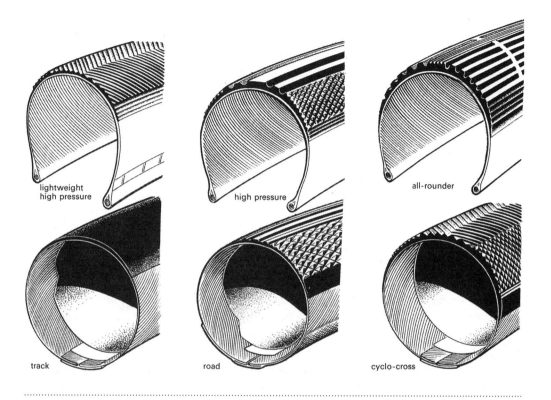

Figure 6.7 Typical sports and racing tires of the late 1960s (R. John Way).

Cushion tires

The difficulty of repairing the early pneumatic tires led to renewed interest in cushion tires, which lasted several years. Cushion tires came in various forms, some (e.g., Metzeler's Bavaria) having multiple air pockets and some (e.g., McDonald's) made of composites of cork and rubber or of sponge rubber. They were more comfortable than solid tires but not as comfortable as pneumatics. They didn't require inflating, and even those versions with air pockets weren't easily punctured, but they had higher rolling resistance than pneumatics. They were, therefore, popular only as long as pneumatics were particularly difficult to repair. Sharp (1896) doesn't mention cushion tires in his chapter on tires, and there is only one indexed reference to them in his book. Nonetheless, cushion tires remained in use in the UK on some carrier cycles as late as 1950, and they still return to the market periodically. Raleigh had high hopes for its Cairfree tire (a patent application for which was filed in 1972), but it proved unsuitable for adult machines owing to its high rolling resistance. Greentyres has had more success with its one-piece cushion tires made of micro-cellular polyurethane. Most of Greentyres' products are exported, many for use on wheelchairs and on wheelbarrows. Greentyres also has a surprisingly wide range of bicycle tires.

SPRUNG SUPPORTS FOR SADDLES

Even a first-generation draisine had a padded saddle. To improve both comfort and ergonomics, Drais equipped his second-generation machine with a sausage-shaped, leather-covered suspended saddle that was adjustable for height.

The next step in improving comfort was to mount the saddle on springs. By 1818, a French velocipede had been built with the rear of the seat suspended on double leaf springs. It is shown in the second edition of Ernest Deharme's 1874 book *Les Merveilles de la Locomotion*.

The saddle of a Michaux-style velocipede of the 1860s was typically fixed to a long leaf spring. The ends of the spring were fixed by pivots, one on the back of the head tube and the other attached to the top of a pair of stays rising from the rear of the frame.

The geometry of the high-wheeler made a long leaf spring such as that of a Michaux-style machine impractical. Shorter leaf springs were tried, but a more practical solution was to incorporate the springing into the saddle itself and clamp the saddle directly to the backbone of the machine.

With the coming of the safety bicycle, sprung seat posts (sometimes called seat pins or seat pillars) were tried. A "spring-gooseneck" seat post was made of thin, relatively flexible steel rod. Typically such a post emerged from the seat tube, then ran horizontally for several inches before curving up through 180° and again running horizontally. The saddle was mounted on the "beak" of the "gooseneck." This system typically provided too much springing

Figure 6.8 Left: Metzeler's Bavaria cushion tire, with air voids. Right: Section through McDonald's cushion tire, with cork inner core, soft rubber above and below it, and hard rubber tread and carcass (*Polytechnisches Journal* 296, 1895, 205 and 204).

Figure 6.9 The suspended saddle of a second-generation draisine (Hans-Erhard Lessing).

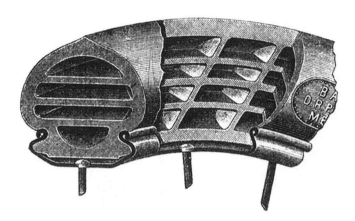
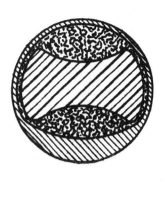
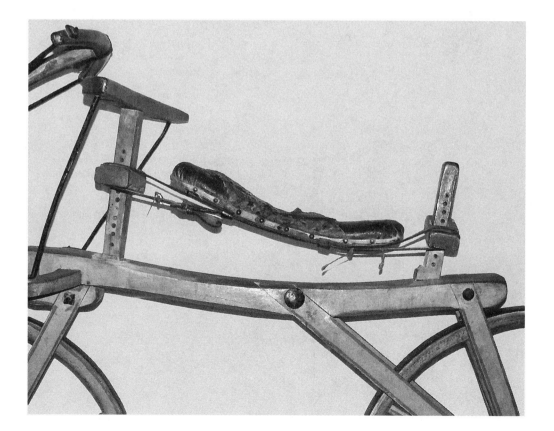

Figure 6.10 An 1818 French velocipede with leaf-spring seat suspension (Deharme 1874).
Figure 6.11 A German tricycle, based on a Michaux-style velocipede, with the saddle mounted on a single-leaf spring (R. John Way).

and necessitated a low frame to enable the rider to mount the saddle. In addition, the saddle sagged considerably when loaded, as the "gooseneck" flexed.

A better solution was a simple telescopically sprung seat post. One early example, designed by Harold Serrell of New Jersey in 1895 (US patent 562,203 of 1896), had a coil spring within the seat post. The spring could be adjusted to suit the rider's weight by means of a screwed plug in the base of the post. The saddle was mounted on a horizontal bar pivoted at the top of the post in such a way that it acted on the spring in the post by means of a cam.

Another approach, proposed by Charles Little of Michigan (US patent 584,944 of 1897), involved bolting one end of a C-shaped spring to a bicycle's frame and the other end to a standard seat post. But sprung seat posts didn't achieve commercial success until the 1990s, when the mountain bike revived interest in suspension systems. A British firm called Ultimate Sports Engineering introduced its first Shokpost in 1990.

Although sprung "folding" parallelograms and other designs have been tried, today's suspension seat posts are almost all telescopic, the suspension provided by an elastomer, a coil spring, or compressed air within the seat post.

Suspension seat posts are the easiest form of suspension to retrofit (apart from that built into the saddle itself) but have two major disadvantages. The first is that the whole weight of the bike (apart from the saddle) is unsprung. The second is that, as with a sprung saddle, the rider's knees are made to flex involuntarily as the seat post moves up and down relative to the bottom bracket.

In the 1890s, when the cycle industry was opting for standardized saddles that could fit almost any bicycle, the British-based Danish inventor Mikael Pedersen designed a bicycle around his "hammock" saddle (British patent 18,371 of 1893). Pedersen, an accomplished rider, was said to have ridden 5,000 miles in a year. "The part of the machine in general use which I found most imperfect," he wrote, "was the seat." He described his solution as follows:

The seat which I have devised is, as you will observe, made of strings of different degrees of tension, running from a point in front to a cross steel bar giving the requisite width behind. In order to give the right width and form, cross strings are interwoven. The seat is suspended between two supporting points about two feet from each other; and running from the cross steel bar to the rear supporting point are several spiral springs, which afford the required elasticity. It will be seen that this seat (called by some the "hammock," and by others the "network" seat) can never become hard or too wide at any point, although it give the rider more space than do other seats. As, moreover, it "gives" in every direction, the weight is always evenly distributed. . . . Its weight is not more than four ounces, as against the (about) 3 lb of an ordinary saddle." (Evans 1978, 10)

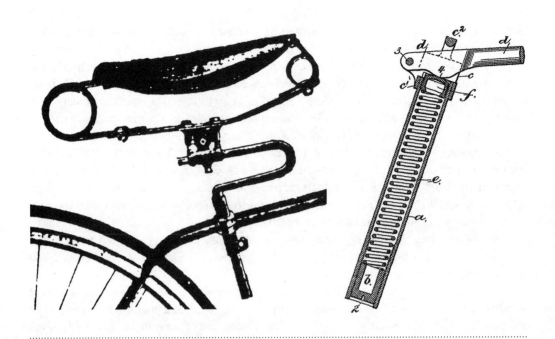

Figure 6.12 Left: A flexible gooseneck seat post, circa 1890 (National Cycle Library). Right: Serrell's sprung seat post of 1895 (patent drawing).

The Pedersen bicycle met with some commercial success and has its devotees to this day. Pedersens were made in England from 1897 until 1914 and from 1920 until 1922. From the 1970s until the present day, various small-scale and specialist makers have, at various times, produced limited numbers of Pedersen replicas or derivatives in England, Denmark, Germany, and the Czech Republic.

In the 1990s, another attempt to provide enhanced saddle suspension also ended up working best with a specially designed frame. This was the Allsop Beam, designed by James Allsop and David Calopp of Bellingham, Washington (US patent 4,934,724 of 1990) and later sold in various versions under the brand name Softride. The saddle was mounted on the end of a nearly horizontal cantilevered beam, typically made of carbon fiber and shaped like a flattened S, that pivoted in the vertical plane from a point just behind the head tube. A few inches behind the pivot point, the beam rested on a fulcrum. The springy beam provided simple and effective suspension for the saddle. The fulcrum was adjustable to vary the beam's tilt and thus the saddle's height.

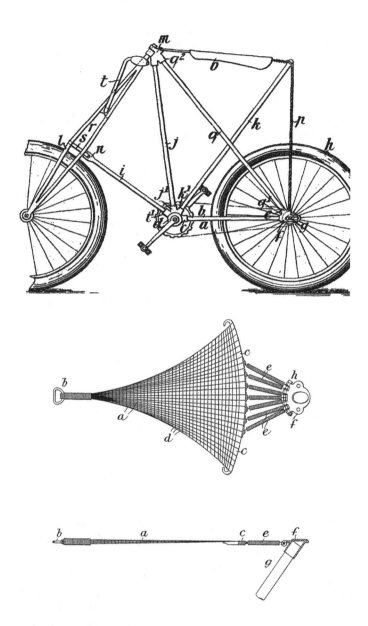

Figure 6.13 A Pedersen bicycle and its suspended "network" or "hammock" saddle (patent drawings).

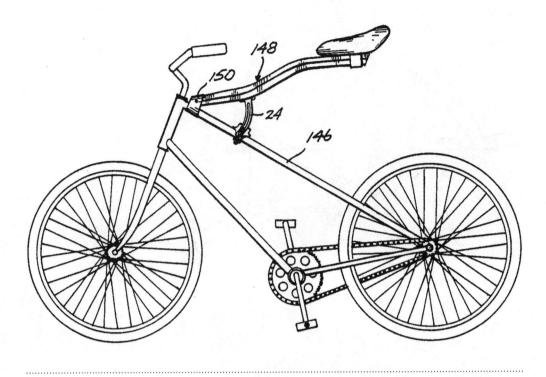

Figure 6.14 The Allsop/Softride beam (patent drawing).

The Allsop/Softride system was the most successful seat-suspension system of its kind, remaining in production until 2006. Particularly popular among ultra-marathon and triathlon riders, it was banned in 1999 when the Union Cycliste Internationale made conventional seat tubes mandatory.

Although originally conceived as suitable for retrofitting to a conventional diamond frame, a Softride could cause frame damage, especially to thin-walled butted top tubes. Some bicycle manufacturers, notably Cannondale, warned against the use of such a system. It worked best on a frame designed specifically for it, which limited its appeal and its market. One slightly disconcerting characteristic was that the beam moved not only up and down but also, to an extent, from side to side.

The Australian mountain bike champion Rod Evans used a Softride and a special frame in a 1992 race from the west coast to the east coast of Australia that entailed riding 2,200 miles across the middle of the Outback on unpaved roads. The frame broke halfway through the race, and Evans rode a conventional mountain bike until another Softride bike was flown in from Sydney. He completed the last 1,000 miles on the replacement Softride machine.

In the 1990s, presumably inspired by Softride's success, a builder in Oregon called Bike Friday introduced two folding bikes (the Air Friday and the Air Glide) that used a cantilevered titanium beam to suspend the saddle. Instead of tilting the beam to adjust the saddle's height, Bike Friday used a conventional adjustable seat post in a truncated seat tube clamped to the end of the beam.

On the development of saddles, including their integral springing, see chapter 9.

SPRUNG HANDLEBARS

Various methods of springing handlebars have been tried. The Whippet bicycle of the mid 1880s had the whole section of the frame carrying the handlebars, the seat, and the cranks sprung as a single unit. In 1887, James Copeland of Connecticut patented rubber-sprung handlebars (US patent 367,368). In 1889, Charles Collings of Ohio patented left and right handlebars independently sprung from their conjunction with the stem (US patent 409,143). In 1896, Lucien and Charles Barnes of New York patented a handlebar that rotated against a coil spring in the stem (US patent 568,082). In 1897, Henry Christy of Illinois patented handlebar grips decoupled from the handlebar by coil springs (US patent 583,457). In 1941, Norton Motors and Edgar Franks obtained British patent 531,716 for another method.

Although none of the inventions mentioned above were commercially successful, the idea of springing handlebars achieved some fleeting popularity in the early 1990s, especially among mountain bikers. The simplest and most successful implementation was Robert Girvin's Flex-stem, invented in 1988 (US patent 4,939,950 of 1990), which was inexpensive, easy to fit, robust, and very effective at reducing shocks and vibration caused by small, high-frequency irregularities in road surfaces. Like Copeland's 1887 design, it used elastomers for both the main springing and the rebound springing.

For most of the bicycle's history, riders have simply used various types of padded handlebar grips to add a little comfort. Wood, solid cork, rubber, leather, rigid plastics, polyethylene, fabric tape, cork tape, plastic tape, foam rubber, and foam plastic have all been used.

On the development of handlebars in general, see chapter 9.

Figure 6.15 A Linley & Biggs Whippet bicycle (R. John Way).

Figure 6.16 Left: Copeland's elastomer-sprung handlebars (patent drawing). Right: A Girvin Flexstem (catalog illustration).

WHEEL SUSPENSION

Some general points about suspension

In the pursuit of comfort, as Sharp pointed out (1896, 487), the aim should be to minimize the unsprung mass of the machine and the rider so as to minimize the loss of forward momentum through shock.

Wheel suspension involves more than just interposing a spring between the wheel and the frame. Damping allows a suspension system to react quickly to the initial shock but return to its normal position in a controlled manner, without oscillating. Preload (whereby the spring is compressed to allow for the rider's weight) may be useful in preventing excessive sagging of the suspension when the rider mounts the machine. Steps should be taken to minimize stiction (sticking friction), which impairs smooth operation of a suspension system. Early suspension designers didn't necessarily consider all these factors.

Some early systems had an inherent element of damping—for example, multiple leaf springs provide some damping through friction as the leaves slide against one another. But a single leaf spring, such as that used to mount the seat of a Michaux-style velocipede, has no inherent damping. A suspension pivot could be fitted with a series of friction discs that were tightened or loosened to adjust the damping, as on early Bentley cars. This simple but effective system was used in the rear forks of some Moulton bicycles in the 1960s and has been used in the leading-link forks of some Moultons since the 1980s. In some of the better mountain-bike suspensions, damping is applied (as in most automobile and aircraft shock absorbers) by forcing air or a fluid through a valve. Elastomer springs have some inherent damping and can sometimes be used without additional damping, as in the rubber rear suspension of the Brompton folding bicycle.

A particular problem faced by designers of bicycle suspension systems is the oscillation of the rider's power input. An enthusiastic rider "honking or "dancing" on the pedals is likely to bounce the bike up and down on its suspension, wasting energy that should be translated into forward motion. For this reason, a suspension, particularly that of the front wheel, sometimes has a "lock-out" facility that enables the rider to deactivate the suspension (wholly or partially) at will. Suspension systems tend to work best for riders who stay in the saddle and have a smooth rotary pedaling action.

Harmonic oscillations of any kind are to be avoided in sprung suspension systems. They can be introduced not only by the rider's pedaling but also by unstable loads on the front of the bike. For example, early space-frame Moultons (such as the AM7, introduced in 1983), could develop front-wheel wobble (shimmy) as a result of oscillations induced by a load on the front-mounted luggage rack. In the late 1980s the leading links of the front suspension were stiffened, and from 1993 on stiffer forks were fitted (Hadland 1994).

The development of bicycle suspension systems

After the adoption of solid rubber tires, some bicycle makers tried to improve comfort further by adding suspension to the wheels. Mounting the saddle on a leaf spring had substantially improved saddle comfort. The next priority was the rider's hands, which were not yet protected from road shock to any great extent.

In 1869 Eugène Dufeutrelle obtained French patent protection for two types of twin-fork front suspension using leaf springs. The wheel was held in the inner fork, which could move up and down relative to the outer fork, to which it was attached by slides in the outer fork legs and the steerer. Velocipedes with this feature were advertised for sale by the Compagnie Parisienne, and examples survive in museums in Lyon and Saint-Étienne. Another form of velocipede front suspension, featured in a Compagnie Parisienne catalog, had a telescopic steerer with a "hairpin" spring above the fork crown (Reynaud 2008, 124ff).

René Olivier, founder of the Compagnie Parisienne, obtained an American patent for four forms of front wheel suspension for velocipedes (US patent 97,683 of 1869). Like Dufeutrelle, Olivier used a sprung inner fork, which he called an "auxiliary compensating fork," sliding within the main fork. The main differences lay in the springing media.

Olivier's first type used semi-elliptical leaf springs below the axle; his second type had India rubber bands in tension in front of and behind the axle; his third variant had lenticular rubber or other springs immediately above the axle; his fourth version had a single coil spring within the steering head. His patent also covered use of the same springing methods for the rear wheel.

Some designers thought that the small rear wheel of a high-wheeler should be suspended. Small wheels tend to drop deeper into potholes and to fall and rise more quickly over bumps, thus giving a rough ride unless sprung. Henry Kellogg of Connecticut devised a sophisticated self-adjusting telescopic air suspension system for the rear wheel (US patent 283,612 of 1883). But the rider of a high-wheeler was, in reality, well isolated from vertical movements of the rear wheel, and the large front wheel gave a relatively smooth ride, so suspension systems for high-wheelers didn't catch on.

....

Figure 6.17 An 1869 Compagnie Parisienne velocipede with leaf-spring front suspension (Musée National de la Voiture et du Tourisme, Palais de Compiègne/Studio Caterin).
Figure 6.18 Olivier's suspension variants (patent drawings).

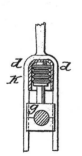

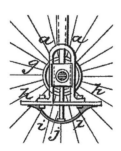

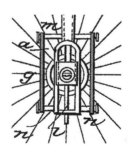

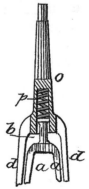

Lenticular spring
above axle

Leaf spring
below axle

Rubber bands fore
and aft of axle

Coil spring in
steering head

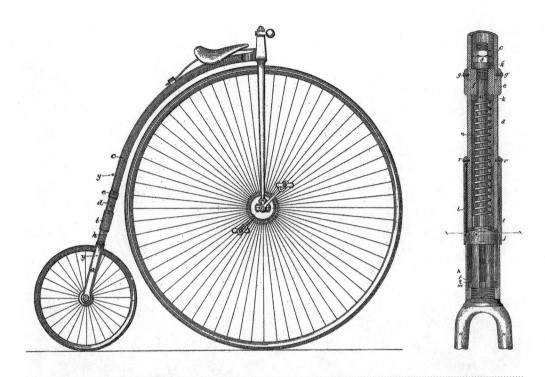

Figure 6.19 A high-wheeler with Kellogg's self-adjusting air suspension on the rear wheel (patent drawings).

It was the solid-tired safety bicycle that prompted a burst of suspension innovation. Many kinds of suspension systems were patented, some for front wheels and some for rear wheels. Some achieved a measure of commercial success. We have already mentioned Linley and Biggs's Whippet bicycle. For several years, beginning in 1887, the American Victor (men's) and Victoria (ladies') bicycles featured the Victor spring fork.

Columbia offered a coil-sprung leading-link suspension on the front fork. In the UK, Rudge patented and produced a "Non-vibrating Spring Fork," another coil-sprung leading-link design. Some other makers, including Raleigh, offered cycles with a telescopic steerer tube that had a coil spring between the top of the fork crown and the bottom of the head tube. Humber's offerings included a spring-frame bicycle with leading-link front suspension and a sprung cantilever rear fork, both with coil springs. Humber's Patent Anti-Vibrator (British patent 12,491 of 1885) was a sophisticated telescopic front fork with three coil springs—a short-travel hard spring, a long-travel soft spring, and a rebound spring.

In 1889, Hugo Auguste Becker of Blaenavon, South Wales invented a dual-suspension bicycle (US patent 439,095 of 1890). The rear suspension featured, on each side of the rear wheel, pivoted chain stays and seat stays, with short pivoted links between the rearmost ends of these stays. The seat tube, the seat stays, the link, and the chain stays formed a pivoting quadrilateral. A coil spring was fixed in tension between each chain stay and the seat stay. When the rear wheel moved upward, the coil spring was stretched. Becker's front suspension also used a coil spring in tension. The more advanced of the two front suspension arrangements shown in his patent had a sprung pivoted quadrilateral linkage between the suspended front fork and the head tube. The linkage was similar in principle to Becker's rear suspension, but much more compact. As the fork was floating on this suspended linkage ahead of the head tube, the fork's steerer had to be connected to the handlebar's steerer by means of a bridle rod system. Becker's design was plainly less than robust, and he seems to have had no appreciation of the need for damping. Not surprisingly, his bicycle doesn't appear to have been put into production.

A somewhat more practical dual-suspension bicycle invented by Charles McGlinchey of Chicago (US patent 465,599 of 1891) had stiff short-travel vertical coil springs in compression. The rear suspension had a cantilevered trailing fork with integrated bottom bracket, pivoted from the lowest point of the frame, a few inches ahead of the bracket. The coil spring was directly above the bottom bracket, acting on an abutment on the back of the seat tube. McGlinchey's front suspension had short leading links on the front fork, each acting on a short coil spring, and the tension of the springs could be adjusted. The design wasn't commercially successful.

Some of the early suspension designs that were put into production were still available in the mid 1890s, but they were fast becoming rarities as pneumatic tires increasingly dominated the market.

After the universal adoption of the pneumatic tire, bicycle suspension systems of various kinds continued to be invented from time to time. Owing to the pneumatic tire's effectiveness and simplicity and the rapid improvement of road surfaces in the West during the first half of the twentieth century, they saw little commercial success. In the remainder of this chapter, we highlight a few noteworthy of suspension systems of the early twentieth century.

The idea of air suspension, first proposed in Kellogg's 1883 patent, was occasionally revived, usually with a small inflatable cushion as the spring. In 1900, John Stewart of Edinburgh patented a safety bicycle with air-cushion suspension on both wheels (British patent 17,515 of 1900). It was put into production by the inventor's own firm, the Polwarth Cycle Manufacturing Company (Campbell 1903).

In 1920, a simple and easy-to-fit dual telescopic (sliding-column) front fork was devised by George W. Sage Jr. of Port Chester, New York (US patent 1,429,107 of 1922). It used short-travel coil springs in the upper section of each telescopic fork blade. Telescopic suspension for bicycles wasn't new; as was noted above, there had been several single telescopic

Figure 6.20   Left: The Victor sprung fork (*The Data Book*, Van der Plas, 2000). Right: Humber's triple-coil-spring front suspension (National Cycle Library).

systems in the 1880s. But Sage may have been the first to patent a dual telescopic fork for a pedaled cycle. Seventy years later, the dual telescopic fork became the most widely adopted form of bicycle front suspension; it remains so at the time of writing.

In the few cases where suspension was fitted as original equipment, it was often on bicycles designed to appeal to young people with features that hinted at motorcycle technology. For example, Schwinn fitted crude "springer" forks (US patent 2,160,034 of 1939) to some cruisers in the post-World War II years and to some "Krate" high-rise bikes in the 1960s. (This was a poor design, as the wheel went back and forth more than up and down.)

Some makers of lightweight bicycles occasionally offered suspension. For example, the English maker Carlton marketed a sprung front fork in the 1930s.

In the late 1940s and the early 1950s, various bicycles with integral suspension or add-on units were demonstrated at the big European national cycle shows. H. C. Webb & Company

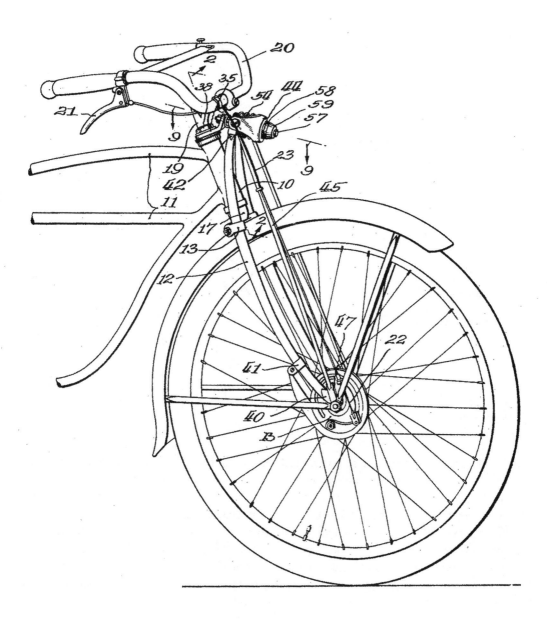

Figure 6.21 Frank Schwinn's "springer" fork (patent drawing).

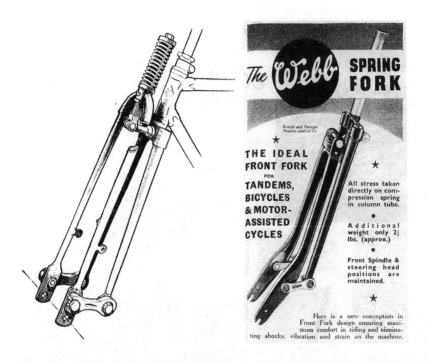

Figure 6.22 Left: A Carlton sprung fork of the 1930s (National Cycle Library). Right: A Webb Spring Fork of 1952 (advertisement).

of Birmingham introduced a well-engineered example at the 1952 British Cycle Show. It had a parallelogram action, as some motorcycles' forks do, and a coil spring within the steerer tube. Around the same time, Palco of London introduced an add-on suspension unit for use on the front or the rear wheel of any bicycle. Light, adjustable, and easy to fit, it was still on sale in the mid 1950s. One disadvantage of the Palco suspension was that, as it responded to bumps, the wheel rim moved up and down relative to the brake blocks. The maker, however, claimed the product improved braking, reduced skidding, eliminated broken spokes, lessened tire wear, and protected lamp bulbs from premature failure. The Palco units certainly received some good reviews, one of them from F. J. Camm, editor of *The Cyclist*.

By 1960, youngsters in the Darlington area of northeastern England were riding "bog-wheels"—home-made off-road bicycles equipped with front-wheel suspensions taken from mopeds. In the United States, in the 1960s and later, Dan Henry designed and rode suspension bicycles. But none of these innovations made a significant impact on the market.

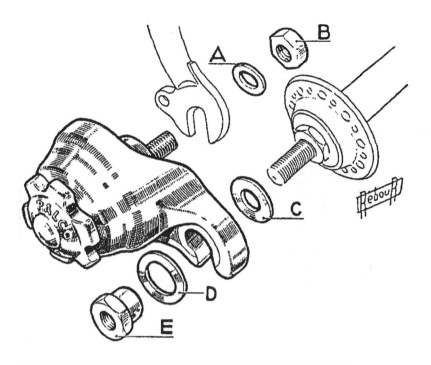

Figure 6.23 A Palco suspension unit (National Cycle Library).

In 1963, the Moulton small-wheeler began to appear in British cycle shops. It was the first dual-suspension bicycle for adult use to achieve respectable sales figures. The original Moulton's telescopic front suspension was neatly concealed in the steerer. At its heart was a rubber column (the main spring) surrounded by a steel coil spring. Compression of the suspension caused the rubber to bulge between the coils of the steel spring, thus damping the suspension. A separate coil spring dealt with rebound. The rear suspension was a simple trailing arm with a cleverly designed rubber spring that worked in shear and compression at the same time. This provided a rising spring rate, so that the more heavily the bike was loaded the stiffer the spring became. Thus the rear suspension was, to some extent, self-adjusting for load. The only maintenance normally needed was occasional bearing replacement.

Although the Moulton had a major effect on the British cycle industry, it didn't lead to a renaissance in bicycle suspension. That would come with the development of the mountain bike, discussed in chapter 14.

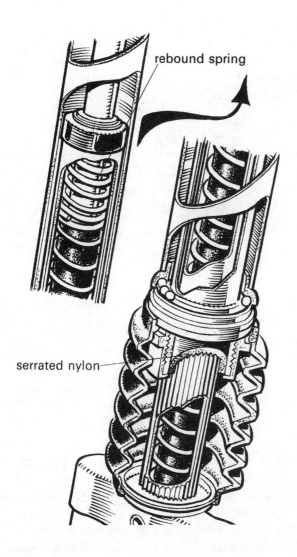

rebound spring

serrated nylon

Figure 6.24 The front suspension in
the steering head of the Moulton bicycle,
launched in 1962 (R. John Way).
Figure 6.25 RockShox suspension forks
(1997 SRAM Corporation catalog).

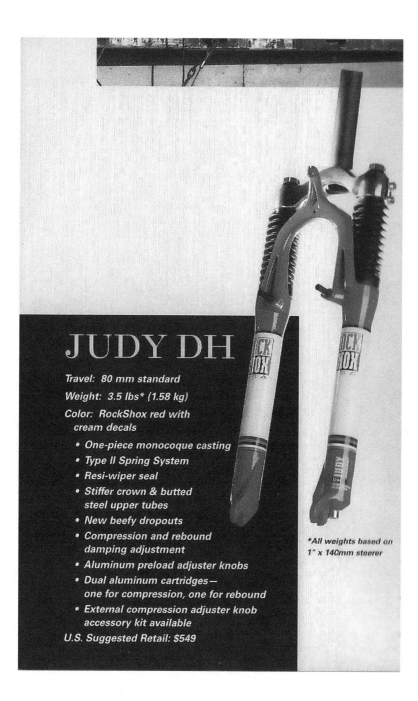

JUDY DH

Travel: *80 mm standard*

Weight: *3.5 lbs* (1.58 kg)*

Color: *RockShox red with cream decals*

- One-piece monocoque casting
- Type II Spring System
- Resi-wiper seal
- Stiffer crown & butted steel upper tubes
- New beefy dropouts
- Compression and rebound damping adjustment
- Aluminum preload adjuster knobs
- Dual aluminum cartridges— one for compression, one for rebound
- External compression adjuster knob accessory kit available

U.S. Suggested Retail: $549

*All weights based on 1" x 140mm steerer

IMPROVING TRANSMISSION

We discussed the evolution of the primary drive system in chapter 4. In this chapter we examine two ways in which transmission has been improved to more effectively match the limited power output of the rider to the desired speed of travel, taking account of factors such as gradients and wind direction.

One approach is multi-speed gearing. As the magazine *Cycling* put it in 1903, the ability to select a lower gear when encountering hills or headwinds enables the rider "to overcome the increased resistance by a steady flow of energy spread over the longer period caused by the sacrifice of speed."

The other transmission technology—the automatic freewheel—is so universal that it is taken for granted. But its evolution was a long and complex process.

EVOLUTION OF THE AUTOMATIC FREEWHEEL

The idea of the freewheel goes back to the dawn of cycling, but freewheels didn't become common until brakes and gears had been perfected. In 1821, Lewis Gompertz attempted to improve Denis Johnson's velocipede by using the rider's arms to drive the front wheel by means of a quadrant and pinion (Gompertz 1821; Bowerman 1993). No examples of the Gompertz machine or detailed drawings of his hub survive, but clearly it involved an automatic freewheel or a unidirectional clutch, a device that was common on winches and other machinery, such as the winding mechanism of a watch.

Before the era of the cranked velocipede, quadricycles and tricycles generally had fixed drive. When two-wheelers came back into fashion, inventive minds again took up the subject of drive. Tom Burgess included plans for fitting a "ratchet-catch" in his 1869 instructions on how to build a velocipede (Velox 1869). In the United States, William van Anden patented a freewheel with a single sprung ratchet in March of 1869 (US patent 88,238). Two months later, in France, François Nicolet of Tarare patented a freewheel device (French patent 85,439), and soon a man in Tarare named A. Boeuf was advertising freewheel-equipped velocipedes:

> Mountains and plains are covered with the same ease on the velocipede with pedals separate or at rest using the Nicolet system. On descents the leg movement is discontinued without the feet leaving the pedals. . . . By pressing a simple button one renders the pedals fixed again within a second.

In December of 1869, a London patent agent named W. E. Gedge secured a patent (British patent 3,570) on behalf of Boeuf and Nicolet, but we find no record of freewheel velocipedes' having been made or sold in Britain. Velocipedists, it seems, preferred to retain the fixed wheel for better control of their machines; instead of freewheeling, they put their legs on the leg rests during descents.

The first high-wheelers had foot rests cantilevered out from the forks and/or supported from the head. Resting the rider's legs on these added considerable weight in the wrong place and tended to make headers more likely. William Henry James Grout patented retractable toe rests in 1874 (British patent 1,173). These were much lighter and kept the rider's weight farther behind the axle. Toe rests rapidly gained popularity until people began hearing of headers caused by the rider's catching a heel in the spokes while searching for the rest. By 1878, toe rests had been all but abandoned.

The freewheel as an alternative to footrests or toerests for coasting was an attractive concept. Jules-Pierre Suriray and Eugène Meyer, two important French makers, manufactured

Figure 7.1 Gompertz's velocipede of 1821, with a pawl-and-ratchet freewheel in the front hub (*Polytechnisches Journal*, June 1821).

high-wheelers with freewheels (Kobayashi 1990). (Examples exist in the Musée des Arts et Métiers in Paris and in the Musée d'Art et d'Industrie in Saint-Étienne.) The reason freewheels didn't catch on then was that most riders of high-wheelers preferred to use the fixed wheel to control their speed on descents, since the brakes that were available weren't sufficiently reliable.

The brakes of high-wheel tricycles were more effective than those of high-wheel bicycles. The brake of a tricycle was applied with the full force of one arm, or occasionally a heel. With most models there was no risk of a forward upset. J. Monteith's lever-driven tricycle had a freewheel on at least one of its wheels (British patent 2,436 of 1876). In 1879, Frederick Warner Jones fitted freewheels to his Devon tricycle (British patent 3,086 of 1879) (Roberts 1991, 14; Scholes 2011, 38). The Coventry Machinists' Cheylesmore tricycle of 1881 also had a free-wheel. Instead of a ratchet mechanism, this freewheel had steel balls in tapered cavities formed in the crankshaft ends, around which the crank fitted. These cavities were circular at one end. Because the balls rested loose in the cavities, the crankshaft could rotate freely if the rider stopped pedaling. But when the cranks were turned, the balls jammed solid in the narrower tapered part of the cavities, locking the cranks to their shaft (British patent 512 of 1881). The Cheylesmore tricycle also had a separate mechanism to allow the drive to be locked manually for back-pedal braking.

Other two-chain tricycles made similar use of freewheels. If each driven wheel of a pair had its own freewheel, one wheel could rotate faster than the other during cornering. Dual-freewheel drive for tricycles reemerges from time to time; it is a simpler and cheaper way of achieving two-wheel drive than a differential gear. (See chapter 3.)

When safety bicycles of the Rover type began to replace both high-wheeler bicycles and tricycles, nearly all of them retained the fixed wheel. Coasting on a safety bicycle with one's feet on pegs attached to the front forks was exhilarating and relatively safe. Pneumatic-tire safeties of the early 1890s were similarly equipped. There was little demand from cyclists for a more comfortable system until the mid 1890s, when pneumatic-tired safety bicycles became popular. In England and in the United States, during that boom, a large number of fashionable bicyclists, including many women, were more interested in parading and being seen on bicycles, and in comfort and ease of riding, than in competitive cycling. In the US, these forces encouraged inventors to turn their attention to the development of in-hub back-pedal brakes. Of course direct-drive bicycles were braked largely by back-pedaling, and all bicycles at this time were direct-drive machines, but the in-hub braking mechanism provided assistance in slowing and stopping the bicycle. The next step was to add a freewheel action to the in-hub back-pedal brake to create a "coaster brake." That was accomplished by 1897. (See chapter 8.)

One of the first commercially produced gear systems for changing the speed of a bicycle was the four-speed Protean, invented in England by Linley, Biggs, and Archer (British patent

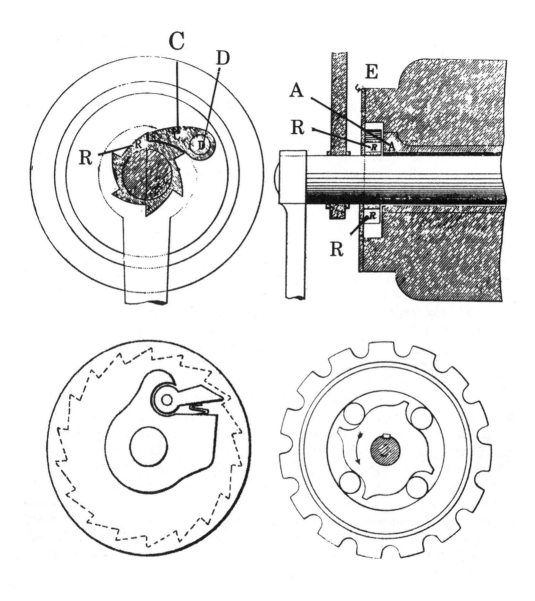

Figure 7.2 Above: Boeuf and Nicolet's pawl-and-ratchet freewheel (patent drawing). Below left: Van Anden's freewheel with spring-loaded pawl acting on a ratchet track (patent drawing). Below right: A Cheylesmore freewheel with balls in tapered cavities (patent drawing).

17,908 of 1894), which was an expanding chainwheel. The fact that the rider changed gears by back-pedaling necessitated the reintroduction of the freewheel. Once riders of machines multiple-speed machines had experienced the pleasure of keeping their legs still when coasting, riders of single-speed machines wanted to experienced it too.

The lack of the fixed wheel's back-pedal braking necessitated the introduction of alternative braking systems. The principal alternative in the UK was the use of rim brakes on both wheels. Coaster brakes became popular in in North America (where they had been invented) and in Germany, whereas rim brakes were preferred in the United Kingdom and in France.

Most major British cycle manufacturers adopted the freewheel around 1900. In 1901, catering to riders who were uncertain about the freewheel, Raleigh introduced a freewheel hub that could be locked. Such uncertainty was short-lived, however, and soon the freewheel was a standard feature.

Many early freewheels, such as those used by Sunbeam in 1900, worked on a principle similar to that of the Cheylesmore mechanism discussed above. However, instead of balls they typically had rollers, which, when drive was applied, were drawn up ramps by friction, thus locking the sprocket to the hub. The rollers were freed when the hub rotated faster than the sprocket. The roller ramp system was silent in use but tended to be erratic in action, especially when worn or badly lubricated. For this reason, the rollers in some of these freewheels had springs to ensure positive take-up of drive. By 1913, the roller ramp freewheel was considered obsolescent in single-speed applications, though it was still used in some hub gears and coaster brakes (Jones 1913).

The Micrometer freewheel, another silent design, was popular in the early 1900s and proved reliable. It used crescent-shaped unsprung pawls. Freewheeling was accomplished by a rocking action of the pawls when they passed "ramps" and "valleys" on the sprocket. Rocking pawls made a brief and unsuccessful comeback in the mid 1950s in the Sturmey-Archer SW three-speed hub. In that application, rocking pawls proved very unreliable. (Tiny, highly loaded components of that sort have to be designed and manufactured with great care.)

Other freewheels used spring-loaded pawls acting on a ratchet. Though noisier than earlier freewheels, these rapidly became the standard, simply because it was easier to make a cheap and reliable freewheel with sprung pawls than with friction rollers. Thus, the principle proposed by the early freewheel inventors of the 1860s turned out to be the best. Nonetheless, friction roller freewheels reemerge occasionally.

Figure 7.3 Changing gear with the Protean expanding chainwheel necessitated freewheeling (catalog page, National Cycle Library).

LOW GEAR, 18 Teeth. Right Foot Back.

HIGH GEAR, 21 Teeth. Right Foot Forward.

Figure 7.4   Raleigh's "Free Wheel at Will" (National Cycle Library). Adjustment of the bolt labeled A selected fixed wheel or freewheel.
Figure 7.5   Left: A roller ramp freewheel with spring-assisted rollers. Center: A Micrometer rocking-pawl freewheel. Right: A Hyde sprung-pawl freewheel, popular in the 1910s. (All from National Cycle Library.)

THE EARLY DEVELOPMENT OF MULTI-SPEED GEARING

The concept of multi-speed gearing goes back a long way. In 1784, James Watt described a multi-speed transmission for steam carriages in which a cog on the steam engine's output shaft meshed with a cog on the axle of the driving wheel. Watt used two or more selectable pairs of cogs of differing diameters "in order to give more power to the engine, when bad roads or steep ascents require it" (British patent 1,432 of 1784).

Lay shafts, belts, and pulleys

Riders of three-wheel velocipedes didn't have to worry about balancing, and could concentrate on the most effective way to transfer their exertions to the road. When they wanted to climb steep hills, they had to dismount and push the heavy machines. For this reason, various ideas for multi-speed tricycle velocipedes arose.

As early as 1819, it was proposed that a tricycle operator standing on treadles connected to cranks in a lay shaft could choose between two speeds. A Liverpool surveyor named B. Smythe, designer of the British Facilitator or Traveling Car, used the standard belt-transmission technique of the time. Each rear wheel had a pair of pulleys, which were connected by a belt. By means a kind of clutch, the crankshaft was connected either to the right wheel's pulley (for higher speed) or to the left wheel's pulley (for lower speed, e.g. on gradients) (Street 1998). Whether Smythe's vehicle was ever built isn't certain. Thirty or more years later, commercial makers of multi-track velocipedes, including Willard Sawyer of Dover, were content with single-speed drive. With the regained dominance of the direct-drive single-speed vélocipède bicycle of the 1860s came a French patent for a two-speed transmission and a manufactured two-speed bicycle. Two manufacturers in Nérondes, France, Alphonse Barberon and Joseph Meunier, began to equip their velocipedes with a two-speed drive system (French patent 86,459 of 1870; British patent 2,626 of 1869). The front hub rotated freely on the pedal shaft, which was either connected directly to the hub by ratchets or connected by a belt to a small lay shaft on top of the front wheel. Merely by back-pedaling, a velocipedist could double his speed without having to pull a lever or press a button. An 1870 addendum to their patent even described a three-speed variable drive system in which either a belt or a chain would be shifted from one set of discs to another by means of a lever. Alas, the Franco-Prussian War and ensuing civil war ended the venture. (Belt transmission made a comeback in early automobiles such as Karl Benz's two-speed motor velocipedes.)

A system for varying crank length "on the fly" was proposed around the same time as Barberon & Meunier's early ideas. The cranks were mounted on a variable-eccentricity mechanism, as shown in figure 7.10. Longer cranks enabled the rider to exert more leverage when climbing a hill but required more leg movement for each rotation of the wheel; shorter cranks worked better with lighter loads (as on a flat) and required less leg movement. Although the idea was claimed to be patented, no patent has been found, and the inventor's name isn't known. However, the Compagnie Parisienne advertised a bicycle with this feature in April of 1870 (Reynaud 2008, volume 1, 125). In some ways the system was comparable to the variable-leverage treadle system used later in Paul Jaray's J-Rad recumbent. (See chapter 16.)

Lay shafts and cogs

Barberon & Meunier had thought about using cogs on the front wheel of a velocipede, as an alternative to a belt, in 1870. They described a compact arrangement of a large internally toothed wheel (fixed to the crank) which engaged with a pinion on a short layshaft. This layshaft carried another pinion which engaged with a pinion on the hub. This looked superficially similar to an epicyclic gear. The same idea appeared later in the Boudard gear.

Even earlier, in 1868, Constant Hazard had patented the idea of having the pedal spindles become lay shafts (French patent 79,748). On the pedal spindles were gearwheels fixed to the cranks, meshing with a smaller cog connected to the hub of the front wheel, thus increasing the speed at which the front wheel turned when pedaled backward. Alternatively, by pressing a button, the rider could lock the cranks to the front wheel to drive it directly when pedaling forward.

A velocipede of unknown origin (now in the Musée du Vélo at Domazan, France) has two gearwheels and two crank sets on each side, pivoting on the fork. This gave a choice of using the pedals on either the upper or the lower set of cranks, depending on the rider's leg length. But the machine had only one speed, and the rider had to pedal backward to move forward.

James Starley and William Hillman's Ariel patent called for a two-speed gear using lay shafts (countershafts) on both sides, requiring eight cogs. There was no need to pedal backward with this design. A ratchet between the axle and the hub was overridden when the cogs were engaged for the high gear. With the lay shafts lifted upward, the cogs disengaged and the ratchet locked the hub to the crankshaft (British patent 2,236 of 1870). Perry's front-driving gear of 1892, a single-sided version, was used simply as a single-speed drive to increase the effective "diameter" of the front wheel (Sharp 1896).

Riders who wanted to race high-wheelers adopted larger-diameter front wheels. Cogs were rarely seen on high-wheelers. A curious epicyclic gear used on the Geared Facile of 1887

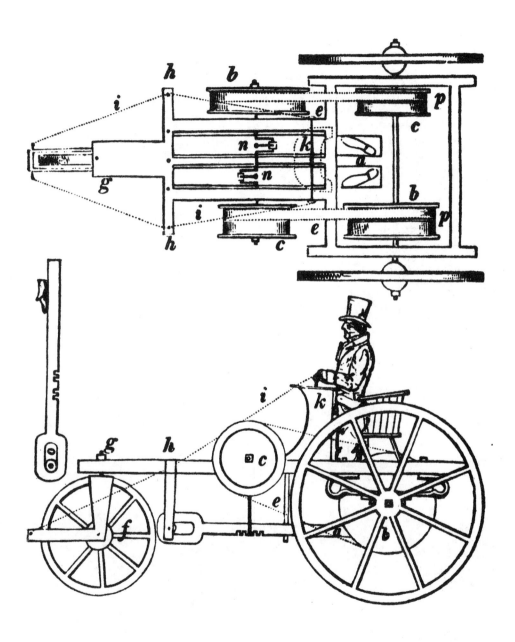

Figure 7.6 Smythe's British Facilitator (*The Imperial Magazine*, May 31, 1819).

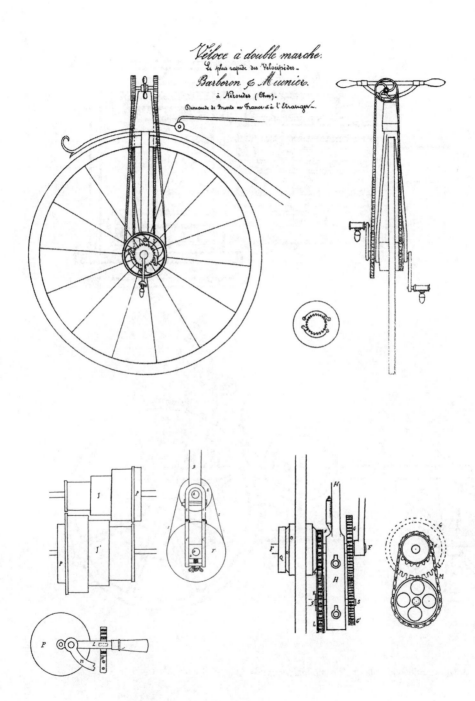

Figure 7.7 Barberon & Meunier's belt gearing on a cranked velocipede (*Le Vélocipède*, 2008).
Figure 7.8 Patent drawings of Barberon & Meunier's three-speed belt transmission (left) and the chain version (right).
Figure 7.9 A two-speed belt system on an 1898 Benz automobile (Baudry 1899).

geared the 40-inch driving wheel up to an equivalent of 60 inches. With the cranks fixed to the planet cogs, the pedals moved in a vertical ellipse, so the rider's feet moved more in an up-and-down fashion than in a circle (Sharp 1896).

Most tricycles had chain drive, but the Excelsior Tricycle of 1882 used three cogs instead of a chain to transmit the pedal power to the left rear wheel. With a total of six gear wheels, the Dual tricycle built by William James in Christchurch in 1882 provided two speeds by driving either the left or the right wheel. Several cog-drive machines were built by the Zephyr Bicycle & Tricycle Company in Coventry and described by the cycling press (Street 1979). An all-cog transmission was even tried on bicycles of the Rover type, but chains provided greater efficiency and were less subject to breakage.

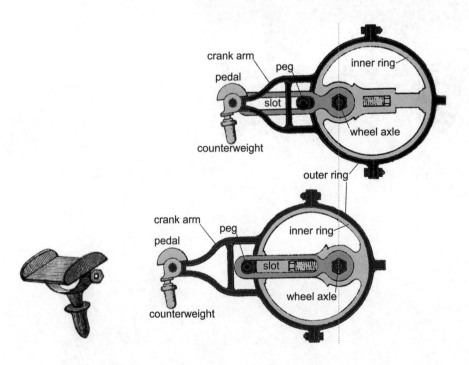

Figure 7.10 Adjustable-length cranks as used on a Compagnie Parisienne velocipede of 1870 (Tony Hadland). The outer ring, integral with the crank arm, could be rotated relative to inner ring, thus varying the length of the crank from 10 cm to as much as 20 cm. Rotation of the outer ring was controlled by a clutch (not shown), which was operated via a cord from below the handlebar. Below left: a perspective view of the single-sided, counterbalanced pedal.

The success of the Rover and similar safety bicycles initiated a rush of patents for multi-speed gears all over the world. At first the lay shaft was put either within a bulky bottom bracket (as in Marcel Boudard's 1896 design, used for some time by Humber & Company) or within a bulky rear hub (as in the Dursley-Pedersen design of 1904 or Peugeot's retro hub of 1907) (Henry 1998; Berto 2009). But by the mid 1890s, patentees were avoiding such bulky arrangements by putting epicyclic gears inside a compact hub. Bicycle manufacturers used standardized bracket hangers so as to be able to switch suppliers easily. The bulky hangers that lay-shaft gears required impeded the exchangeability of crank axles and their bearings. Yet Adler, in Frankfurt, began producing bicycles with a three-speed hanger gearbox (German

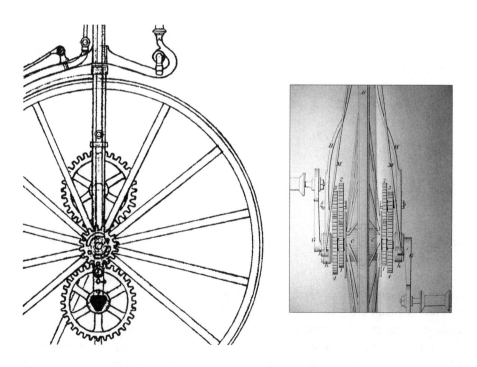

Figure 7.11 Left: Hazard's two-speed gear (Raymond Henry). Right: Starley & Hillman's two-speed gear (patent drawing).

patent 650,386 of 1935) as late as 1935 and was still making them after World War II. French predecessors had been around since the 1900s.

EPICYCLIC GEARING

A simple epicyclic change-speed gear typically involves a fixed "sun" pinion (a pinion being a small cog); several "planet" pinions that roll around the sun, meshing with it; and an annulus, an internally toothed ring that surrounds the whole assembly and meshes with the planets. The planets are held in a cage. If the cage is rotated, the planets pick up motion by engaging with the sun and pass this motion on to the annulus. This makes the annulus rotate faster than the planet cage. If the drive is fed into the planet cage and out of the annulus, a gear ratio higher than direct drive is obtained. Conversely, if the drive is fed into the annulus and out of the planet cage, a gear ratio lower than direct drive results. Hence, a simple epicyclic change-speed gear can provide three speeds. Two-speed epicyclic gears use only two of these three speeds. Epicyclic gears with more than three speeds have more than one epicyclic train.

In high gear, a simple epicyclic train with a 20-tooth sun and a 60-tooth annulus will cause the wheel to rotate at $(20 + 60)/60 = 4/3 \times$ direct drive—an increase of 1/3. The reduction offered by the same configuration is the inverse, 3/4—a reduction of 1/4. The size and number of the planet pinions makes no difference to the ratios; the planet pinions merely act as intermediaries, relaying motion between the annulus and the sun.

During the tricycle boom of the 1880s, a number of American and British epicyclic gears for tricycles came on the market, mostly two-speeds. Beveled cogs, like those on a hand drill, were used in some early epicyclic gears, such as Robert Charles Jay's three-speed (British patent 2,957 of 1883).

In 1883, Emmit and Adrian Latta of Friendship, New York applied for a patent for a three-speed epicyclic hub gear for front-drive bicycles or tricycles (US patent 294,641 of 1884). One version used bevel gears and required the rider to pedal backward in two of the three speeds. A more user-friendly version, also described in the patent, used pinions and an annulus.

In the 1880s, Crypto-Dynamic epicyclic gears, made by the London firm Shaw & Sydenham became market leaders, and for a while "Crypto principle" became the generic term for epicyclic gears. In the 1890s, as front-drive bicycles fought a rear-guard action against rear-drive safeties, Shaw & Sydenham introduced a single-speed epicyclic hub gear that allowed the use of a smaller front wheel. This was a developmental blind alley, because front-drivers soon went off the market.

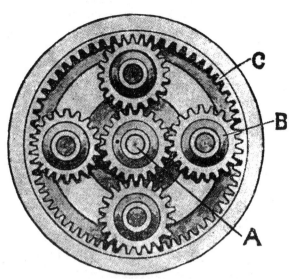

Figure 7.12 This explanation appeared in a booklet published by *Cycling* circa 1909.

THE ESSENTIAL PARTS OF AN
EPICYCLIC GEAR.

A, the sun pinion, which, when prevented
from rotating, forms a fulcrum for the
planet pinions (B) when the member carrying them is driven, thus giving an increased
speed to the internally-toothed ring (C).

Designers occasionally returned to the idea of a front-drive machine with epicyclic gears. The French engineer Louis Debuit used epicyclic gears in a design for a recumbent bicycle that he created in the 1940s (US patent 2,505,464 of 1950). In 1984, an Australian company called Acrow announced a small-wheeled front-drive bicycle that could be converted into a tricycle (US patent 4,389,055 of 1983 for Paul Cockburn). Bearing some resemblance to the early Crypto Bantam (Hadland 1987, 14), it had a two-speed coaster hub, direct crank drive, and back-pedal shifting. About 100 pre-production samples were made, but series production didn't proceed. In 1998, Thomas Kretschmer of Berlin applied for a patent for a direct-drive multi-speed epicyclic hub (German patent 19,824,745). A few years later, Jeremy Garnet of Ottawa designed and built a direct-drive recumbent with a modified Schlumpf SpeedDrive epicyclic chainwheel gear (Garnet 2008). The Kris Holm/Schlumpf two-speed unicycle hub could be used in a similar way.

Epicyclic chainwheel gears, often referred to as "bracket gears" though not actually in the bottom bracket, usually don't require a non-standard frame with an oversize bottom bracket or an external gear casing. They enjoyed some popularity in Britain in the Edwardian era, when Sunbeam and Centaur both made two-speeds and James made two-speeds and three-speeds. Sunbeam offered bicycles with a combination of its own two-speed chainwheel gear and either a Villiers two-speed or a Sunbeam three-speed hub; the former combination pro-vided four speeds and the latter six, all by means of fully enclosed epicyclic mechanisms (*Cycling* 1909).

Compact hub gears

During the cycling boom of the 1890s, epicyclic gearing began to be used in its most success-ful and enduring application: the compact hub gear for a rear-drive safety bicycle.

In 1891, the market leaders in epicyclic gearing, Shaw & Sydenham, introduced a compact two-speed rear hub gear. In June of that year it was reviewed enthusiastically in *Cycling*. Its neatness was contrasted with earlier "complicated and unwieldy" epicyclics. It appears never to have been listed in a catalog, actively marketed, put into series production, or commented

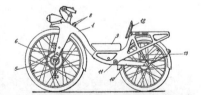

Figure 7.13 Left: The Acrow semi-recumbent, whose front drive allowed easy conversion to tricycle mode (Paul Cockburn). Above right: Louis Debuit's 1943 front-drive recumbent, patented in the US in 1950. Below right: Jeremy Garnet's front-drive recumbent (Jeremy Garnet).

Figure 7.14 A Schlumpf two-speed unicycle hub in a Kris Holm unicycle (Kris Holm Unicycles and Schlumpf Innovations).

Figure 7.15 Left: A Sunbeam two-speed epicyclic chainwheel gear (1904 catalog). Right: A Schlumpf Mountain-Drive, a modern two-speed chainwheel epicyclic gear (Schlumpf Innovations).

on thereafter by journalists, though it deserved to succeed. Its potential lay in the fact that a safety bicycle's chain drive gears up for speed (typically by a factor greater than 2), rather than down for torque. Because the torque is therefore proportionately lower at the hub than at the crank, a gear in the hub can be made smaller and lighter than a gear at the crank (in the bottom bracket or integral with the chainwheel).

By 1895, a machinist in Indiana, Seward Thomas Johnson, had invented a compact two-speed hub (British patent 12,681 of 1895). This apparently was the basis of the J & R hub, which was reviewed by Archibald Sharp in 1896. The J & R (not commercially successful) was soon followed by The Hub, a two-speed model designed by William Reilly of Salford.

Reilly's first patent application for The Hub was filed in March of 1896, and the gear was put into production in 1898. In its original form, it gave fixed-wheel drive in either gear, but, like some other gears, it had a selectable freewheeling mode when no gear was engaged. A later version had automatic freewheeling in high gear and fixed-wheel drive in low gear. By 1901, The Hub's reputation was firmly established and the feasibility of compact hub gears had been demonstrated. Reilly went on to design the first Sturmey-Archer three-speed hub gear, which for contractual reasons was patented in the name of his colleague James Archer. Launched in 1902, it had automatic freewheeling in all gears.

In the UK around the turn of the twentieth century, the new gearing systems that seemed to have a chance of catching on included the New Protean and Gradient derailleurs, the Collier bracket gear, the Paradox expanding chainwheel gear, the Garrard two-speed epicyclic gear (which screwed onto a standard hub), and The Hub. But within seven years compact epicyclics (particularly those made by Sturmey-Archer) completely dominated the British market, and they continued to do so for many decades. The Sturmey-Archer type X wide-ratio hub of 1910, made under license by BSA until 1955, set a standard for epicyclic three-speeds that arguably has never been surpassed.

Hub gears were adopted widely, especially by utility riders in non-mountainous industrialized areas of Britain, Germany, the Netherlands, and Denmark. In some of these countries, especially the Netherlands, hub gears still have a significant market share. In Britain, hub gears were used for many years by some racing cyclists, and even for point-to-point record breaking. From the 1930s until the early 1960s, Sturmey-Archer produced hubs specifically for club cyclists. (The term "club cyclist" covers a wide spectrum of cycling enthusiasts who belong to cycling clubs, ranging from leisurely tourists to record-breaking racers.)

....

Figure 7.16 Above: The Hub (*Cycling*, October 3, 1903). Middle: The first Sturmey-Archer three-speed hub (Sturmey-Archer Heritage). Inset: William Reilly, inventor of these two hubs (National Cycle Library). Below: A Fichtel & Sachs Universal Torpedo four-speed with coaster brake of 1912 (company brochure).

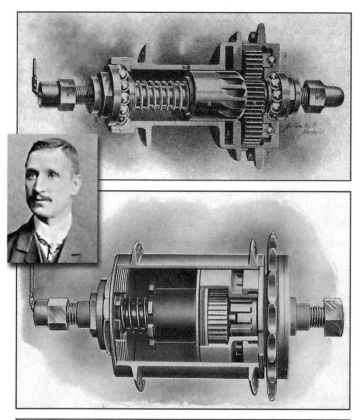

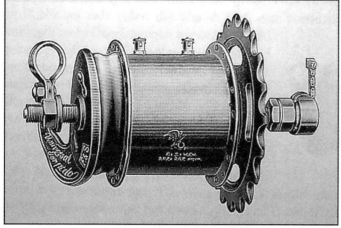

Three-speed hubs were popular, particularly in Britain, because they combined low cost, ease of shifting (even when stationary), high efficiency (better than 90 percent even in the least efficient gear), and low maintenance requirements. There were few calls for more than three speeds, and the British technical press was dismissive of the need for more and wider ratios. In 1912, when Fichtel & Sachs launched a four-speed hub designed by Franz Winkler (German patent 1,045,236 of 1912), the former racer Frederick Thomas Bidlake dismissed it as something that would "best appeal to pass-stormers." And when Henry Sturmey patented and successfully prototyped a wide-ratio five-speed (British patent 188,178, application filed in 1921), nobody would manufacture it. For a long time, many sporting cyclists preferred single-speed machines. (A double-sided rear hub, with a fixed sprocket on one side and a differently sized freewheel on the other, was favored by many.)

Gradually, the number of gears offered in epicyclic hubs increased. Sturmey-Archer introduced four-speed hubs in the late 1930s and a five-speed model (patented in the 1930s) in the 1960s. In the 1990s, three makers launched seven-speed hubs. (Sturmey-Archer had patented a seven-speed hub in 1973.) In 1995, Sachs launched the heavy and short-lived Elan twelve-speed hub. At the time of writing, hub gears can be bought with two, three, five, seven, eight, nine, eleven, and fourteen speeds.

Epicyclic hubs with more than three speeds can be quite inefficient in some gears and are more expensive than derailleurs. The king of hub gears, made in Germany, is the fourteen-speed Rohloff 500/14, launched in 1998. It approaches the efficiency and range of a modern derailleur and provides more evenly spaced ratios, better reliability, and longer service life.

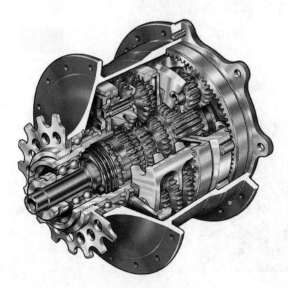

Figure 7.17   A Rohloff Speedhub 500/14 hub gear (Rohloff AG).

DERAILLEURS

In many countries today, the dominant form of multi-speed gearing is the derailleur. Different ratios are selected by shifting the drive chain across up to twelve sprockets on the rear wheel and up to three chainwheels on the crankshaft. Quadruple chainwheels have been offered, for example by Alex Singer in France in 1973 (Rebour 1976) and more recently by Chris Bell of Highpath Engineering in Wales, but have never been popular.

In 1868, Charles Dubos patented a tandem tricycle whose chain could be manually shifted from one chainwheel to another to give two or more speeds; it lacked a chain tensioner to take up the slack. In 1869, Barberon and Meunier designed a three-speed system in which a belt or a chain could be shifted between two sets of pulleys or sprockets. These designs were early ancestors of today's derailleurs.

By the mid 1890s, amid a plethora of multi-speed patents, some designs for true derailleurs had appeared. In 1895, Jean Loubeyre, a French national, patented a two-speed system that he called the Polyceler. Though it was advertised the following year, the Polyceler wasn't commercially successful. Two early British derailleurs did achieve some success, however: Edmund Hodgkinson's three-speed Gradient, first displayed in 1899, and Linley & Biggs's New Protean gear, a two-speed system that was patented the same year.

The Gradient incorporated a sprung chain tensioner arm under the bottom bracket. The gear was changed by back-pedaling, which caused two arms to lift the chain clear of the sprockets. Moving a lever slid the sprockets sideways; pedaling forward then dropped the chain onto a different sprocket. The chain always ran in line. By 1901, the chain was lifted automatically. The Gradient didn't catch on in the UK, where three-speed epicyclic hubs were in fashion, and in 1904 Hodgkinson sold the patent to the Terrot company of Dijon.

The New Protean used a chain with arched links, reminiscent of a toothed belt, which eased sideways shifting of the chain from one sprocket to the other. The sprockets and the chainwheel were flanged to keep the chain from falling off. The New Protean's chainwheel was twice as wide as a conventional one, to allow the chain to run in line when either sprocket was selected. The New Protean gear was used on Linley & Biggs's Whippet bicycles and subsequently became known as the Whippet gear; in its home market it followed the Gradient into oblivion, but, like the Gradient, it was taken up in France. By 1905, Terrot was making a version of the Gradient, the Terrot Model H (the H standing for Hodgkinson), and Paul de Vivie (a.k.a. Vélocio) was experimenting with a Whippet gear.

The evolution of the derailleur from the early commercial offerings described above to the smooth-running and highly efficient devices available today is far too complex to cover here in

Figure 7.18 Dubos's patent drawing, clearly showing a double chainwheel on the crankshaft.

detail. (For a more detailed discussion, see Berto 2009.) In the next hundred years, numerous small refinements were made, and every decade or two an additional sprocket was squeezed in.

The main factor in the derailleur's early evolution was the increasing awareness, especially among French engineers, that a drive chain could be made to run acceptably efficiently even when out of line. Even Dubos, in his 1868 patent, seems to have appreciated this. It was a crucial insight.

However, out-of-line running was anathema to British engineers and was avoided in both the Gradient and the Whippet gear. Indeed, the British generally treated derailleurs with disdain until Sir Hubert Opperman's sporting successes in the mid 1930s started to swing opinion. Raleigh, which owned Sturmey-Archer and thus had a big vested interest in hub gears, didn't offer a derailleur on any of its bicycles until the mid 1950s.

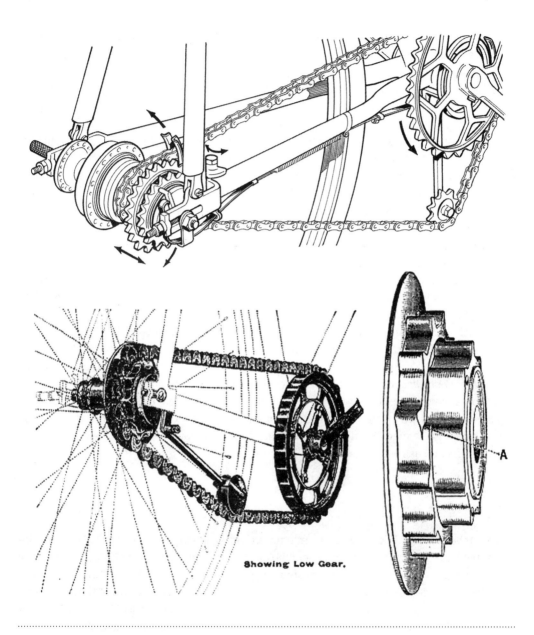

Showing Low Gear.

Figure 7.19 Above: Hodgkinson's Gradient three-speed derailleur (R. John Way). Below: The New Protean two-speed derailleur, later known as the Whippet gear. (All from National Cycle Library.)

Improvements in chain design have allowed out-of-line chains to run with increasing numbers of sprockets. Narrower chains are more flexible than wide ones and can therefore accommodate more sprockets. The 1900s saw the ¼-inch chain give way to the ³⁄₁₆-inch chain, which could be used with two sprockets. In the 1920s, the ⅛-inch chain became standard; such a chain could be used with as many as four sprockets. In 1936, the British firm Brampton introduced the ³⁄₃₂-inch chain, which permitted five and eventually even more sprockets. Later, the introduction of the bushingless chain was another big step in progress toward efficient derailleurs. (The bushingless Sedisport became widely available in 1981.) Omitting bushings between a chain's pins and their rollers makes the chain more flexible, and today all derailleur chains are bushingless. Today, nominal chain widths like the ones mentioned above (based on the matching sprocket widths) are not used with eight-to-twelve-speed derailleurs; other dimensions (including outer plate width and pin width) are considered more important.

Also important in the early development of the derailleur was the proximity of major French centers of engineering, such as Saint-Étienne, to mountainous terrain. A cursory comparison of the topography of the Massif Central and the rolling landscape of the English Midlands suggests why French cycle engineers were more interested in having a wider spread of gears than their English counterparts.

French involvement in developing chain-shifting gears is reflected in the English adoption, in the 1920s, of the French word "dérailleur," eliminating its accent and Anglicizing the pronunciation. The word is now so well established in the Anglophone world that the *Oxford Hachette French Dictionary* gives "derailleur" as the English translation of "dérailleur." Recent American attempts to further Anglicize the word to "derailer" have met with little success. In any case, no rails are involved. A more logical English name would be "chain-shifter," which would echo the German "Kettenschaltung." But after about 90 years, "derailleur" is too well established to be easily displaced.

Indexed shifting

Indexing the shifting of derailleurs was attempted a long time ago. It was relatively easy to index a three-speed derailleur, as high gear (cable tight) and low gear (cable slack) are effectively self-indexing; only the middle gear requires a detent mechanism. The 1949 British Hercules Herailleur, a three-speed derailleur, had indexed shifting, as did a three-speed Huret unit sold in the early 1980s. But indexing gears with more than three sprockets proved difficult. The lack of positive shifting was a major deterrent to the widespread adoption of derailleurs in some markets, especially those hitherto dominated by hub gears.

In 1969 SunTour offered a five-speed indexed gear, and from 1980 on that company marketed Mighty Click indexing. In 1975, Shimano introduced the Positron indexed system, the first to achieve significant market share but still not a great success. Shimano's 1981 indexed Aero AX derailleurs weren't very successful either. Sachs-Huret launched its indexed Commander in 1983, but it was Shimano's SIS (Shimano Indexed Shifting) system, launched in 1984, that set a new standard and really started the popularization of indexed shifting. The development of the SIS system was facilitated by new technology and by the bringing together of several earlier technical refinements after considerable investment in research and development. The SIS system had a computer-optimized rear mechanism with two sprung pivots and a recently out-of-patent SunTour innovation, the slant parallelogram. SunTour applied for a patent for the slant parallelogram in 1964 (US patent 3,364,762 of 1968). One of the most important innovations in the history of the derailleur, it permits the jockey pulley to position the chain very close to the sprocket cluster regardless of which gear is selected. This is critical for reliable indexed shifting.

In 1989, Shimano improved SIS shifting further with the introduction of HyperGlide sprockets, which have specially modified teeth to form optimized shifting paths for the chain when moving from one sprocket to another. Shimano's innovations in indexed derailleur shifting were supported by comprehensive installation documentation, a zero-defects approach to quality assurance, timely delivery, and skillful marketing.

Shimano's innovations, first introduced on the company's upscale products, eventually trickled down to the whole product range and were widely copied. Today, even the cheapest derailleur, regardless of the manufacturer, has reliable indexed shifting, if properly installed and adjusted.

In 1978, six years before the introduction of SIS, Shimano launched the Freehub, combining the freewheel with the rear hub. It was an old idea, introduced by the British firm Bayliss Wiley in 1937, that Shimano perfected. The Freehub was emulated by rival manufacturers and rapidly gained in popularity on better bikes. Whereas screw-on freewheels were once the norm, they are now found only on the cheapest derailleur-geared bikes.

AUTOMATIC AND CONTINUOUSLY VARIABLE GEARS

For more than a century, inventors have tried to devise automatic or continuously variable gears for bicycles. An early example of a transmission that was both automatic and

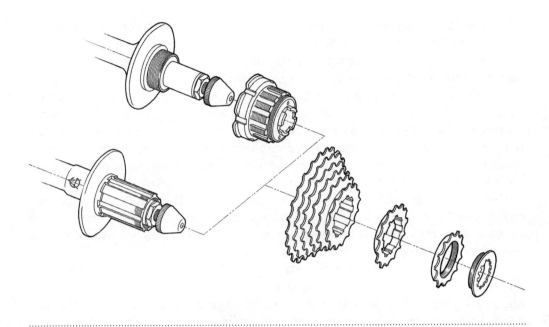

Figure 7.20 A traditional screw-on freewheel (top) and a Freehub-style hub (below) with integrated freewheel (Geoff Apps).

continuously variable was the Dieterich gearless "variable-power transmitter," designed by the Austrian Ludwig Dieterich, who resided in Hartford, Connecticut (US patent 634,327 of 1899). It was a variable-eccentricity lever-drive mechanism. The version for bicycles was housed in an oversize bottom bracket. It wasn't commercially successful.

Most of the continuously variable gears that have made it to series production have been hub gears or expanding chainwheels.

Continuously variable hub gears

Any system that required a non-standard frame, as Dieterich's did, was at a disadvantage. A gear in the hub was a better bet commercially, as it could be adapted to almost any bicycle. Archibald Sharp, the London-based engineer and patent agent who authored the classic book *Bicycles & Tricycles*, invented a manually controlled continuously variable hub gear and applied for a patent for it in 1900 (British patent 22,574). Like Dieterich's "variable-power transmitter," Sharp's system wasn't epicyclic. It was "an apparatus for varying the speed ratio of two shafts continuously between certain limits." An input crank and an output crank, connected by a link, revolved around separate centers. The input crank moved in a normal circular fashion, but, because of the link, the output crank moved elliptically. By means of a series of rapidly switching clutches, a nearly constant output could be taken from any particular point on the ellipse, to give circular output motion. Output speed depended on where on the ellipse output was taken. Raleigh intended to manufacture the device, but Sharp never got it to work properly (Hadland 2011). In the mid 1930s, a similar principle was used in the Milpat gear, manufactured in France. However, the Milpat's mechanism was within the chainwheel, not the hub. It gave a range of 191 percent in twelve steps (Whitt 1979).

G. F. Taylor of Birmingham devised another continuously variable hub gear. Promoted as the All-Speed, it had a sun-and-planet mechanism with the planet pinions mounted in such a way that an adjustable cam plate could give them additional rotary motion, simulating an increasingly large sun pinion. The cam plate was controlled by a handlebar twist grip and gave a continuously variable range from direct drive to an increase of 50 percent. Although this device was widely reported and was expected to appear on the market in 1907, only two examples have been found. It doesn't appear to have gone into series production (Hadland 1987; *Cycling* 1909). In the 1970s, a somewhat similar system called the Arcu was produced in the United States. Another American system of this type was the Paradigm hub gear, announced in the autumn of 1991, designed by Bill Terry and marketed by CV Posi-Drive of Redmond, Washington.

A different approach to infinitely variable epicyclic gears was taken by George Ripley III in his design for an epicyclic gear mounted outboard of the rear wheel (US patent 467,653 of 1974). In this system, the chain drove the planet cage, the sun drove the bicycle wheel, and the annulus was allowed to rotate to a varying extent by a mechanical or a hydraulic brake. With the annulus completely unbraked (rotating freely), a 1:1 transmission ratio was achieved; with the annulus fully braked (stationary), the ratio was about 4:1. Thus a stepless range of about 400 percent was offered, controlled solely by the amount of slippage allowed to the annulus. This system doesn't appear to have been marketed.

In 2006, Fallbrook Technologies Inc. introduced the NuVinci continuously variable bicycle hub gear, a ball-and-cone traction drive that transmitted rotating power from an input cone to an output cone by means of a set of balls. The balls engaged with the cones by means of friction. Tilting the balls changed their contact diameter, increasing it relative to one cone and decreasing it relative to the other and thereby varying the speed ratio. The typical range was 360 percent. The NuVinci, which was relatively heavy and was less efficient than a derailleur system, was the first continuously variable step less gear to achieve some commercial success.

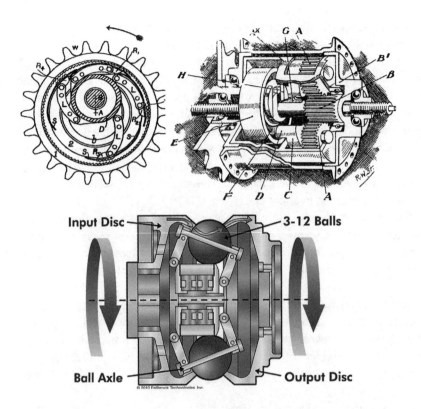

Figure 7.21   Above left: Section through Sharp's continuously variable hub gear (patent drawing). Above right: Cutaway drawing of the All-Speed continuously variable hub (*Cycling*, 1909). Below: The NuVinci ball-and-cone traction drive (illustration used under license from Fallbrook Technologies Inc.).

Expanding chainwheels have been used in a variety of variable gear systems. Although we have classed these as continuously variable gears, these systems often used detents to provide specific gear ratios. This was partly for the rider's convenience but also because, in some designs, each change in diameter had to equate to a whole number of chainwheel teeth. In 1894, the Linley & Biggs Protean gear incorporated two half-chainwheels that could be spread to increase the effective diameter, giving four closely spaced gears. The chainwheel being oval in all but the lowest gear. (Many years later, Frank Whitt, co-author of *Bicycling Science*, made himself a similar gear.) The Protean soon went out of production, superseded by the New Protean derailleur, later known as the Whippet gear.

In 1903, a more sophisticated expanding chainwheel was launched. William Dyson Wansbrough's Paradox incorporated a complex mechanism to achieve a circular expandable chainwheel. Like the Protean, it worked in one-tooth steps, but it had seven detents rather than four. Not commercially successful, it was discontinued after one season.

The Mitchell Any-Speed combined elements of variable eccentricity and the expanding chainwheel. To achieve the effect of increased diameter, the chainwheel could be raised off center by a system of arms and clutches. Contemporaneous with the Paradox, it was no more successful.

The Bilis, a French expanding chainwheel introduced in 1925 and used by the winner of the Ploy de Chanteloup, soon faded from memory (Berto 2009, 128). In 1936, the Nealeson, another British expanding chainwheel gear, was favorably reviewed in *Cycling*. It had a 200 percent range in several steps and was available from F. W. Evans, a famous builder of lightweight bicycles in London. It doesn't appear to have been put into series production (Whitt 1979).

A resurgence of interest in expanding chainwheel gears began in the 1970s. The 1974 Hagan All-Speed system, produced in the United States, had six small freewheel sprockets mounted in slots in a drive plate. A control disc, coaxial with the drive plate, had spiral slots that engaged with the sprockets. Rotation of the control disc moved the sprockets up and down their slots in the drive plate, thus varying the effective chainwheel diameter by 285 percent.

Arguably the most interesting expanding chainwheel gear was the automatic Deal Drive, invented by a Frenchman named Michel Deal (British patent 2,062,142 of 1981). It had six spring-loaded sliding segments and a range of about 200 percent. As pedal force increased, the springs in the segments compressed and the segments moved inward, reducing the effective diameter of the chainwheel and thus lowering the gear. Sixteen distinct gears were provided and the spring loading could be adjusted to suit the rider. By 1983 it was being promoted to the cycle trade, and soon several UK manufacturers exhibited bikes equipped with it. However, production costs in the UK were too high. Attempts to make the gear in countries where the costs were lower came to nothing. This, coupled with the limited range of the gear (less than that of a five-speed hub) and its weight, sealed its fate.

The Excel Cambiogear, contemporaneous with the Deal Drive but less sophisticated, also gave sixteen speeds, but with a 300 percent range. It wasn't successful either.

A simple, efficient, lightweight manually controlled expanding rear sprocket called the HettlageDrive Variator was developed by the German engineer Eckart Hettlage between 1996 and 2002. Versions were made for chain drive and for belt drive. Although it did not sell in large numbers, it was still in production in the 2010s.

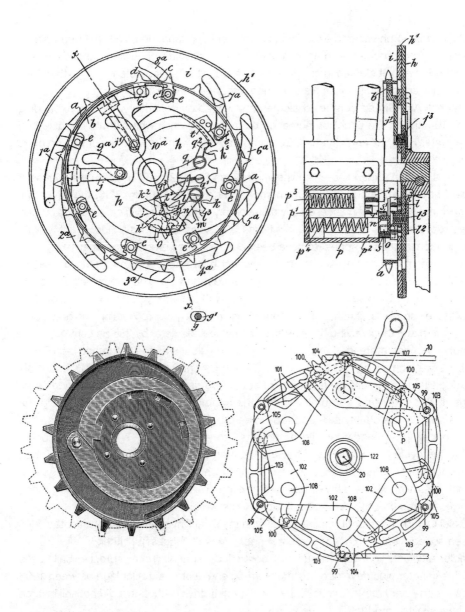

Figure 7.22 Above: A Paradox expanding chainwheel (patent drawing). Below left: A Protean expanding chainwheel, shown here in low gear with the high-gear mode shown by broken lines (National Cycle Library). Below right: A Deal Drive automatic expanding chainwheel (patent drawing).

Figure 7.23   A HettlageDrive Variator (Eckart Hettlage).

Automatic shifting

Automatic transmission for bicycles can be traced back at least as far as 1899, when the Dieterich system was patented. According to the complex patent application, in which a total of 39 claims were made, it was "a mechanism whose resistance may vary owing to variations in the load upon it, the speed of the driven mechanism being reduced upon an increase of its resistance or load and increased upon a reduction of such resistance or load at will or automatically." The automatic function involved two mechanical "transmitting devices," one between the drive input and the variable-eccentricity lever-drive mechanism and the other between the drive mechanism and the drive output. Each device produced a "rectilineal resultant force." If these two forces went out of equilibrium, the axis of the variable-eccentricity drive system was shifted until equilibrium was restored, changing the gear.

Dieterich wasn't the only early inventor of a self-shifting bicycle gear. Another was Charles Thompson of New Jersey, who patented a two-speed "automatic hub" in 1903 (US patent 734,008). The fact that it shifted whenever the rider freewheeled probably contributed to its commercial failure. Rather than a true automatic, Thompson's gear was really a predecessor of two-speed hubs that were shifted by back-pedaling; hubs of that sort have made at various times since the 1960s by Fichtel & Sachs (now SRAM), Bendix, and Sturmey-Archer. But unlike these later hubs, Thompson's didn't allow a rider to freewheel without shifting.

For automatic shifting, a device is needed that responds to increased torque in the drive system (as in Dieterich's system) or to increased road speed. Centrifugal shifting mechanisms have been used in both hub gears and derailleurs to give automatic shifting. They are essentially similar to a centrifugal speed governor on a steam engine or on the motor of a clockwork gramophone, but instead of applying a brake they shift gears. At the heart of such a mechanism are spring-loaded weights that are moved outward from the center of rotation by centrifugal force as the wheel's speed increases, thus actuating gear shifting at one or more predetermined speeds.

Probably the neatest and most successful application of centrifugal shifting was the Fichtel & Sachs Automatic two-speed hub, introduced in 1966 and produced until about 1980. The first patent application relating to this hub was filed in Germany in 1961 by the company's principle gear designer, Hans-Joachim Schwerdhöfer (German patent 1,169,798 of 1964; US patent 3,143,005 of 1964). The gear had an integral centrifugal mechanism that shifted from low gear to high at about 9 miles per hour. (Separate versions were made for bicycles with standard-size wheels and for small-wheeled bicycles.) A hold-off mechanism prevented downshifting until pressure on the pedals was eased, thus preventing "hunting" between gears. In the early 1970s, Shimano produced a similar hub, also called the Automatic. Invented in 1967 by Keizo Shimano and Takashi Segawa (US patent 3,494,227), and made in only one version, it had an adjuster disc inboard of the sprocket that allowed the rider to choose any shifting speed between the hub's high and low settings to suit different wheel sizes and the taste of the rider.

In 1962, William Nelson of Florida applied for a patent for another automatic two-speed compact hub gear with centrifugal shifting (US patent 3,388,617 of 1968).

Both Shimano and Fichtel & Sachs had other patents for centrifugally controlled hub gears in addition to those mentioned above. In 2011, SRAM (successor to Fichtel & Sachs) announced a new two-speed automatic hub called the Automatix.

Centrifugal technology was also used in the Autobike Smartshift 2000 (later sold as the LandRider AutoShift), a self-shifting derailleur rear mechanism that was still advertised as available on LandRider bikes in 2013.

Figure 7.24 A Fichtel & Sachs Automatic two-speed hub of 1966. In this cutaway, the pointed end of one of the centrifugal weights is visible halfway along the hub (SRAM Deutschland GmbH).

Electronic shifting

In the late 1990s, Shimano introduced a microprocessor-controlled system for its four-speed hub gear. Sold as the Nexus Auto D, it sensed wheel speed by means of a magnet fixed to a spoke (as with an electronic odometer) and shifted accordingly. The rider could use a controller to select from three shifting modes: normal, sport, and manual. The Nexus Auto D was used successfully on electrically assisted bicycles in Japan. For the 2001 season, Shimano launched a simpler three-speed version, with no manual control option, in the Japanese market.

In 1994 and 1995, Mavic produced a microprocessor-controlled electric rear derailleur called the ZAP; it was used by some professional riders. Push buttons activated a battery-powered solenoid that caused a jockey pulley to shift to predetermined positions, using the pulley's own rotation to provide the shifting force. The system (which wasn't automatic) proved temperamental in wet weather and was soon discontinued. In 1999, Mavic introduced another electronic derailleur, the Mektronic; it was wirelessly controlled and incorporated a cyclometer. It was discontinued in 2002.

In 1997, the twelve-speed Browning Red Shift derailleur was marketed with the option of fully automatic electronic control. The first of Browning's unconventional derailleurs had "swinging-gate" multiple chainwheels, each chainwheel having a hinged segment to smoothly move the chain to the adjacent chainwheel. (The "swinging-gate" principle can be found in John Wilson's British patent 3,843 of 1892.) Invented in 1974 by Bruce Browning (a grandson of John Browning, famed designer of machine guns), the Browning derailleur went on sale in 1982. Eight years later it became the SunTour BEAST (Browning Electronic Accushift Transmission). In 1997, SunTour's business having failed (see Berto 2009), the system was relaunched with a three-speed swinging-gate chainwheel and four-speed swinging-gate freewheel, thus offering twelve speeds. The Red Shift offered manual or electronic fully automatic control. It worked well but was far too expensive to be commercially successful.

A specially built automatic three-speed Browning transmission was tested on USA Cycling track bikes in 1995. Designed to be used in the 1996 Olympic 1,000-meter time trial, it automatically shifted at crank speeds exceeding 100 rpm. The first lap time was about a second faster with the Browning transmission than with a fixed gear. This would be enough for a racer to go from fifth to first place in the 1,000-meter sprint. The Union Cycliste Internationale ruled the Browning transmission illegal (*Cycling Science*, winter 1995, 11).

Fallbrook's Harmony electronic control system, introduced in 2012, was an option for use with the continuously variable NuVinci hub. It gave the rider the option to shift automatically or manually, either seamlessly or in preset steps. In 2009, Shimano introduced manually controlled derailleurs with programmed electronic shifting (the Dura-Ace Di2, joined in 2012 by the cheaper Ultegra Di2). In 2011, Campagnolo did likewise (the Super Record EPS and Record EPS). In 2012, the Italian maker Tiso launched a twelve-sprocket wirelessly controlled derailleur.

BRAKING

8

....

We saw in chapter 7 how the automatic freewheel necessitated better brakes to compensate for the loss of back-pedal braking provided by fixed-wheel transmission. In this chapter we consider the evolution of the various types of brakes.

TAKING THE HEAT OUT OF SPEED

All commonly used bicycle braking systems work by converting the forward kinetic energy into heat, then dissipating it to the atmosphere. The heat is generated by friction between the brake surfaces—for example, brake blocks acting on a wheel rim, or brake shoes acting on a drum in a wheel hub.

Air braking, by increasing the frontal area of the bicycle and rider to increase air resistance, is only used inasmuch as riders may occasionally sit more upright to slow themselves down a little. Air brakes, in the form of flaps or parachutes, are not used. There have, however, been patents for bicycle drag chutes, principally as novelties (e.g., US patent 3,993,323 of 1976).

TIRE BRAKES

Shoe, spoon, and roller brakes

The first bicycle, Drais's running machine, had a pivoting brake shoe that acted on the steel tire of the rear wheel. The rider applied the brake by pulling a cord under the armrest. (Drais wisely avoided using a braking method that was common at the time on horse-drawn vehicles: swinging a "skid shoe" under a wheel to stop it rotating. Subsequent inventors proposed this method for stopping a bicycle as late as the 1890s; two examples are Charles Challand's Swiss patent 11,429 of 1895 and Preston Helmon's US patent 583,371 of 1897.)

A typical front-drive velocipede of the late 1860s had a rear brake quite similar to Drais's, acting on the running surface of the solid steel or rubber tire. The brake shoe was typically of metal, sometimes with a wearing surface of leather or rubber. As on Drais's machine, a cord linkage was used, but usually it was actuated by twisting the straight handlebar. To double the pressure of the brake shoe, a kind of brake servo was devised by Michaux & Cie. (French patent 80,637 of 1868): the brake cord went through a block and tackle. The brake had a return spring to hold it clear of the tire when not in use. (Return springs are used in almost all bicycle brakes, to limit losses caused by light rubbing of braking surfaces when the brake isn't applied. The reader may assume that there are return springs in all the brakes described in this chapter.)

The early velocipede brake was an auxiliary device, most of the braking being done by back-pedaling of the direct-drive front wheel. It was the rider who got hot, not a mechanical brake.

An early brake shoe was typically curved in one plane only, to match the curvature of the flat metal tire. With the development of solid rubber tires with rounded cross-sections, the spoon brake evolved. The concave spoon-like shape fitted the rounded tire section better, making fuller contact with the tire.

The draisine and the velocipede of 1869 both used a robust shoe, operating on the face of the large rear wheel. Turning the handlebar of the latter, and thus tightening a connecting cord, applied a considerable braking force without danger of upset. The coming of the high-wheeler overturned this equilibrium in two ways. First, the large front wheel demanded that the rider, in

Figure 8.1 An isometric drawing of Drais's 1817 plate, showing the brake (arrowed) and its cord (Lessing 2003a).

order to reach the pedals, sit farther forward, nearly over the front axle. Second, the now nearly redundant rear wheel, carrying little weight, was made smaller, shortening the wheelbase and lightening the machine. This greatly diminished the rear wheel's braking potential. Rear wheels, which averaged 34 inches in diameter in 1869, were down to 24 or 26 inches in 1871, and by 1876 the fashionable size was 18 or 20 inches. The little wheel skipped along behind, less effective as a restraint. In consequence, brakes became an urgent topic of discussion.

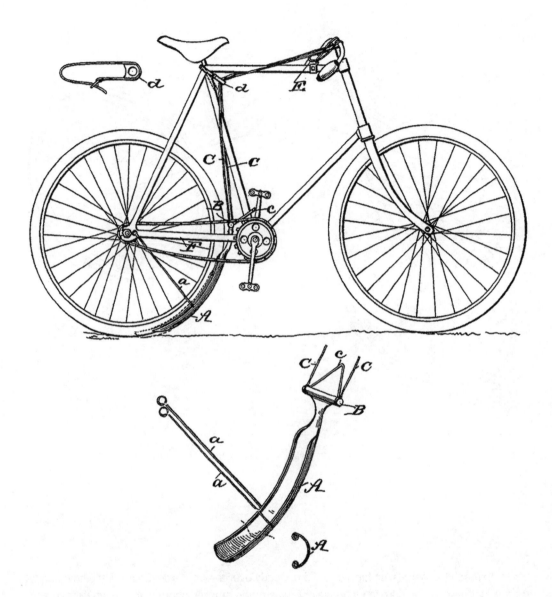

Figure 8.2 Helmon's skid shoe brake, shown here in a patent drawing, was like dropping a fender under the back wheel.

Figure 8.3 A machine with a block and tackle below the saddle, which increased the amount of force that could be applied to the brake (*Le Centaure*, September 1868).

Barberon & Meunier devised a novel alternative actuating mechanism for a rear brake (addendum to French patent 86,459 of 1870). The brake shoe was mounted on a spring-loaded plunger within the spine tube of the bicycle's frame. The shoe was held away from the tire by a cord running through the frame, over a pulley, and up to the handlebar. The cord was attached to, and wrapped around, the handlebar, and was held in tension by a leaf spring acting on a flattened portion of the handlebar. To apply the brake, the rider twisted the handlebar grips to release tension on the cord and allow the spring to push the shoe onto the tire. To release the brake, one reversed the process. This system wasn't widely adopted (Besse and Henry 2008, 153).

One bonus of the new forward riding position was that back-pedaling became more effective. A rider could safely apply weight behind the front axle with little risk of a header. For this reason, many cyclists preferred to use machines without brakes, and to rely entirely on back-pedaling. This worked as long as the bicycle was kept firmly under control, but it provided no way of slowing while coasting with the legs over the handlebar, or when the inclination of a steep hill overcame the desperately back-pedaling rider. The result of a mishap was often unpleasant. A correspondent to *The Field* wrote the following in the summer of 1872:

> I have a new 41-inch Ariel, with roller brake, which I find of very little use; in descending a steep hill, in fact, I do all the work of restraining the machine with my legs, so that really it is just as fatiguing going down a bad hill as going up. I am quite satisfied that with the large driving wheel no power supplied to the back wheel will be sufficient. We need a brake to both wheels, so that going at full speed down hill the machine can be readily stopped, at all events in fifty yards. Let anyone imagine himself going at nearly twenty-five miles an hour downhill with his legs on rest; he turns a bend in the road, and sees a couple of wagons, or anything else—sheep for instance, blocking the way, what can he do to prevent a bad accident? With the present style of brake he is powerless, and must either take a header into the hedge, or charge the obstruction. The old style of bicycling certainly had the merit of a thoroughly effective brake, so that now, when going where I know there are bad hills, I always use my old machine in preference to my Ariel. (*The Field*, July 6)

Much ingenuity was expended on overcoming this weakness. For a while, rear-wheel roller brakes of various designs, controlled by means of a wire or a cord connected to the rotating handlebar, were used. Carter's Trailing Brake was the first to have a hardened lever, pivoted on the rear forks near the axle, that could be dragged down against the roadway (British patent 2,893 of 1875). Carter's brake had the same disadvantage as the rear roller: if the operating cord snapped, the rider was on his own:

> The trailer has undoubtedly a power superior to the roller, it as certainly requires such strength in the cord by means of which it is worked that until something more reliable than silk or steel wire is found, the strong point of the trailer becomes its weakness. When it is remembered that with cords, wires, and chains which are liable to give way, and do in point of fact frequently crack at critical moments, the trailer is not only no better but actually rather worse than a roller. (*Bicycling News*, October 27, 1876)

All kinds of ground brakes—even those that were fail-safe, such as Simpson's Safety Slipper brake (British patent 3,779 of 1877) and Fournier's (British patent 2,720 of 1876)—were limited in effectiveness because road surfaces varied. Furthermore, the clattering against the roadway was annoying.

Somewhat surprisingly, it was the front-wheel brake that gradually took over. The Nonpareil, introduced in 1875 by London manufacturer Stassen, was the first machine to have both a front-wheel brake and a standard rear-wheel roller. A "handsome bronze eccentric" on the revolving handlebar pushed a roller down onto the front wheel. Other makers followed suit. In late 1876, the Surrey Machinists' Company introduced a double-lever spoon brake, with the spoon hinged in front of the head and pressing down on the front tire. The design wasn't patented. With variations (e.g., the brake lever being pushed with the thumbs or pulled with the fingers), it became the predominant style of brake for the remaining years of the high-wheeler. When the brake lever was gripped in panic, a header could easily result; however, a rider sitting well back on the saddle might, if circumspect and lucky, hope to restrain his machine on most of the hills he was likely to encounter.

Spoon or roller brakes were also used on the front wheels of the better early pneumatic-tired safety bicycles. (Racers relied solely on the fixed rear-wheel drive for braking.)

Roller brakes first appeared on Michaux-style velocipedes such as the rubber-tired Rousseau machine now in the Velorama Museum at Nijmegen. The Timberlake roller brake appeared circa 1880. An advantage of the roller brake was that it was less damaging to the surface of the tire, at least in theory.

After the introduction of expensive and relatively fragile pneumatic tires, the roller brake was developed further. Edward Rockwell of Connecticut patented an improved roller brake, with tapered rubber-tired rollers (US patent 524,839 of 1894). Other American examples include Francis John Cole's 1894 design, with a single roller tapered at both ends (US patent 540,637 of 1895); William Stewart's roller brake of 1896, which had extended roller axles so that the rider could apply his feet to them for extra force (US patent 576,912 of 1897); and Abram Duck's 1897 design, which used two angled rubber rollers (US patent 594,234 of 1897).

Pneumatic brakes

In the 1890s, rod linkage was the norm for brakes. However, pneumatic technology was also tried.

In an 1893 design by the British engineer John George Kitchen, the rider compressed air by squeezing a rubber ball on the handlebar; the air traveled through a thin rubber hose to a

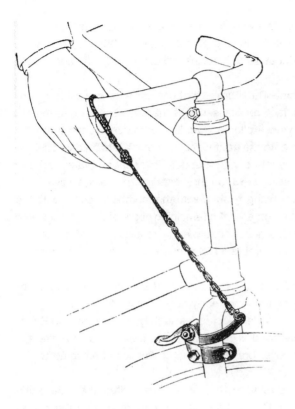

Figure 8.4 A simple, lightweight spoon
brake of circa 1900, actuated by pulling a
chain (Noguchi-san 1998).

Figure 8.5 Left: In the Duck roller brake,
shown here in a patent drawing, two rollers
(*H*) pressed down on the tire (*L*). Right: The
Timberlake roller brake of 1880 (National
Cycle Library).

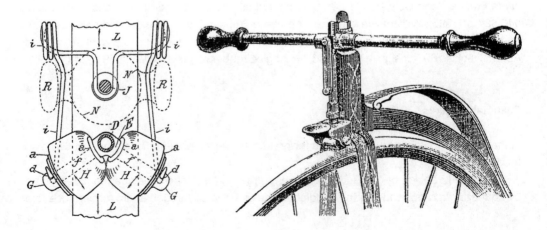

small inflatable brake block that, when inflated, acted on the top of the tire (Sharp 1896, 528; British patent 16,581 of 1893).

Four years later, John Bowman of Pennsylvania applied for a patent for a more sophisticated pneumatic brake (US patent 610,796 of 1898). Like Kitchen's brake, Bowman's had a bulb on the handlebar that was squeezed to compress air. But instead of an inflatable brake pad, the compressed air moved a piston, which pushed a brake shoe onto the rear tire.

One perceived advantage of pneumatic brakes was the convenience of routing thin, flexible rubber hoses from the handlebar to the brake. When Archibald Sharp wrote his famous treatise on bicycles and tricycles, pneumatic brakes seemed to have an assured future (Sharp 1896, 528). But more reliable solutions to the linkage problem were on their way. Pneumatic brakes proved to be a passing fad. They made a reappearance in the 1950s but didn't catch on.

Later plunger brakes

With the coming of pneumatic tires, spoons and rollers initially gave way to simple rubber brake blocks in metal mounts, still called "spoons" although they no longer were spoon-shaped. In some countries these simple "plunger brakes" continued to be used for many years. They were still being fitted to some new bicycles in Germany in the 1960s.

....

Figure 8.6 Left: A vertical section through the inflatable brake pad of Kitchen's pneumatic brake (patent drawing). Right: A contemporary advertisement for the Pneumatic Cycle Brake showing the inflatable brake pad and the squeeze bulb.

Figure 8.7 A simple plunger brake, circa 1900, with direct rod linkage and a rubber "shoe" acting on the top of the tire (Noguchi-san 1998).

RIM BRAKES

Bowden cables versus rod linkage

By the early 1900s, in the UK and in many other places, the plunger brake's days were numbered. With the widespread adoption of the pneumatic tire, rim brakes were a better solution. They caught on quickly.

Rim brakes were patented as early as 1869 by the Lyon-based manufacturer Gervat (addendum to French patent 85,428 of 1869). The Gervat design was known as the frein á pincette (Besse and Henry 2008, 153). Other rim brakes followed in the early 1870s but were not widely adopted. The idea was resurrected in the early 1890s. In 1893, James Bickford of Pennsylvania patented a center-pull caliper brake, which he claimed was superior for use with pneumatic tires (US patent 510,766 of 1893). Bickford also claimed that it offered better braking and reduced tire wear.

In 1896, Ernest Monnington Bowden applied for a patent for a flexible control cable housed in an easily bendable sheath. It was eventually to become a world standard. The drawing that accompanied the first patent already showed it connected to a rim brake (British patent 25,325 of 1896). Bowden's German patent application, filed in 1897, showed a fully specified center-pull caliper brake acting on the rim (German patent 101,470 of 1899) but had the disadvantage that the brake blocks acted on the rolled edge of the Westwood-style rims then in use, which made alignment difficult. Early in 1898, Bowden applied for a patent for a completely different rim brake; later that year, he offered such a brake for sale (British patent 1,196 of 1898). The brake blocks were mounted on a horseshoe-shaped steel stirrup that, when raised by a Bowden cable actuated by a twist grip or a lever on the handlebar, brought the blocks into contact with the inside surface of a wheel's rim.

With the widespread and rapid adoption of the automatic freewheel around 1900, British cycle manufacturers simultaneously adopted rim brakes and two-wheel hand-operated braking. Many makers used rod linkage rather than pay royalties to Bowden—and also because of distrust of the flexible cable. For example, in 1900 Sunbeam introduced its own patented rod-operated stirrup brake. However, Frank Bowden of Raleigh (not related to Ernest Bowden) joined Ernest Bowden's syndicate. That enabled Raleigh to use Bowden cables to operate brakes on its bicycles and, in 1902, to operate the new Sturmey-Archer three-speed hub gears.

It was sometimes suggested that Ernest Bowden didn't invent the Bowden cable and that it was actually the work of Sir Frank Bowden or of Ernest Bowden's associate George Frederick Larkin. In 2012 Nick Clayton comprehensively demolished these suggestions in a paper titled "Who invented the Bowden cable?"

Materials used for brake blocks

Among the materials used for early brake blocks were solid vulcanized rubber, vulcanized compressed fiber, and cork. Leather was also sometimes used, for example by Ernest Bowden in the late 1890s. Depending on the source and the curing process, leather can be durable; it also grips wet shiny steel surfaces well and conforms well to the shape of a braking surface. But it wasn't long before vulcanized rubber became the most widely used brake-block material, despite losing as much as 90 percent of its friction coefficient when wet (Wilson 2002, 13).

Many decades later, leather made a limited comeback as a result of safety legislation in the United States. In the late 1970s, Raleigh designed and patented laminated brake blocks with a braking surface of chrome-tanned leather on an elastomeric backing (such as rubber). These brake blocks, marketed by Raleigh under the name Rain-Check, were particularly effective on chromium-plated steel rims in the wet. Today, most manufacturers overcome the

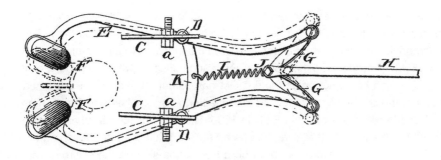

Figure 8.8 Above: Bickford's center-pull caliper brake (patent drawing). Below: A Bowden cable, with spiral-wound steel wire casing coated in Bowdenite (National Cycle Library).

Figure 8.9 An early Bowden stirrup brake (National Cycle Library).

problem of poor wet braking by specifying aluminum rims for use with rim brakes. However, the sidewalls of such rims can wear away quite rapidly, particularly in wet conditions. Worn aluminum rims can fail suddenly, resulting in an instantaneous puncture and possibly a locked wheel or loss of effective steering control. Wear indicators are sometimes provided on aluminum rims, but they are not necessarily checked by users. Many accidents result from exploding aluminum rims, something that didn't happen with steel rims (Wilson 2002, 13–17).

In the early 1970s, David Gordon Wilson and his students at MIT discovered that a material used for aircraft brake pads had about the same coefficient of friction when wet as when dry. However, it wasn't suitable for use with standard brakes, as it required much higher leverage and wide clearance between the blocks and the rim. Wilson's team therefore devised a revolutionary brake caliper mechanism, named the Positech, that had two sequential leverages: one to quickly move the blocks into position and one to apply braking leverage (US patent 3,870,127 of 1975). It worked superbly on steel rims, but it didn't overcome the problem—inherent in all rim brakes—of potential overheating of the rims on long steep descents, which can lead to instantaneous tire deflation (Wilson 2002, 15–17). The Positech design was rejected by every company to which it was offered.

Roller-lever stirrup brakes

As was noted above, bicycle rims of the early twentieth century were generally of the Westwood pattern or a similar pattern. The best surface for brake blocks to contact was the flattish inside surface of the rim, between the spokes and the rolled edge of the rim.

Between 1900 and World War I, various brake designs were tried with Westwood rims. Nearly all of them had a stirrup holding the brake blocks. Some used thumb levers, some pull-up levers; some used rod linkage, some Bowden cables.

It was the roller-lever brake that emerged as a world standard. In this design, the levers were integral with a roller running along the front of the handlebar. Pulling the lever caused the roller to rotate, actuating a rod linkage that pulled the brake stirrup, thus applying the brake blocks to the rim. The rod linkage from the roller to the front wheel was very simple. That to the rear wheel was more complex, involving rods and bell cranks.

Caliper brakes

A caliper brakes has a pair of pivoted brake arms that act on the sides of a wheel's rim. Some have a single pivot, some two pivots. There are center-pull cables and side-pull cables.

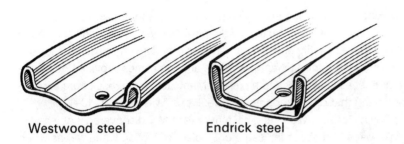

Westwood steel   Endrick steel

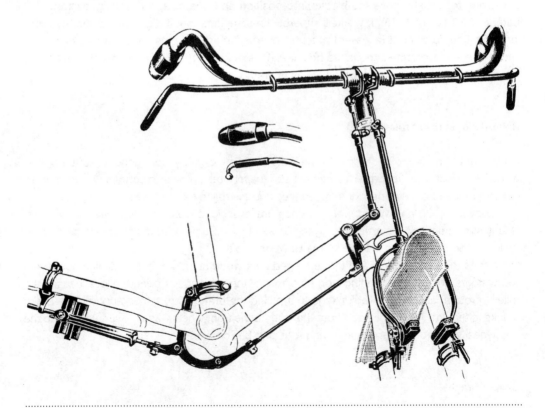

Figure 8.10 A drawing showing the basic difference between Westwood and Endrick rims (R. John Way).
Figure 8.11 A classic roller-lever stirrup brake (Noguchi-san 1998).

Calipers were considered for use on Michaux-style velocipedes in the late 1860s (Roberts 1991, 70). At least one example of a velocipede with calipers exists, but there is no evidence of widespread use. In the high-wheeler era, Thomas Browett and W. H. Harrison of Manchester patented a center-pull, dual-pivot caliper brake (British patent 3,700 of 1876). It even had a power-modulator to prevent the rider from braking too hard on the front wheel and taking a header. Caliper brakes didn't catch on at that time, but interest was revived in the 1890s, with designs such as those of James Bickford and Ernest Bowden.

Caliper brakes work particularly well with Bowden cables. However, they do not work well with Westwood-style rims, as the brake blocks have to act on the rolled edge of the rim, and they are less effective if the caliper has to straddle a tire with a large cross-section, owing to the reduced mechanical advantage and increased flexing of the long brake arms. Another two decades would pass before flat-sided rims (such as those on the Endrick pattern) started to become popular. For these, caliper brakes were ideal. Most of the calipers were of side-pull design, with the ends of both arms on the same side of the bicycle. With the widespread adoption of the caliper brake, many bicycle makers began to provide holes for the pivot bolts in the fork crown and the brake bridge.

By 1938, Raleigh had been producing significant numbers of bicycles with caliper brakes for about a decade. However, Raleigh also was producing even larger numbers of bikes with roller-lever brakes. In an effort to rationalize, Raleigh introduced a hybrid rim profile—the so-called Westrick—that was suitable for use with brakes of both types.

For many decades, simple single-pivot side-pull calipers have been the norm in most developed countries. In post-World War II Britain, calipers rapidly displaced roller-lever brakes on the majority of roadsters.

Dual-pivot side-pull calipers have been around for many years. They are more effective than single-pivot calipers, having greater mechanical advantage. Typically, one arm is pivoted from the central fixing bolt (as on a single-pivot caliper) and the other arm is pivoted from the side opposite the cable connection. Dual-pivot side-pull calipers are used on most modern racing bicycles. They use the same fixing holes as single-pivot calipers and therefore can be interchanged with them.

The Weinmann PBS 300 side-pull caliper was a novel design introduced around 1990. Weinmann, with facilities in Germany, Switzerland, and Belgium, was a long-established component manufacturer and was particularly noted for aluminum alloy wheel rims and brakes. PBS stood for Progressive Braking System. The inner brake cable was anchored to a fast-threaded spindle. ("Fast threaded" means having a screw thread with a steeper pitch than normal, so that rotation of the spindle creates greater lateral movement.) When the cable was pulled, it rotated the spindle, which moved inward, pushing the brake block onto the wheel rim. At the same time, the "passive" brake block on the other arm of the stirrup was pulled

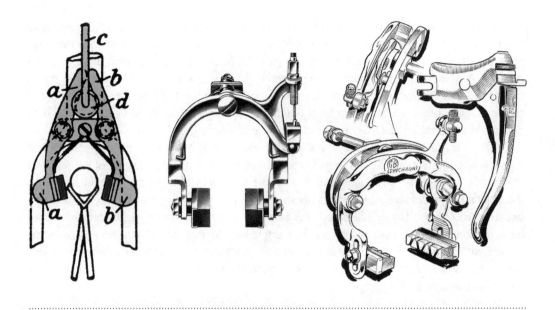

Figure 8.12   Left: Browett and Harrison's 1876 dual-pivot caliper (patent drawing). Center: A Webb steel caliper of the 1930s (National Cycle Library). Right: A GB Synchron dual-pivot caliper of the 1960s (R. John Way).

onto the rim by the stirrup pivoting on the brake bolt. A return spring moved the spindle back to its rest position when the brake cable was slackened. The "passive" brake block's mounting was fitted with a large knob for easy adjustment.

The two symmetrical brake arms of a center-pull caliper are pivoted separately. Typically they are linked by a straddle wire that passes above the tire and connects to a central control cable. Center-pull calipers are easily centered and retain alignment better than side-pulls. However, they cannot accommodate slightly buckled wheels, as side-pulls can.

As was noted above, Browett and Harrison patented a center-pull caliper in 1876, and Bickford and Ernest Bowden both patented center-pull calipers in the 1890s. But, like side-pull calipers, they didn't start to become popular until the 1920s. Since then, most center-pull calipers have used the same fixing holes as single-pivot calipers. Today on racing bikes, center-pulls have largely been superseded by dual-pivot side-pulls.

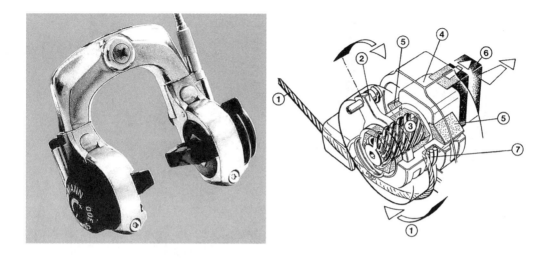

Figure 8.13   Left: A Weinmann PBS 300 threaded-spindle side-pull caliper (National Cycle Library). Right: A diagram of PBS 300 caliper showing the fast-threaded spindle (3), the brake block (6), the inner brake cable (1), the inner cable's anchorage point (2), and the return spring (7) (Ryde International BV).

The U-brake, a variant of the center-pull caliper, was popular on mountain bikes in the early 1990s. In contrast with conventional center-pulls, the arm pivots of U-brakes were attached directly to the fork or the frame.

The delta brake, another variant of the center-pull caliper, has the cable connected to a parallelogram linkage. Pulling the cable shortens the parallelogram vertically and spreads it horizontally, pushing out the brake arms so that the brake pads, which are below the pivot points, move inward toward the wheel rim. The basic concept dates back to the Edwardian era. In the 1980s Campagnolo led a revival of this design, but neither that company nor any of its rivals now makes them. That isn't surprising, as they tend to be heavy, expensive, complicated, and not particularly effective.

Self-adjusting bicycle brakes are rare. One successful design, introduced by Raleigh around 1974, had a self-adjusting mechanism similar to those used in automobile drum brakes. As the

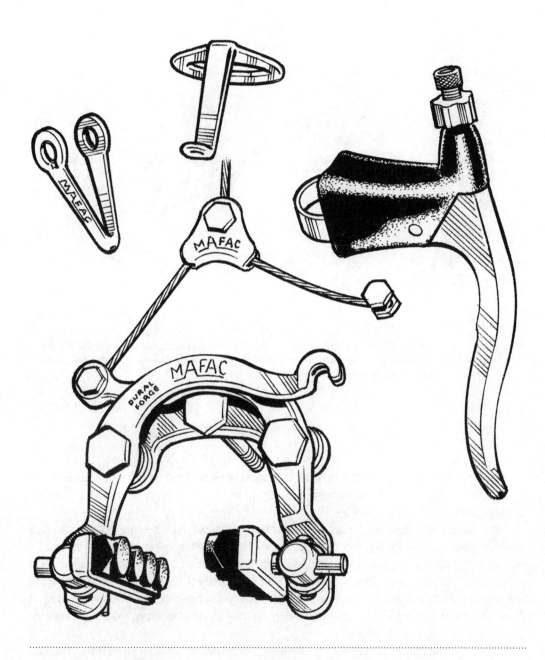

Figure 8.14 Mafac center-pull calipers, popular in the 1960s (R. John Way).

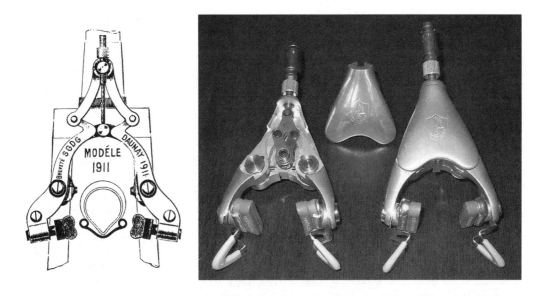

Figure 8.15 Right: A pair of early Campagnolo Delta brakes, showing the internal parallelogram linkage (Wingnut). Left: A 1911 Daunay center-pull brake (Noguchi-san 1998).

brake blocks wore, the travel of the brake lever increased. When it exceeded a certain amount, a ratchet tightened the Bowden cable. Although it earned Raleigh an award from the British Design Centre, this system seems to have confused bicycle mechanics. It soon went out of production.

Cantilever brakes

Cantilever brakes, invented considerably earlier than U-brakes, are center-pull brakes with their arm pivots attached to the fork or the frame. The arms protrude outward, and their ends are connected to a straddle wire; that wire is connected to the control cable. In 1929, an English firm called Resilion began to produce a particularly successful range of cantilevers that had a separate Bowden cable for each brake block (British patent 329,211 of 1929). These brakes, sold for more than 30 years, could be clamped onto a wide range of forks and stays without the need for brazed-on fittings. Later cantilevers, such as the Mafacs that achieved popularity in the 1960s, required brazed-on mounting points.

Cantilever brakes were standard on mountain bikes for some years. They are powerful, and they work well with wide tires. However, the protruding brake arms are more susceptible to damage and more likely to cause injury than many other brake designs. The need for a separate cable stop made complicated their use with suspension. And they can be very dangerous if the straddle wire connecting the two front brake arms drops onto a front tire with knobby tread, as can happen if the front brake cable goes excessively slack because a cable casing fulcrum stop fails, or a pulley over which the inner cable runs breaks off, or the clamp that holds the inner cable to midpoint of the straddle wire works loose, or if the brake cable simply parts. If the straddle wire catches on a knobby tread, the front wheel can lock, instantaneously pitching the rider over the handlebars. This is particularly likely to happen as a result of hard application of the brake, at the very time when the rider most needs effective, controllable braking. For example, in April of 1991 a student at Penn State University was approaching a red light at about 6 miles per hour on his mountain bike. He applied his brakes. The front brake's pulley mechanism suffered a fatigue fracture and allowed the straddle cable to catch on the tread of the knobby tire. The bike stopped suddenly, throwing the rider over the handlebars. A broken neck and a spinal-cord injury rendered him a quadriplegic (Hadland 2011, 279). This type of brake should therefore be used with a fender, a reflector bracket, or some other device to prevent the straddle cable from snagging the tire in the event of any of the mechanical failures mentioned above.

David Gordon Wilson has highlighted the risk of fatigue failure in straddle cables that are rigidly fixed to brake arms. The rotation of brake arms relative to their straddle wires almost guarantees that the cables will eventually fail, usually without warning, during hard braking—a potentially fatal situation. This risk can be designed out by the use of a freely pivoting clamp or a retrofittable curved washer that puts the cable through a gentle bend where it bolts to the brake arm (Wilson 2002, 10–13).

As was mentioned above, center-pull calipers also have straddle wires, and some designs may be susceptible to problems similar to those relating to cantilever brakes.

A variant of the center-pull cantilever is the roller-cam brake, developed by a Californian mountain biker named Charlie Cunningham in the early 1980s. This uses a double-sided sliding cam, pulled by the cable, to force the two brake arms apart. Side-pull variants have also been made.

Center-pull cantilevers have been largely superseded by direct-pull cantilevers. (One model, produced by Shimano, is called the V-brake.) The cable connects the ends of the two brake arms, running horizontally. Instead of bending the usual flexible cable sheath through a sharp angle to run it to the brake lever, the last few inches of the sheath are replaced by a

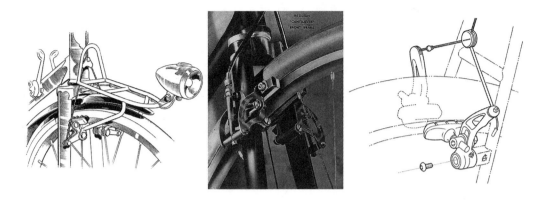

Figure 8.16 Left: Mafac Criterium cantilevers, here used as mounting points for a front rack (R. John Way). Center: A 1934 catalog illustration of the Resilion cantilever brake (National Cycle Library). Right: A cantilever brake of the sort used on mountain bikes in the 1980s (Geoff Apps).

"noodle"—a rigid metal tube that turns through about 90°. This neatly and efficiently leads the cable from a near vertical position to a horizontal position without imposing side force on the brake or protruding from the bike. Direct-pull cantilevers are efficient and unobtrusive. They are also easy for the manufacturer to fit, even to bikes equipped with suspension.

Hydraulic rim brakes

In 1968, Keizo Shimano and Yuji Fujii invented a hydraulically operated dual-pivot caliper brake system (US patent 3,554,334 of 1969). A single brake lever operated the front and rear brakes sequentially. Each caliper had a horizontal hydraulic cylinder and piston. The lever had a two-chamber, two-piston master cylinder, which would continue to work on one brake if the other brake's cylinder leaked. The German company Magura became a market leader in hydraulic rim brakes; at the time of writing, it remains so. Magura's brakes have blocks directly connected to compact pistons, rather than using calipers. The market for hydraulic rim brakes has been small but is growing. Their complexity, vulnerability, and cost have been perceived as offsetting the advantages of almost lossless transmission of force between brake lever and brake block.

Figure 8.17 The Shimano DXR V-brake, a direct-pull cantilever design (Shimano Inc.).

Figure 8.18 A well-used Magura hydraulic rim brake (Christoph Eckert).

BRAKES IN OR ATTACHED TO THE HUB

Coaster brakes, drum brakes, band brakes, and disc brakes all have been installed in or attached to hubs. Unlike rim brakes, they all impose considerable torque on the wheel during braking. This "wind-up" is in the opposite direction to the torque imposed by the drive train. Consequently, wheels with hub brakes—especially rear wheels—must have strong spokes.

Coaster brakes

In the 1890s and the early 1900s, a variety of braking systems actuated by back-pedaling— including spoon brakes, roller brakes, and drum brakes—were available. Some were outboard units that could be retrofitted to an existing hub. But only the neat and tidy coaster brake was an enduring success.

Canadians and Americans did most of the work that led to development of the first coaster brakes. By 1900, coaster brakes were found on most of the new bicycles manufactured in the United States and Canada, and they were readily available for retrofitting to older machines.

Various inventors in North America who were vying for priority in the development of improved braking systems that would appeal to the average bicycle rider were involved in the invention and development of these in-hub back-pedaling brakes. For a comprehensive listing of these inventors, and the companies that employed them and exploited their inventions, see Sanderson 2012b.

A variety of braking mechanisms were used in early in-hub coaster brakes. Some, such as the Doolittle (US patent 576,560 of 1897), had no freewheel action. However, coasters soon settled into two main categories, all with automatic freewheeling.

One category has multiple friction discs. In this type, alternate discs are keyed to the hub shell and therefore rotate with the wheel; the rest are locked to the axle and therefore don't rotate. When the rider is pedaling forward or freewheeling, the friction discs are clear of each other. Back-pedaling causes a clutch to push the plates together, causing friction and slowing the wheel.

The other widely used coaster mechanism typically has a split cylindrical metal brake band, often made of brass or phosphor-bronze. Back-pedaling causes a cone to be pushed

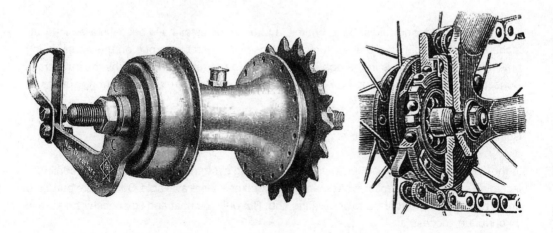

Figure 8.19 Left: A New Departure coaster brake of the early twentieth century (National Cycle Library). Right: A Trebert retrofit outboard back-pedal brake of 1899 (contemporary advertisement).

into the end of the cylindrical brake band, expanding it to press against the inside of the hub shell and thus slowing the wheel. In some variants, instead of a single brake band, two, three, or four segmented brake shoes are used.

The metal-to-metal braking surfaces of coaster brakes require lubrication, which can be burned off by sustained heavy use, as in descending a mountain. But in normal utility use, coasters are very reliable, aren't affected by wet weather, and require little maintenance.

The torque arm of a coaster brake's hub has to be fastened securely to the chain stay to keep the brake band, the brake shoes, or the fixed friction discs from rotating during braking.

Precursors of the coaster brake included various back-pedal brakes not contained within the hub. Herbert Bailey of Chicago applied for a patent for a back-pedal band brake in 1893 (US patent 517,996 of 1894). This had an external actuating mechanism connected to the chain, and so was not a self-contained coaster hub. From 1897 on, patents were granted for various designs for back-pedal brakes. Alexander Morrow of the Eclipse Cycle Company in Elmira, New York came up with a particularly neat early design (British patent 18,105 of 1897). However, in this design, as in many other early designs for back-pedal brakes, the brake was actually a spoon type.

The first design that put a coaster brake entirely within the hub of the rear wheel, invented by James Copeland of Hartford (its priority date was April 4, 1898), was assigned to the New Departure Manufacturing Company. New Departure coaster brakes became very popular in the United States, especially in the 1930s and the 1940s.

The British bicycle industry was less enthusiastic about coaster brakes than the North American. Despite some patents of British origin, there is little mention of them in the literature until 1902 (Sanderson 2012b). For example, the upmarket British maker Sunbeam introduced the freewheel in 1900, but initially paired it with a back-pedal rim brake rather than a coaster hub. Sunbeam's 1900 catalog included this cautionary note: "Cyclists are warned against free-wheeling with only the ordinary front wheel brake; it is essential for safety to have brakes both on the front and back wheel." This highlights the point that, unlike North American safety bicycles, British ones typically had hand-operated front brakes, even in the fixed-wheel era. Reliance solely on rear-wheel braking is, in any case, not a good idea, because "the retardation with rear braking is less than half the value at which, using the front brake to the maximum safe limit, the rider would be about to go over the handlebars," and "brakes that operate on the rear wheel only, however reliable and effective they may be in themselves, are wholly insufficient to take care of emergencies" (Wilson 2004, 243ff.).

Raleigh's directors monitored American technical developments closely. In 1899 they discussed coaster hubs at length, but they chose not to offer a coaster option until well into the Edwardian era. Raleigh's chairman, Frank Bowden, disliked coaster brakes. "Like every cyclist I know," he wrote (1913), "I prefer two hand brakes." Coaster brakes never became very popular in the UK. But in the Netherlands and Germany coaster brakes rapidly gained large followings. To this day they are still somewhat popular in those countries.

The most famous European coaster hubs were the Torpedo models made by Fichtel & Sachs of Schweinfurt, Germany. The company was founded in 1895 by Karl Fichtel (a businessman) and Ernst Sachs (a bicycle mechanic). Around that time, Sachs obtained several patents for applications of ball bearings, and the company was to become famous for its ball bearings. In 1898, Sachs demonstrated his first back-pedal brake in London and sold 500 units to an English company. After a bigger order from a Munich firm, the device became known as the Freilauf mit der Münchner Brems (freewheel with the Munich brake).

In the next few years, Fichtel & Sachs continued to develop back-pedal brakes. A 1900 Sachs brake (German patent 129,301 of 1902) was similar in many respects to an 1899 design by Henry Trebert of Syracuse, New York (US patent 671,409 of 1901). But whereas Trebert simply used metal-on-metal braking surfaces, Sachs used a fiber brake ring, with tapered edges, that acted on a metal surface.

According to company literature, Ernst Sachs moved his developers into tents in the Austrian Alps to do braking tests on grades, and returned with the first Torpedo coaster brake. In reality, the inventor was Johann Modler, Sachs's engineer since 1901. By 1903 Sachs had an improved coaster hub, the basis of the first Torpedo, which he patented in his name (German patent 216,985 of 1903, US patent 777,811 of 1904). Sachs denied a 2 percent royalty to Modler, who then left Sachs, invented the spherical roller bearing (US patent 1,226,785 of 1917), and founded his own engineering works. Since then, company lore has attributed the Torpedo achievement to Sachs alone. (Sachs is known to have paid a license fee of 3 million marks to the New Departure Company, but for exactly what feature isn't known.)

Torpedo coaster brakes, in various forms, were produced throughout most of the twentieth century—a total of 280 million units—until 1977, when SRAM (the American company that acquired the bicycle department of Fichtel & Sachs) discontinued the name "Torpedo." (The name was later revived for a switchable fixed/free hub, a neater option than a double-sided or "flip-flop" fixed/free hub with a fixed gear on one side and a freewheel on the other. This Torpedo was erroneously claimed by SRAM to be the world's first fixed/free hub. Fichtel & Sachs made a more sophisticated one in 1901 that that could be switched while riding. That same year, Raleigh made a simpler one that required a spanner. The present SRAM product requires a screwdriver.)

In Britain, the most important makers of coaster brakes in the twentieth century were BSA (which made the Eadie coaster brake from 1907), Perry, and Sturmey-Archer. Fichtel & Sachs, Sturmey-Archer, Shimano, and other manufacturers sometimes combined coaster brakes with hub gears.

Coaster brakes impose considerable stress on the chain and chainwheel fixings, especially during long and steep descents. This could be enough to shear small-diameter alloy bolts

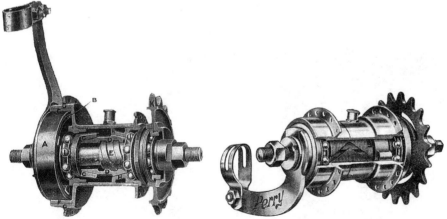

Figure 8.20   The first Torpedo coaster hub (catalog picture). Inset: Johann Modler, the true designer of the Torpedo coaster brake (Johann Modler GmbH).

Figure 8.21   Left: A catalog illustration of BSA's Eadie coaster brake, circa 1910. Right: A 1930s catalog illustration of a Perry Coaster (National Cycle Library).

used in chainwheels such as the Williams AB77 of the 1960s. However, most bicycles fitted with coaster brakes had non-detachable steel chainwheels, so this problem was rarely encountered.

Band brakes

A design for a band brake for a horse-drawn carriage appears in James Smith's 1818 book *The Mechanic, or Compendium of Practical Inventions,* and band brakes were already in use on some tricycles by the 1880s. Soon afterward, the development of band brakes for bicycles was encouraged by the desire to reduce damage to the newly introduced and expensive pneumatic tires.

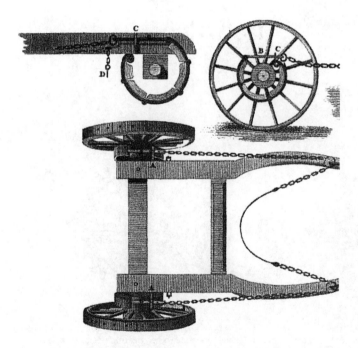

Figure 8.22 Rapson's design for a band brake, circa 1818.

In a typical band brake, a friction band was fixed at one end to a bicycle's frame and passed around a brake drum fixed to the hub on the opposite side to the chain drive. The other end of the band was connected by a rod linkage to the brake lever. Pulling the brake lever tightened the band around the drum, creating friction and slowing the wheel. Mud, grit, and other debris could easily get trapped between the brake band and the brake drum, thus slowing the rider when the brake was not in use. A neater design for a band brake (British patent 474,051 of 1890) by Richard Morriss Woodhead and Paul Angois, founders of the Raleigh bicycle brand, addressed this problem. In their design, a two-part band surrounded the drum almost completely, restricting the amount of debris that could be drawn into it. Some years later, William Taylor devised a simpler version with a one-piece belt (British patent 6,780 of 1897).

Around 1909, the British company Triumph produced an adapted version of the Sturmey-Archer three-speed, to which Triumph added its own large-diameter spoked brake wheel in place of the more common compact drum (*Cycling 1909*, 15).

Band brakes were not hugely popular in Western countries and were soon displaced by other solutions, such as the coaster hub or improved rim brakes. However, enclosed band brakes, such as the Chinese Jinyu, were and still are widely used in parts of Asia.

Royce Husted of Illinois devised a modern variant of the band brake (US patent 5,052,524 of 1991). Instead of a small-diameter brake drum, it had a Kevlar-coated stainless-steel cable acting on a channel that was integral with the wheel's rim. Used on an unusual bicycle of that era called the Yankee, it may have been the only band brake that could also be described as a rim brake.

Internally expanding hand-operated drum brakes

Most internally expanding hand-operated drum brakes for bicycles ("drum brakes") are broadly similar to automobile drum brakes. Such a brake has a pair of pivoting brake shoes lined with a heat-resistant non-metallic friction material. (Asbestos was typically used before the health hazards of that material were fully appreciated.) When the brake is applied, the shoes act on the inside face of a drum. Unlike modern automobile drum brakes, in which the shoes are forced apart and against the brake drum by a hydraulic cylinder, bicycle drum brakes typically use a mechanical cam, actuated by a brake lever through a rod linkage or a Bowden cable. Like a coaster hub, a drum brake has a torque arm that has to be firmly attached to a chain stay or to a fork to keep the fixed brake assembly (shoes, mounting plate, and cam) from rotating with the drum during braking.

What may have been the first drum brake for a bicycle was patented by W. R. Mortimer (British patent 3,279 of 1881). But bicycle drum brakes didn't catch on at that time.

The British Hub Company launched drum brakes in the UK in 1926. Their popularity peaked in the 1930s. British Hub's Cyklbrake range used Ferodo brake linings and was available with 3¾-inch drums for solo bikes and with 4-inch drums and wider brake shoes for tandems. By 1931, T. F. Blumfield Ltd. of Birmingham had also introduced hub brakes. Thomas Frederick Blumfield had applied for a patent in 1926 for improving the water resistance of drum brakes by standing the torque arm away from the drum on spacers and providing a deflector plate between the arm and the drum (British patent 284,743 of 1928). A version of Blumfield's brake was made to be mounted outboard on a double-sided hub. Such hubs, popular with club riders in Britain at the time, offered a choice of a differently sized sprocket on each side and/or one sprocket fixed and one free.

In 1931, Raleigh licensed Perry to combine a Perry drum brake with a Sturmey-Archer K-series three-speed. Sturmey-Archer soon began making its own range of hub brakes. These were broadly similar to the British Hub and Perry products, and were also offered in combination with various hub gears. The British market for drum brakes had shrunk quite considerably by the end of the 1930s, but large numbers were exported. Drum brakes became popular in the Netherlands, in Germany, and in Denmark. Sturmey-Archer, now under Taiwanese ownership, continues to make a wide range of drum brakes to this day, as does SRAM, the American-owned descendant of the German hub maker Fichtel & Sachs.

Shimano's drum brakes are modular roller brakes of Shimano design. Some Shimano front and rear hubs (including multi-speed hubs) are fitted with splines on the left side, onto which the roller brake fits, outboard of the hub. Like coaster brakes, roller brakes use metal-on-metal braking; three metal brake shoes are forced against the inside of the brake drum by a cam-and-roller system.

Roller brakes are designed so that, when the braking surfaces have worn out, the whole modular unit can easily be removed and replaced by a complete new unit. A complete new unit can be bought for as little as $40. Utility versions look quite similar to modern Far Eastern band brakes. Upmarket versions, some with cooling discs, can be considerably more expensive.

Disc brakes

Instead of a brake drum, a disc brake typically has a metal disc, also known as a rotor. Disc brakes' main advantage is better cooling of the braking surface, which is not enclosed. Better cooling reduces "brake fade."

The Birmingham automaker Frederick William Lanchester patented an automobile disc brake in 1902 (British patent 26,407) but wasn't able to popularize it at the time. Early disc brakes performed poorly after exposure to dust and other road debris. This was a major reason

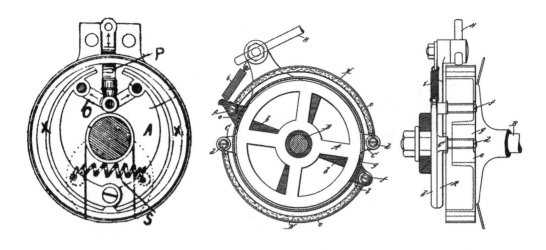

Figure 8.23 Left: Mortimer's drum brake of 1881 (patent drawing). Center and right: An improved band brake designed by Woodhead and Angois of Raleigh, 1890 (patent drawings).

why they were not widely adopted for automobile use until the second half of the twentieth century, by which time many more roads had sealed surfaces.

Disc brakes for bicycles predate Lanchester's patent by nearly ten years. In 1893, Joel Hendrick and Arthur Fay, both of Massachusetts, applied for a patent for a disc brake with an aluminum rotor and with pads made of vulcanized rubber or vulcanized fiber (US patent 526,317 of 1894). Commercial success was not achieved with this design.

In 1969, Masayoshi Kine of Shimano applied for a patent in Japan and was also granted a US patent (3,680,663 of 1972). In 1971, two New York residents, Karl Frei and Edwin Elliott Hood, filed their own application for a disc brake patent. However, there was little interest in the technology until well into the mountain bike boom. Detractors argued that a caliper rim brake was already a form of disc brake—one with a disc of the biggest possible diameter.

Around the end of the twentieth century, interest in disc brakes exploded after they were adopted by downhill mountain bike racing teams. At the time of writing, simple cable-operated disc brakes can be found on mountain bikes selling for as little as $200. Hydraulic disc brakes can be found on bicycles costing less than $800.

At the top end of the market, downhill racers go for expensive hydraulic systems with multiple caliper cylinders. The discs, often only 2 millimeters thick, are usually made of stainless steel, but aluminum and titanium are also used. Unlike the pads of disc brakes used on

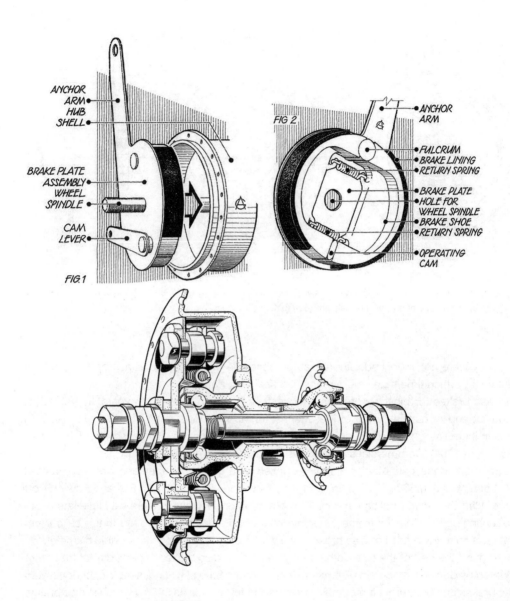

Figure 8.24 Above: The working parts of a typical internally expanding drum brake (Geoff Apps). Below: the Sturmey-Archer BF, a classic drum brake designed in the 1930s (Sturmey-Archer Heritage).

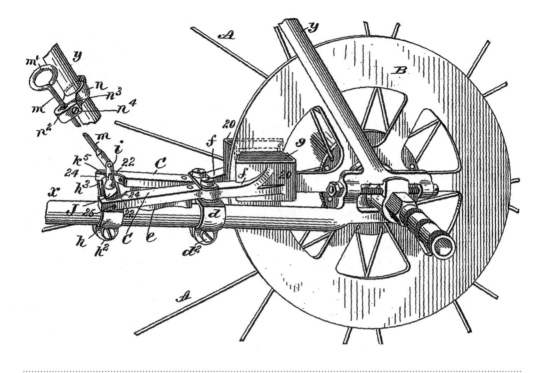

Figure 8.25 An 1894 design for a bicycle disc brake by Hendrick and Fay (patent drawing).

motorized vehicles, those in bicycle disc brake move clear of the disc when the brake isn't in use, to eliminate pad drag.

Disc brakes, like other hub brakes, have the advantage that the braking surfaces are farther away from mud and other debris than are the wheel rims. Even when the brake pads are retracted, they remain very close to the disc, so there is less chance that debris will be trapped between the braking surfaces than there is with a rim brake. Brake discs are harder than wheel rims, and disc brakes' pads are harder than rim brakes' blocks, so greater braking force can be used without the risk of excessive wear to the wheel rim. A brake disc is perforated, not just for lightness but also to allow debris and water to escape from between the brake pads and brake disc. Disc brakes can easily be used with very wide tires and with suspension. They also reduce the risk of instantaneous tire blow-outs caused by brake-wear-induced failure of the rim sidewalls or by overheating of the rims on long steep descents.

Today disc brakes are regarded as the most effective bicycle brakes available. Used almost universally in mountain biking and downhill racing, they are increasingly found on road bikes despite their added weight, cost, and air resistance. Contrary to early experience with automobile disc brakes, today's bicycle disc brakes perform exceptionally well when wet or covered with dust or mud.

Unlike rim brakes, but like other hub brakes, disc brakes cause considerable torque at the hub. This tends to "wind up" the wheel, putting stress on the hub flanges, the spokes, and the rim. To cope with this, a heavier-than-normal wheel is required, with a special hub on which to mount the brake disc. To accommodate the width of a front disc brake, either dished spoking or an extra-wide front fork must be used. Because the disc brake exerts a large bending force on the fork, an extra-strong fork may be necessary. Under some circumstances, hard use of a front disc brake can cause a conventional front-wheel quick-release mechanism to work sufficiently loose from conventional dropouts that the wheel comes out of the fork. However, these problems rarely arise except when disc brakes have been retrofitted to a bike not designed to accommodate them. Any bicycle made for use with disc brakes should have been designed with these factors in mind.

SADDLES, PEDALS, AND HANDLEBARS

9

Because the points of contact between rider and machine are important for a comfortable and efficient ride, prospective purchasers often look at a bicycle's saddle, pedals, and handlebar first. Experienced sellers know this and make sure that a second-hand bike's handlebar grips, saddle, and pedals are in good condition. In this chapter, we explore the development of those components.

SADDLES

As was noted in chapter 6, Drais's first machine had a padded saddle fixed to the main beam. The second-generation draisine had a padded, sausage-like suspended saddle. The simple rope suspension made it possible to adjust the saddle's height but also contributed to comfort by isolating the saddle a little from the main beam.

The next step to improving rider comfort was to mount the saddle on springs. A Michaux-style velocipede's springing was an integral part of the machine, something that wasn't easy to do with a high-wheeler. An early high-wheeler's saddle was, therefore, typically mounted on a simple, rigid iron frame, with the nose (peak) and back of the leather saddle top riveted to it. The stretched leather provided the only springing. Since there was no way to adjust the tension, the saddle became increasingly uncomfortable as use caused the leather top to sag. Tension adjustment by means of a screw—a method still used today—was therefore incorporated into leather saddles.

Some riders of high-wheelers wanted more springing than a tensioned leather saddle cover alone could offer. Various sprung mountings were tried. One practical solution was to incorporate the springing in the saddle itself and to clamp the saddle directly to the backbone of the machine. An important early example was the sprung saddle designed by John Harrington of Coventry in the mid 1880s. This was followed by a spate of innovative saddles with

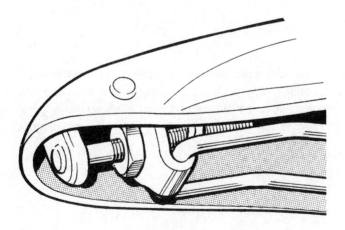

Figure 9.1   A saddle tensioner—a simple device still used on modern leather saddles (R. John Way).

built-in springing, including some pneumatic models, such as the Henson Anatomic and the Guthrie-Hall. The Automatic even enabled the rider to adjust the tilt of the saddle while riding.

The new saddles attracted the attention of the medical press. In the March 28, 1886 issue of the *British Medical Journal*, a surgeon named E. B. Turner responded to a reader's query as follows:

> The comfort of any cycle saddle depends on adjustment only. The Guthrie-Hall sad-
> dle is very comfortable for short rides, but after a certain number of miles it is apt to
> get very hard and hot, and unless the air tension is most carefully regulated and the
> "tilt" adjusted, causes a good deal of discomfort. The Burgess seat has not been tried
> much as yet, but its success, too, would depend entirely on sufficient pains being
> taken to adjust it to the individual using it. A saddle of the same sort, peakless, and
> shaped, is the Anatomical or "Henson's seat," which is pneumatic, with depressions
> for the ischial tuberosities, and this also, if properly tilted, is very good. But for an
> ordinary healthy man a common saddle with spring adapted to his weight, and so

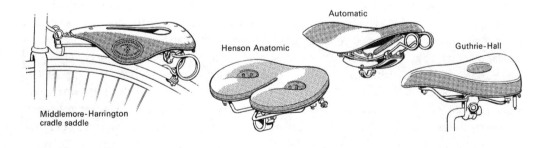

Figure 9.2 Early sprung saddles (R. John Way).

adjusted that he sits on ischial bones, and is not hung up on his perineum, is as good as any. Such a saddle is the "Brooks B28, size 3." I have ridden hundreds of miles on saddles of this pattern without the slightest inconvenience. If a saddle without a peak is required, I should recommend the "Henson" in preference to any other.

With the evolution of the safety bicycle, the mass-produced sprung saddle, which could be clamped to almost any seat pin, rapidly became the standard. The cover was typically of leather and the frame of round-section steel wire with steel pressings. Most saddles not made for sports models now had coil springs, typically two at the back, and sometimes a coil or loop spring at the front.

For sporting purposes, less springing was desirable. Riders didn't want to put their effort into repeatedly compressing saddle springs. Sports saddles depended for their limited springing on the slight give in the frame's wire rails and the inherent flexibility of the tensioned leather saddle top. However, not all saddles had wire rails: some instead used flat steel or aluminum strip, which had no give whatsoever.

Leading early makers of saddles included Brooks, Middlemore, and Mansfield in the UK, Idéale in France, and Lepper in the Netherlands. Some of these brands still exist.

As was mentioned in chapter 6, the British-based Danish inventor Mikael Pedersen went against the flow in pursuing his goal of a more comfortable saddle. When the cycle industry was opting for standardized saddles that could fit almost any bicycle, he designed a bicycle specifically around his "hammock" saddle. But he was very much the exception.

In 1973, John Marchello of Michigan invented a smaller, simpler hammock saddle that could be mounted on a standard seat post (US patent 3,874,730 of 1975). It didn't catch on.

In the 1930s, "mattress" saddles became popular. Instead of a leather top, these had "leather cloth" (a plastic-coated fabric) on a layer of felt. This was supported by a multiplicity of small-diameter coil springs, with one set arranged in a fan shape from the cantle plate at the back of the saddle to the middle and another set running from the middle to the nose. Leading makers included Lycett and Terrys. Mattress saddles became the norm for utility riders in many markets for 40 or 50 years. Later examples sometimes had a top made of nylon or similar semi-rigid plastic, covered with a thin layer of foam and a soft vinyl outer cover.

Saddles with hard plastic tops began to gain popularity with racing cyclists in the 1960s. The first was probably the Italian Nitor Model 1960, made by Unica. These saddles were considerably lighter and cheaper than traditional leather saddles, required no maintenance, were inherently waterproof, and didn't require breaking in—more accurate, they were so rigid that they couldn't be broken in. By the early 1970s, more comfortable plastic saddles had been developed. The Milremo Super de Luxe had a plastic shell topped with a thin layer of upholsterer's foam and a soft leather cover. By the 1980s, saddles of broadly similar construction had all but displaced the mattress saddle among utility riders.

No. 30.

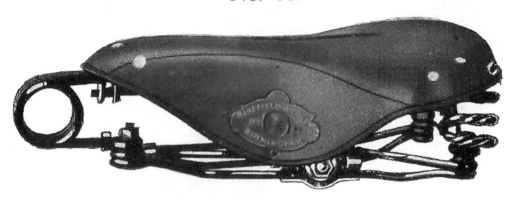

Size, 12 in. x 9½ in.

No. 50.

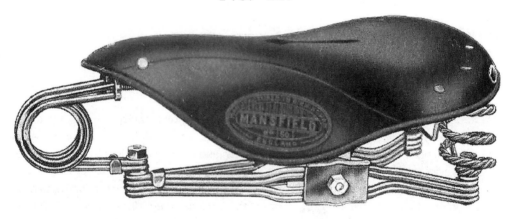

Size, 12 in. x 9½ in.

The extra large seat makes these saddles ideal for heavy riders.

Figure 9.3 Mansfield roadster saddles from about 1930 (National Cycle Library).

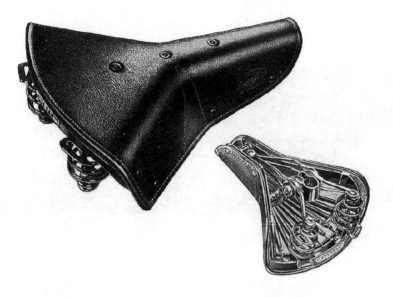

Figure 9.4   A Lycett mattress saddle (National Cycle Library).

Today, most saddles have a shell of a plastic such as nylon (or carbon fiber at the top end of the market), usually topped by a layer of foam or gel, and an outer cover of vinyl, leather, or Lycra. Versions are still made specifically for men and for women, though some are usable by either sex.

To relieve pressure on nerves and blood vessels, many saddles designed for males have a center groove. In September 1997, the editor of the American magazine *Bicycling*, Ed Pavelka, published an article reporting his impotence from riding long distances. The article was widely quoted by the general press. This led to a sudden increase in the sale of anatomical saddles with a center groove. The Specialized Body Geometry saddle, designed by a physician named Roger Minkow, was especially popular. (Sales of recumbents also surged.)

Traditional leather saddles are still made by Brooks and Lepper. Some of these have changed little since the 1890s.

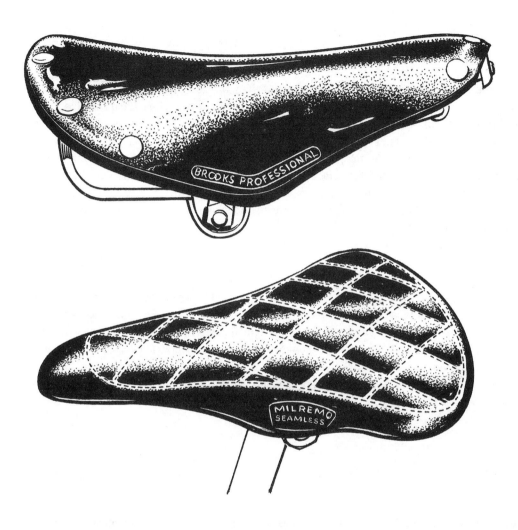

Figure 9.5 The timeless Brooks Professional leather saddle and a Milremo Super de Luxe from around 1970 (R. John Way).

SEAT POSTS

With the introduction of the safety bicycle and standardized, mass-produced saddles, the means of fixing the seat to the bicycle also became standardized. The saddle was fixed to the seat post by a clip, which permitted the angle of the saddle to be adjusted. A typical example was the Brooks-style clip, in which serrated discs were clamped together by a bolt. The seat post became a hollow metal tube, usually reduced in diameter at its top to keep the saddle clip from slipping down. It fitted telescopically into the seat tube and was held by a clamp with a binder bolt. As with many other metal components, aluminum alloy came to be used increasingly for seat posts, although steel remained in wide use, especially on cheap bicycles and traditional roadsters.

By the 1960s, seat posts with integral saddle clamps, offering more subtle adjustment, were available from Campagnolo, Zeus, Simplex, Unica, and other makers. Today, micro-adjusting alloy seat posts are commonplace on bicycles sold in Western countries. In most modern designs, a single vertical bolt is used to adjust the saddle's angle and to secure the clamp.

Since the 1990s, carbon-fiber seat posts have been available. Some of these are genuinely aerodynamic, following the style set by the British designer Mike Burrows and featured in Giant's TCR racing bikes of the 1990s. "I have always felt that airflow at this point was critical," Burrows has written (2000, 89). "For as we tend to scoop up the air with our bodies, there will be a high pressure area created. The gap between our legs is where it ends up. Not filling this area with a round seat pin and seat stays, etc., seems like a good idea."

PEDALS

Karl Drais didn't have to worry about pedals; he simply propelled his machine by scooting along the ground. The treadle-driven tricycles and quadricycles of the 1850s often had sandal-like overshoes for the rider's feet, fixed onto the treadles.

Velocipedes were pedaled with the instep rather than the ball of the foot. The rider sat well back and placed one foot's instep on the pedal. The pedals had flanges to hold the rider's shoes. The pedals of Michaux's machines had an "acorn" plumb bob to keep the flat side upward. Pierre Lallement included counterbalanced pedals in his 1866 velocipede patent (US patent 59,915 of 1866). The "acorn" later found use as an oil reservoir for the pedal pin (French patent 80,637 of 1868). Another pattern of pedal had three flat faces (a triangular

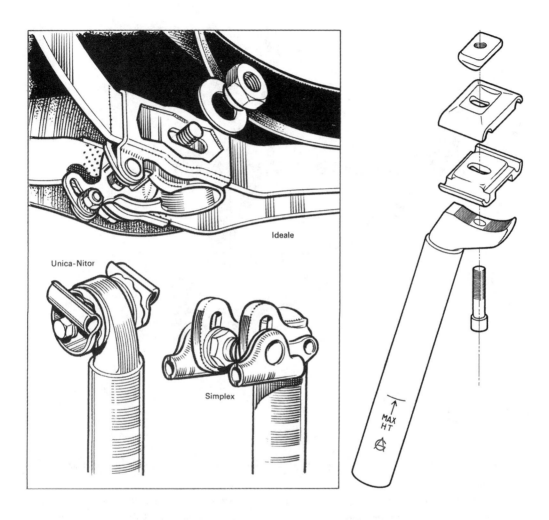

Figure 9.6 Above left: An Idéale saddle of the 1960s with rigid aluminum alloy rails and a separate clip for fixing to a seat post. Below left: Seat posts of the 1960s with integral saddle clamps (R. John Way) Right: A micro-adjusting seat post (Geoff Apps).

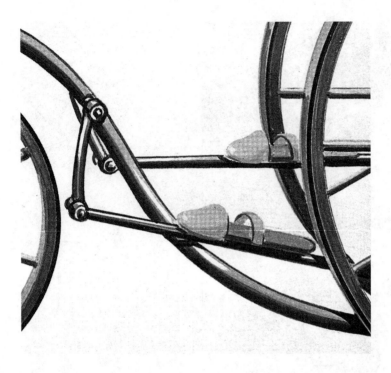

Figure 9.7   A treadle drive with "overshoes" (R. John Way).

cross-section). Thus, one face was always near enough to horizontal that the foot would engage with it easily.

The high-wheeler demanded a new riding style. James Moore, recalling his win at Wolverhampton's Molineux Park in August of 1870, wrote "I was riding a 43[-inch] Meyer tension-wheel bicycle and used toe pedals, while my opponents were yet pedaling from the instep." Meyer pedals were neat two-sided bronze castings with pedal rubbers, turning on a tapered, steel pedal pin, a design he was still making ten years later.

William Henry James Grout patented rubber-clothed flat pedals (British patent 1,468 of 1871), but a more important improvement came in 1881: the use of ball bearings in pedals. Both William Bown and Daniel Rudge, suppliers of wheel bearings to the trade, also supplied ball-bearing-equipped pedals. Sturmey (1887) reported that "nearly every maker now makes his own [ball-bearing pedals]" and "there exists practically but little difference in any."

Lightweight "rat-trap" pedals were introduced for racing by John Keen in 1876 (*Bicycling News*, July 1876). These were condemned for road use as being "prone to wear out the boots." Similarly, whereas racers used toe clips, the risk of falling while still attached to one's machine wasn't welcomed by the average club rider or tourist.

Some early ball-bearing pedals had exposed spindles, which made it easy for water and grit to get into the bearings. By the mid 1890s, this problem had been designed out by surrounding the spindle with a steel tube connected to the pedal's end plates. This not only gave better protection to the bearings, but also strengthened the pedal.

Quill pedals, in which the metal cage is formed in one "wrap-around" piece, were available by 1896, an example being Bown's Aeolus Butterfly. Thus, by the end of the nineteenth century double-sided pedals recognizably similar to many found today had evolved. One could even buy a pedal—the Velox Combination—that was like a rubber pedal on one side and like a rat trap on the other.

Counterbalanced single-sided pedals have occasionally reappeared on the market, though not with the ornate and pendulous counterweights used on the French-style velocipedes of the 1860s. For example, in the late 1890s, Reed and Curtis sold a self-balancing pedal with a relatively small horizontal cylindrical counterweight. In the 1980s, Shimano marketed even neater counterbalanced pedals.

The 1898 Ramsey swinging pedal was inherently self-righting. It was mounted on a large-diameter flat bearing in such a way that it was considerably displaced from the normal pedal spindle axis. The aim was to avoid the "top dead center" (TDC) problem caused by the fact that downward force on a pedal that is directly in line with the crank produces no leverage. With the Ramsey swinging pedal, because the rider sat behind the crank, the foot would automatically push the pedal beyond the normal TDC point. The makers claimed that the suspended pedal made hill climbing 25 percent easier, and offered a money-back guarantee, but in reality the TDC problem still occurred when the pedal was in line with the crank; the TDC point was slightly different.

One noteworthy design was the elegantly minimalist Lyotard platform pedal, invented by French racing cyclist Marcel Berthet around 1930.

Over the decades, it became commoner for the better pedals to have bodies of aluminum alloy rather than steel. In the late 1960s and the 1970s, some bicycle makers, including Raleigh, used plain, non-adjustable, oil-retaining bearings on their cheaper pedals. Cheap pedals were also made with non-adjustable ball-bearing races, for example by Union in Germany. Plastic bodies became increasingly common for cheaper pedals.

Folding pedals of various designs are used on many portable bicycles. A particularly robust and successful design is the folding left pedal of the Brompton bicycle. In the early 2000s, MKS introduced a range of quick-release pedals, removable from the crank arm without the need for tools.

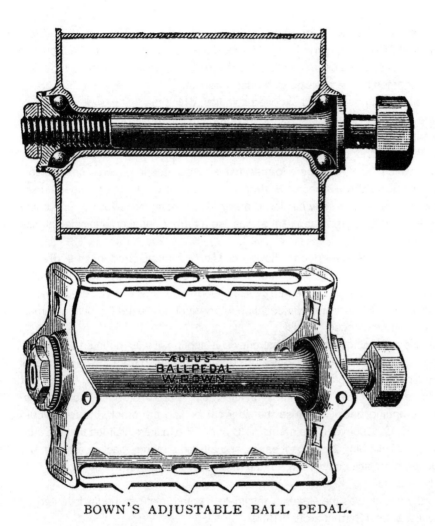

BOWN'S ADJUSTABLE BALL PEDAL.

Figure 9.8 Early rat-trap pedals with ball bearings (Sturmey 1885).

BALL PEDALS.

No. 842.

Best, **16**/- pair.   Medium, **10**/- pair.

TOE CLIPS.

No. 843, **1/9** per pair.

WATERSON'S PATENT PEDALS.

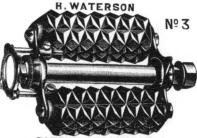

PATENT 17940 1893

(Adjusts to any width of Boots).

Price **Extra,** if fitted on Sunbeams in place
of ball pedals, usually supplied, **19**/-

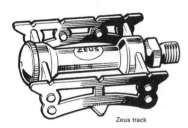

Zeus track

Campagnolo road

Lyotard platform

Figure 9.9   Pedals shown in Sunbeam's 1894 catalog.
Figure 9.10   Racing pedals of the pre-clipless era (R. John Way).

Toe clips

Keeping the rider's feet on the pedals isn't difficult when the rider is a leisurely commuter wearing "sensible shoes," but for an enthusiastic rider, especially a racing cyclist, a system to hold the foot on the pedal more securely is desirable. The sandal-like overshoes fixed to the treadles of 1850s tricycles and quadricycles provided one way of doing this.

In the late 1880s, interest in toe clips began to increase. For example, the patent drawing shown here in figure 9.11 shows toe clips on a high-wheeler. By 1894, Sunbeam was listing toe clips as a standard accessory. That same year, Raleigh offered the Zimmerman toe clip (named for Raleigh's star rider, the American Arthur Zimmerman). From the mid 1890s on, as the safety bicycle developed rapidly, there was a flurry of patents for various types of toe clips, some incorporating strapping systems. Elastic, leather, and metal straps were all tried. One product that reached the market was the Whaley Adjustable Bicycle Stirrup. This combined a steel clip (to stop the toe of the shoe from sliding forward) with a broad steel-edged leather band that wrapped around the forward part of the shoe.

For many decades, most toe clips were simple in design and made of wire or pressed steel. (A few were made of aluminum alloy.) Adjustable leather straps were used. Buckled straps were used from about 1900 on. Self-clinching buckles became popular in the 1930s. A later refinement of the self-clinching buckle, the Binda buckle (named for the racing cyclist Alfredo Binda), incorporated a brass or plastic roller.

The more serious riders added cleats to the soles of their shoes. These were slotted to engage with the pedal cage when the strap was tightened, thus locking the rider's foot into the toe clip. Cleats (also known as shoe plates) were made of various materials. Steel and aluminum alloy cleats were most common, but wood, rubber, leather, and plastic cleats were available at various times. Plastic toe clips were popular for a while among riders of mountain bikes and are still available at the time of writing.

Half-clips, with the front end of a conventional toe clip but without an extension to accommodate a strap, have been produced intermittently throughout the history of the toe clip and have been used by riders who considered straps an encumbrance. The clips listed by Sunbeam and Raleigh in 1894 were of this pattern. Half-clips still have a small following, particularly among urban riders and casual mountain-bike riders.

Clipless pedals

Confusingly, at the heart of each and every so-called clipless pedal is a clip. Such pedals are called clipless because they don't have an external toe clip. Instead, they have fastener, which

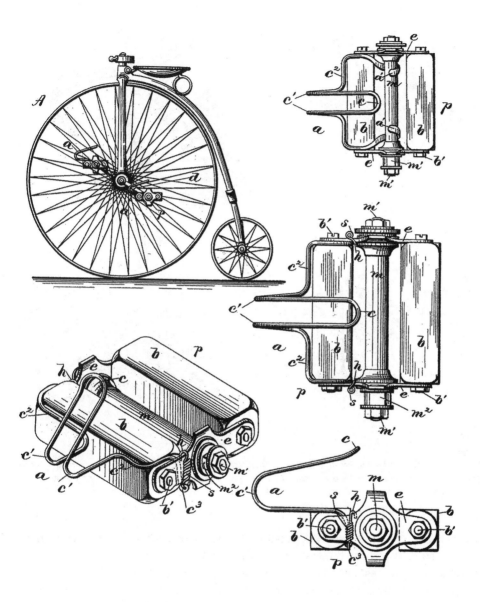

Figure 9.11 An 1889 patent drawing by William Rankin of Rhode Island, who was awarded US patent 425,697 of 1890.

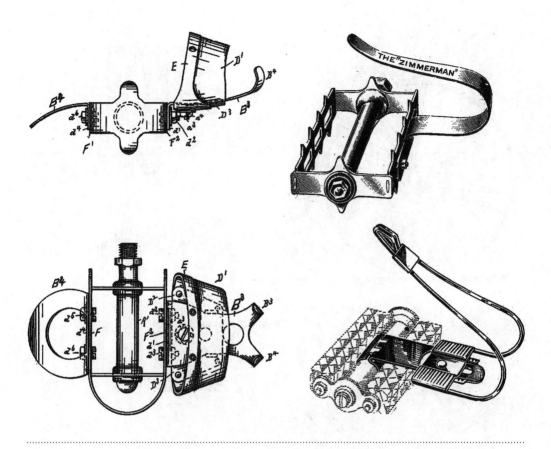

Figure 9.12 Left, above and below: Patent drawings of Whaley's toe clip. Above right: A 1894 Zimmerman toe clip made by Raleigh (catalog illustration). Below right: An adjustable toe clip for use with rubber block pedals, circa 1950 (reprinted, with permission, from *Every Cyclist's Pocket Book* by F. J. Camm, published by Newnes in 1950).

a special cleat on the sole of the shoe locks onto. (The more technically correct terms "step-in" or "clip-in" are sometimes used but are not widely known.)

The explosion of interest in pedal-clip design that began around 1894 led to a number of patents for clipless systems. Charles Hanson of Rhode Island is credited with the first patent (US patent 550,409 of 1895); it involved a four-spoke cleat on the shoe and a plate with four matching hooks on the pedal. A slight twist of the ankle engaged the cleat with the pedal plate.

Hanson's device was quite fragile and awkward to use. An alternative devised by Elijah Harris and Albert Reed of Chicago (US patent 554,686 of 1896) used suction cups on the

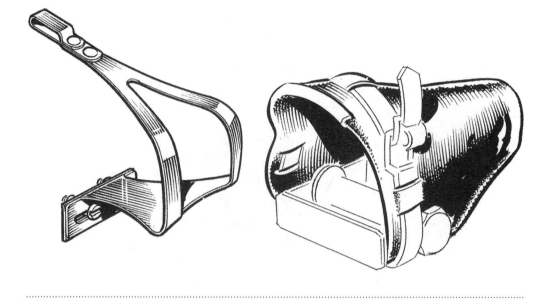

Figure 9.13   Left: A typical steel non-adjustable toe clip. Right: Shoe covers for winter riding (R. John Way).

pedals. This required the use of smooth soles to push the air out of the suction cups, creating a vacuum that would hold the shoes onto the pedals. More practical was the simple system designed by Marmaduke Matthews of Ontario in 1895 (US patent 590,685 of 1897). Each side of the pedal had a metal plate with gripping teeth, which engaged with recessed cleats in the soles of the rider's shoes. However, unlike Hanson's design, this had no "float" to allow the foot to rotate slightly relative to the pedal. It would have necessitated very precise alignment of foot and pedal to get the clip to engage. And it probably was very hard to get out of once clipped in.

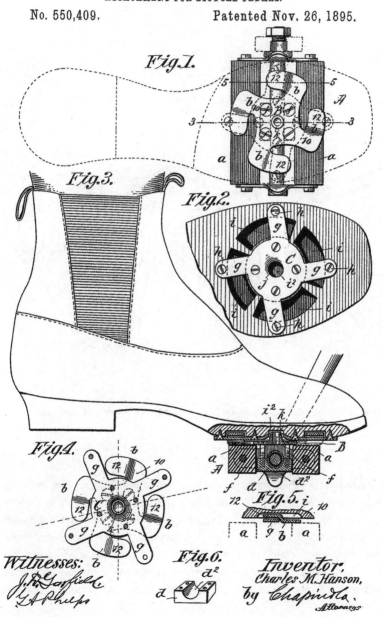

C. M. HANSON.
ATTACHMENT FOR BICYCLE PEDALS.

No. 550,409.

Patented Nov. 26, 1895.

Fig.1.

Fig.3.

Fig.2.

Fig.4.

Fig.5.

Fig.6.

Witnesses:

Inventor.
Charles M. Hanson,
by Chapin&Co.
Attorneys

Magnetic pedal attachments were designed in 1896 by Henry Tudor of Boston (US patent 588,038 of 1897). The pedals were fitted with permanent magnets, which magnetically engaged with soft iron plates strapped to the soles of the rider's shoes.

Many other clipless designs were produced, but none was commercially successful. For many decades, the simple toe-clip-and-strap system was the standard; serious sportsmen also used shoe cleats. But in the 1970s, interest in clipless pedals revived. In 1970, Cinelli introduced the M71 clipless pedal, which had a plastic cleat that slid into grooves in the pedal. Over the next dozen years, various inventors patented clip systems, some drawing inspiration from those used in ski bindings. Contak of Italy, NaturaLimits of the United States, and Keywin of New Zealand all introduced new clip systems, none of which sold particularly well.

A 1983 invention by Jean Bernard and Michel Mercier (US patent 4,686,867 of 1987) led to production of a clipless pedal by a company called Look. Bernard Hinault won the 1985 Tour de France using prototype Look pedals. He and Greg Lemond used Look pedals in the 1986 Tour de France and came in first and second respectively. Look's clipless pedals were the first to achieve significant commercial success.

Other makers continued to develop clipless designs, including Elger, Puma, CycleBinding, Avenir, Sampson, Aerolite, MKS, and Campagnolo. The Time pedal, patented in 1988 by Jean Beyl, reintroduced rotational float, a feature that was inherent in Hanson's 1894 design. Other notable designs were Richard Bryne's Speedplay X (1989) and Masashi Nagano's Shimano SPD mountain bike pedals with recessed cleats (1990).

Shimano's first clipless road pedals were made under a license from Look, but in 1993 Shimano introduced its own SPD (Shimano Pedaling Dynamics) road pedal, which had an exceptionally small cleat. The SPD system eventually became the market leader.

Henry Tudor's 1896 idea of a magnetic clipless pedal was revived a century later in the form of the Exus Mag Flux pedal, made in Taiwan. Mavic of France and the American company Proton Locks subsequently introduced magnetic pedals. The MPSG (Magnetic Pedal System Germany) was based on a 2005 design by Germans Wolfgang Duerr and Norbert Sadler (Taiwan patent 1,279,356 of 2007).

Nearly all racing cyclists adopted clipless pedals, which were much easier to disengage from than traditional toe clips used with cleats. However, touring cyclists who didn't use cleats, and didn't tighten their toe straps fully, didn't necessarily find them easier to use. Most clipless pedals required a twist of the ankle to disengage the pedal. That wasn't the first instinctive

Figure 9.14 Hanson's clipless pedal of 1895 (patent drawing).

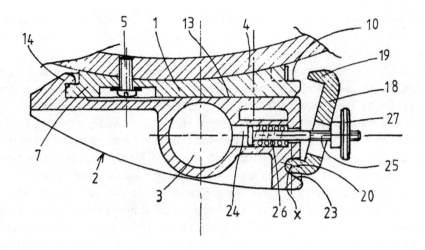

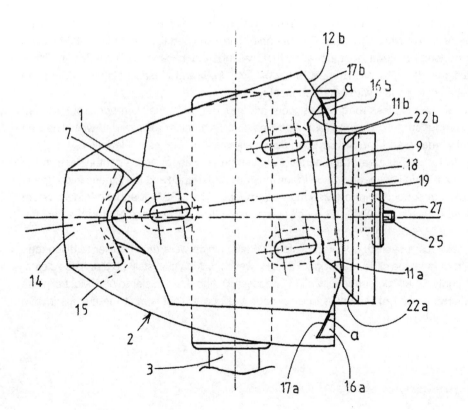

reaction, and a failure to disengage quickly enough could lead to a fall—especially if an emergency stop was required. The first instinctive reaction—to snatch the foot backward—could work well with traditional toe clips, but only if all four of the following conditions applied: the sole of the shoe was smooth, cleats weren't used, the straps weren't tightened fully, and the straps were placed around or ahead of the widest part of the foot.

For riders who weren't certain whether clipless pedals would suit them, combination pedals were available that could be used in clipless mode, or with traditional toe clips and straps, or without any form of clip.

At the International Cycle History Conference hosted by Shimano in Sakai, Japan in 2000, a questioner asked senior Shimano executives whether the company had ever been unsuccessful in developing an innovative idea and bringing it to market. The reply was Yes: this had happened when the company had tried to develop a clipless pedal for the everyday cyclist.

HANDLEBARS

Materials

The first handlebars, created by Karl Drais, were made of wood. Some cheap American bicycles had wooden handlebars as late as the 1890s. But most early bicycles had iron or steel handlebars, typically formed from round-section rod. With the development of the safety bicycle came the adoption of tubular steel handlebars. Later, those seeking lighter weight adopted handlebars made of aluminum alloy.

Aluminum alloy wasn't rapidly adopted in all markets. Though lighter, it was usually more expensive and always more susceptible to failure through fatigue cracking. Track riders stuck with steel for its strength. Some other riders were cautious about adopting aluminum alloy for handlebars or stems well into the 1960s (Way 1973, 59). National tastes and the influence of market-leading firms on those tastes also came into play. For example, by the 1960s, while makers of British roadsters used steel components exclusively, Belgian manufacturers of utility bikes were using alloy extensively, including for the handlebars. In Italy, steel is still widely used for roadster handlebars.

Figure 9.15   The first Look clipless pedal, designed in 1983 (patent drawing).

During the Cold War, the Soviet Union and the United States reserved considerable quantities of titanium for strategic military use. Titanium was therefore scarce, expensive, and rarely used for bicycle components. This situation changed after the fall of communism, and Russia began exporting large quantities of titanium for civilian use. Titanium handlebars became available; they were light, strong, and still relatively expensive.

Today there is considerable interest in carbon-fiber handlebars among racing cyclists, who appreciate its lightness and strength. Stefan Schmolke of Germany, who had made the first carbon-fiber handlebars, founded a company to manufacture them (Schmolke Carbon) in 1992. But steel and aluminum alloys are still the most widely used handlebar materials.

Configurations

Many different handlebar bends have been tried. Riders and designers soon became aware that, although an upright riding position was more comfortable, a stooped position reduced air resistance and made it possible to go faster. As was mentioned in chapter 3, drop handlebars of a sort were invented by 1879, in the high-wheeler era. Bars with an element of "drop," so the hands could be placed lower than the point at which the bars connected with the handlebar stem, were used on very early safety bicycles in the late 1880s and the early 1890s.

Figures 9.16–9.18 show some handlebar configurations that were popular in the United Kingdom at various times. Figure 9.16 shows a selection of handlebars offered by Raleigh at the beginning of the twentieth century, when the company categorized these broadly as "flat," "upturned," and "dropped." Figure 9.17 shows bars that were popular in the 1930s and the 1940s. Figure 9.18 shows some bar styles of the 1960s. The Maes drop pattern (bottom left), named for Belgian racer Sylvère Maes, was popular among racing cyclists. Porteur-style flat bars and "comfort" bars gave way to the straighter "all-rounder," which was typically fitted to sports light roadsters (sometimes referred to in North America as "English three-speeds").

Today there is a wide choice of handlebars. Drops are still around, the ergo or anatomic patterns being particularly popular. These have a flat section on the lower part of the drop curve. Aerobars can be bolted onto drop bars; they enable the rider to crouch very far forward, with both hands close together for a more aerodynamic profile, and are often used in time trials and in triathlons.

The handlebars on most mountain bikes are straight or nearly straight. Raised mountain-bike bars have a dip in the center where they connect with the stem, so that the riding position is a little higher.

North Road bars (named for London's North Road Cycling Club) and similar swept-back upright bars are popular on city bikes in Germany and the Netherlands. Butterfly bars,

Box 9.1

THE HANDLEBAR

In 1880 *The Cyclist* had this to say about the variations of handlebars in the high-wheeler era:

Perhaps no single portion of the bicycle marks the general improvement of the age so much as the handle-bar, for by looking at this alone the experienced eye is almost enabled to give the year in which the machine to which it is attached was turned out. The present season is remarkable for the length to which these have attained, and we have reason to believe that the limit in this respect that is in a general way is by no means yet reached. The climax in the direction of shortness was reached three years since, when few handles were turned out exceeding 18 inches in length, and we remember about that time riding a 54 inches [front wheel diameter] with handles scarcely 15 inches long, so short in fact that our hands came over the middle of our legs. The length of the handle-bars has seen a gradual contraction and subsequent extension to far beyond their original limits, for when bicycles first came into common use makers were sensible enough to affix rudders with a fair leverage, and found an almost universal measurement in 21 inches and 22 inches—sometimes more but rarely less; then as back-wheels grew smaller, riders, hitherto accustomed to considerable weight behind, finding themselves relieved of this, took to frequent croppers in consequence, and then began to find to their cost that when performing an involuntary dismount their legs were cramped up and caught by the handle-bar, to the great detriment of their facial extremities; this set the writers of the period thinking, and a persistent advocacy of very short steering-rods induced manufacturers to adopt them, and vie with each other in the shortness of these appendages to their machines, the theory being that in the case of a cropper the legs could be easily freed, and the rider alight on his feet. This was all very well during the summer months, and short handlebars were all the rage for the space of one season, but when the winter came on and the

Box 9.1
(Continued)

roads became plentifully interspersed with ruts, hard mud, and loose stones, the lack of sufficient leverage told its tale in the increased difficulty and danger of getting out of ruts and avoiding obstacles, and the greater amount of work required from the arms. Then, too, riders gained experience, and became accustomed to the small, light wheels behind, riding more carefully and not mounting with a rush and a jump, and as a matter of course were safer upon their machines, and could go out for a spin without the expectation of 'coming a cropper' four or five times before their return. The necessity therefore of providing so carefully for their safety in this respect grew less, and makers last season added a couple of inches to their handle-bars, and as cyclists grew still more to be parts of their machines and to work automatically with them, so did the handle-rods grow in length, until the present season finds few road machines provided with handles less than 22 inches long and few racers with less than 24 inches, and we think we can foresee that two additional inches will be the rule for next season, for a long handle-bar not only gives greater command over the machine in guiding it clear of stones and ruts, but by straightening the arms enables the rider to exert his power with much greater ease, comfort, and effectiveness when riding hills or putting on a spurt, as well as conducing to a freer and less cramped attitude when on the machine, and a consequently greater expansion of the chest. It must not, however, be forgotten that very much further elongation of the rudder is not advisable, as when the handles are too long for the rider's length of arm he is obliged to stoop forward in order to reach them, an action tending to contract the chest and produce the 'bicycle back' so lately thrown at us by a certain captious critic, which although ridiculous under the present circumstances, may not after all be so absurd in the future if handle-bars are allowed to exceed the range of reason.

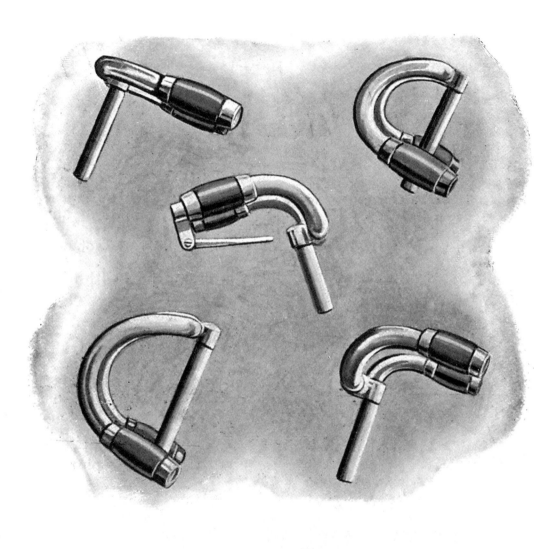

Figure 9.16   Raleigh handlebars of 1903 (catalog illustration).

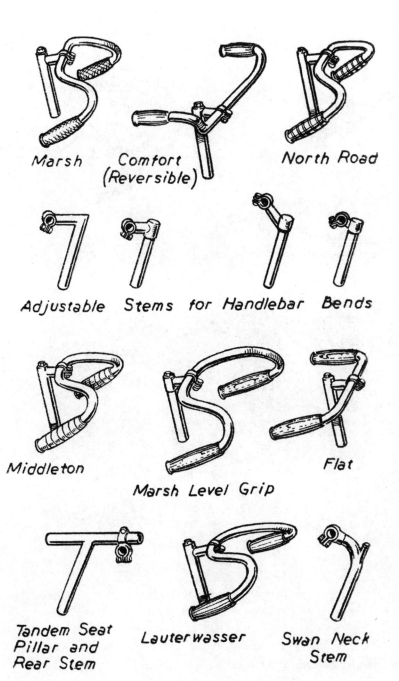

Marsh

Comfort
(Reversible)

North Road

Adjustable   Stems   for   Handlebar   Bends

Middleton

Marsh Level Grip

Flat

Tandem Seat
Pillar and
Rear Stem

Lauterwasser

Swan Neck
Stem

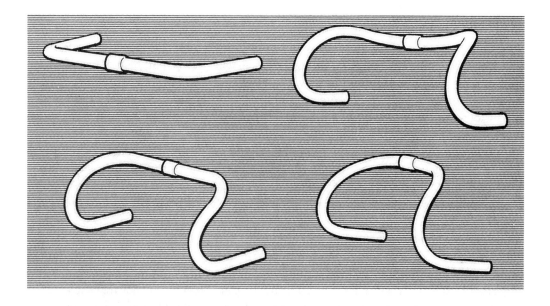

Figure 9.17 Handlebars and stems popular in the 1930s and the 1940s (reprinted, with permission, from *Every Cyclist's Pocket Book* by F. J. Camm, published by Newnes in 1950).
Figure 9.18 Handlebar bends popular in the 1960s (R. John Way).

which resemble a figure eight with a gap in it, offer a wide variety of hand positions without necessitating bending down as far as drop handlebars. They are popular in northern Europe, especially on trekking bikes.

Ape-hanger or high-rise bars may have been first used in the United States on youngster's bikes designed so that a sack of newspapers could fit in the dip. They became popular in the US during the high-riser craze of the 1960s, when bicycles styled to resemble customized motorcycles were in fashion. The American high-riser craze, promoted by Schwinn, was followed by the British Chopper craze of the 1970s, instigated by Raleigh.

Tracker bars (somewhat similar to ape-hangers, some with a bracing bar) were sold in the UK during a cycle speedway boom in the years after World War II. Dawes used the Hi-Lo (a more compact version of the high-riser bar) from the 1960s to the 1980s on its Kingpin bikes; it allowed some fore and aft adjustment to suit riders of different sizes. A bar with a similar bend is standard on most Brompton folding bicycles; it allows the use of a shorter folding headstock.

Handlebar stems

With mass production of the safety bicycle, handlebar stems became increasingly standard-ized. For many decades, nearly all stems were adjustable for height; many of those made today still are. Although external clamps were sometimes used, most stems were held in the steerer tube telescopically by an expansion mechanism. Typically, a pinch bolt pulled a cone into a slotted section at the base of the stem, thus expanding its diameter to grip the inside of the steerer. Later designs, popular from the 1980s on, used a tapered wedge nut, which was less likely than a cone to jam. These systems are still used, but another system is also now commonplace. Used in the increasingly prevalent threadless headsets, it was invented in 1990 by Homer J. Rader III of Dallas (US patent 590,575 of 1992) and was originally sold by Dia Compe as the Aheadset. In this design, the steerer extends beyond the top of the bicycle frame's head tube. In a departure from traditional practice, it isn't externally threaded. Instead, the handlebar stem clamps onto the steerer, holding the steering bearings in place. A headset of this design is very strong, and the bearings rarely require attention. The major disadvantage is that the height of the stem can't be changed easily. One can reduce the height by removing spacers between the upper steering bearing and the stem, then cutting down the steerer. But one can increase the height only by using a stem canted at a steeper angle, by fitting a com-plete new fork with a longer steerer, or by using a rather inelegant adapter.

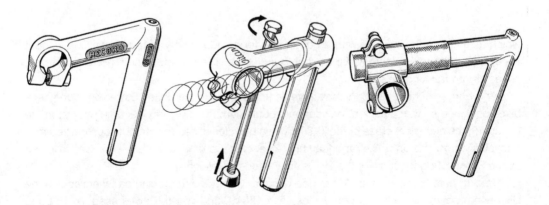

Figure 9.19 Alloy stems of the 1960s. The middle illustration shows the range of different extension lengths offered and the expander bolt and cone. The Cinelli stem on the right is adjustable for extension length (R. John Way).

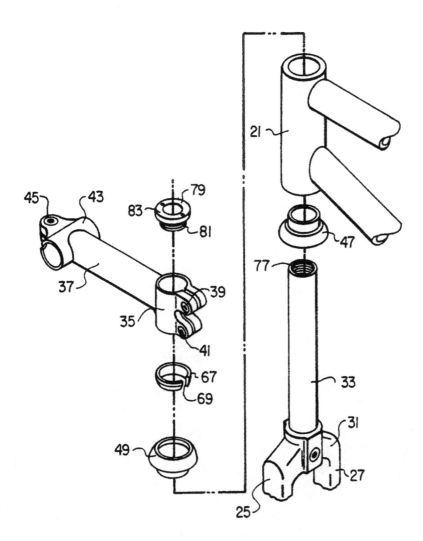

Figure 9.20 Patent drawing for Homer J. Rader's Aheadset.

LIGHTING 10

....

The need for lighting as an aid to night riding was felt from the earliest days of bicycling. This chapter recounts how new methods of lighting were pressed into service for cyclists and how those applications evolved thereafter.

CANDLE LANTERNS AND OIL LANTERNS

Candles were long the standard means of lighting doors, rooms, or coaches. They were cheap, and they were easy to store and replenish. Wooden candle housings with glass sides were widely forbidden in the eighteenth century as fire hazards; they were superseded by safer sheet-metal lanterns. Two engravings preserved in Germany are thought to show candle lanterns in use on velocipedes in 1817, and several candle lanterns appeared as options in the 1869 price list of the Compagnie Parisienne's front-cranked velocipedes.

Candle lanterns continued to be used by cyclists into the twentieth century, although they often served merely to fulfill legal requirements as "navigation lights." Candles for cycle lanterns were made of stearin, a glyceryl ester of stearic acid with a melting point higher than 50°C (122°F). The relatively solid top of the candle was pressed upward against a collar by a small coil spring. As the stearin was consumed, the base of the candle moved upward until the candle was used up. A spherical mirror behind the flame and a lens in front of it served to focus the light beam. A heavy jolt could extinguish the flame by splattering liquid stearin onto the candle's wick; the cyclist then had to dismount and light the candle again. Some candle lamps had weatherproof compartments in which matches could be stowed.

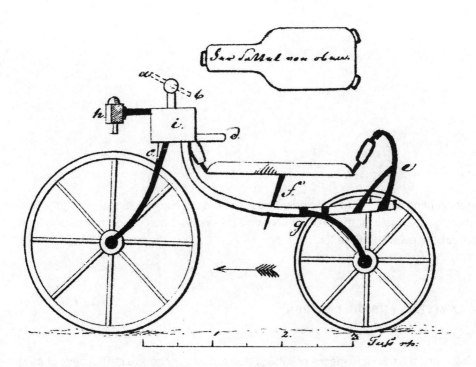

Figure 10.1 An 1817 drawing of a velocipede with a candle lantern (from Lessing 2003a).

In an early improvement patented by Biémont & Cie., a manufacturer of wagon lanterns, the housing of a candle lamp was suspended between two vertical coil springs to damp its bobbing on bumpy roads (French patent 85,346 of 1869). Another manufacturer, Henri Masson, made lamps of a similar design based on French patent 86,283 of 1869. Lamps with side windows of colored glass helped to make a velocipede visible from the side at night.

Oil lamps, with a wick held within the central hole of a lid covering the vessel or even floating on the oil, had been common since Roman times. The Argand lamp, introduced in 1783, was substantially brighter than a simple oil lamp; it produced a larger, brighter flame by drawing air from inside the tubular wick as well as from the outside. A glass cylinder around the flame provided an upward airflow that nourished the flame and protected it from wind gusts. The Argand lamp, brighter and less susceptible to flickering than earlier types, was soon in widespread use in the rooms of well-to-do people, then on their coaches. Olive oil, whale oil,

Figure 10.2 Riemann Germania lamps, candle and oil (Gerd Böttcher).

Figure 10.3 A Société Biémont candle lantern of 1869 (Reynaud 2008, ii).
Figure 10.4 A Lucas Silver King oil lamp (Gerd Böttcher).

or purified rape-seed oil was burned. Special lamps made to burn kerosene (called paraffin in the UK and petroleum on the Continent), which burned at a higher temperature, were built, but the unpleasant-smelling kerosene had impurities that caused it to produce a lot of soot. Moreover, it tended to sweat through any gasket.

Some riders of high-wheelers undertook long tours that included night riding. In Vienna, where riding was forbidden altogether until 1885, night riding was a way to evade the police. Cyclists who use oil lamps took care not to let the wick drown in the oil. Some began to mount their lamps on sprung parallelogram holders that damped the oscillations caused by riding on bad roads.

The front lamp holder that was standard on most British bicycles until the late twentieth century had an upward-facing "blade" onto which the lamp body slid. Adjusting the height of the wick by means of a knob on the side of the lamp allowed a rider to regulate brightness.

Breathing in the hot fumes rising from an oil lamp mounted near the handlebar wasn't pleasant. The hub lamp, introduced in the 1870s, mitigated the unpleasantness some. Edward Salsbury of the Salsbury Lamp Works in Long Acre, the wagoner's area in London, claimed to have invented the hub lamp (Card 2008). By 1878, Joseph Lucas of Birmingham was also making hub lamps. By 1880 he had developed the "divided style" hub lamp, which could be unfolded, squeezed through the spokes, folded back together, and hung from the front hub. (See figure 10.5.) Unfolding also made it easier to clean the lamp and to trim a crusted wick. The upper clamp that hugged the hub loosely was lined with felt; this provided damping, so the lamp that swung from the hub like a pendulum, wouldn't get whirled around, and would remain fairly vertical. The light (still rather feeble) had the advantage of being nearer to the road than that cast by a handlebar-mounted lamp. On the minus side, the rim and the tire blocked the center section of the beam, casting a shadow on the road.

Demand from the high-wheeler avant-garde substantially increased business for oil lamp manufacturers in many countries during the 1880s. A particularly famous brand of hub lamp was the King of the Road, made by Joseph Lucas & Son Ltd. Another company's lamp—the Monopol, made to be mounted on a cycle's steering head—had a circular wick and a glass cylinder for wind protection, as an Argand lamp did. With these lamps, sheet-metal production techniques entered the bicycle sector on a large scale.

BATTERY-POWERED LAMPS

Long before the British had electricity in their homes, electric lamps for their bicycles were available. At the 1888 Stanley Show, Joseph Lucas & Son of Birmingham introduced the New

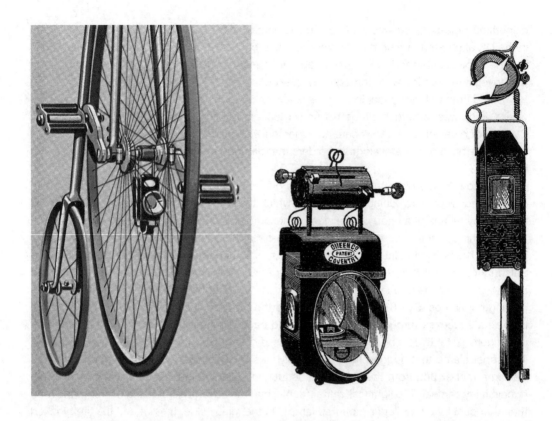

Figure 10.5 Left: A high-wheeler with a hub lamp (R. John Way). Center: The Queen of Lamps, an oil lamp made to hang on the front hub. Right: A Queen of Lamps made slender to slip between the spokes (Silberer 1883).

Patent Electric Lamp, priced at 55 shillings—more than a month's pay for some workers (Card 2006). There were two reasons for the high price: the cost of the bulb and the fact that Lucas had to pay royalties to Edward Vaughton, a Birmingham goldsmith. (Vaughton's British patent, number 14,622, had been awarded in 1887.) Vaughton's improved accumulator protected the cell plates from jolt-induced fractures by infilling the space between them with porous plates of asbestos. The New Patent Electric Lamp disappeared from the Lucas catalog after only a year. Two examples have survived; they resemble oil lamps of the period. Inside was a Bunsen element, consisting of a carbon cathode and an amalgamated zinc plate anode immersed in sulphuric acid. Opening the lid gave access to the terminals, which were connected to wires for recharging. The New Patent Electric Lamp's lack of commercial success may have been due in large part to the lack of electrical outlets in homes. To charge the battery, one would have to take it to one of the few shops or service stations that generated their own electricity. Forty years would pass before Lucas would launch its next battery lamp.

The Arabian Electric Cycle Lamp, first advertised in 1895 by the Arabian Oil Company of London, was also of the Bunsen type, but it differed from the New Patent Electric Lamp in that the housing (plated with zinc on the inside) served as one of the two electrodes; the other electrode, made of carbon, was again immersed in sulphuric acid, which could be obtained from any drugstore or pharmacy.

The Electric Portable Lamp Company of Elmira, New York introduced its Chloride lamp in 1896 (Card 2006). It consisted of a circular hard rubber container, with a screw-on lid, into which one placed zinc plates and special salts dissolved in water. The carbon-filament bulb would then glow for about four hours. Afterward, the rider would discard the liquid and rinse the plates with water. Before the next ride, new salt would have to be dissolved in water and put into the lamp with the plates.

Similar in design to the Chloride lamp was the Eclipse lamp, introduced by the Electric Lamp Company of Buffalo in 1896; it was powered by a salt powder ("electric sand") and diluted sulphuric acid.

Dry-cell batteries, which became available in 1898, were used to power La Marquette, a lamp manufactured by the Portable Electric Light Company of Chicago. A battery suspended from a cycle's top tube in a leather pouch could power La Marquette for about twenty hours (*The Electrical Engineer* 25, 1898, 566).

More brands of electric cycle lamps arose, but the advent of the acetylene-gas lamp sent the pioneer companies into oblivion. The carbon-filament bulbs used in the electrical lamps had been too sensitive to jolts and too costly to replace. Male bicycle enthusiasts liked to tinker with complicated acetylene lamps. Women, the ideal customers for the clean and silent electric lamps, had yet to take up cycling in large numbers. Not until 1911, when jolt-resistant tungsten-filament bulbs were introduced, did battery lamps for bicycles begin to reappear. They have remained in production ever since, sometimes evolving slowly and sometimes rapidly.

Bulb technology has advanced considerably since the 1980s. Halogen bulbs, though expensive, provided a significant improvement. Metal halide (non-incandescent) bulbs, used in the CatEye Stadium system of the 1990s, were better still but even more costly. Light-emitting diodes have improved gradually and are now widely used in bicycle lamps, usually in clusters of three or more. LEDs have proved very reliable and can run for very long periods on much smaller batteries than incandescent bulbs require.

Figure 10.6   The Electric Portable Lamp Company's Chloride model (*Scientific American*, May 1896).

ACETYLENE LAMPS

The year 1895 saw the beginning of industrial production of calcium carbide, which surpassed oil and candles for purposes of lighting. Dripping water on calcium carbide generated acetylene gas that burned with a bright flame that was compared by the marketing men to sunlight. This was, however, accompanied by a bad smell generated when impurities of the carbide reacted with the water. Acetylene bicycle lamps soon appeared, meant to be mounted at the steering head or aside the front wheel of a safety bicycle. A claim that an acetylene lamp was manufactured by F. H. Fuller in 1895 under the auspices of the Illinois Acetylene Company remains unsubstantiated (Card 2008). The first such lamp known to have been available, an

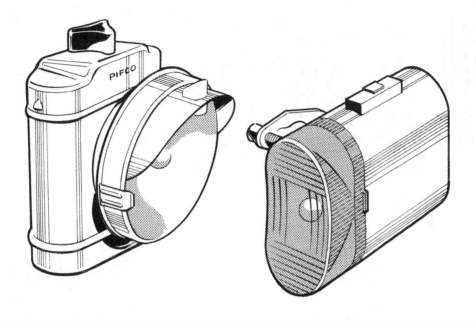

Figure 10.7 Typical British battery lamps of the 1960s and the 1970s (R. John Way).

acetylene lamp named the Solar, was introduced by the Solar Acetylene Lamp Company of Chicago in 1897. The English Lucas firm introduced its Acetylator in the same year. Lamps of this type were subsequently produced in all Western countries and are still produced in India today.

An acetylene lamp could explode if the gas was allowed to accumulate and then was ignited by a nearby flame. There are reports that some acetylene lamps made of copper exploded when struck during use (Dyer 1940). Precarious situations could arise after a night ride if the wet carbide hadn't been used up and continued to generate acetylene. It was wise to estimate how long a night ride would take and how much carbide would be needed. Upon getting home, a cyclist usually put the lamp outside a window to let the carbide use itself up and the acetylene escape unburned into the air. The lamp had to be removed from the bicycle in

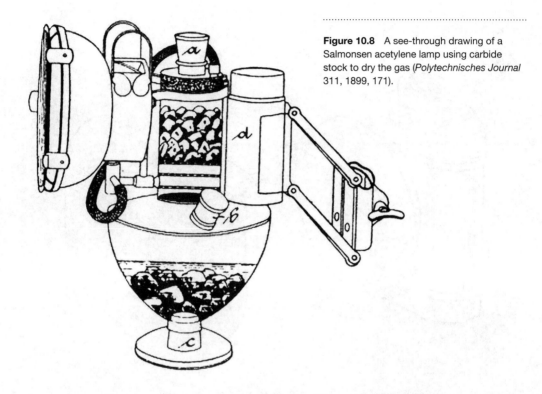

Figure 10.8 A see-through drawing of a Salmonsen acetylene lamp using carbide stock to dry the gas (*Polytechnisches Journal* 311, 1899, 171).

any case, since the carbide, having reacted, baked solid and stuck to the housing. A thorough cleaning was needed after every ride. Eventually, pre-packaged carbide cartridges for rides of different durations were offered. The paper wrapper of such a cartridge allowed clean removal of the carbide slurry after a ride, even if it was wet.

Many ingenious acetylene lamps were put on the market. The basic arrangement was a carbide vessel at the bottom covered by a sieve to hold the carbide down during out-gassing. Water dripped from a reservoir above through a thin central tube onto the carbide. A flexible hose directed the gases through a filter to the ceramic burner, which had two or more bores. Provision was made to facilitate clearing the bores by blowing air through them with the standard bicycle pump. (See figure 10.9.) By squeezing the hose, the flame could be extinguished. The central tube had a valve that could be opened by turning it counterclockwise by means of a knob, whereupon the water would begin dripping down. A rider could adjust the speed of dripping, and therefore the generation of acetylene and the brightness of the flame, by means of the valve. Some brands solved the problem of administering the carbide for a shorter ride by means of a sectored carbide container that the rider could turn. If the carbide in a sector was nearly used up, the rider would turn the container to the next sector. Some lamps allowed a rider to relight an extinguished flame without dismounting. Turning a handle on the side of a lamp called the Triumph (manufactured in Berlin by Max Retemeyer) caused a hammer to strike a band of percussion-activated primer and thus to reignite the acetylene. (See figure 10.9.)

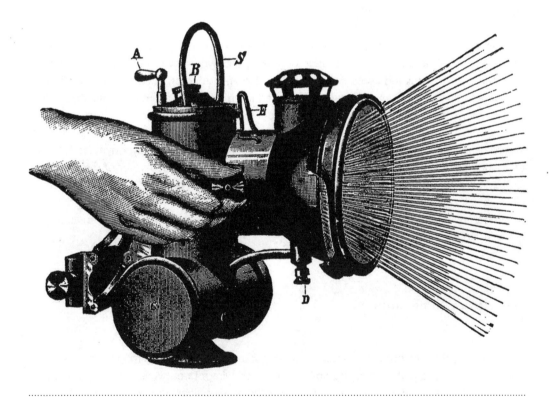

Figure 10.9 A Retemeyer Triumph acetylene lamp (*Polytechnisches Journal* 313, 1899, 188). Hand wheel reignites extinguished flame. A bicycle pump cleans burner via D.

TIRE-DRIVEN DYNAMOS

In the 1880s, once carbon-filament bulbs were available, a new possibility occurred to some inventors who were interested in cycling: Why not have the rider drive a tiny dynamo that would provide electricity for a lamp? This idea was taken up and turned into reality by a mechanic in Leipzig named Richard Weber. He may have been inspired by Sigfried Marcus of Vienna, who obtained a patent for using a gas-motor-driven dynamo to generate electricity for the motor's ignition system (British patent 2,423 of 1882). Weber obtained two British patents (5,078 in 1886 and 16,603 in 1887) for a miniature dynamo in a rectangular box with a friction wheel that could be pressed sideways by a spring onto the tire of the high-wheeler or tricycle. He then tried to sell his Excelsior Electric Lighting in the run-up to the First Grand General Exhibition of Bicycles and Cycleparts of Germany at Leipzig in 1889 (Wolf 1890).

Weber's first patent utilized the dynamo principle, discovered by Werner Siemens and Charles Wheatstone in 1866. Both the stator and the rotor consisted of bobbins on soft-iron cores. A lever allowed a cyclist to engage or release the dynamo while riding. A commutator consisting of two insulated contact rings with brushes, mounted on the axle opposite the friction wheel, allowed the current that was generated to be carried to a lamp. The second patent led to a more compact dynamo and to the use of a parabolic reflector for the lamp.

Electrical generators used on bicycles are usually referred to as dynamos. Although both everyday speech and major dictionaries allow the use of "dynamo" as a synonym for "generator," electrical engineers typically reserve "dynamo" to describe a generator of direct current (DC). Most later bicycle dynamos, such as the classic Sturmey-Archer Dynohub, were actually alternators, producing alternating current (AC). In this chapter, we generally use the term "dynamo" in its looser, everyday sense; we differentiate between a dynamo and an alternator where the distinction is important.

EARLY DYNAMO DESIGNS

A typical early dynamo had, as a stator, a powerful fixed permanent-field magnet, between the poles of which an armature carrying coils of insulated wire rotated. When rotating, the armature coils "cut" the lines of magnetic force, inducing an electrical current. The metal frame of the bicycle was often used as a part of the circuit to carry the current from the dynamo to the lamp, so that only one wire was needed.

Figure 10.10 Illustrations of Richard Weber's tire-driven dynamo lighting system from the drawings for his 1886 British patent. Inset: A portrait of Weber (Gerd Böttcher).

In 1892, longer-lasting bulbs with filaments of osmium and tantalum became available. A flurry of activity among bicycle dynamo inventors in the northeastern United States began in 1894, but there was no initial consensus on how to drive the dynamo.

One early patent, held by George Mayr of Brooklyn (US patent 521,721, granted in 1894), entailed fixing a dynamo to the seat tube and speeding up the rotation of its armature by means of a gearbox driven by a lightweight chain from a sprocket on the rear wheel.

Another early patent was held by Ernest Tillmann, a Frenchman living in New York (US patent 532,840 of 1895). Tillmann's design, like Mayr's, put the dynamo on the seat tube, but Tillmann proposed the use of a friction-driven pulley and a belt. A conical rubber roller on the pulley's axle was to engage with the inside of one wheel's rim.

Figure 10.11 Patent drawings from the 1890s by (from top down) Tilmann, Mayr, Libbey, and Magee. As these drawings show, there was no consensus on where to place a dynamo on a bicycle or on how to drive it.

Hosea Libbey of Boston came up with yet another drive system (US patent 567,719 of 1896). His dynamo, which had electromagnets instead of the permanent magnets, was placed over the front wheel and driven, by means of bevel gears, by a friction wheel in contact with the running surface of the tire. Alfred Rodriguez of Brooklyn (US patent 568,209 of 1896) also placed a dynamo over the front wheel. He used a pair of self-centering tapered rubber-faced friction rollers running on the top of the tire to drive the dynamo by means of a pair of pulleys and a short belt. His dynamo was combined with a headlamp. Rodriguez also patented a combined dynamo and headlamp that could be mounted just above the front axle. This dynamo was driven by a flexible shaft from a friction pulley running on one sidewall of a tire (US patent 583,945 of 1897).

Francis Magee of Brooklyn proposed mounting a dynamo under the saddle, on the backs of the seat stays, and driving it with a long belt from a pulley on the rear wheel (US patent 572,430 of 1896). Magee's design incorporated an anti-overload device to prevent the bulb being burned out by excessive voltage. At a certain speed, a centrifugal switch doubled the internal electrical resistance of the armature, thus reducing the output current.

Malcolm Ryder of Westfield, New Jersey invented another combined dynamo and headlamp. It was clamped to the top of a fork blade and driven by the action of the running surface of the tire on a friction roller (US patent 586,399 of 1897).

Edwin Wilson Farnham of Chicago patented a dynamo in which the armature was fixed but the magnets rotated with the dynamo's cylindrical casing (US patent 591,623 of 1897). The casing was a horizontal drum that doubled as a friction roller, driven by the top of the front tire. Farnham claimed that his design offered better protection of the dynamo from dust and dirt. Sidney Latham Holdrege of Boston made similar claims for his dynamo (US patent 643,095 of 1900), which also took the form of a horizontal drum running as a friction roller on the top of the front tire. None of these designs appears to have been a significant commercial success, although Farnham's was advertised.

Another 1897 design, by Paul Wagner of Strasbourg, involved a dynamo driven by a belt that took power either from the inside of the rim of either wheel (by means of a friction pulley) or from a groove on the edge of a specially made wheel rim (British patent 16,919 of 1897). This complicated approach wasn't commercially successful.

TOWARD THE DOMINANCE OF THE "BOTTLE" DYNAMO

An enduringly successful early dynamo was the Voltalite, first marketed in 1895 and made by Ward & Goldstone of Salford, near Manchester. The Voltalite was well established by 1912,

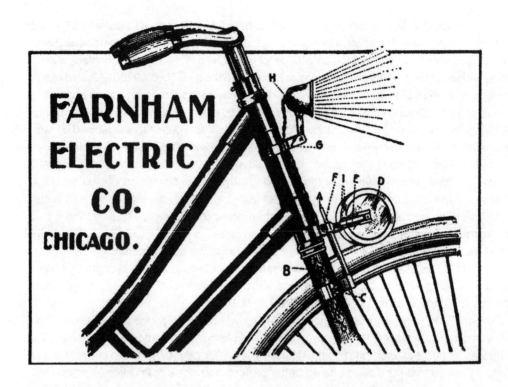

Figure 10.12 An 1898 advertisement for a Farnham dynamo.

and as late as 1926 it was still the main brand of dynamo stocked by the major British distributor, Brown Brothers. The Voltalite had a horizontal armature with a friction pulley running on the inside of the front wheel rim. In a 1912 advertisement it was claimed to be "the most successful electric cycle lamp invented" and to give "equally brilliant light at walking speed as at 50 miles per hour."

But it was the "bottle-shaped" vertical dynamo, driven by a friction pulley running on one sidewall of a tire, that was eventually to prove the most commercially and enduringly successful dynamo design. James Wilson of Battle Creek, Michigan designed such a dynamo in 1901 (US patent 699,734 of 1902). Meant to be clamped to the top of one blade of the fork, it had a friction pulley below its body and a headlamp above it.

Once the basic form had been established, many of the patents relating to bicycle dynamos were for refinements (friction pulleys, bearings, anti-overload protection, mounting devices,

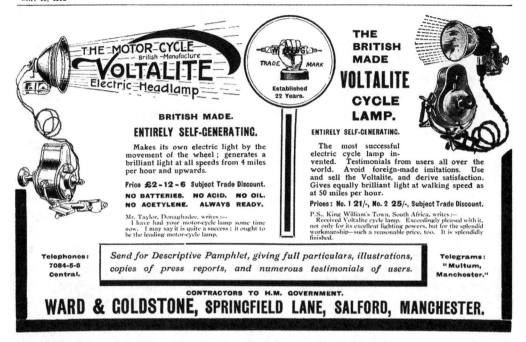

Figure 10.13 A 1912 advertisement for Voltalite dynamos (National Cycle Library).

sprung pivots, and so on) rather than radical breakthroughs. Occasionally, however, an alternative drive system was proposed. For example, Harry Van Deventer of Sumter, South Carolina patented a combined dynamo and headlamp that was to be driven, like a mechanical speedometer, by a flexible cable from a bevel gear clipped onto the hub of the front wheel (US patent 1,355,581 of 1920).

More dynamo patents specifying flexible drive appeared between the 1890s and the 1930s. A design by Carl McDermott of Freehold, New Jersey specified stationary field coils and an armature comprising centrifugally controlled permanent magnets (US patent 2,088,029 of 1937). As the speed of rotation increased, the centrifugal mechanism partially withdrew the magnets from the coils, thus maintaining a safe voltage.

The use of a centrifugal device to limit voltage wasn't new. In 1919, the French cycle maker Peugeot had designed a bottle dynamo with a centrifugal regulator. At speeds above

10 kilometers (about 6 miles) per hour, metal blades moved under centrifugal force to shunt the magnetic field and keep it more or less constant. Peugeot's British patent was, however, voided at provisional stage (British patent 145,010 of 1920).

In 1919, Rudolf Frauenfelder of Grenchen, Switzerland designed a bottle dynamo combined with a headlamp in a compact casing (British patent 148,277 of 1920). The armature shaft was in a threaded sleeve that secured the horseshoe-magnet stator to the housing. Three years later, Helliwell of Birmingham was selling a dynamo combined with rear lamp. Called the Helco, it had a die-cast aluminum body, built-in overload protection, and a horizontal armature shaft. The friction pulley ran on the inside of one wheel's rim. The design was protected by a provisional patent (British patent 12,144 of 1922). Soon, however, the bottle dynamo eclipsed it.

In 1923, Miller of Birmingham introduced a lighting set with a bottle dynamo. Charles Albert Miller and Frederick John Miller obtained British patent 192,798 in the same year, having applied in 1921. This patent covered various improvements to the mounting and the spring loading of friction-driven dynamos.

By 1927, Lucas, Britain's largest maker of electrical equipment for cars and motorcycles, had introduced its King of the Road bottle dynamos. A dozen years later, Brown Brothers stocked a wide range of bottle dynamos, and no longer stocked Voltalites and other dynamos of older design. Brown Brothers' 1939 catalog included dynamos from the leading British makers, Miller and Lucas, from Belmag, Challenge, and Lucifer of Switzerland, from Soubitez of France, from Berko and Bosch of Germany. Among the other brands listed were Arclyte, Bemo, Impex, Jux, Mandaw, Philidyne, and Seeco.

After World War I, the Robert Bosch Company of Germany patented a combined lamp and dynamo with a flexible shaft (German patent 325,243 of 1918). Bosch also proposed using a freewheel to let the dynamo spin like a flywheel and continue to generate power when the bicycle wasn't in motion, but it was never produced.

In the mid 1930s there was a flurry of interest in dynamos with flexible drive shafts. The aim was to avoid the need for the body of the dynamo to pivot to engage its friction pulley with the tire sidewall. Instead, the dynamo could be permanently fixed in an accurately aligned position, and only the pulley would move on its flexible shaft. Albert Victor Lafbery of Raleigh designed a dynamo of this sort in 1935 (British patent 452,940 of 1936). Alfred Huyton of Joseph Lucas Limited also designed one; the patent (British patent 462,678 of 1937) was applied for only four months after Raleigh's. Both designs had the friction roller below the body of the dynamo. Carl McDermott of Freehold, New Jersey proposed a flexible a drive shaft connecting a dynamo mounted under the frame's top tube to a friction pulley running on the rear tire sidewall (US patent 2,299,762 of 1942). Despite its recurring appeal to inventors, flexible drive was an inefficient "blind alley" and never caught on. The simple bottle dynamo was to prove a very enduring design.

The "Helco" Dynamo

(Combined Dynamo and Rear Lamp)

Cycle Lighting Set

(Prov. Patent No. 12144/22).

Solves the Rear Light Question.

The "Helco" Dynamo Lighting Set is designed and manufactured by engineers, is beautifully made, and can be fitted to any cycle in five minutes.

The dynamo and rear lamp are enclosed in an aluminium die casting, highly polished. The front lamp is brass, heavily plated.

The Set lights at **SLOW** walking pace, and **CANNOT BURN OUT AT ANY SPEED.**

We will replace, free of charge, any of our dynamos that prove unsatisfactory through faulty materials or workmanship.

The Rear Lamp.
"it never fails."   Showing Set fixed on Cycle.

Don't worry about your rear light! Use the "Helco," and **know positively** that if the head lamp is all right, the rear lamp **MUST BE!**

18/6

Postage 9d.

Stocked by all the leading Cycle Agents, or direct from the manufacturers—

HELLIWELL & CO.,
349, Bristol Rd., Birmingham.

Figure 10.14 A 1922 advertisement for a Helco dynamo (National Cycle Library).

MILLER CYCLE DYNAMO SET.

The Miller Cycle Dynamo Set embodies all the good points necessary to make this form of lighting successful. Full details are given in separate booklet, which will be forwarded on application.

The lamp is supplied complete with bracket, clips, and wiring, ready for attachment to bicycle, an operation which can be performed in a very few minutes.

Price :
No. 56C.D.,
Head Lamp and Dynamo,
£1 2 0

Cable Code : 00110.

No. 57C.D.,
complete with Tail Lamp,
£1 5 0

Cable Code : 00111.

The Lamps that won't go out

Figure 10.15   Left: A 1923 advertisement for a Miller dynamo (National Cycle Library). Right: The Bosch Rad-Licht dynamo set, introduced in 1923 (Robert Bosch GmbH).

Figure 10.16   A few of the Lucas dynamo lighting sets in Brown Brothers' 1939 catalog (National Cycle Library).

201

LAMPS (DYNAMO ELECTRIC)—*continued*
"LUCAS" CYCLE DYNAMO ELECTRIC LIGHTING SETS
LESS BATTERIES
Complete with Bulbs and 6 volt, 0·5 amp. or 3-watt Dynamo.

LUCAS
No506 SET

LUCAS
No503 SET

LUCAS
No505 SET

Model No. 506.

Chromium Plated Head Lamp, streamlined rust-proof Brass Body, special rubber socket shock absorbing Bracket. Domed Glass, Green side glasses, Switch on top. Dynamo **C25PU**, with improved trigger release, universal Carrier Bracket and built-in Rear Lamp with realite Reflecting Glass) incorporated in Dynamo. Complete with Cables and Bulbs.

No. 25/L76a/1608 .. .. per set 25/-

Front Head Lamp only, with Bulb (less Battery), No. 506 C.P.

No. 25/L76b/504 .. .. each 9/6

Model No. 503.

Ebony Black Head Lamp, with deep Chromium Plated Rim, Green side glasses, streamlined rust-proof Brass Body, special rubber socket shock absorbing Bracket. Domed Glass, Switch on top, Dynamo C25PU, with improved trigger release, universal Carrier Bracket and built-in Rear Lamp (with realite Reflecting Glass) incorporated in Dynamo.
Complete with Cables and Bulbs.

No. 25/L76d/1508 .. .. per set 23/6

Front Head Lamp only, with Bulb (less Battery), No. 503B C.P.

No. 25/L76e/504 .. .. each 8/-

Model No. 505.

Chromium Plated Head Lamp, streamline rust-proof Brass Body. Domed Glass, Green side glasses. Switch on top, with metal adjustable Bracket, with C25PU Dynamo. Complete with Cable and Bulbs.

No. 25/L76f/1508 .. .. per set 23/6
Front Head Lamp only with bulbs (less Battery), No. 505 C.P.
No. 25/L76g/504 .. .. each 8/-

LUCAS
No504 SET

25/L79m

Model No. 504.

Head Lamp, Ebony Black, and deep Chromium Plated Rim, with C25PU Dynamo. Complete with Cable and Bulbs.

No. 25/L76k/1400 .. .. per set 21/-
Front Head Lamp only, with Bulbs, No. 504B C.P.
No. 25/L76l/404 .. .. each 6/6

Details of Bulbs, see page 225.
For Dynamos only, see pages 231 to 233.

Model No. 586.

Improved design, smoothly contoured Head Lamp, non-Battery type, Ebony Black with deep Chromium Plated Rim, with Green side glasses, with C25J Dynamo with universal Bracket built into base of Dynamo. Complete with Cable and Bulbs.

No. 25/L79m/1103 .. .. per set 16/-
Model No. 586LR, less Rear Lamp.
No. 25/L79n/1002 .. .. per set 14/6
Front Head Lamp only, with Bulb, No. 586R C.P.
No. 25/L79r/210 .. .. each 4/-

LUCAS
No507 SET

Model No. 507.

Smoothly contoured Head Lamp, Ebony Black with deep Chromium Plated Rim, metal adjustable Bracket, Green side glass, deep domed front glass of special design, operating switch on top of lamp, with C25HF Dynamo with universal Carrier Bracket, 6 volt, 3 watt, complete with Rear Lamp 49, fitted with realite Reflecting Glass.
Complete with Cable and Bulbs.

No. 25/L80m/1308 .. .. per set 19/6
Model No. 507LR, less Rear Lamp.
No. 25/L80n/1208 .. .. per set 18/-
Front Head Lamp only, with Bulbs, No. 507B C.P.
No. 25/L80r/306 .. .. each 5/-
Model No. 507/6.
As above, but with Head Lamp without operating switch, with C25HF Dynamo as above.
No. 25/L80w/1203 .. .. per set 17/6
Model No. 507/6LR, less Rear Lamp.
No. 25/L80x/1103 .. .. per set 16/-

Branches:
Aberdeen, Acton, Belfast
Birmingham Bournemouth
Bristol, Cardiff Carlisle
Croydon, Dublin Dundee
Eastbourne, Edinburgh
Glasgow Inverness

Head Offices and Warehouses, Wholesale only:
GREAT EASTERN STREET, LONDON, E.C. 2
126 GEORGE STREET, EDINBURGH. 2

Branches:
Hull, Leeds, Liverpool
London, W.1
Manchester, Newcastle
Nottingham Southampton
Stoke-on-Trent
Wolverhampton

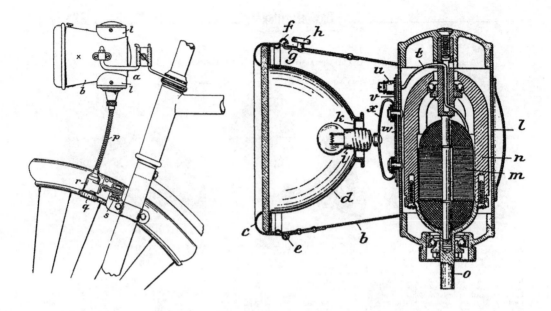

Figure 10.17 Patent drawings of a Bosch combination dynamo/lamp of 1918.
Figure 10.18 A 1937 advertisement for the Sturmey-Archer Dynolamp (Sturmey-Archer Heritage).

HUB DYNAMOS

A major design breakthrough in bicycle lighting came in 1935, when the Raleigh Cycle Company and George William Rawlings (an independent inventor living in Kenilworth, near Coventry) applied for a patent for a hub dynamo (British patent 468,065 of 1937, US patent 2,104,707 of 1938). This was the first of several patents in Rawlings's name, or jointly with Raleigh, relating to hub dynamos. Eventually they led to the famous Sturmey-Archer Dynohub range. (Sturmey-Archer was then a wholly owned subsidiary of Raleigh.)

In his original patent application, Rawlings pointed out that, to deliver a sufficiently high and steady light output, a generator mounted on a bicycle had hitherto had to rotate much faster than the bicycle's wheels. "Where the generator has been built into the hub," he noted, "this has

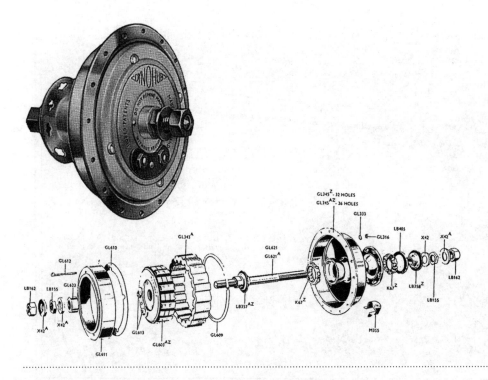

Figure 10.19   A Sturmey-Archer GH6 Dynohub (Sturmey-Archer Heritage).

involved the use of gearing." Rawlings's Dynohub had a powerful multi-pole ring magnet in the hub. This magnet rotated around a wound multi-pole stator, which was fixed to the stationary axle. There were no gears, no brushes, and no commutator. The drive couldn't slip, and the light output was reasonable for the time. The main advantages were reliability and low drag. There was a minute amount of magnetic drag when the lights were off, and a little more when the lights were switched on, but the extra effort involved was imperceptible to most riders. Some bottle dynamos produced considerable drag, and some were noisy; the Dynohub was silent.

The first Dynohubs, produced in 1937, put out 12 volts. An 8-volt unit followed in 1938; Sid Ferris used one when he broke the British 24-hour Road Records Association record.

By the end of 1938, Lucas and Miller had exhibited their own hub dynamos at Britain's national cycle show. This resulted in legal action, but because of World War II the matter wasn't resolved until May 1949, when, as a result of a successful challenge from Miller, the original

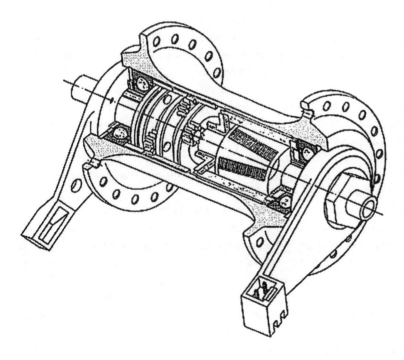

Figure 10.20   A cutaway drawing of a Renak Enparlite 2 geared hub dynamo (Renak GmbH).

Dynohub patent was amended to cover only a specific design of hub dynamo, not the general idea of a generator in the hub. Now other manufacturers could enter the market without fear of litigation from Raleigh.

Other inventors soon turned their attentions to hub dynamos. In 1938, Albert Rabl of Wiener-Neudorf in German-occupied Austria designed a compact speed multiplier for hub dynamos (British patent 533,160 of 1941). Instead of a gearing system, it used a compound series of driving sleeves with slotted curved cams housing ball bearings. In 1939, George Schwab of Denver invented a hub dynamo with an internally toothed wheel and pinions to speed up the rotation of the generator (US patent 2,265,454 of 1949). In the late 1940s, a French hub dynamo was demonstrated. None of these designs seems to have been commercially successful.

Sturmey-Archer's GH6, a 6-volt front Dynohub introduced in 1946, had a 90-millimeter drum rather than the 111-millimeter drum of the 12-volt and 8-volt versions.

Ever since the Dynohub's introduction, there had been efforts to increase its light output. Legislation, especially in Germany, forced the pace of those efforts. In 1967, Raleigh and Tony Hillyer, then Sturmey-Archer's product design manager, applied for a patent for a geared front hub dynamo (British patent 1,244,726 of 1971) that used a mechanism somewhat similar to George Schwab's to rapidly rotate the field poles in the opposite direction to the wheel. The gear train could be manually de-clutched to reduce drag when light wasn't needed. Hillyer's design also incorporated an internal freewheel to enable the field poles to continue rotating if the bike had to stop suddenly. But, as he conceded, there were problems with "gear lash jump due to the magnetic effect of lamination to magnet at walking speed." Consequently, the design never went into production.

In 1982, a new Dynohub with a thirty-pole ceramic magnet was prototyped. It was said to be four times as efficient as a typical tire-driven dynamo and to exceed the latest international lighting standards. But it never went into production.

In 1984, Sturmey-Archer ceased all Dynohub production. With demand falling, the company and its parent, TI Raleigh, were unwilling to invest in the new plant necessary to produce improved versions that would meet new lighting standards. Other makers eventually entered the market. In 1992, Wilfried Schmidt began making his high-quality SON hub dynamos. (SON stands for Schmidts Original Nabendynamo—in English, Schmidt's original hub dynamo.) SON dynamos gained a reputation for quality and reliability, and were supplied in a variety of models for different types of cycles. Another German maker, Renak (a descendant of an East German spinoff from Fichtel & Sachs), began making lightweight hub dynamos called Enparlites in 1994. Enparlites are characterized by a very small hub diameter and the use of a three-stage epicyclic gear to increase the speed of the rotor to 22.5 times that of the road wheel. The rider can de-clutch the gearing by operating a small lever at the side of the hub. The gearing hums when in use, and the claimed efficiency of 40 percent is low by hub-dynamo standards, but amateur racers like the absence of dynamo resistance when the gearing is disengaged.

Shimano, SP, Sanyo, and SRAM began making hub dynamos in the 1990s. Shimano's hub dynamos proved particularly successful in the market. An early Shimano patent relating to that company's move into this market concerns a design by Kazunori Nakamura of Sakai, applied for early in 1996 (US patent 5,828,145 of 1998).

Sturmey-Archer, after being acquired by SunRace of Taiwan, reintroduced a hub dynamo to its product range for the 2006 season, after a break of more than 30 years. It was in a front hub, and it was combined with a drum brake—an idea Sturmey-Archer had proposed in the 1930s but hadn't put into production then. Like most modern hub dynamos, the new Sturmey-Archer hub didn't use internal gearing to speed up the rotor. Instead, it relied principally on improved magnetic materials to achieve considerably higher output than the original Dynohub.

SPOKE DYNAMOS

Dynamos made to fit onto the side of a hub, rather than forming part of the hub itself, have been produced. These were called "spoke dynamos," because they took their drive from an arm driven by a wheel spoke. Their principal advantage was that they could be retrofitted to existing wheels and that they were less susceptible to drive slippage than bottle dynamos. The best-known spoke dynamo was the German Aufa (formerly FER), which went out of production around 2008. Spoke dynamos were significantly less efficient than true hub dynamos.

BOTTOM-BRACKET (ROLLER) DYNAMOS

From time to time, friction-driven dynamos made to be mounted behind a bicycle's bottom bracket have been produced. They were particularly popular in the 1980s, when the Sanyo Dynapower and rival products from Union and Soubitez came on the market. These units were typically clamped to the chain stays. A special brazed-on fitting could be used for a neater, lighter installation. The dynamo's rotor was encased by a roller that made contact with the running surface of the rear tire.

Figure 10.21 An Aufa spoke dynamo (user "ocrho," Wikipedia Commons).
Figure 10.22 A Sanyo NH-T10 bottom-bracket dynamo (Peter Jon White).

Although highly regarded when they first appeared, these dynamos often suffered from drive slippage and rapid deterioration due to their exposure to water and grit thrown up from the road wheels. (It was to avoid such problems that Farnham put his 1897 roller dynamo run on top of the wheel.)

BATTERY BACKUP

Throughout the history of bicycle dynamo lighting, various battery-powered backup systems have been devised. The simplest of these consisted of a separate battery carrier and a switch. Sometimes the batteries were housed in a headlamp. More sophisticated versions had automatic switching. Some even used the output from the dynamo to charge the batteries.

Perhaps the best-known and most commercially successful battery backup systems were those made by Sturmey-Archer from the 1940s until the 1980s. Shortly after World War II, Sturmey-Archer introduced a rechargeable battery system for use with Dynohubs. Known as the DAU (Dry Accumulator Unit), it consisted of three 2-volt dry accumulator cells in a tubular holder that could be fixed to the seat tube and a rectifier unit that converted the Dynohub's AC output to DC for charging purposes. When the cyclist came to a halt, the DAU automatically cut in to maintain illumination. However, the "dry" accumulator cells had to be topped up with distilled water every two to four weeks, and were prone to leakage of battery acid. The DAU was soon superseded by the DBU (Dry Battery Unit), which used ordinary disposable flashlight batteries.

The DBU could be fitted with an optional Filter Switch Unit (FSU). This contained a small rectifier unit and associated circuitry to provide automatic and progressive switchover from Dynohub to dry batteries when the bicycle wasn't moving. Feeding a small current through the cells in the reverse direction to normal extended the batteries' life, apparently by depolarizing the cells. The FSU was based on a 1949 invention by Lesley Arthur Holliday of London (British patent 662,678 of 1951). The first version was introduced around 1951; about four years later it was superseded by a version in which diodes were used. More than 750,000 FSUs were made between 1965 and 1983 (Hadland 1987, 133).

LUGGAGE

11

The ability of bicycles to carry luggage has been acknowledged since the machine's earliest times. Karl Drais's machine was intended as a horse replacement, and therefore Drais provided luggage-carrying facilities, starting a practice that continues to this day.

In some developing countries, particularly in the Far East, stupefying loads are regularly carried on very ordinary bicycles. The Viet Cong moved vast amounts of equipment along the Ho Chi Minh Trail. At the other extreme, some Western cyclists advocate "credit-card touring," in which the rider carries little more than a credit card with which to pay for food and overnight accommodations.

In this chapter we explore the development of the many ways of transporting luggage by bicycle.

SIMPLE HORIZONTAL REAR RACKS

One of the oldest, simplest, and most commonplace means of carrying luggage is the basic horizontal rack, often known in the UK as a carrier. It provides a platform to which luggage may be strapped or tied. It can also form a firm base for a box, a basket, or a bag. Most simple racks are fitted horizontally over the rear wheel. The idea goes back as far as Drais.

A typical draisine had an upstand or "horn" at the back of its main beam. A cylindrical leather or canvas bag, a rolled-up coat, or a bedroll could be strapped or tied across the beam, behind the rider, and the horn would keep the luggage from rolling off the back. A transverse luggage platform made of wood could be added to provide better support to such items of luggage.

The long, thin, flexible, saddle spring of the Michaux-style velocipede wasn't a good mounting point for a luggage rack. However, racks were occasionally fitted, as on the Rousseau velocipede in the Velorama collection (Reynaud 2008, 169). Rather than fit a rack, it was easier to strap a cylindrical bag along the top of the spring, using simple bolt-on fittings (ibid., 113). The Compagnie Parisienne des Vélocipèdes listed a range of luggage and accessories (ibid., 107).

Carrying luggage wasn't a strong point of the French velocipede's successor, the high-wheeler. Some items could be attached to the handlebars. An overcoat or small tent could also be strapped to a high-wheeler's "spine," facing rearward. However, a rider had to ensure that the luggage could not swing around and jam the front wheel. Occasionally a rear rack was mounted over a high-wheeler's small rear wheel.

As the design of the safety bicycle stabilized, simple rear racks, typically made of flat steel strip or steel tubing, came on the market. Usually the front of a rack was bolted onto the seat stays near their top. A support strut on either side of the wheel ran from the back of the rack down to a point near the base of the seat stay, to which it was bolted or clamped.

In some designs, the bottom of the strut was bolted to the axle for a stronger fixing, although this made wheel removal awkward. Clamps that fit around seat stays were used from time to time, but eventually it became standard practice to use a fender eyelet as the lower fixing. The front of the carrier was typically clamped to the seat stays, though later the brake bridge, the brake bosses, or brazed-on threaded rack mounts were used.

Figure 11.1 The "horn" and the transverse luggage platform of a draisine (H.-E. Lessing).

Figure 11.2 An 1869 Michaux with a handlebar bag and a bag on a saddle spring (Musée National de la Voiture et du Tourisme, Palais de Compiegne/Studio Caterin).

The "Gentleman's" Roadster,

Fitted with Luggage-Carrier and Registered Bag (patent Lock), constructed to carry a change of linen, a suit of clothes, shaving and dressing tackle, road-map, and a macintosh or cape.

Figure 11.3 A high-wheeler with rack-mounted rear panniers (Noguchi-san 1998).

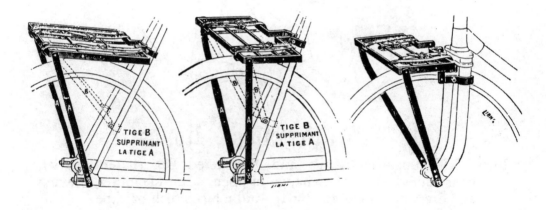

Figure 11.4 French racks of 1907 (Noguchi-san 1998).
Figure 11.5 Sunbeam racks for ladies' bicycles, as shown in a 1915 catalog.

FRONT AND REAR CARRIERS.

The war has brought parcel carriers into fashion. Ladies are now using bicycles for shopping, and these Carriers have been

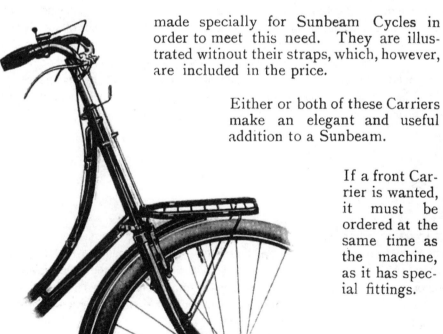

made specially for Sunbeam Cycles in order to meet this need. They are illustrated without their straps, which, however, are included in the price.

Either or both of these Carriers make an elegant and useful addition to a Sunbeam.

If a front Carrier is wanted, it must be ordered at the same time as the machine, as it has special fittings.

A luggage platform might have a spring-loaded parcel clip, straps, or elastic cords. The infill of the luggage platform might consist of thin steel rods, flat steel strips, or perforated steel sheet.

World War I boosted the demand for luggage carriers. A 1915 catalog issued by the upscale cycle maker Sunbeam noted that the war had "brought parcel carriers into fashion" and that ladies were "using bicycles for shopping."

Simple rear racks are still commonplace. Today many such racks are made of aluminum alloy. As with other cycle components, however, the transition from steel to alloy has been gradual.

In some countries which in the past had unusually rough roads (Belgium, for example), brazed-on tubular steel racks were popular.

BEAM RACKS

In the late 1990s, largely in response to a lack of mounting positions for traditional rear racks on full-suspension mountain bikes, beam racks were introduced. A rack of this kind is supported by an integral beam that clamps to the seat post. The leading maker of such racks, Topeak, introduced its first beam rack in 1997. Being cantilevered, beam racks may be less rigid than other racks when loaded, and typically such racks are suitable for loads no greater than 15 or 20 pounds. One advantage of using a beam rack on a bike with rear suspension is that the suspension protects the load. Racks with side panels to which small panniers can be attached are available.

FRONT RACKS

Although the vast majority of simple horizontal racks are fitted over the rear wheel, similar racks can be used over the front wheel. Front racks emerged in the early days of the pneumatic-tired safety bicycle. Raleigh's 1894 front racks bolted to the head tube and provided a platform and back frame for a front bag. It was, however, more common for a front rack to be attached to the fork. Front racks became more popular in some countries, such as France, than in others. They have always been rare in Britain.

When a front rack is attached to the fork, the top fixing may be a tabbed washer, held between the locknuts of the upper steering race. Brake bosses are also sometimes used as

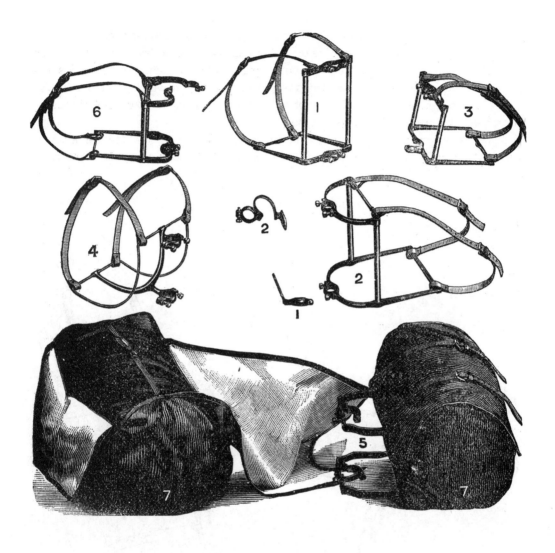

Figure 11.6 Raleigh's 1894 range of front racks, and holdalls to fit them (Raleigh).

upper fixing points. The lower ends of the struts can be fixed to the fork blades using clamps or fender eyelets. The axle can also be used, but this is unusual today, principally because it complicates wheel removal but also because it may not be compatible with "lawyers' lips" (projections around the dropout intended to keep a front wheel from working loose if the quick-release skewer comes undone). This problem does not occur with "lawyers' tabs" (washers with a bent tab that engages in a hole in the fork).

A heavy load placed on a simple platform-type rack fixed to the front fork can affect the bicycle's handling. A front rack fixed rigidly to the bicycle frame, so that it doesn't turn with the

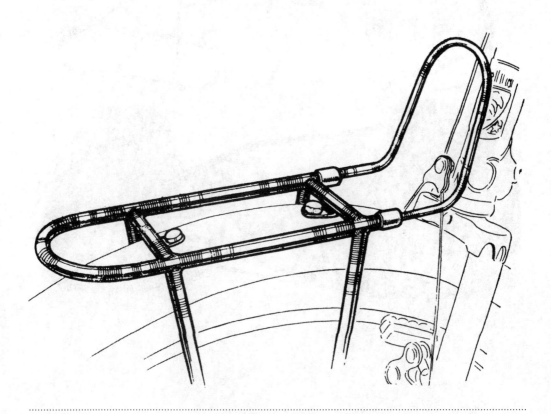

Figure 11.7 A small front rack, partly supported by the fender, on a French Stella bicycle of 1954 (Noguchi-san 1998).

handlebars, is less likely to compromise handling than a fork-fixed rack. However, on many modern bicycles it is difficult to install a strong and rigid frame-fixed front carrier of useful size in such a way that the load doesn't get in the way of the handlebars and the control cables. Frame-fixed front carriers have been used successfully with small-wheeled bicycles, many of which have much longer head tubes and more space between the top of the front wheel and the handlebars than larger machines. The Moulton small-wheelers of the 1960s had brazed-on mounting points in the head tube and on the main beam for a wide cantilevered tubular steel rack that could carry 20 pounds of luggage. This was copied in the Royal Enfield Revelation, and a similar approach was used in one version of the Raleigh Twenty. However, some riders find a frame-fixed front rack disconcerting if it doesn't turn with the handlebars.

The Brompton folding bicycle has an unusual but effective frame-fixed front rack system. The rack, which has a large backrest and a small supporting ledge, is easily detached from its wedge-shaped plastic mounting block, which is bolted to the front of the head tube. Most Brompton racks are made to be used with the company's proprietary luggage. Options include a folding metal shopping basket, a leather attaché case, and a heavy-duty waterproof expedition holdall.

Small front or rear racks for light items, such as a cape, have sometimes been mounted on top of metal fenders (mudguards). Such racks were often seen on French touring bikes of the 1940s and the 1950s.

FITTINGS FOR SPORTS EQUIPMENT

From time to time, special fittings have been produced for carrying rifles, camping stoves, golf clubs, or hockey sticks on bicycles. In the leafier English suburbs, from the 1930s until the 1960s, a common sight on a bicycle's front fork was a small spring-loaded felt-lined clip made to hold a tennis racket; the German company Abus now makes a modern equivalent.

PANNIERS

Bicycle panniers comprise a pair of bags hanging either side of the bicycle frame or a luggage rack. Leather panniers could be fitted to the triangular spaces between the supports for the front wheel of a draisine, one on each side of the wheel. Panniers also could be attached to the sides of the main beam, just behind the rider.

Panniers weren't often seen during the days of the French velocipede and the high-wheeler. Since the advent of the safety bicycle, panniers have always been around, but generally in quite small numbers. Their popularity has varied from country to country; one was much more likely to see them in France than in the UK, for example. Even among tourists, they have not always been particularly popular. Much cycle tourism was done by means of the youth hostel system, started in Germany in 1909 by Richard Schirrmann. By the mid 1930s, New England and most of the countries in Central and Northern Europe had networks of youth hostels, which provided cheap accommodations and meals or kitchen facilities. Cyclists who used hostels didn't have to carry camping equipment, so they generally found panniers unnecessary. Only two of the sixteen bags listed in a Brooks catalog of the late 1930s are panniers.

Rear panniers must be sized and shaped so as not to interfere with the brakes, the gears, the chain, and the control cables. They must also provide adequate clearance for the rider's heels.

Front panniers are generally smaller than rear ones, partly to avoid making the steering too heavy but also to avoid hitting the rider's toes. Front panniers have been produced that fit behind the head tube and on either side of the top and down tube, without the need for a rack. The need for knee clearance limits their size.

Most modern panniers have metal or plastic hooks that fit onto the top rail of a rack and a bungee cord that hooks onto the bottom of the rack. This arrangement isn't always sufficient to keep a pannier from wobbling when loaded, so additional straps are sometimes provided.

Draisine panniers were made of leather. Various other materials have been used, especially linen or cotton based canvases. Most of the panniers now made by the British suppliers Carradice and Brooks are of canvas. Ripstop nylon is a popular alternative. Plastic-coated textiles (such as leatherette) were popular in the past but are out of fashion now. Commuter panniers have been made of rigid plastic and of lightweight corrugated plastic.

A pannier usually has a main compartment and pockets in which tools, rainwear, and snacks can be put. Some panniers come with removable waterproof covers.

Panniers can often be fitted to simple horizontal racks, but many standard racks are too flimsy and will "whip" when loaded with panniers. This can induce very unpleasant speed wobble, especially on fast descents. And many panniers, unless fitted with substantial internal stiffening (such as a plywood board or corrugated plastic sheet), aren't rigid enough; their lower extremities can get caught in the spokes. Hence, a rack made specifically for panniers will typically be stiffer than a standard rack and will have side frames to keep the bags away from the spokes.

Since the mid 1980s, low-mounted front pannier racks have become increasingly popular. Jim Blackburn, the founder of Blackburn Designs, researched the stability of loaded bicycles

Figure 11.8 A front pannier on a draisine (Tilman Wagenknecht).

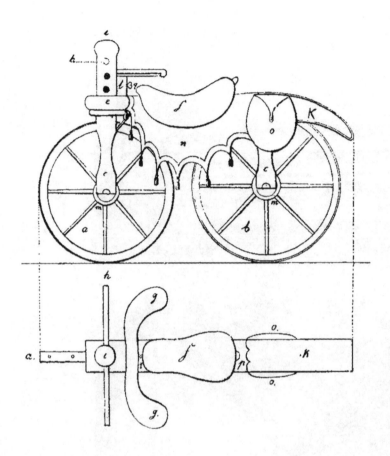

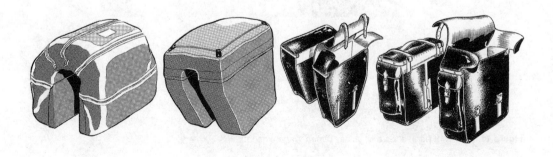

and found that the optimum way to carry a heavy expedition load was with conventionally (high) mounted rear panniers, low-mounted front panniers, and very little load on the handle-bars. However, Blackburn also found that conventional high-mounted front panniers were quite acceptable. This was good news for the minority of intrepid riders who wish to ride on tricky off-road trails with front panniers, as low-mounted bags can easily get caught on rocks.

BASKETS

Baskets were used on the main beams of draisines, both behind and ahead of the rider. They are still used by some cyclists today.

In Britain, wicker baskets with rounded fronts and open tops, attached to the handlebars by short leather straps and buckles, were popular on ladies' roadsters from the 1920s until the 1950s. They worked well with the upright riding position and the roller-lever brakes then in use. They were big enough to carry a few library books and some groceries home. (In those days, local grocers, greengrocers, and butchers would deliver bulky goods to people who had accounts with them.)

Wicker baskets are still available, some with quick-release fixings and a carrying han-dle. Steel wire or mesh baskets have become widely available. Wicker baskets for rear racks have been less common but are an option. They are occasionally used for transporting small dogs. Steel wire or mesh baskets for rear racks are also available, including pannier-style side-mounting models.

Figure 11.9 A Schwalbach velocipede with small rounded panniers behind the saddle (*Miscellen zur Belehrung*, November 28, 1817).
Figure 11.10 Typical panniers of the early 1970s (R. John Way)

Figure 11.11 A velocipede (builder unknown) with baskets fore and aft of the rider, as depicted in the *Moden-Zeitung* in November 1817 (von Salvisberg 1897).

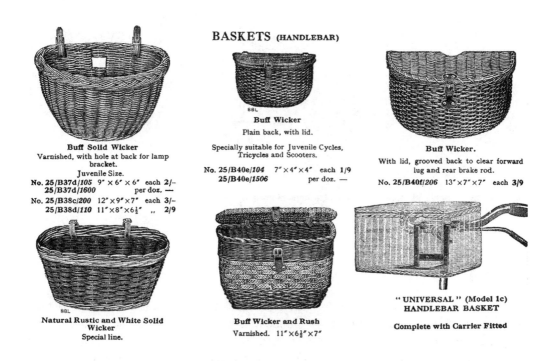

BASKETS (HANDLEBAR)

Buff Solid Wicker
Varnished, with hole at back for lamp
bracket.
Juvenile Size.
No. 25/B37d/105 9″ × 6″ × 6″ each **2/–**
    25/B37d/1600   per doz. ——
No. 25/B38c/200 12″ × 9″ × 7″ each **3/–**
    25/B38d/110 11″ × 8″ × 6½″ ,, **2/9**

Buff Wicker
Plain back, with lid.
Specially suitable for Juvenile Cycles,
Tricycles and Scooters.
No. 25/B40e/104   7″ × 4″ × 4″ each **1/9**
    25/B40e/1506   per doz. ——

Buff Wicker.
With lid, grooved back to clear forward
lug and rear brake rod.
No. 25/B40f/206 13″ × 7″ × 7″ each **3/9**

**Natural Rustic and White Solid
Wicker**
Special line.

Buff Wicker and Rush
Varnished. 11″ × 6½″ × 7″

**" UNIVERSAL " (Model 1c)
HANDLEBAR BASKET**

Complete with Carrier Fitted

Figure 11.12   Some of the many different types of bicycle baskets available in Britain in the 1930s (National Cycle Library).

SADDLEBAGS

The transverse saddlebag, suspended from the rear of the saddle and strapped to the seat post to minimize swaying, was the classic British item of cycling luggage. Such bags were simple to fit and easy to remove. In the interwar years, a wide range of saddlebags were produced in a variety of materials, qualities, and sizes. The bigger ones typically had side pockets for items needed on the road, such as tools and snacks.

Those who took their cycle touring seriously used the biggest and best saddlebags. Utility riders commonly used cheaper and smaller versions. By the 1960s, low-end saddlebags were typically made of vinyl, stiffened with cardboard, and were generally of poor quality.

Figure 11.13 Typical saddlebags and handlebar bags of the early 1970s (R. John Way).

Since the 1960s, traditional-style transverse saddlebags have become rare in Britain. Nonetheless, Brooks and Carradice still produce them, and they have their devotees. Bag supports were produced for the larger saddlebags from the 1930s on, and versions are still made. Brooks's catalog for 1939 illustrated sixteen different types. These typically fitted onto the seat stays or the seat post, sometimes with lightweight stays clamped to the seat stays, and were intended to prevent a large, heavily laden bag from swinging from side to side or sagging onto the rear fender. (The latter was more likely to be a problem for a shorter rider, whose saddle would be closer to the fender.)

In recent decades, smaller, more streamlined saddlebags have been popular. These are held onto the saddle rails by Velcro straps or buckles, by a quick-release tongue and socket, or by a T-bar that locks onto the rails of the saddle chassis. Most of these bags are large enough only for small items. Some can be expanded by unzipping a central gusset.

HANDLEBAR BAGS

Handlebar bags became increasingly popular in the late twentieth century. They could be used on most types of bicycles, they fitted neatly onto the drop handlebars of a touring bike, and they provided easy access to snacks, cameras, maps, and rainwear without the need to dismount. Many had proprietary quick-release systems, such as Rixen & Kaul's Klickfix, that made it easy to use a single bag on several different bikes. However, they could adversely affect steering if heavily loaded.

RACK-MOUNTED HOLDALLS

Purpose-made holdalls that mount on the rear rack have rarely been big sellers, perhaps because it was so easy to use a bag or box made for another purpose. Some people made their own luggage. A wooden box bolted to the rack was a useful accessory for a workman. Even Raleigh's chairman, Frank Bowden, a very rich cycle tourist with a vested interest in selling cycle accessories, made his own holdalls. In the 1913 edition of his popular book *Cycling for Health*, Bowden explained his method:

> Get a piece of strong ordinary waterproof "American cloth" [varnished cotton cloth] that will not stick in hot weather, size 36 by 24 inches. Cut off 36 by 15 inches, and bind the edges. From the remainder cut two round pieces nine inches in diameter bind and sew them to each side of the first piece, commencing nine inches from its end, until you have sewn a little more than half-way around the discs. In the center of each unsewn portion of the discs, sew a piece of black tape. Put your baggage in the bag thus formed, tie the two ends of tape across the top to keep it neatly in, tuck the nine-inch flap over, roll up the hold-all and put it on the carrier, where a couple of straps will secure it, or, as I often do to save weight, dispense with the carrier and strap the hold-all to the handle-bar. If carrying but little, and you do not trouble to make a hold-all, roll up your parcel in waterproof cloth and strap it to the handle-bar.

The Moulton small-wheeler of the 1960s had unusually large racks fore and aft. The company offered a range of holdalls made specifically for its bikes, including a touring version with side pockets, an expandable lid, and fittings for a tent on top. Competitors emulated the Moulton's large rear holdall. Raleigh's RSW 16 small-wheeler went Moulton one better with a large quick-release holdall. Large rear holdalls with capacities approaching 45 liters were made for later upscale Moultons. The rack-mounted holdalls that were available for conventional bikes tended to be smaller, with a typical capacity of about 12 liters.

TOOL BAGS

Small bags specifically for tools have been made since the earliest days of cycling. The same materials were used as for other bags, though leather was particularly popular in earlier times, being resistant to perforation by the tools inside. A tool bag was commonly fitted to the rear of the saddle. Another popular position was in the angle formed by the top tube and the seat tube.

Tool rolls made of leatherette or canvas, with a pocket for each tool, were also popular. Rolled up and strapped or tied to the frame, the rack, or the saddle, a tool roll held the tools securely and compactly. Unrolled, it presented the tools clearly and kept them from rolling away when the bike was being worked on.

CHILD SEATS

The idea of carrying a child on a bicycle dates back to the days of the draisine. A illustration from that era (figure 11.14) shows a child riding behind an adult. A strap passes around the waists of the child and the adult, and the child's feet are in small panniers fixed to the side of the machine's main beam. It didn't become common for adults to carry children on bikes until the popularization of the safety bicycle, however.

A number of patent applications for child seats were filed during the late 1880s and the 1890s. There were four main approaches: bolt-on top tube saddles, seats over the rear wheel, seats over the front wheel, and sidecars.

Charles Harvey of Philadelphia filed one of the very first patent applications for a child seat (US patent 409,964 of 1889). It was for a seat mounted on the main beam of a cross-frame safety bicycle, so that the child sat between the adult rider's arms. The rapid evolution of the standard men's diamond frame made it easy to fix a saddle on the top tube, in the position suggested by Harvey.

In a design that became popular in Britain, a small saddle was clamped onto the top tube of a men's roadster, and a footrest was bolted onto the down tube, near its junction with the head tube. The child sat on the little saddle, with its feet on the footrest and its hands on the handlebars. In one version, the seat was mounted on coil springs and had a detachable wire backrest. The August Maier child seat (made in Germany since the late 1940s, still in production today, and known as the Bulldog) fitted in a similar position but had a quick-release plug-in mount so that it could be used on men's or ladies' bicycles (Briese 2008, 44). Seats of this

Figure 11.14   An 1817 drawing showing a child being carried on a Schwalbach velocipede (Wikipedia Commons).

type were inexpensive and unobtrusive and gave the child a good forward view and a feeling of security. They didn't add much weight to the machine, and, with the additional load well within the wheelbase, the effect on handling was minimized. However, low-speed maneuvering could be impeded—large movements of the handlebars could be obstructed by the presence of the child between the adult rider's arms.

A seat over the rear wheel is the enduring solution to the problem of carrying a child on a bicycle. Some early designs, such as that of Ernest Batchelder of Chicago (US patent 615,783 of 1898), involved adding a framework to support a simple saddle and footrests. But without the adult's arms around the child, this wasn't safe for small children. It was soon recognized that a backrest and side rails were needed.

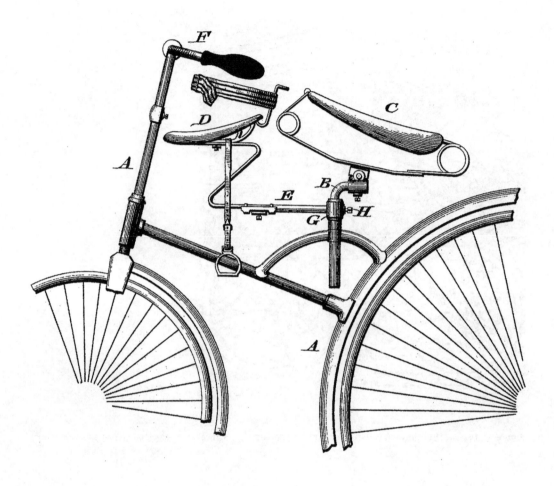

Figure 11.15 Harvey's 1889 child seat (patent drawing).

In the interwar years, a wicker child seat that fitted "sidesaddle" onto a rear rack was marketed in Britain but wasn't widely adopted.

A child seat that was popular in the UK from at least the 1940s until the 1970s was made of riveted steel strip. The stays were firmly fixed to the rear axle. The child faced forward, with a close-up view of the parental posterior. The slightly padded seat had a backrest and side rails, and guard plates protected the child's feet from the spokes. The child could be strapped in with a harness. When a child wasn't being carried, the seat could be folded down and used as a large luggage rack.

Today child seats are available in a wide range of designs, almost invariably with molded plastic shells, padded linings, and integral safety harnesses. Some face forward, some backward. Some can be reclined for sleeping. The mounting is typically onto a "hairpin" of steel rod, which is clamped to the seat tube or seat post. The seat is fixed to the cantilevered "hairpin" (which is slightly springy, and angled about 30° to the horizontal) by means of a quick-release mechanism.

Figure 11.16 Batchelder's 1898 child seat (patent drawing).

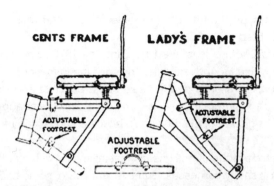

GENTS FRAME   LADY'S FRAME

ADJUSTABLE FOOTREST.

ADJUSTABLE FOOTREST.

ADJUSTABLE FOOTREST.

"TRIPPA" UNIVERSAL MODEL CHILD CARRIER

Spring model with foot-rests to suit both Gent.'s or Lady's Cycles.

No. **25/C187L/604**   ..   .. each **8/6**

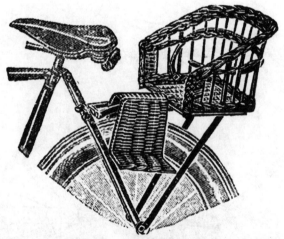

REAR CHILD CARRIER TO RIDE ASTRIDE

Black enamelled metal framework. Varnished Buff Wicker Basket.

No. **25/C188L/608**   ..   .. each **10/–**

Figure 11.17   British cycle carriers of the 1930s (National Cycle Library).

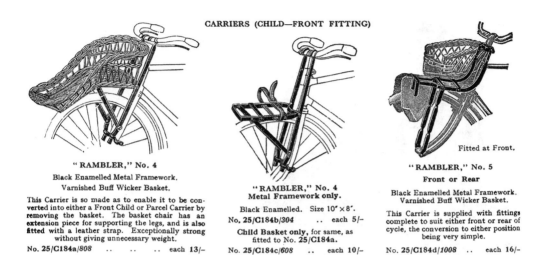

CARRIERS (CHILD—FRONT FITTING)

" RAMBLER," No. 4

Black Enamelled Metal Framework.
Varnished Buff Wicker Basket.

This Carrier is so made as to enable it to be converted into either a Front Child or Parcel Carrier by
removing the basket. The basket chair has an
extension piece for supporting the legs, and is also
fitted with a leather strap. Exceptionally strong
without giving unnecessary weight.

No. 25/C184a/808   ..   ..   .. each 13/-

" RAMBLER," No. 4
Metal Framework only.

Black Enamelled. Size 10″ × 8″.
No. 25/C184b/304   .. each 5/-

Child Basket only, for same, as
fitted to No. 25/C184a.

No. 25/C184c/608   ..   each 10/-

Fitted at Front.

" RAMBLER," No. 5
Front or Rear

Black Enamelled Metal Framework.
Varnished Buff Wicker Basket.

This Carrier is supplied with fittings
complete to suit either front or rear of
cycle, the conversion to either position
being very simple.

No. 25/C184d/1008   ..   each 16/-

Figure 11.18   Front-fitting child seats sold in the UK in the 1930s (National Cycle Library).

Seats over the front wheel are rare today, but one of the earliest patents for a child seat, granted to an inventive English bicycle maker and hotelier named Dan Albone, was for a design of this type (British patent 7,300 of 1891). The seat shell was of wicker supported on a steel framework. Child carriers similar to Albone's (although with much less elegant supporting frames) were available in Britain until World War II. They were also available from the Berlin-based manufacturer Adolf Lofmann, whose 1914 range included versions for front, rear, and top-tube mounting (Briese 2008, 46).

Occasionally, designers have turned their attention to harnessing the energy of a child passenger to contribute to a bicycle's motive power. Various add-on drive systems have been devised, referred to generically as "kiddie cranks." In the 2010s, the American firm Precision Tandems offered a complete add-on drive train. Said to be suitable for children between the ages of 2½ and 9 years, it was priced at nearly $500.

Figure 11.19 Dan Albone's 1891 child seat (patent drawing).

SIDECARS

In 1893, a French army officer called Bertoux won a prize in a newspaper competition for designing a child-carrying sidecar for a safety bicycle (Sheldon 42–43). Thereafter, sidecars for carrying children were occasionally used in the UK and on the Continent, particularly during the interwar years. A family outing could be accomplished on a tandem bike equipped with a seat over the back wheel for a child up to about 9 years old and a sidecar for a baby or a toddler, but such configurations were never common. Trailers (discussed below) were more popular than sidecars for transporting children.

During the 1920s and the 1930s, bicycle sidecars with plywood boxes, wicker baskets, or slatted side panels were produced for tradesmen in the UK and on the Continent. Brown Brothers and Watsonian were well-known British makers. The advantage of sidecars was that they could easily be coupled to a conventional bicycle. Their major disadvantage was the width of the slow-moving ensemble. Bicycle sidecars were rarely seen in Britain or mainland

Europe after World War II, when the streets were increasingly dominated by motor vehicles. They are, however, widely used in the Far East.

TRAILERS

Some bicycle trailers have two wheels, some a single wheel. Most of the single-wheelers are low-slung cargo trailers or trailer-cycles. (A trailer-cycle carries a pedaling passenger, usually a child.)

A design devised by Henry Mathew Hunt of Indianapolis in 1896 (US patent 598,872 of 1898) was intended to convert a standard safety bicycle into a tandem for two adults. It didn't achieve commercial success, though it was similar in some respects to the better-known trailer-cycle developed by British frame builder Bill Rann in the interwar years. Rann's trailer, like Hunt's, resembled the back end of a bicycle and had a saddle, a drive train, and handlebars. It enabling a larger child to take an active part in the ride. Unlike Hunt's, Rann's trailer didn't link the "stoker's" handlebars to the "pilot's."

The physical connection between a bicycle and any trailer has to cope not only with horizontal turning but also with the need for the bicycle to lean (pitch) into a turn. Bill Rann recognized that the turn pivot should ideally be directly above the rear axle of the bicycle. To achieve this, he used a frame that resembled a rear luggage rack. (In fact, it could usually double as one.) Rann also placed the pitch pivot above the bike's rear axle.

Rann's trailers were widely copied but were rarely seen in Britain after the 1950s. In the 1980s, a man named Hannington revived them. Hannington's versions were often referred to as Hann trailers, a play on his name and Rann's.

Like a Rann trailer, the Piccolo trailer-cycle, made in the 2010s by the American company Burley Design, used a turn pivot above the bicycle's rear axle. But unlike the Rann, it had the pitch pivot on the trailer. This made it easier to park than a Rann trailer, which can flop over when the bike is pushed backward.

Interest in trailer-cycles increased in the 1980s, and in the early twenty-first century they were readily available. Many inexpensive ones were made in Asia. Most designs used the simple and cheap expedient of coupling the trailer to the bicycle's seat post. This could work reasonably well if the pivot was vertical and was bracketed out from the seat post clamp toward the rear axle. If, however, the pivoting was around the seat post, the geometry was very bad, the trailer being made to lean out of the turn while the bike leaned in. And some seat posts weren't strong enough to cope with the loads.

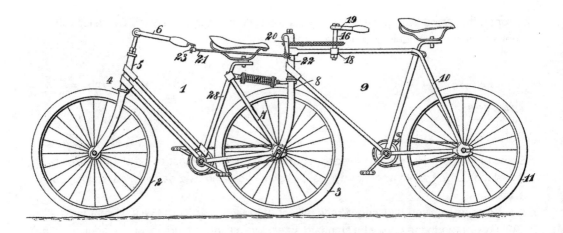

Figure 11.20 Henry Mathew Hunt's 1896 trailer-cycle (patent drawing).
Figure 11.21 A Rann-style trailer by Hannington (Graham Brodie).

Two-wheeled trailers appeared on the British market around the beginning of the twentieth century. In 1900, John Marston and J. Herbert obtained a patent for a passenger-carrying
trailer. The next year, they introduced the Sunbeam Ricksha at the National Cycle Show. The
body was made of wicker or cane woven onto a tubular steel frame mounted on elliptical steel
springs. The hitching arm of the trailer had a ball-and-socket joint, to cope with turning and
pitching, and was fastened to the bicycle by a quick-release clip on the seat post. The Ricksha
weighed about 33 pounds (Pinkerton and Roberts 2002, 97).

In 1903, the Star Cycle Company (which, like Sunbeam, was based in Wolverhampton)
launched a line of trailers. The Trailing Carriage had a wicker seat; the Tradesman's Carrier had
a large wooden box (with the option of a zinc lining) with a lockable zinc lid.

In later years, lightweight trailers were sometimes available from specialist builders. In the
1950s and the 1960s, Jack Taylor Cycles of Stockton-on-Tees offered a low-slung trailer with
a single small-diameter wheel. The wheel was suspended. A balloon tire was used. The trailer

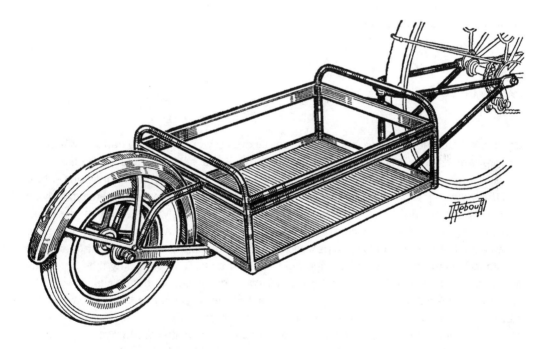

Figure 11.22   A 1953 CMDC Monosport trailer (Rob van der Plas).

was pivoted from a "head tube" mounted behind the bicycle on a triangulated framework attached to the rear axle and the seat binder bolt. All the attachments were of the quick-release type. The trailer weighed only 11 pounds but could carry ten times that weight.

Burley Design, founded in Eugene, Oregon in 1978, became a world leader in the field of child trailers. Burley's trailers, which came in one-child and two-child models, had roll-up weather-protection covers. Some doubled as strollers. Burley also made a variety of cargo trailers, including a camping version, a flatbed, a city trailer, and a pet carrier. Most Burley trailers attached to a hitching point retained by the bicycle's rear axle. The coupling incorporated an elastomer to accommodate pitching.

In 1980, the Bike-Hod was introduced. This compact British design remained in production for more than 30 years. A Bike-Hod was attached to the bicycle's seat post. It was available in standard, touring, and commercial versions, with 12½-inch or 16-inch wheels and cushion or pneumatic tires.

Among the other trailer manufacturers active in the early twenty-first century were Weber, Carry Freedom, Chariot, Human Powered Machines, Pashley, and Raleigh (which offers trailers under the brand name Avenir).

CARGO BIKES

Cargo bikes are also known as freight bikes, carrier cycles, work bikes, and tradesman's bikes, and are sometimes referred to generically as delibikes, baker's bikes, or butcher's bikes.

In the early twentieth century, two basic patterns of cargo bikes emerged: the equal-wheel pattern and the "low gravity" pattern. In the equal-wheel type, both wheels were typically 26 inches in diameter. Bikes built on the "low gravity" pattern typically had a 26-inch rear wheel and a smaller front wheel (between 14 and 20 inches). Both types had substantial frame-fixed front racks, but the "low gravity" type's rack was considerably deeper. There was usually a substantial twin-arm prop-stand, hinged from the front rack. The heavy-duty tires were wide and sometimes were of the cushion type rather than pneumatic, so that deliveries would be less likely to be delayed by punctures. In the past a single speed was the norm, but many modern versions have hub gears and a few have derailleurs.

Raleigh began making cargo cycles in substantial numbers after World War I, soon found that 1/8-inch chains weren't strong enough, and switched to 3/16-inch chains, which then became the norm for British cargo cycles. Brown Brothers and Pashley also made cargo cycles. Raleigh continued making them into the 1970s, and Pashley into the twenty-first century.

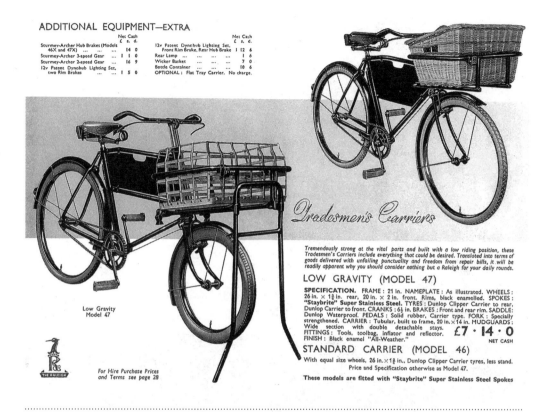

ADDITIONAL EQUIPMENT—EXTRA

	Net Cash £ s. d.		Net Cash £ s. d.
Sturmey-Archer Hub Brakes (Models 46X and 47X)	14 0	12v Patent Dynohub Lighting Set, Front Rim Brake, Rear Hub Brake	1 12 6
Sturmey-Archer 3-speed Gear ...	1 1 0	Rear Lamp	1 6
Sturmey-Archer 2-speed Gear ...	16 9	Wicker Basket	7 0
12v Patent Dynohub Lighting Set, two Rim Brakes	1 5 0	Bottle Container	10 6
		OPTIONAL: Flat Tray Carrier. No charge.	

Tradesmen's Carriers

Tremendously strong at the vital parts and built with a low riding position, these Tradesmen's Carriers include everything that could be desired. Translated into terms of goods delivered with unfailing punctuality and freedom from repair bills, it will be readily apparent why you should consider nothing but a Raleigh for your daily rounds.

LOW GRAVITY (MODEL 47)

SPECIFICATION. FRAME: 21 in. NAMEPLATE: As illustrated. WHEELS: 26 in. × 1¾ in. rear, 20 in. × 2 in. front. Rims, black enamelled. SPOKES: "Staybrite" Super Stainless Steel. TYRES: Dunlop Clipper Carrier to rear, Dunlop Carrier to front. CRANKS: 6½ in. BRAKES: Front and rear rim. SADDLE: Dunlop Waterproof. PEDALS: Solid rubber, Carrier type. FORK: Specially strengthened. CARRIER: Tubular, built to frame, 20 in. × 14 in. MUDGUARDS: Wide section with double detachable stays. FITTINGS: Tools, toolbag, inflator and reflector. FINISH: Black enamel "All-Weather." **£7 · 14 · 0** NET CASH

STANDARD CARRIER (MODEL 46)

With equal size wheels, 26 in. × 1¾ in., Dunlop Clipper Carrier tyres, less stand. Price and Specification otherwise as Model 47.

These models are fitted with "Staybrite" Super Stainless Steel Spokes

Low Gravity Model 47

For Hire Purchase Prices and Terms see page 28

Figure 11.23   Raleigh low-center-of-gravity and equal-wheel carrier cycles of 1939 (Raleigh).

Another classic style of cargo bike is the Long John, which resembles a "low gravity" cargo bike that has been stretched to allow a long, low cargo platform to be placed between the front wheel and the rider. The handlebars are in the normal position, and steering is done indirectly by means of a bridle rod system below the load platform. Long Johns originated in Denmark circa 1930 and were manufactured by several Scandinavian companies. Companies producing Long Johns or machines of similar design in the early twenty-first century included Monark of Sweden and Human Powered Machines of Oregon.

In 1978, Georg Ruffer of Germany prototyped his Fahrroller, a bi-scooter that had a conventional rear wheel, a small front wheel, luggage racks fore and aft, and a step-through frame with

Figure 11.24 Above: A 1991 Long John by SCO (Velo Zuerich GmbH). Below: A 1978 prototype Fahrroller by Georg Ruffer (Wolfgang Siol).
Figure 11.25 A Burrows 8 Freight (Hugh Swire).

a low luggage platform midway along the wheelbase (German patent 2,831,289 of 1978). The platform provided an excellent way to carry a compact but heavy load, such as a narrow beverage box. Moreover, the platform allowed the rider to use the bike like a scooter for easier starting or moving in pedestrian precincts, where cycling is forbidden, and to take a buddy along.

The 8 Freight, a long-wheelbase cargo bike designed by Mike Burrows of England, had the rider at the front, and a long, low cargo platform behind. Steering was direct, and 20-inch BMX-format wheels with wide-section tires were used. Both wheels had single-sided supports, so tires could be changed or repaired without removing the wheels.

Some European postal services made considerable use of cargo bikes during the twentieth century. These machines were built to the postal services' own demanding specifications but were usually based on cargo-bike designs that were common in the countries concerned. In the late 1990s and the early 2000s, Deutsche Post in Germany, La Poste in France, bpost in Belgium, and Royal Mail in the UK all commissioned more radical cargo bikes. For example, Pashley's 2001 Royal Mail Mailstar (also available in civilian form as the Pronto) had a 26-inch rear wheel, a 24-inch front wheel, a large frame-fixed front rack, and a heavy-duty rear pannier rack. The frame was of step-through design but was very rigid. Sadly and inexplicably, in 2010 Royal Mail announced it would drastically reduce its fleet of cargo bikes for "health and safety" reasons.

A more recent development in cargo bikes was the "longtail," a fairly conventional diamond-frame bicycle with a greatly extended rear triangle that lengthened the wheelbase so that large panniers could be fitted and long loads could be carried on top of the rear rack. Longtail models of the early 2010s included the Kona Ute, the Sun Atlas Cargo, and the Surly Big Dummy.

RACING BICYCLES

In Britain, machines inspired by the draisine were often called "hobby-horses" or "dandy horses." Racing such machines became a minor craze in 1819. In March of that year, two riders in Essex competed to see which could ride farther in an hour, the winner achieving nearly 8 miles. A month later, on a bet, a rider in Kent covered 6 miles in just over 51 minutes. Later that year, in Cornwall, a rider managed 26 miles in less than 4 hours, averaging more than 7 miles per hour (Street 2000, 77). In three-mile races in the Ipswich area, average speeds were said to approach 12 miles per hour. In 1819, there was a 50-mile race around the outskirts of London; there was also a race in the Nottingham area, in which a donkey rider defeated a man on a hobby-horse (Street 2000, 77–82).

The only documented draisine race in Germany—run secretly to evade the authorities—took place in 1829 and ran from the outskirts of Munich to the Nymphenburg Palace. The winner rode 11 kilometers in 30 minutes (*Münchner Tagsblatt*, April 23, 1829).

After the widespread suppression of the draisine, bicycle racing ceased for nearly 40 years, until the coming of the Michaux-style velocipede reignited interest. By the early summer of 1868, at least six race events had been held at Saint-Cloud, near Paris, and another at Hendon, west of London. An Englishman named James Moore had won a one-kilometer race at Saint-Cloud on May 31, achieving about 14.4 miles per hour. The following year, Moore won the Paris-to-Rouen race, believed to be the first long-distance road race (Roberts 1991, 64ff.). From then on, there was continual development of racing bikes.

THE EVOLUTION OF FRAME GEOMETRY

The quest for speed was the main reason for the evolution from the Michaux-style front-drive velocipede to the high-wheeler. A larger front wheel produced a higher speed at a given pedal cadence; a small rear wheel saved weight and shortened the overall length of the machine. To accommodate the change in wheel sizes, the main beam of the French velocipede rapidly evolved into the elegant, thin, curved spine of the high-wheeler. During this period, hollow metal tubing became increasingly used in bicycle construction. (On the early development of hollow tubing, see chapter 5.)

The direct-drive high-wheeler was an efficient machine. Record breakers on solid-tired high-wheelers achieved 50 miles in well under 3 hours, 100 miles in less than 7 hours, and 259 miles in 24 hours (RRA 1965, 31). But direct front drive proved a developmental blind alley.

The development of the safety bicycle led, in the early 1890s, to a new breed of diamond-frame racing bicycles. One example, Sunbeam's 1892 Special Light Road Racer, had a diamond frame with a rearward-sloping top tube made of seamless steel. It weighed 27 pounds. Two years later, Sunbeam offered a Track Racer with a guaranteed weight of just 22 pounds. Despite recurring claims from decade to decade of "lightest yet," bicycles didn't get much lighter until the adoption of carbon fiber.

By 1899, rearward-sloping top tubes were out of style. The new Scorching Sunbeam came with a horizontal top tube. Top tubes then began to slope forward. We see this in Raleigh's 1907 Road Racer and more so in Raleigh's 1911 racers. After World War I, horizontal ("parallel") top tubes came back into fashion and remained the norm for many decades. In the 1930s, the fashion was for lower top tubes, the idea being that the less frame there was, the lighter the bike would be.

Early racing bikes tended to have short rear triangles and seat-tube and head-tube angles of about 68°. Gradually, steeper frame angles were adopted. By the late 1930s, the Carlton

Flyer (a hand-built road racer) was offered with head-tube angles from 73° to 75° and seat-tube angles of 71° to 73°. A hundred years after the first diamond-frame safety racers, parallel head-tube and seat-tube angles of about 73° were the norm for medium-size riders, with 72° recommended for shorter people and 74° for taller ones.

Frame builders generally tried to keep the wheelbase reasonably short for good handling while at the same time keeping the front wheel clear of the rider's toes. Wheelbases of about 40 or 41 inches were common; wheelbases shorter than 39 inches or longer than 42 inches were rare.

Since 1997, racing frames with rearward-sloping top tubes and compact rear triangles have become popular. The British designer Mike Burrows was the pioneer in this field; his Giant TCR

Figure 12.1   A late lightweight ordinary, the Raleigh Racer of 1891 (Raleigh).

got a lot of publicity when the Spanish ONCE team used it in the Tour de France. Today, the typical Tour de France machine has a carbon-fiber frame with geometry broadly similar to that popularized by the TCR.

HORSES FOR COURSES

Over time, more and more different kinds of bicycle races were held. There were mass-start events, time trials of various kinds, cyclo-cross events, and a wide variety of track races. There were also endurance events, such as reliability rides, randonnée cyclosportive (gran rondo), and audax; though not races as such, these have strict time limits and therefore encourage the use of fast machines. Different types of bicycles have been developed for these activities.

Figure 12.2   An 1892 Sunbeam Special Light Road Racer (catalog illustration).

Figure 12.3 A 1939 Carlton Flyer (Raleigh).

Figure 12.4 A Giant TCR (Giant).

Time trials take various forms, including short prologues (as in the Tour de France), timed long-distance individual and team races, and timed individual mountain climbs. British time-trial rules were devised for races on unclosed public roads over set distances of 10, 25, 50, and 100 miles, always returning to the start point ("out and home"). There were also 12-hour and 24-hour time trials. Regular road racing bicycles were often used, sometimes with bolt-on accessories.

In the 1980s, frame builders began making low-profile time-trial machines, using a smaller front wheel (nominally 24 or 26 inches), a forward-sloping top tube, a shorter wheelbase, and "cow-horn handlebars" or tri-bars (also called aerobars). The aims were lighter weight and reduced frontal area, to minimize air resistance. Variants of this design were also used in pursuit time trials on hard tracks. When the use of aerobars in time trials became common, the rider was able to rest body weight on the elbows. Rider comfort may therefore have been better, even with a shorter wheelbase and smaller front wheel. In 2000, the Union Cycliste Internationale ruled that both wheels had to be the same size (UCI Rule 1.3.006).

Wheels with an overall diameter ranging from 55 to 70 centimeters (21.65 to 27.56 inches) are still permitted by the UCI. This, however, rules out most commercially produced high-performance small-wheelers, such as Moultons and Bike Fridays.

In cyclo-cross (a form of cross-country competition, usually in the autumn or the winter), the rider sometimes has to carry the bike. Therefore, the cyclo-cross bike evolved into a light, easy-to-handle machine with a minimum of protuberances. A modern cyclo-cross bike often has a rearward-sloping top tube (with the cables on top, to make it easier for the rider to carry the underside of the top tube on one shoulder), and a shorter seat tube and more relaxed frame angles than a road bike.

Different forms of track-racing bikes evolved for racing on different surfaces (hard, grass, cinders) and for different types of racing. Races held on hard tracks, such as velodromes, included two-man and four-man sprints, team sprints, Keirin (mass-start sprinting with a paced start), various types of time trials, elimination racing (such as "win and out" and "devil take the hindmost"), and Six Day racing. Bikes for grass or cinder track racing needed wider tires and bigger tire clearances. Dual-purpose road/track bikes were popular in Britain from the 1930s into the 1950s.

In a motorcycle-paced event, the cyclist or "stayer" follows the motorcycle as closely as possible, to maximize the aerodynamic "drafting," and sits forward on the bike. The bike has reverse-rake forks and a 24-inch front wheel.

Motor pacing of another kind is occasionally used for speed-record attempts. In 1899, Charles Murphy used a specially designed bicycle to achieve 60 miles per hour by riding immediately behind a railway train on smooth plywood sheeting that had been laid between the tracks. His close proximity to the rear of the train meant that he had to overcome little or no air resistance. Hence he achieved a speed comparable to that of a fast motorcycle of the era and earned the nickname "Mile a Minute Murphy."

Subsequent paced records were usually achieved on closed freeways or salt flats. At the time of writing, the Dutch cyclist Fred Rompelberg was the holder of the motor-paced world speed record for cycling, having achieved nearly 170 miles per hour on the Bonneville Salt Flats in Utah in 1995. He rode a special bicycle behind a dragster fitted with a large air shelter. Bicycles for this purpose typically have a very long wheelbase, extremely high gearing, and motorcycle tires. Rompelberg's bike, with a wheelbase of 57 inches and telescopic front suspension, traveled more than 114 feet per pedal revolution.

"Tourer" (or "tourist") is a name bicycle makers have often applied to machines that were, in reality, roadsters. However, there was also another breed of tourers, more closely related to racing bikes. In the interwar period, some British makers began offering lightweight bikes

Figure 12.5   A Condor track bike of the 1960s (R. John Way).

produced specifically for touring. In comparison with racing bikes, these had relatively relaxed frame angles (about 70°) and a longer wheelbase (typically 42 inches). Generous clearances were provided for wider tires and fenders. A typical pre-World War II example was the Carlton Tourist. The Dawes Windrush, introduced in the mid 1950s, soon evolved into the classic Galaxy, a model name that survives to this day. Claud Butler made the Cape Wrath tourer. In 1987, Raleigh introduced the Randonneur, another classic tourer. These bikes were similar in many respects to clubmen's racing machines. However, they tended to have slightly longer wheelbases, larger clearances for toes and mudguards, and more provisions for carrying luggage. And their frame angles were typically a little less steep than those of racing machines.

The bikes referred to today as sportive are specifically designed for audax, randonnée cyclosportive (gran rondo), and similar events. Their frame geometry tends to be somewhere between that of a lightweight tourer and that of a road-racing bike. Though not designed for out-and-out racing, neither are they intended for major expeditions with full luggage.

Figure 12.6   A Gazelle stayer bike, circa 1980, with saddle brace and adjustable handlebar reach (Raleigh).

Specialized frames also are made for other forms of competition, including triathlon, cycle speedway, and polo.

FRAME MATERIALS

Steel tubing was the dominant material for racing frames until relatively recently. In the 1880s, there were more than 180 patent applications for seamless tubing alone; one of the most famous patents was the one granted to the German brothers Reinhard and Max Mannesmann (US patent 389,585 of 1888). As early as 1892, pneumatic-tired racers were built from seamless steel tubing rather than the heavy seamed tube used in cheaper machines. By the 1930s,

Figure 12.7 A typical tourer of the early 2000s (Geoff Apps).

low-alloy chrome molybdenum steel tubing, which had been developed for the aircraft industry, was being used in the better bicycle frames. In 1939, the British lightweight specialist Carlton advertised "ALL our Racing models are completely built of Aircraft tubing." Carlton was using Reynolds 531 tubing for the butted tubes, forks, and stays of its top models. (Butted tubes are thicker internally at the ends, where greater thickness is necessary to maintain strength during brazing, but thinner for most of their length to save weight. Butted stays and forks are tapered internally and are more correctly described as taper gauge. Reynolds's numbers, such as 531, are brand names.) Over time, Reynolds added even lighter tubing to their range, including the highly regarded type 753 in 1975. Rivals to Reynolds, such as Columbus and Falck in Italy, Vitus in France, and Tangye and Ishiwata in Japan, ensured that frame builders had a good choice of steel tubing.

Steel tubing was usually joined by brazing it into steel lugs, sometimes very ornate ones. Lugless frames, welded or fillet brazed, were rarer. Fillet brazing can produce a very elegant lugless frame, but achieving a good appearance is labor intensive. Raleigh tried acetylene welding for racing frames in the early 1920s but suffered an unacceptably high rate of failures, caused by brittle joints. By the mid 1930s, the frames of Tour de France bikes were routinely arc welded and some British lightweight builders, such as Paris Cycles and Holdsworth, were using arc welding too. In 1941, Russell Meredith of Los Angeles invented Tungsten Inert Gas (TIG) welding (US Patent 2,274,631 of 1942), and it was subsequently adopted by some frame builders. After World War II, two British firms, Royal Enfield and Dayton, used flash pressure welding, a fast method of electrical resistance welding that doesn't require cosmetic finishing.

In the earliest days of the pneumatic-tired safety bicycle, aluminum was tried as a frame material. "Many attempts have been made to employ it in cycle construction," Archibald Sharp wrote (1896, 287), but "no alloy containing a large percentage of aluminium, and therefore very light, has been found to combine the strength and ductility necessary for it to compare favourably with steel." The St. Louis Refrigerator and Wooden Gutter Company showed aluminum bicycles in New York in 1895 and claimed to have made racing versions weighing about 16 pounds. Three years later, the British firm Humber introduced a 22-pound diamond-frame bike built of aluminum tubes mechanically clamped together with steel lugs. This necessitated inserting steel liners in the ends of the frame tubes. The Humber machines weren't durable and were soon discontinued.

Aluminum only has about one-third the stiffness (modulus of elasticity) of steel. To achieve stiffness and maintain low weight, the diameter of the tubing has to be increased. But for many decades the few bicycle makers who built aluminum frames typically used tubing similar in diameter to that in steel frames. Another drawback of aluminum is that, unlike steel, it has no fixed fatigue limit and can fail under fairly low stress with enough repetitions. Owing to aluminum's deficiencies in stiffness and resistance to fatigue, frames made of it were inferior to steel frames, even if they were somewhat lighter.

A few French makers produced beautiful aluminum frames, such as Caminade's Caminargents of the late 1930s. In 1948, the British firms Holdsworth and Hobbs both exhibited all-welded aluminum-alloy frames, but they don't seem to have manufactured them in large quantities. In 1949, Raleigh exhibited a 16-pound bicycle of similar construction. It got a lot of publicity, but wasn't series produced.

In 1967, the British Aluminium Company (BACo) undertook research for its sister company Raleigh. (At the time, both were owned by Tube Investments.) BACo made a study of past aluminum racing bicycle frames and found that all had been based on the conventional triangulated tubular steel design. It concluded that the few commercially successful machines had had mechanical joints with tapers and/or clamps, and that, used in this way, aluminum didn't offer advantages over steel as a frame material. BACo and Raleigh later built an experimental aluminum monocoque prototype; series production did not follow. An alternative approach to monocoque aluminum construction was demonstrated in 1986 by the Italian designers Fabrizio Carola and Carla Matessi. Their Aluetta commuter bicycle (Italian patent 19,748A of 1986) had a frame made up of two half-shells of honeycomb-core aluminum. In the late 1980s, Raleigh America made lightweight frames of aluminum but stayed with the lugged diamond frame design and used the Technium system of adhesive bonding.

In the early 1990s, TIG-welded aluminum frames with large-diameter tubes, mostly made in the Far East, became widely available and fashionable, having been pioneered in the United States by Cannondale and Klein a decade earlier. TIG welding was found to work well if a much larger fillet was used at the joint than would be used with steel. Most TIG-welded aluminum joints looked a little crude, but, as with steel, improving the appearance was a manual job that cost time and money.

Few cycle makers in the West were able to manufacture aluminum frames as cheaply as their competitors in the Far East, and this hastened the demise of frame making in North America and Europe. The Heinz Kettler company in Germany, however, has produced TIG-welded aluminum city and trekking bicycles since 1977.

Because aluminum has much poorer fatigue performance than steel, the cheaper aluminum frames were overbuilt to avoid warranty and liability problems. Such frames were often therefore no lighter than steel ones.

Figure 12.8   An 1898 Humber aluminum bicycle (National Cycle Library).

Figure 12.9 A 1986 Aluetta—not a racer, but an interesting honeycomb-core aluminum monocoque (Carla Matessi/Fabrizio Carola and patent illustrations).

Titanium weighs half as much as steel but has a similar tensile strength. It is an expensive material with limited availability and a restricted choice of grades and sizes. Because it has a lower modulus of elasticity than steel, titanium is often said to give a flexible and soft ride; however, no fully triangulated diamond frame made of any metal can perceptibly absorb shock in the vertical plane.

Speedwell of Birmingham, an early maker of titanium frames, is thought to have used a fusion welding process as early as 1972. Raleigh later used Speedwell's Dynatech system, employing lugs with adhesive bonding. Most subsequent titanium frames were TIG welded.

In 1972, the American firm Teledyne introduced a titanium-frame bicycle called the Titan. It was raced with some success for several years (notably by Ron Skarin), but its forks and bottom brackets were subject to fatigue cracking and failure (probably traceable to corrosion), and it was discontinued around 1982.

There have been attempts to build racing bikes with frames of cast magnesium. Magnesium, not quite as strong as aluminum alloy, is the lightest readily available structural metal. The main frame of a racing bike called the Kirk Precision was made up of three magnesium castings glued together. Designed by the British automotive engineer Frank Kirk, it was the subject of several patents, the first applied for in 1984 (British patent 2,164,300A of 1988). Kirks were seen in some professional cycle races, including stages of the Tour de France. There were numerous frame failures, and the Kirk wasn't commercially successful despite investment from Norsk Hydro (the world's largest producer of magnesium) and marketing by Dawes Cycles.

Carbon fiber was developed in the late 1950s and the early 1960s in Britain, in the United States, and in Japan. Crucial work was done by the Royal Aircraft Establishment at Farnborough in 1963. Carbon fiber comprises tows (bundles) of very fine fibers which are held in place by cotton stitching or adhesive film, or are woven into a fabric, or are knitted into a three-dimensional shape. The fibers are then impregnated and coated with resin, which, after curing by heating or by chemical reaction, gives the material its strength. Often the material is placed in a mold under pressure during the curing process.

Frames partly built of carbon fiber first came on the market in the 1970s, but the best-known early carbon-fiber bike was the Peugeot PY10FC of the early 1980s. Its frame consisted of carbon-fiber tubes bonded into external aluminum lugs in a traditional diamond configuration.

In 1986, Kestrel of California launched the first series-produced all-carbon bicycle frame that wasn't of lugged tube design. Other makers followed suit, notably Trek and Giant. Giant's MCR was designed by a British engineer named Mike Burrows, who in 1982 had made what was probably the first true carbon-fiber monocoque frame. Burrows didn't built a complete bike until 1985; it was first raced on May 1 of that year. In 1986, Burrows built a version with a

Figure 12.10 A typical aluminum-framed racing bike of the early 2000s (Geoff Apps).

monoblade rather than a front fork. A derivative of that machine, the Lotus 108, was used by Chris Boardman to win the 4,000-meter sprint in the 1992 Olympics. On a Giant MCR, Andy Wilkinson set world time-trial records for 12 hours, 24 hours, 50 miles, and 100 miles.

Today, carbon-fiber frames are standard in professional cycle racing. The bikes, though typically described as monocoque, usually have curvaceous one-piece diamond frames.

Carbon fiber and other composites (including aramid and glass fiber) have a huge weight advantage over other frame materials. Their downside is that when they fail, they don't merely bend; they shatter. But they are very resistant to fatigue, and they are easy to repair.

Figure 12.11   Mike Burrows on his 1986 carbon-fiber Windcheetah monocoque (Hugh Swire).

AERODYNAMICS

In achieving high speed on a bicycle, air resistance is a much more important factor than weight or the number of gears available. At racing speeds, most of the rider's energy goes into fighting air resistance. Moreover, air resistance, unlike rolling resistance, increases exponentially with speed—that is, by the square of the velocity. Hence, anything that can be done to reduce air resistance is helpful.

Wind-tunnel tests conducted in 1957 by Tony Nonweiler of Britain's Cranfield College of Aeronautics showed the effects of equipment and rider position on air resistance (Nonweiler 1957). In 1958 and 1959, a faired streamlined bicycle called the Sputnik, built by the Swiss racing rider Oscar Egg, was raced at Manchester and proved faster than a four-man pursuit team. Such teams achieve higher speeds than solo riders because the riders follow one another closely to minimize aerodynamic drag, and because each rider takes a turn as the leader, who has to overcome the greatest air resistance (Abbott and Wilson 1995). In 1962, Alex Moulton tested two differently constructed fairings on prototypes of his 16-inch-wheel bicycle (Hadland 1981). The following year, Moulton applied for a patent for a bicycle with a large front fairing, a 16-inch front wheel, and a 22-inch rear wheel (British patent 1,018,962 of 1966). (The machine was never produced.) In 1980, Moulton sponsored wind-tunnel tests of his streamlined fairings by Douglas Milliken (Moulton, Hadland, and Milliken 2006).

Chester Kyle was a professor in the Mechanical Engineering Department of California State University at Long Beach. In 1973, he and some of his students conducted coastdown tests on a number of bicycles to measure air and rolling resistance. One of the machines they tested was a racing bicycle whose frame and wheels were covered with Mylar plastic sheeting (Kyle, Crawford, and Nadeau 1974). Later, Kyle performed coastdown tests of several streamlined vehicles that he and his students had built (Kyle and Edelman 1974). On November 11, 1974, with Ron Skarin as the rider, Kyle's streamlined Teledyne Titan broke four bicycle speed records on a runway at the Los Alamitos Naval Air Station ("New World Speed Record," *Bicycling*, January 1975), garnering worldwide publicity. Later, Kyle and his students learned that the Union Cycliste Internationale would not recognize records set with streamlined bicycles.

In 1975, Kyle, Jack Lambie, and Paul MacCready organized an open race for human-powered vehicles (HPVs) that wasn't limited by the UCI's rules. Announced in *Bicycling*, it was the first such race since one held in 1914 in Berlin. The fourteen entries included six streamlined standard bicycles, two long-wheelbase supine recumbent bicycles, three supine recumbent tricycles, two prone recumbent bicycles, and a prone recumbent tricycle. In 1976, after the *Guinness Book of World Records* refused to recognize the records set by the HPVs without the approval of some official organization, Chester Kyle and Jack Lambie organized the International Human Powered Vehicle Association. Open races for HPVs have been held yearly throughout the world since 1975, and HPV clubs have been established in various countries outside the United States. There are eleven national associations in Europe.

The pioneering work by Kyle and his collaborators in the IHPVA had a profound effect. In 1974, the bicycle industry ignored aerodynamics and alternative bicycle designs almost entirely. There were no airfoil-shaped tubes, no aero rims, no disc wheels, no aerodynamic components, no new riding positions, no aero helmets, no skin suits, no streamlined bicycles, and no commercially produced recumbents—items that are common today. Racing cyclists were still riding traditional bicycles of designs that were decades old.

After 1975, there was a sudden surge of public and commercial interest in bicycle aerodynamics. Builders of time-trial bikes began to use some streamlined elements. In 1978, Shimano introduced its first group of streamlined components, including streamlined seat posts and pedals. Other manufacturers introduced airfoil-shaped tubes, and "cow-horn" handlebars became popular. Racers in the Eastern European countries began wearing stream-lined helmets, shoe covers, and tight rubberized skin suits.

After the 1984 Olympic Games, in which Italian and American riders using disc wheels and aero bikes won gold in the individual pursuit and the 100-kilometer time trials and took medals in all rest of the time trials, bicycle racing was never the same. The Italian Olympic bikes had been designed by Antonio dal Monte, the American ones by a group led by Chester Kyle. They were the first examples of modern aero bikes, lacking only aero-bars, which were developed later (Abbott and Wilson 1995).

Even with the rules the UCI introduced in 2000 to restrict the use of aerodynamic com-ponents, all elite racing bicycles and their riders now use a variety of legal aerodynamic components to increase speed, including disc rear wheels, aero-spoke front wheels, airfoil-shaped frame tubing, aero-bars, shoe covers, streamlined helmets and wind-tunnel tested aerodynamic clothing, such as Nike's Swift range.

RIDING POSITION AND AERO-BARS

Even before the aerodynamics of the bicycle began to be properly understood, it was apparent that stooping to reduce one's frontal area had a noticeable beneficial effect on one's speed, and thus a racing bike often had a lower handlebar position than a road bike. Many different styles of drop handlebars have been used since the days of the high-wheeler. Subtle variations on old themes continue to be produced, often in newer materials such as carbon fiber.

The development in the 1980s of "aero-bars" or "tri-bars" for triathlon and ultra-marathon riders was part of a move to refine the riding position for better aerodynamic advantage. Tri-bars have handgrips well ahead of the rider and close together, and also have elbow supports. They permit a variety of forward-stooped riding positions, ranging from the traditional triathlon stance to the forward-stretched "Superman" stance.

Pete Penseyres of the United States was a pioneer of aero-bars; he used them on his record-breaking ride in the 1986 Race Across America. However, it took many years for them to become common in bicycle racing. Triathlon competitors, who tend to be less traditional than competitors in other events, were the first to use them. One early adopter of aero-bars for standard racing was Chris Boardman of Great Britain, who won gold in the 4,000-meter individual pursuit in the 1992 Barcelona Olympics.

The most famous of all bicycle world records, that for distance traveled in one hour, was broken five times between 1984 and 1988 by Francesco Moser of Italy, who used standard cow-horn bars.

The first rider to break the hour record using aero-bars was Graham Obree, in 1993. Obree, an English-born Scottish bicycle mechanic, self-taught engineer, and amateur bike racer, was one of the most creative bike designers in the UK. In 1993, he invented a new riding position—arms folded under the shoulders and resting on the bars—and built a bike to suit it. In 1993, riding his own bike, Obree rode 51.596 kilometers in an hour, breaking Moser's 1988 record. The UCI soon banned Obree's position and voided any subsequent records set with his position. Chris Boardman then broke Obree's hour record, achieving 52.27 kilometers with standard aero-bars. In 1994, Obree invented the "Superman" position and set a new hour record of 52.719 kilometers. From 1994 until 2000, when the UCI banned it, the Obree "Superman" position was used to break dozens of records in time trials, including the Olympic and World records for 4,000 meters.

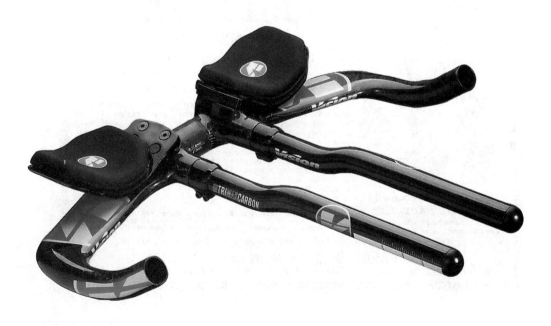

Figure 12.12 A catalog picture of a Vision TriMax Carbon SI Aerobar.

OTHER AERODYNAMIC COMPONENTS

Aerodynamic accessories for bicycles were first marketed in the early days of the pneumatic-tired safety bicycle. In 1893 B. Larue & Cie. sold a demountable transparent fairing called Le Papillon. This was an early forerunner of devices such as the demountable polycarbonate Zzipper fairings developed in California by Glen Brown from the mid 1970s on (US patent Des. 248,638 of 1976).

In the late 1890s, Archibald Sharp advocated a cycle cape that could double as an aerodynamic shape when attached to a bicycle. Capes for this purpose, incorporating inflatable rims to hold them in shape, were commercially available around that time (Wilson 2004, 185).

Figure 12.13 An 1893 advertisement for the Larue Papillon fairing

Étienne Bunau-Varilla designed and constructed a Vélo Torpille (Torpedo Bike) that had a "teardrop-shaped" fairing that enclosed the rider's whole body other than the lower legs (British patent 22,510 of 1913). In 1913, using this machine, Marcel Berthet set a new world record, completing 5 kilometers on Paris's Vel d'Hiv track in 5 minutes and 39.3 seconds—about 33 miles per hour. The German cycle makers Brennabor and Göricke copied the Vélo Torpille, but in 1914 the UCI banned aerodynamic devices in normal cycle racing.

After World War I, there were other aerodynamic experiments. Oscar Egg fitted himself with a tail cone. A much more serious effort was the Vélodyne, designed by the aerodynamicist Marcel Riffard, a French citizen born in Argentina. Riffard had worked on Bunau-Varilla's Vélo Torpille. By the 1930s he was employed by the French aircraft firm Avions Caudron. The Vélodyne had an aerodynamic shell made from spruce and tulipwood. Inside was a bicycle

Figure 12.14   A press clipping showing Étienne Bunau-Varilla supporting Marcel Berthet in the Vélo Torpille (Arnfried Schmitz).

Figure 12.15 Marcel Berthet and Marcel Riffard with the Vélodyne (Arnfried Schmitz).

similar to a stayer (a motorcycle-paced bike), with a backward-facing fork and a smaller front wheel.

In 1933, at Le Parc des Princes in Paris, Marcel Berthet in the Vélodyne broke the UCI hour record for "special bikes with device to reduce air resistance." Then 45 years old and well past his prime, he covered 48.604 kilometers at an average of about 30 miles per hour. He estimated that the fairing gave him a speed advantage of 30 percent over the same machine unfaired. Thereafter, because they were banned in normal racing, fairings were more or less consigned to history until the coming of the HPV movement in the 1970s.

Although it has sometimes been disputed, wind-tunnel and field tests have shown that aerodynamic frame tubes have less air drag than conventional tubes. Any tube that is "teardrop shaped" or elliptical in cross-section is aerodynamically superior to a round tube of equal diameter (Hoerner 1965). Aero frame tubes with a 2.31:1 ratio have a 26 percent lower drag coefficient than round tubes of equal diameter. The UCI currently specifies 3:1 as the limit for frame tubes. Tubes with that ratio have a 53 percent lower drag coefficient than round tubes (Abbott and Wilson 1995, 152).

For optimal streamlining, the cross-section of a tube should be approximately "teardrop shaped," with the rounded (blunt) end facing forward. The cross-section should be three to four times the maximum width (a "fineness ratio" of between 3:1 and 4:1). Such tubes are difficult to incorporate into a standard racing bicycle. However, it is quite easy, using composites, to make a seat post with a 4:1 section ratio. Such seat posts were pioneered in the early 1980s by Mike Burrows, whose interest in aerodynamics was greatly stimulated by the IHPVA. Composite 4:1 aero seat posts were introduced in the early 1990s by Giant (for whom Burrows then worked); other makers, including Pro-Lite, followed suit. Burrows also demonstrated that similar airfoil sections could be used in handlebars constructed from composites; modern handlebars of this type include the Vision TriMax Carbon SI Aerobar and the USE Tula Aero Base.

Burrows also applied the 4:1 airfoil approach to wheel supports, creating the aerodynamic monoblade to replace the traditional fork. James Starley had used monoblades as early as 1872, J. Keen had used them a few years later, and J. S. Smith of the Surrey Machinists Company had used them in 1889 (Bartleet 1931, 87). Examples of more recent series-produced monoblade machines are the Strida folding bicycle, designed by Mark Sanders in the 1980s, and the Giant Halfway folder, designed by Mike Burrows in the 1990s. But in none of these cases was the monoblade adopted for aerodynamic reasons.

Aerodynamic design has been applied to wheels more than to any other bicycle component. The British inventor Arthur Comings Hide, who applied for a patent for sheet-metal wheels in 1892 (British patent 496,937 of 1893), was less interested in aerodynamic advantage than in strength and light weight. Hide mentioned defensively that his wheel didn't have materially higher air resistance than a plain disc wheel, which suggests that he had some appreciation of aerodynamics. However, he wasn't aware that his wheels might have possessed an aerodynamic advantage.

A disc rear wheel was tried on the 1913 Vélo Torpille (Schmitz 2000, 3). Soon afterward, disc wheels were used on both the front and the rear of the Brennabor Fish ridden by Piet Dickentman in a race in Berlin on April 4, 1914. The front wheel was unstable in cross winds, and Dickentman lost the race to the Göricke Bomb ridden by Arthur Stelbrink (Abbott and Wilson 1995, 100).

Figure 12.16 USE Tula Aero Base handlebars and levers (USE).

Interest in disc wheels increased in the 1980s. Discs that could be added to conventional spoked wheels achieved some popularity in BMX competition. Such discs were typically made from lightweight moldable materials, such as rigid polystyrene. Wind-tunnel testing increased understanding of bicycle aerodynamics and especially of the effects of spoke turbulence. Flat-bladed spokes were found to have lower drag than round spokes (Abbott and Wilson 1995, 149).

In early 1984, Francesco Moser used disc wheels when he broke the hour record. Around that time, applications for patents for true disc wheels began to appear. An application filed in 1985 by Antonio Monte of Rome (US patent 4,732,428 of 1988) was for a streamlined wheel formed by two hollow half-shells coupled to form a biconvex lenticular shape with a groove for a tire around its circumference. This design was good aerodynamically. Many disc wheels that reached the market were less efficient, being flat sandwiches of foam in a composite shell.

Figure 12.17 The Vélo Torpille with a disc rear wheel (Arnfried Schmitz).

Others had a double conical cross-section, which was better than a flat disc but less efficient than the lenticular design.

In 1985, the French firm Mavic introduced full disc wheels of either carbon fiber (the Comete) or aluminum alloy (the Challenger). In 1988, Compositech, based in Indianapolis, introduced its Zipp carbon-fiber disc wheels, and Corima of France also entered the market. Full disc wheels are used only on the rear, except on indoor tracks where crosswinds are not a problem.

An alternative to the solid disc is the three-spoke, four-spoke, or five-spoke composite aerodynamic wheel with an aerodynamic rim 30–75 millimeters deep. The purpose of such a wheel is to try to approach the aerodynamic advantage of a full disc while presenting less sail area to destabilizing crosswinds. A patent application for a composite wheel with a deep aero-section rim and true airfoil-section spokes was filed in 1988 by Mark Hopkins and Frank Principe of Delaware; the patent (US patent 4,919,490 of 1990) was assigned to the DuPont company. Wheels made according to this patent were marketed first by Specialized and later by Hed. Steve Hed and Robert Haug filed their own patent application in 1989 (US patent 5,061,013 of 1991). Hed's company became one of the world leaders in this field, along with Zipp, Corima, and Mavic. Zipp started making a three-spoke wheel in 1989, Corima launched a four-spoke wheel in 1990, and Mavic introduced a three-spoke wheel in 1992.

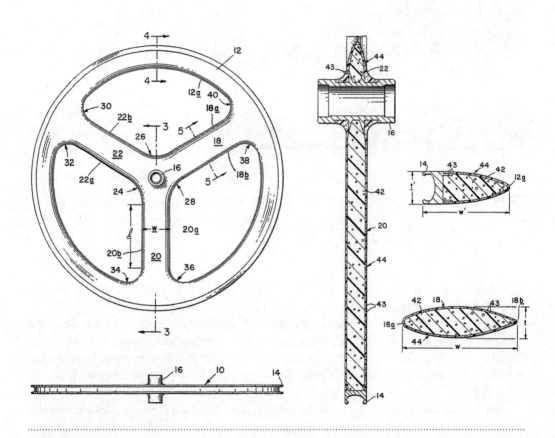

Figure 12.18   Left: Elevation and plan views of the DuPont aero wheel. Right: Sections through spokes, hub, and rim (patent drawings).

A third aerodynamic wheel style, which evolved during the same period, again used a deep aerodynamic rim but had tension spokes. The rim could be either rolled or extruded aluminum or molded composite, with a metal sub-rim if a braking surface was needed. This style of wheel had less aerodynamic advantage but was also less affected by side winds. It was therefore more suitable for use in road races.

THE EFFECT OF REGULATIONS

Cycle sport has long been governed by various national and international bodies, some of which lay down rules affecting the design of bicycles. The best-known and most restrictive organization involved is the Union Cycliste International, founded in 1900 and based in Switzerland. The UCI produces rules for many different types of cycle racing, some of them very complex; for example, the 2011 rules for track racing alone took up 96 pages. UCI rules are often also very arbitrary, and some (such as the rule enforced in the 2011 Tour de France that the saddle must be exactly level, with no tilt whatsoever) appear to be pointless. The UCI forbids recumbent bicycles; it also rules out many small-wheeled machines and various aerodynamic aids, such as fairings.

The International Human Powered Vehicle Association's rules for land vehicles, only 232 words long, are devoted mostly to precluding non-human power sources, energy-storage devices, remote control, and sails. Apart from that, you can do what you like.

The UCI states that its mission is "to develop and promote cycling, in close collaboration with National Federations, be it as a competition sport and its associated values (effort, well-being, and fair play), as a healthy recreational activity or as a means of transport." There is, however, a strong case to be made that the UCI has been a major impediment to the development of human-powered transport and the bicycle in particular. Other bodies, such as the International Triathlon Union, govern certain types of cycle sport and tend to be more permissive than the UCI in matters of bicycle design.

For a comprehensive account of the conflict between technological development and the UCI, see Kyle 2001.

MILITARY BICYCLES 13

In this chapter we trace the history of the bicycle's use and adaptation for military purposes. This is a topic that captured the imagination of certain inventors and military strategists, particularly before armies were motorized. But although bicycles have been widely used by some armies for short-range transport away from combat zones, they have rarely been used to any great extent in combat situations. The most impressive military use of bicycles has been the use of standard diamond-frame utility versions to move troops and supplies.

EARLY MILITARY USE OF BICYCLES

The earliest known depiction of military use of a bicycle, published by Karl Drais (1817a), is an artist's impression of a Badenian army staff messenger. Quite a few years were to pass before bicycles evolved sufficiently to attract the interest of the major armies, although there seems to have been some discussion of a military use of the early velocipede in the 1830s—Drais informed the grand duke in 1833 that "draisine corps shall be raised in the great planes of America according to newspapers" (Rauck 1983, 331), and Thomas Stephens Davies asserted in his 1837 lecture on the velocipede at the Royal Military Academy of Woolwich that "several foreign writers were of opinion that such machines might afflict the march of bodies of infantry, by enabling the soldier not only to get over ground more rapidly and easily, but also carry his arms, provisions and ammunition, with less trouble or inconvenience . . . the advantage of taking this weight from the shoulders of the man and placing it upon two wheels appears obvious."

After the Franco-Prussian War, military interest in cycling increased rapidly. By 1875, cycle messengers were used in Italian military maneuvers. Cyclists were soon performing similar roles in Austria-Hungary, Switzerland, Germany, Britain, and France. They were also used as scouts. Formal military cycling sections were established in several armies; both Britain and Spain did so in 1887 (Brun 2010, 157).

When rear-drive safety bicycles came on the market, the British army set up a committee to consider specifications for military bicycles. Fifty-one cycle makers contributed ideas. In the spring of 1888, the committee announced this conclusion:

> If it were intended that volunteer cyclists should be employed solely as messengers . . . the ordinary bicycle [i.e., high-wheeler] would fulfill most of the requirements of a military machine, but as we are aware that the wish of the War Office authorities is that volunteer cyclists shall be efficient Infantry soldiers, capable of rapidly moving considerable distances in compact bodies, and carrying their aims, a large amount of ammunition, and their kits, on all kinds of passable roads, and of conveying their

Figure 13.1   A plate, published by Karl Drais in 1817, depicting a Badenian army staff messenger (Drais 1817c).

Die Laufmaschine des
Freiherrn Carl von Drais.

machines when dismounted over any kind of country, we at once abandoned all thoughts of the ordinary bicycles, and decided in favor of the rear-driving safety bicycle, which by reason of its diminished height and longer wheelbase, is to be preferred to the ordinary bicycle; while in that it occupies less space . . . is lighter, more speedy and easier to handle, the rear-driving safety bicycle is better adopted to the use of the rank and file than even a tricycle.

Unable to recommend any of the machines submitted, the committee drew up its own specifications for a military bicycle. By this time, the British army was seeking to use cyclists not only as messengers and scouts but also as a mobile fighting force. Some experts thought that

Figure 13.2 A Hillman, Herbert & Cooper military cross-frame bicycle of 1888, as illustrated in the London journal *Engineering*. Unusually, the chain is on the left side.

cyclists would be able to travel greater distances—up to 100 miles a day on good roads—and more quietly than cavalry. And they wouldn't have to feed and water horses, or to hold them during fighting. However, because cyclists could not easily fight while mounted, they would be at a disadvantage when pursuing an enemy who suddenly beat a retreat. Other nations, meanwhile, continued to use cyclists mainly as messengers in garrison towns and large military camps (M.H., "Cads on castors, part I," *The Boneshaker* 104, 1983).

In the early 1890s, the great cycle maker Colonel Albert Pope tried to persuade the US Army to adopt bicycles. By 1892, he was supplying a special Columbia safety bicycle, with cushion tires and rifle clips on the top tube, to the First Signal Corps of the Connecticut National Guard (Herlihy 2004, 258). Four years later, American Lieutenant James Moss formed

Figure 13.3 French military cyclists, as depicted in *Scientific American*'s issue of November 30, 1889.

Figure 13.4 Two 1896 Pope military bicycles: a solo machine equipped with a Browning machine gun and a tandem fitted with pistols and a rifle (*Polytechnisches Journal* 301, 1896, 179).

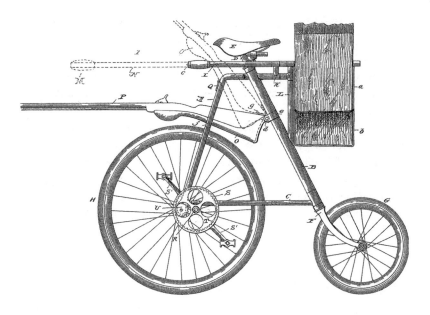

Figure 13.5 James Anderson's seat-steered military bicycle of 1899 (patent drawing).

and led the 25th Infantry Bicycle Corps. Their rugged bicycles were built to Moss's own speci-fication and included full chaincases. In 1897, Moss successfully led twenty soldiers on a 2,000-mile expedition across five states. But he failed to impress his superiors, and the corps was disbanded (ibid., 292–293).

Pope created other bicycles for military use. In 1896, he offered a safety bicycle for use with a Browning machine gun and a military tandem that could carry a repeater rifle, two pis-tols, ammunition, a signal flag, and two greatcoats (Kielwein and Lessing 2005, 89).

In France, Métropole offered a folding military diamond-frame bicycle with shaft drive, the Model 152 Acatène Militaire (Métropole catalog, 1897).

A more radical design came from James Anderson of Illinois (US patent 633,745 of 1899). This was a geared front-driver with a small rear wheel, over which was a large equipment rack. Rear-wheel steering, operated by swiveling the saddle, left the hands free for shooting. At least one example was made (Fitzpatrick 1998, 47).

In the Boer War (1899–1902), the British army deployed cyclists mainly as dispatch riders. In World War I, British cyclist battalions were used to rapidly reinforce weak points in a battle line; by that time, however, the attraction of the bicycle for mass troop movements was waning, as motorized transport had become more effective and was in wider use. In World War II, several armies adopted folding bicycles for parachutists, though they didn't see much use. Also in World War II, German troops on bicycles fought partisans in the mountains of Norway, and large numbers of Japanese troops on bicycles successfully circumvented bridges blown up by the retreating British in Malaya.

In Vietnam in 1954, the defeat of the French by the Viet Minh at Dien Bien Phu was due largely to the insurgents' ability to transport large quantities of food, medical supplies, and ammunition through the jungle on "pack bikes" ("xe tho" in Vietnamese). A pack bike, laden like a mule with sacks that could carry 440 pounds or more of military supplies, was pushed along rather than ridden. The pilot used two stiff bamboo sticks, one attached to the handlebars as a tiller and the other extending upward from the seat tube to aid balancing and braking (Chen 2002).

DESIGN FEATURES OF MILITARY BICYCLES

The most effective military use of bicycles in actual combat situations—for example, by the Japanese in Malaya and the Viet Minh in Vietnam—involved cheap, more or less standard utility bicycles. The various fanciful special designs that were proposed were often impractical in reality. (If you were a machine gunner, would you rather be a sitting target astride a bicycle, or hiding behind a rock or in a trench?)

In World War I, bicycles that were actually adopted for widespread military use, as distinct from those that were merely prototyped, often differed from basic roadsters only inasmuch that they were more robust and had clips for carrying a rifle. The 1915 Military Sunbeam is typical (Pinkerton and Roberts 2002, 302–303). In World War II, major cycle manufacturers in the UK and the US produced standardized bicycles for military use, often without any fittings to carry weapons. The "Bicycle, Military, Universal" adopted by the US Ordnance Department in 1942 was a rugged version of the Westfield Columbia roadster and was made by both Westfield and Huffman. In the UK, the BSA Mark V military roadster was produced by BSA, Raleigh, and other manufacturers. Raleigh alone produced 200,000 bicycles—a mix of roadsters and folding bikes—for military use in World War II (Hadland 2011, 99).

The most enduring military bicycle was the Swiss army's MO 05 (short for Model 1905), introduced in 1905 and nicknamed the "Drahtesel" ("wire donkey"). It remained in production until 1981. In all, about 68,000 were produced by five or six different makers. The MO 05 remained in use, with only minor specification changes, until the early 1990s. A single-speed

Figure 13.6   Above: A Sunbeam Military model of 1915 (catalog illustration). Below: Indian troops of the British army with BSA military bicycles during World War II (National Cycle Library).

Figure 13.7 A Swiss MO 05 (VeloSolo).

machine weighing more than 50 pounds, it had 28-inch wheels and a heavy-duty ³⁄₁₆-inch chain. The front brake was a plunger, the rear a coaster. After World War II, a second rear hub brake, operated by a cable, was fitted. Luggage bags could be fitted between the top, seat, and down tubes and between the rear mudguard, the seat stays, and the seat tube. Front and rear luggage racks could be fitted, too (Van Helden 2011; George and Surber 1995).

In 1993 the MO 05 was replaced by a new model influenced by mountain bike design, the MO 93. Slightly lighter, it had hydraulic brakes, a seven-speed derailleur, and very rugged racks (the rear one welded to the frame). Tubular frames to hold panniers could be fitted. The paint was invisible to infrared night vision glasses (Van Helden 2011; George and Surber 1995).

The MO 93's proposed replacement, evaluated in 2011, also showed mountain bike influence; it had hydraulic disc brakes and an eight-speed hub gear (Van Helden 2011).

FOLDING OR SEPARABLE MILITARY CYCLES

Some of the best-known military bicycles could be folded. Why this complication? The idea was that a soldier would carry his bike, folded, on his back when traversing a fence, a wall, a ditch, a stream, soft ground, or some other obstacle or stretch of difficult terrain. The earliest military folder is said to have been created in 1893 by a lieutenant in the Belgian army (Brun 2010, 157).

The first foldable bike to attract significant military attention was designed by Capitaine Henry Gérard, author of *Infanterie cycliste en campagne*, an 1898 treatise on the use of bicycles by infantrymen. While a lieutenant in the French army, Gérard was garrisoned at Grenoble. There he collaborated with a local industrialist named Charles Morel. Together they applied for a French patent for a folding military bicycle in January of 1896. At first the machine (then called the Capitaine Gérard) was manufactured by Morel's company, but by 1901 it was a Peugeot product called La Pliante (The Folder) and marketed to the general public as well as the military. The unusual frame lacked a top tube and had two parallel telescopic folding down tubes attached to a curved telescopic tube that extended from the bottom bracket to the top of the seat stays. The seat stays were pivoted at their base and doubled as seat tubes, the saddle being supported on a pair of thin seat posts held in the seat stays. This arrangement allowed the fore-and-aft position of the saddle to be varied relative to the bottom bracket and the handlebars.

Foldable military bikes made in other countries followed the French lead but were generally folding versions of the increasingly popular diamond frame. The first patent application for a folding diamond frame seems to have been filed in 1893 by Michael Ryan of Boston (US patent 518,330 of 1894). A simpler approach was used in the Faun folding cycle, which went on sale in Britain in 1896. Its diamond frame folded around a vertical hinge forming a brace between the top tube and down tube. Although the Faun wasn't a military machine, several subsequent military folding safeties incorporated similar arrangements, combining a vertical frame hinge with a brace between the top and down tubes. Ryan soon developed an even simpler design for a folding diamond frame; it dispensed with the brace and had separate hinges in the top and down tubes (US patent 599,016 of 1898).

In 1898, Lieutenant T. L. Wagtendonk of the Dutch army designed a shaft-drive folding bicycle. Like the Capitaine Gérard, it came with shoulder straps to enable a soldier to carry it on his back. But it had a much simpler diamond frame, which could be folded in half by means of a vertical tube connecting the top and down tubes. The Wagtendonk cycle was manufactured in Deventer. Another Dutch maker, Simplex of Amsterdam, made simpler diamond-frame military folders. In 1909, yet another Dutch manufacturer, Fongers of Groningen, produced a

Figure 13.8 Depictions of French soldiers carrying folding Capitaine Gérard bicycles, of the variable geometry of the Capitaine Gérard, and of a folded Capitaine Gérard with shoulder straps (National Cycle Library).

prototype of a small-wheeled military folder. Six years later, Fongers unveiled a version with standard-size wheels. Both Fongers machines had frame-folding arrangements broadly similar to Wagtendonk's. The Dutch army didn't adopted either of them (Drouen 1993, 10–16).

In England, the Danish inventor Mikael Pedersen designed a portable military version of his hammock-saddle bicycle. This version had smaller wheels (24 inches) than Pedersen's civilian models, and the frame was lower and the seat farther back so that the rider could shoot from the saddle with both feet on the ground. The Pedersen Military was a separable machine rather than a true folder; the front fork, with the handlebars and the wheel, was fastened to the frame by a single strap and could be quickly detached. Unlike most other military bicycles, which stowed the rifle longitudinally on the frame between the rider's legs, on the Pedersen the rifle was carried vertically on two sprung brackets. The claimed weight of a production model was a mere 19 pounds. Pedersen failed to persuade either the British or the Danish army to buy his machine (Evans 1992, 39–40).

In 1902, the British War Office adopted cycle fittings made by Birmingham Small Arms for all its military bicycles, regardless of what company assembled the complete machine. In 1910, BSA began making bicycles under its own name for the first time. From 1911 to 1913, BSA offered the Territorial model, which had rifle supports. It was apparently intended for private sale to members of Britain's Territorial Army—that is, army reservists.

In December of 1908, Captain A. H. Trapmann of the 25th (Cyclists) Battalion, part of the London Regiment, gave a lecture ("The Cyclist in Warfare") in which he commented on the use of military bicycles by other European countries:

> Turning to the Continent, we find that France still holds the lead, and has one permanent Company of Cyclists forming part of various rifle battalions, in addition to a liberal supply of cyclist orderlies and scouts in every regiment. . . . The Italians have during the past year turned four companies of Bersagleiri into cyclists, and also greatly increased this establishment during the maneuvers. Large bodies of cyclists operating against cavalry also formed a feature of this year's manoeuvers in Belgium. Germany is still a long way behind the above-named countries in the matter of military cycling. . . .

Captain Trapmann, though a strong advocate of military bicycles and their use in a cavalry role, was vehemently opposed to folders:

> There are, more especially on the Continent, critics who advocate the use of the folding cycle for military purposes. I cannot but believe that these must mostly be people who have never ridden a folding bicycle. It is heavy, lacks rigidity and strength,

entails loss of time in folding and unfolding, and even when it has been folded and is strapped on to the back in such a manner, by the way, that it cannot possibly be unstrapped except by the assistance of a comrade, it is the most unwieldy burthen I have ever carried. (Trapmann 1901)

Trapmann's views echoed comments made in an 1897 book by Hauptmann Julius Burck-hart, Bavaria's chief of military cycling courses: "The use of folding bicycles for military purposes appears to be an error to us. Every bicycle can be carried by two belts across the back." (von Salvisberg 1897, 150) Nonetheless, the Adlerwerke in Germany and the Steyr Waffenfabrik in Austria both produced folding military bicycles. The Austrian company Styria produced a folder for the Swiss army in 1896 and another in 1897; the latter had folding handlebars that proved dangerously unreliable. The Swiss army carried out a thorough appraisal of folding bicycles in late 1902 and early 1903, then decided to reject folding bicycles altogether and develop the MO 05 (George and Surber 1995).

But in Britain opposition to folding military bicycles didn't prevail, despite Captain Trapmann's advice. During World War I, BSA produced two types of folding diamond-frame bicycles. One had a folding mechanism with a vertical tube linking the top and down tubes, as pioneered in the Faun and used subsequently in the Wagtendonk and Fongers machines. (The precise details of the hinges, catches, and levers varied from maker to maker.) The other BSA folder had a hinged joint approximately halfway along the top tube, and another directly below it in the down tube, more like Ryan's later folder. However, there is very little evidence that British troops found the folding capability of these machines useful (Hadland and Pinkerton 1996, 16–17).

The Russian cycle maker Leitner also made folding military cycles during WW1. Leitner used the vertical brace hinge principle, but didn't use a conventional horizontal top tube; the top tube of its machine ran almost parallel to the down tube. An additional tube ran from the top of the seat tube to the hinge point on the top tube.

The Italian maker Bianchi was a major manufacturer of military bicycles. Its 1912 military folder had hinges in the top and down tubes, without a vertical bracing tube, broadly in the manner of Michael Ryan's simplified 1898 design. The 1912 Bianchi had solid tires and light but robust front and rear suspensions. Other interesting design features included a front caliper brake with rod linkage concealed in the steering head and a lightweight rear rack for a bedroll ("Bianchi" at http://bsamuseum.wordpress.com).

In the interwar years, the armies of Germany, Italy, and Britain formed paratroop regiments. Attention was given to the possibility that such forces could use folding bicycles to disperse rapidly from their landing zones. The BSA Airborne Bicycle, probably the best known of all military folders, was created with this in mind. It is often referred to as the Parabike,

Figure 13.9 Left: A Dursley Pedersen Military model (1905 catalog). Center: A Russian stamp depicting a 1917 Leitner folding military bicycle. Above right: Michael Ryan's 1893 design (patent drawing). Below right: A BSA-designed World War I military folder built by Phillips (National Cycle Library).

although that was never its official name; the only product officially known as the Parabike was a non-folding toy version produced by BSA after World War II (Hadland and Pinkerton 1996, 26–29).

In 1940, two employees of BSA, Albert Edward Wood and William Henry Taylor, designed the Airborne Bicycle (British patent 543,076 of 1942). The frame was more an ellipse than a diamond, the curved seat stays and chain stays being continued forward of the seat tube to form twin top and down tubes. The duplex frame design may have been influenced by the Moorson Twin Tube bicycles, which would have been well known to Wood and Taylor and which were designed, patented, and built by another Birmingham bicycle maker, Francis Ernest Moore (British patent 269,418 of 1927).

The first production version of the BSA Airborne Bicycle had twin seat tubes; they were soon superseded by a conventional single seat tube. The pedals were simply tubes for the rider's insteps—acceptable for riding short distances in army boots, but not good for long-distance riding. These pedal tubes could be pushed through the crank to reduce the width of the bicycle. Annular grooves in the pedal tubes helped locate them in either the extended

Figure 13.10 A BSA Airborne Bicycle (National Cycle Library).

or retracted mode. The frame hinges followed the general layout established by Bianchi's 1912 model, with no vertical brace between the top and down tubes.

Although paratroopers were trained to jump with the Airborne Bicycle, in real combat they rarely did so. However, the graceful lines of the BSA Airborne Model inspired imitators. At various times since the end of World War II, bicycles derived from this design were made in Denmark, in Italy, and in the UK. In the 1990s, Pashley introduced bicycles inspired by the BSA Airborne Model. Still in production in 2013, they didn't fold (Hadland and Pinkerton 1996, 26–29).

During World War II, BSA's Airborne Bicycle staved off competition from Raleigh, whose designer Sidney Walter Buxton created a folding diamond-frame military model that was sometimes referred to informally as the Commando. Raleigh ended up making BSA's design.

The American cycle manufacturer Westfield produced a military model during World War II. Known as the Compax, it dispensed with a top tube and relied on a single main beam (an oversized down tube) to link the head tube to the seat tube. Instead of folding, the main beam separated from the seat tube. It was designed in 1937 by Albert Rippenbein of New York (US patent 2,211,164 of 1940). Civilian versions were made before and after the war. There is no hard evidence of use of the Compax in combat situations, but the Marine Corps is known to have tested it.

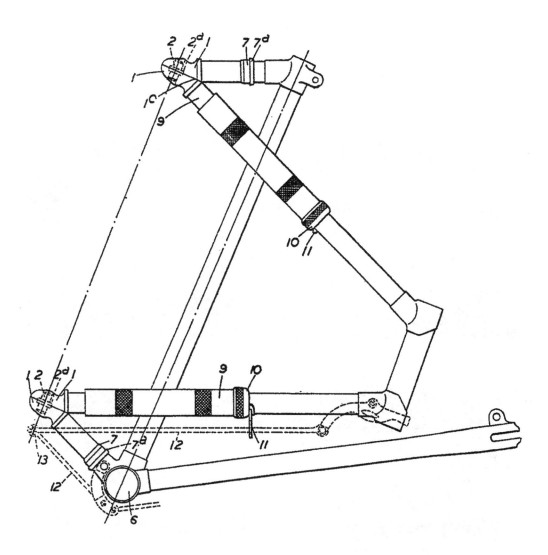

Figure 13.11 Raleigh's prototype military folder (patent drawing).

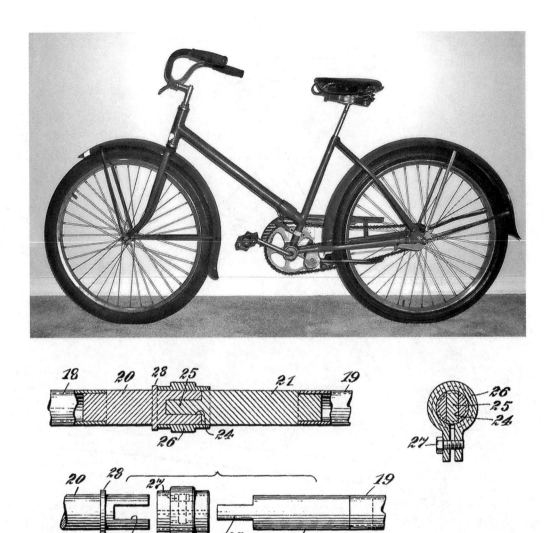

Figure 13.12 Above: A postwar civilian Compax sold as the Paratrooper (Easywind). Below: Details of the frame joint (patent drawings).

Figure 13.13   A Montague Paratrooper (Montague Corporation).

Efforts to design folding bicycles for paratroopers didn't cease with the end of World War II. The best-known recent example is the Montague Paratrooper, produced in Taiwan for the Montague Corporation of Cambridge, Massachusetts. In 1997, Montague received a two-year grant from the US government's Defense Advanced Research Projects Agency to develop an electrically assisted mountain bike. Its frame would have to fold faster and be stronger than Montague's Bi-Frame of the 1980s (a diamond frame with a hinge formed by concentric seat tubes, one fixed to the rear triangle and the other to the top and down tubes). The new frame still hinged around the seat tube but had a single main beam in place of the top and down tubes. This allowed it to be folded using a single catch, whereas the Bi-Frame had two. The US military didn't generally adopt the electrically assisted version. The Montague Paratrooper, a purely pedal-powered derivative, proved more successful, and versions were put on sale to the general public. We have yet to see any evidence that the Paratrooper has been used in combat.

Despite the ingenuity of inventors, unorthodox bicycles designed specifically for military use have been noteworthy for their lack of success. BSA's folding Airborne Bicycles were certainly used during the Allies' invasion of Europe in 1944, but one was more likely to see such a bike wheeled ashore than to see one unfolded by a paratrooper and ridden away (Hadland and Pinkerton 1996, 28). They were mostly used just like any ordinary roadster. The folding option—the very reason for the existence of the non-standard design—was largely superfluous.

EFFECTIVE MILITARY USE OF BICYCLES

On a few occasions, an army has used bicycles to gain a strategic advantage that it would not otherwise have had. Two examples are the Japanese army in Malaya in World War II and the Viet Cong in the Vietnam War. The machines used were essentially conventional diamond-frame bicycles.

MOUNTAIN BIKES

14

In 1869, in the days of the Michaux-style velocipede, a German magazine featured a fanciful drawing of a Gebirgevelocipede (mountain bicycle) being assisted in its climbing by a large hydrogen balloon (Berto 1998, 64). It is doubtful that any such machine was ever built. It is certain, however, that for many years there have been cyclists who have enjoyed off-road riding. An early example was Amos Sugden, who in 1890 took his heavy bicycle over Sty Head Pass in England's Lake District and wrote about his exploits in the *CTC Gazette*.

In the second half of the twentieth century, interest in off-road riding grew. The UK's Rough Stuff Fellowship was founded in 1955. Its members generally used fairly standard bicycles. By 1960, organized off-road trials were regular events in the Darlington area of northeastern England. The riders built their own bikes, often using frames rescued from scrap heaps, and called them "bogwheels." The typical bogwheel had 26 × 1⅜-inch speedway tires, a Sturmey-Archer three-speed or four-speed hub, a specially made 28-tooth sprocket, and a chainwheel (taken from a moped) with 32 to 40 teeth. Some builders fashioned derailleurs that enabled them to switch between a 28-tooth sprocket and a 16-tooth one. The hub gears had doctored springs for better shifting and were fitted with lengths of inner tube around the gear cable and the end of the axle to keep mud out of the toggle chain. Some bogwheels had "ape-hanger" handlebars taken from trials motorcycles, and some had front suspensions taken from mopeds (Hadland 2011, 225–226).

In 1968, also in northern England, Geoff Apps began developing bikes specifically for off-road use. He designed a reinforced diamond frame and used a collection of motorcycle, BMX, and standard bicycle components, including Finnish 2-inch 650B snow tires and French self-adjusting moped brakes. In 1979, bikes designed by Apps went on sale under the name Cleland; they were produced commercially for five years (Hadland 2011, 226).

There were other off-road riders and experimenters at various times in various countries, but their efforts made little impact on the cycling scene. The great exception was a bunch of enthusiasts in California's Marin County in the 1970s.

ORIGINS

Racing of fat-tire "clunkers" began on the tracks and trails of Mount Tamalpais, in Marin County, in 1970. As was noted in chapter 6, Frank Schwinn introduced bicycles with balloon tires to the US market in 1933. Those bikes, typified by the Excelsior, had exceptionally shallow frame angles, a high bottom bracket, and long fork rake (offset). By 1973, it was clear that an older Schwinn frame made for use with balloon tires was the most durable basis for a clunker (Berto 1998, 29–33). By trial and error, clunker riders then found components that were suitable for their purposes. Cantilever brakes superseded coaster and drum brakes. A group of riders in the Cupertino area of Santa Clara County adopted derailleurs in 1973, and by 1976 derailleurs were well on the way to replacing single-speed drives and hub gears on Marin County clunkers (ibid., 32–36).

Joe Breeze's 1976 frame is thought to have been the first purpose-built mountain-bike frame. By 1979, complete new mountain bikes were being made in small numbers. Gary Fisher and Charlie Kelly assembled bikes using frames made by Tom Ritchey. Mass-produced mountain bikes for regular retail distribution, including Mike Sinyard's Specialized Stumpjumper and Bert Lawee's Univega Alpina Sport, appeared in 1982. The Stumpjumper weighed 28 pounds and sold for about $750. (For more on early mountain bikes, see Berto 1998, 43–57.)

Figure 14.1 A signed photograph of a 1961 appearance by some bogwheelers on a BBC telecast (Steve Slater).

Slowly but surely, mountain bikes spread around the world. In the UK only two or three models of mountain bikes were available in 1983; the next year there were about three dozen. A year later, Raleigh launched its Maverick range of mountain bikes (Hadland 2011, 231–232).

The abbreviation ATB (for "all-terrain bicycle") was a widely used alternative to "mountain bike." It was introduced by the American magazine *Bicycling* after the editorial staff decided that "mountain bike" was an unsuitable term and held a competition for a new name. Some makers adopted the term ATB for the reason that many potential customers lived in relatively flat areas. A few years later, MTB became fashionable as the abbreviation for "mountain bike" (Berto 1998, 164).

Figure 14.2 Geoff Apps in 1983 with a Cleland 29-inch-wheel off-road bike (Geoff Apps).

ADVANTAGES

Style, fashion, and peer pressure all figured in the popularization of the mountain bike. For years many male bicyclists in Western countries had felt compelled to ride drop-handlebar pseudo-racers, but the mountain bike made it socially acceptable to ride a comfortable bike with a relatively upright riding position and straight handlebars.

Robust fat tires also proved attractive. Besides making for more comfortable riding, they were significantly less puncture-prone than a racer's narrow-section high-pressure tires, and

Figure 14.3   A typical mountain bike of the early 1990s (Geoff Apps).

less likely to be damaged by, or caught in, potholes, drain covers, and streetcar tracks. Unlike the tires of racers, those of mountain bikes usually had automobile-style Schrader valves. The mountain bike also popularized North American 26-inch (559-millimeter) wheels worldwide. This led to the virtual disappearance of other once-popular 26-inch tires, such as the British 26 × 1⅜-inch and the French 650A (both of which had bead seat diameters of 590 millimeters).

   Two other wheel formats were adopted for full-size mountain bikes and achieved a following, particularly from 2000 on. Both were based on French metric formats and were larger than the standard American 26-inch (559-mm) wheel. The 650B (584 mm), although nominally 26 inches, typically had a diameter of about 27½ inches when fitted with mountain-bike tires.

The 700C (622 mm), when shod with wide tires, was about 28½ inches in diameter and was marketed as a "29-er."

A robust frame was another selling point. Although the cheapest bikes sold as mountain bikes sometimes had frames that differed little from those of light roadsters, true mountain bikes typically had oversize tubes, gusseted frame joints, and unicrown forks (with the two fork blades brazed or welded directly onto the steerer tube). The Aheadset handlebar stem (discussed in chapter 9) added to the robustness.

The popularization of the mountain bike brought a vastly expanded range of gearing and greatly improved braking to even the cheapest bicycles. Where a cheap bike once had either a three-speed hub or an un-indexed ten-speed derailleur with a range little wider than that of a three-speed hub, the "technology trickle down" from true mountain bikes led to low-end bikes' getting indexed eighteen-speed wide-ratio derailleurs. And instead of mediocre side-pull caliper brakes, they got powerful direct-pull cantilevers. Suspension also become commonplace. By 2011, a bicycle with front and rear suspension could be bought for as little as $160.

CHANGES IN SUSPENSION AND IN FRAMES

The early builders of mountain bikes were principally concerned with strengthening the diamond frame and making suitable provision for evolving componentry. The addition of suspension, principally from 1990 on, had further effects. A shock-absorbing handlebar stem and a sprung seat post could be added to any frame (see chapter 6), but proper front and rear suspension necessitated changes in frame design and geometry.

The first series-produced dual-suspension machine to be marketed as a mountain bike was Alex Moulton's space-frame AM-ATB, developed in collaboration with Angle Lake Cyclery of Seattle and introduced in the spring of 1988. *Bicycle Guide*'s 1988 review of new bikes said this about it: "A mountain bike with suspension? You bet, and it works. . . . Expensive and hard to find, a Moulton nonetheless stretches our imagination of what a bike can be." Because the Moulton had 20-inch wheels and was British, many people didn't regard it as a true mountain bike; nonetheless, it was series produced before any 26-inch wheel dual-suspension mountain bike, and it helped stimulate interest in mountain-bike suspension (Hadland 1994, 148ff.).

Among the other companies that pioneered suspension for mountain bikes were Bushido (with help from Roger Piper, who was familiar with Moultons) and Kestrel (with help from Paul Turner and Keith Bontrager). Both Bushido and Kestrel produced prototypes in the late 1980s.

Telescopic front forks of the now commonplace dual-sliding-pillar type were by far the most widely adopted form of front suspension. Among the others were Cannondale's telescopic Head Shok, which had a single air spring within the steering head (US patent 5,320,374 of 1994) and was still in production in 2011, and leading-link designs by Joe Murray, Mert Lawwill, Bob Girvin, and others, none of which achieved widespread lasting commercial success. By 1993, 30 percent of the mountain-bike models sold in the United States had front suspension of some sort and 8 percent had both front and rear suspension.

The market leader in mountain-bike forks for many years was Rock Shox, founded by Paul Turner and Steve Simons in 1989. Early models were air-sprung, with oil damping and travel of just under 2 inches (US patent 4,971,344 of 1990). Some early competitors, such as Manitou, opted for elastomer springing, and Rock Shox too produced elastomer-sprung forks from 1993 on. From 2000 on, however, most Rock Shox forks used air or coil springs. From

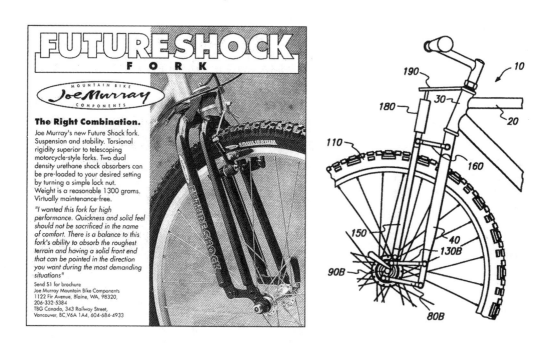

Figure 14.4 Left: A catalog illustration of a 1992 leading-link fork manufactured by Joe Murray. Right: A 1991 patent drawing of a leading-link front suspension design by Mert Lawwill.

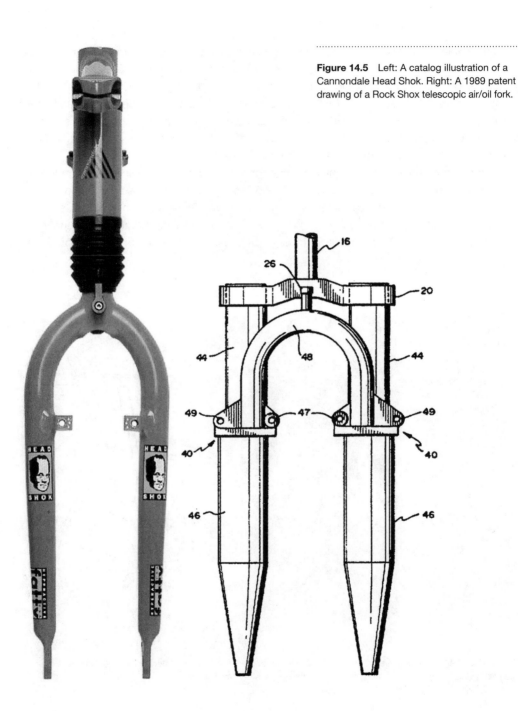

Figure 14.5 Left: A catalog illustration of a Cannondale Head Shok. Right: A 1989 patent drawing of a Rock Shox telescopic air/oil fork.

Figure 14.6   A typical mountain bike of the early 2000s with a telescopic front fork (Geoff Apps).

1995 on there was a trend toward longer-travel front forks for downhill racing. By 2000, Rock Shox was offering forks with up to 8 inches of travel.

Fitting telescopic front forks to standard mountain-bike frames altered the frame angles, and some adjustment for this in the frame geometry was desirable. But it was the introduction of rear suspension that necessitated the most substantial frame redesign.

Mountain bikes' rear suspensions fell, for the most part, into four broad categories: simple pivot designs, multi-link systems, unified-rear-triangle systems, and parallelogram systems.

Simple pivot designs had either a swinging rear triangle (pivoted behind the bottom bracket) or a massive swing arm (pivoted about one-third of the way up the seat tube). Both versions had the merit of simplicity. On the debit side, the swinging rear triangle had to rely on the spring unit at its apex for lateral location, and the swing arm was affected by chain tension, which tended to restrain upward movement of the arm when the wheel hit a bump. With either of these simple pivot designs, the front of the traditional diamond frame—the top, head, down, and seat tubes—could be retained.

Multi-link systems came in many varieties, with the spring units in various positions. In a typical configuration, a swing arm pivoted just behind the bottom bracket. The lower end of each seat stay connected to the swing arm by means of a pivot near the wheel dropout; the upper end of each seat stay connected to a pivot on the end of a rocker arm, which itself pivoted on the seat tube; the other end of the rocker arm acted on the spring unit, which could be fitted vertically above the bottom bracket and just ahead of the seat tube. And there were many other variants. With care, it was possible to design out the need for the rear pivot near the dropout. The first commercially produced mountain bike with a four-bar rear linkage was the 1990 Gary Fisher RS-1, designed by Mert Lawwill of Tiburon, California. Lawwill filed the first of his several patent applications for multi-link rear suspension in 1987 (US patent 4,789,174 of 1988). Another important innovator in multi-link suspension was Horst Leitner of Laguna Beach, California; his first patent application, filed in 1992, culminated in US patent 5,678,837 of 1997. Multi-link suspension had three advantages: the design choices possible for location of the suspension unit, the reasonably good lateral stiffness, and the ability to have a rising suspension rate. The big disadvantage was complexity. Like simple pivot suspension configurations, multi-link systems allowed retention of the traditional top, head, down, and seat tubes.

In a unified-rear-triangle (URT) system, the bottom bracket forms a part of the swinging rear triangle. The pivot can be very close to the bottom bracket or some distance above it. An advantage of this system is that it eliminates chain-tension problems. The disadvantages include lack of suspension movement when the rider is standing on the pedals, increased wear of the pivot bearings, and, with high pivots, fluctuating saddle-to-pedal length. High-pivot URT systems tend to require major frame redesign, with a shortened seat tube and either a raised down tube or—as exemplified by the Klein design of 1995 (US patent 6,109,636 of 2000)—a single beam replacing the top and down tubes. Another frame variant used with URTs is a Y frame, typified by the Trek's 1995 design (US patent 5,685,553 of 1997).

Parallelogram systems were typified by Mert Lawwill's 1990 design (US patent 5,121,937 of 1992). A lower swing arm was pivoted from close to the bottom bracket and connected by pivots to the lower ends of extended rear-wheel dropout plates. The tops of these plates were connected by pivots to the rear end of an upper swing arm. The forward end of the upper swing arm was pivoted from the seat tube. Thus, a compact parallelogram was formed by the two parallel swing arms, the lower part of the seat tube, and the extended rear dropouts. The suspension unit was fitted between the seat tube (near the upper pivot) and a point on the lower swing arm an inch or two behind the bottom bracket. The chain ran midway between the front upper and lower pivots, which were only a few inches apart. This geometry eliminated

Figure 14.7 Top left: A typical mountain bike of the early 2000s with a single-pivot rear suspension (Geoff Apps). Center left: Trek's 1995 Y-frame design (patent drawing). Bottom left: A typical unsprung trekking bike of the early 2000s (Geoff Apps). Top right: Mert Lawwill's 1987 fully suspended design, with multi-link rear suspension (patent drawing). Center right: Klein's 1995 high-pivot unified rear triangle design (patent drawing). Bottom right: Mert Lawwill's 1990 parallelogram rear suspension design (patent drawing).

chain-tension problems yet allowed active suspension under all conditions. However, bearing loads were high, and there were a lot of pivots. With a parallelogram system, the front part of a traditional diamond frame can still be used.

DERIVATIVES OF MOUNTAIN BIKES

Mountain bikes evolved into several specialized categories (including cross-country, touring, downhill, freeride, dirt jumping, and trials machines) and strongly influenced other types of bicycles (notably expedition bikes, which combined the ruggedness of the mountain bike and the characteristics of a traditional touring bike). The most popular derivative of the mountain bike was the hybrid or trekking bike, a cross between a traditional light roadster and a mountain bike. Raleigh and Bianchi pioneered this style in the late 1980s.

It is said that everything that goes around comes around. In 1995, Schwinn celebrated its centenary by producing the Black Phantom, a new model based on the 1949 model of the same name. This fueled a revival of fat-tired bikes of the sort on which many of the early mountain bikes had been based. Manufacturers began making beach cruisers, low riders, choppers, and other models inspired by the American balloon-tired machines of the 1930s, the 1940s, and the 1950s.

Among the other derivatives of mountain bikes were the unusual machines created in California by Dan Hanebrink, a former aerospace engineer and champion cyclist. In the early 1990s, Hanebrink began building mountain bikes with long, squat diamond frames and small-diameter wheels with ultra-wide tires (typically 20 by 8 inches). Hanebrink even built a tandem (the Limo) and some bikes meant to be ridden on ice. By 2011, Hanebrink was concentrating on electrically assisted versions of his machines. A company called Fortune Hanebrink now offers several pedal-powered and electrically powered models.

Figure 14.8 Dan Hanebrink in 1993 with an early example of his ultra-wide-tire mountain bike (Rani Figueroa).

SMALL-WHEELED
BICYCLES

The wheel diameters commonly used on bicycles made for adults have changed little since the evolution of the diamond-frame rear-drive safety bicycle. The 28-inch pneumatic tire was the biggest that could conveniently be accommodated in the robust, uncomplicated, easy-to-manufacture diamond frame. All other factors being equal, a bigger wheel rolls more easily than a smaller one. In an unsprung frame, a bigger wheel also gives a more comfortable ride because it falls less deeply into small depressions in the road surface and, on hitting bumps, rises and falls more slowly. Quite simply, the 28-inch wheel gave the best balance of comfort and rolling resistance that the diamond frame could accommodate. Anything bigger would have compromised the ease of mounting and dismounting that gave the safety bicycle its name.

But despite the enduring dominance of larger wheels, various kinds of small wheels are sometimes used by adult riders:

A small front wheel on a carrier cycle leaves extra space above it for cargo.

A small-wheeled portable cycle requires less space to stow when folded or separated.

A small-wheeled unisex "shopper cycle" has good luggage-carrying capacity over the wheels, and its saddle and handlebars can be adjusted to a wide range of heights.

A BMX bike's small wheels are strong and are conducive to fast acceleration and quick steering.

A small front wheel on a pursuit cycle or one used in motor-paced track racing allows closer drafting of the vehicle ahead.

A small front wheel on a time-trial cycle allows a lower, more aerodynamic riding position (but is no longer permitted by UCI rules).

A small front wheel on a recumbent facilitates convenient location of the cranks and the drive train without impeding steering, and makes it easier to mount a fairing.

Most of these uses of small wheels on special-purpose machines capitalize on one or more advantages of the smaller wheel (see table 15.1) in exchange for certain disadvantages (see table 15.2). Over the years, some powerful arguments have been made for using smaller wheels on standard bicycles too.

EARLY SMALL-WHEELERS

A high-wheeler's rear wheel was very small (typically about 16 inches), and some geared front-drivers (for example, Crypto's Bantam and Bantamette of the mid 1890s) had small wheels.

In 1894, the London-based Pneumatic Wheel Company marketed a rear-drive safety bicycle with 18-inch wheels. This machine, priced at £15, showcased the company's spokeless, rimless pneumatic wheels, designed by Joseph Castle Hall of London (British patent 3,968 of 1891). A wheel of this kind can be thought of as an inflated ball with an axle running through it and a pair of hub flanges squeezing the ball into a wheel shape. In advertisements, the Pneumatic Wheel Company quoted glowing testimonials from champion cyclists and the cycling press. A contemporary photo of the Sharrow Cycling Club of Sheffield shows a rider astride a bicycle with wheels of this type (Barrett 1982, 15). A Birmingham resident named Edmunds—

Table 15.1 Advantages of small wheels (from Hadland 1997).

Contributing factor	Advantage
More space over wheels	Wide panniers either side of wheels not necessary, therefore luggage can be more aerodynamic. Loads more easily carried on center line, improving weight distribution. Greater adjustability of seat height and handlebar height possible. Easier to produce low step-through height where required. Easier to mount handlebars lower for better aerodynamics. Easier to accommodate suspension units.
Easier to incorporate suspension	Suspended small wheel will often give smoother ride than larger unsprung wheel. Roadholding improved through greatly improved tire compliance with road surface.
Wheel takes up less space	Easier stowing, especially of portable cycles. Easier to accommodate fairings. Facilitates lower mounting of drive train in typical recumbent cycle configurations. Wheelbase can be longer or shorter than usual. Allows closer drafting when chasing another rider or pacing vehicle.
Wheel has less mass and at shorter radius, hence lower moment of inertia.	Better acceleration. Reduced flywheel effect aids braking. Lighter steering aids maneuverability. In a suspended bicycle, a lower unsprung mass, hence easier rolling over rough surfaces.
Wheel has smaller frontal area.	Wheel has lower air drag.
Shorter (and often fewer) spokes.	Less spoke turbulence, reducing air drag. Shorter spokes on standard hub form stronger structure.
Wheel has smaller diameter.	Tighter radiused rim inherently stronger. Lower ratio of brake drum radius to wheel radius, so hub brakes work better. Lower torque in driven hub, so hub gears under less stress. Lower gears easier to obtain. Spare tires easier to carry.
Tire has smaller contact patch. (This only applies where higher than normal pressures adopted.)	On good surface, smaller tire has better traction (more "bite" because of higher pressure per unit area).

Table 15.2 Disadvantages of small wheels (from Hadland 1997).

Contributing factor	Disadvantage
Wheel has less mass and at shorter radius, hence lower moment of inertia.	Lower gyroscopic effect reduces steering damping and self-steering tendency. Less flywheel effect at bottom of hill to aid start of next climb.
Hubs nearer ground.	More risk of water and grit penetration.
Wheel has smaller diameter.	Bumpier ride unless wider tires or suspension adopted. Ratio of rim braking radius to wheel radius less advantageous, hence reduced efficiency of rim brakes. (Effect worst with very small-diameter rims and balloon tires—marginal with narrow tires on larger rims.) Higher gears harder to achieve—may necessitate special chainwheels and/or sprockets to obtain higher primary drive ratio. Hub rotates faster for a given road speed, therefore slightly higher bearing friction. Wheel sinks deeper into soft surfaces, greatly increasing rolling resistance. Superior tire construction and careful attention to pressures necessary to approach rolling resistance of larger wheels.
Special tire construction may be necessary for best rolling resistance.	Tire availability limited in some formats. Tires more expensive. Tire pressures more critical. Necessarily light and flexible tires may be less durable. Over rough surfaces, momentum losses due to high-pressure narrow-section small-diameter tire will be higher unless suspension is fitted.
Hubs and rims farther from brake levers.	Longer cables necessary, hence slightly reduced braking efficiency.
Tire has smaller contact patch. (This only applies where higher than normal pressures adopted.)	Less grip on poor surfaces. Greater tire wear.
Tire has shorter circumference.	Tire wears faster.

Figure 15.1 Left: An 1894 First-class Roadster (National Cycle Library). Center: An 1896 Crypto Bantamette (*Polytechnisches Journal* 301, 1898, 176). Right: An 1897 Nitsche und Kausmann Colibri (*Polytechnisches Journal* 306, 1897, 113).

"a racer of some ability"—was later said to have given some youthful challengers "quite a surprise" with his performance on a similar machine (Davison 1939).

In 1897, in Brandenburg, Germany, a company called Nitsche und Kausmann produced a diamond-frame small-wheeler, called the Colibri, that had wheels about 20 inches in diameter with conventional tension spokes and pneumatic tires; it was intended for hunters, the military, and others who wanted a lighter, more compact bicycle (Kielwein and Lessing 2005, 113). About 90 years later, a similar machine became popular in the Japanese market—the Mini Velo, a short-wheelbase diamond-frame bike with wheels about 20 inches in diameter. Mini Velos still have followings in Japan and in Italy (where Bianchi manufactures them).

VÉLOCIO'S EXPERIMENTS WITH SMALL WHEELS

Paul de Vivie (a.k.a. Vélocio), widely thought of as the father of French cycle touring, was an advocate of smaller wheels. In 1911, when he was editor of *Le Cycliste*, he received a letter from a cyclist nicknamed Germain commenting that the German Colibri small-wheeler, with its wheels of "35 to 40 centimeter diameter" (excluding tire thickness), hadn't stayed in production very long. This prompted the following response from Vélocio:

> My own experience has gone no further than to 50 centimeter wheels furnished with 50 millimeter tires [with an overall diameter of about 24 inches], but I can guarantee that in an experiment extending as far as 15,000 kilometers covered, they will not have the smallest disadvantage from the point of view of their running. It simply seems to me they are more prone to skidding, but this is perhaps due to the fact that their tires have no tread and that the bicycle is very short. . . . That universal agreement has fixed on 70 centimeters as the proper size for wheels does not in any way prove that this diameter is best; it simply proves that cyclists follow each other like sheep. (Vélocio 1911)

Vélocio cautioned against assuming that, just because a new invention fails, it is ill-conceived. Often, he noted, an invention fails because it is ahead of its time.

Vélocio seems to have influenced the design of the Hirondelle Passe-partout, a bicycle produced in his home town by Manufacture Française d'Armes et Cycles de Saint-Étienne and advertised in 1911 (the same year in which Vélocio made the statement quoted above). With 24-inch wheels, the men's model was claimed to weigh about 20 pounds, the ladies' about 24 pounds. It was in the tradition of the Colibri, though its wheels were somewhat larger. By this time a general move from 28-inch wheels to slightly smaller ones was already underway in the UK and Vélocio's influence led to a parallel move in France.

In 1913, Frank Bowden, Raleigh's chairman, wrote: "I prefer 1½-inch open-sided Dunlops with puncture-proof band on 26-inch wheels. The lighter tyres and smaller wheels save pounds in weight in the place where it is felt the most, the periphery of the wheels." (Bowden 1913, 55) In the next 25 years, the 26-inch wheel steadily supplanted the 28-inch.

It may have been Vélocio's influence that led to the construction of a mysterious small-wheeler now in the Coventry Transport Museum's Bartleet Collection. Derided by the collector Sammy Bartleet as a "pure freak," it has 20 × 1¾-inch tires and an open frame. It was donated by the widow of P. M. Browne of London, a builder of cycles, motorcycles, and automobiles (Bartleet 1931, 77).

In the 1930s, several experienced British cycle tourists emulated Vélocio's use of smaller wheels. A. C. Davison, *Cycling*'s technical expert, and Medwin Clutterbuck, the Cyclists' Touring Club's consul for Sussex, used tires about 24 inches in diameter and 1⅝ inch in cross-section. Davison covered about 5,000 miles on his "Little Wheels" and declared the bicycle "quite satisfactory" (Davison 1939). Clutterbuck had two small-wheeled cycles built by F. W. Evans of London. On the first of these he toured the Alps, the Dolomites, and Norway, often

Figure 15.2 Left: Vélocio with his Carrosse de Gala small-wheeler in 1907 (Raymond Henry). Above right: A 1911 Hirondelle Passe-partout (National Cycle Library). Below right: A 2011 Fuji Mini Velo (Advanced Sports International).

on poorly paved roads. In England, he covered up to 200 miles a day. Half a century later, he still considered his second Evans-built small-wheeler "the epitome of what a touring machine should be."

The idea of reducing a tire's diameter and increasing its cross-sectional area corresponding-ingly certainly has merit. The volume of air and the pressure remains the same, and the wider cross-section compensates for (and can even improve on) the otherwise harsher ride of the smaller wheel. As for rolling resistance, a reasonable indicator is the length of the inflated tire's contact patch under a known weight divided by the tire's radius (Whitt 1977). For a given pressure and a given load, the contact patch area is constant, whatever the tire's diameter.

In agreement with Vélocio's approach to small wheels, the patch is wider but shorter. Because the rolling resistance is proportional to the length of the contact patch, compensation is thereby obtained for the smaller diameter, provided lightweight tire construction is used. However, this is difficult to achieve—the larger the cross-section, the stronger the carcass must be to hold a given pressure. Vélocio therefore advocated using the thin, flexible canvas-backed tire carcasses that were being manufactured in England—the tires Frank Bowden mentioned in the passage quoted above. Vélocio bemoaned the fact that, for fear of warranty claims, such tires weren't being made in France. Medwin Clutterbuck abandoned his small-wheelers after World War II only because it was no longer possible to have such tires custom made by the Constrictor company.

EARLY PORTABLE BICYCLES

Another wave of small-wheel development was stimulated by attempts to design compact portable bicycles, which had been underway since the time of the high-wheeler. The aim was to make it easier to carry bikes on other forms of transport and to store them in restricted spaces.

Some portable bicycles have had hinges or pivots; others have separated into two or more parts; others have both folded and separated. The last category includes those where the frame folds but it is also necessary to remove a wheel, handlebars or seat post to achieve the smallest stowed size.

The early evolution of portable small-wheelers should be viewed in the context of the development of portable bicycles in general. "The idea of putting a bicycle into a bag," Henry Sturmey wrote in 1881, "is, indeed, a queer one, but of considerable value for all that, in these days of high railway charges." Sturmey was commenting on the Grout Portable of 1878. Designed by William Henry James Grout of London, it was a high-wheeler that could be packed

Figure 15.3   An 1878 Grout Portable (Sturmey 1881).

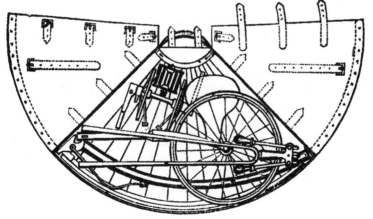

into a bag for transport by train. The spine of the bike folded in half, and the front wheel un-bolted into four quadrants. This took about 10 minutes, and someone who could afford such a machine wasn't likely to grovel around on a railway station's concourse with a spanner; consequently, the Grout Portable didn't sell well, but it did highlight the influence of wheel size on portability (Hadland and Pinkerton 1996, 1–3).

The rear-drive safety bicycle, with two wheels about 28 inches in diameter, made portabil-ity easier. On September 16, 1887, Emmit Latta of Friendship, New York applied for a patent for a folding safety bicycle. When granted US patent 378,253 of 1888, he assigned it to Colo-nel Pope, owner of the Columbia brand. The design specified a combined head tube and seat tube and a front fork that ran, almost horizontally, from just ahead of the bottom bracket to the front hub. With the fork reversed, the front and the and rear wheel would like side by side, making for a compact package. But the handling was very different from a normal bicycle, as both wheels steered, and the bike wasn't commercially successful.

As was noted in chapter 13, Michael Ryan of Boston applied for a patent for a folding dia-mond-frame safety in 1893 (US patent 518,330 of 1894). Ryan's frame was quite complicated and expensive to make. A simpler approach was used in the Faun Folding Cycle, which went on sale in Britain in 1896. Its frame folded around a vertical hinge that formed a brace between the top tube and the down tube. Several subsequent military folding safeties also had a verti-cal frame hinge with a brace between the top and down tubes. Ryan soon developed an even simpler foldable diamond frame that didn't have a brace between the top tube and the down tube (US patent 599,016 of 1898). But making a folded bicycle more compact would require a further reduction in wheel size.

The 1909 Fongers military folder, mentioned in chapter 13, may have been the first small-wheeled folding bicycle to be series produced. However, there was little further development of portable small-wheeled bicycles until the late 1930s. In 1939 the prolific Parisian inventor André-Jules Marcelin came up with Le Petit Bi, a design that called for 16-inch semi-balloon tires (British patent 526,773). The original design didn't specify a folding frame, but the ma-chine could be made quite compact by reversing the fork, folding the handlebars, and sliding the saddle down to its lowest position. The rear rack formed a stand, so the bike could be stood on end in a closet. Famous riders of Le Petit Bi included the philosopher Jean-Paul Sartre and the artist Francis Picabia.

A later version of Le Petit Bi, designed in 1944, had a folding frame (French patent 992,681 of 1951). It may well have been this machine that inspired Norishige Yokomaki of Tokyo to develop the Porta Cycle (US patent 2,777,711 of 1957). Yokomaki, an automotive engineer, designed the bike for his own commuting in 1951. The design was later sold to a company called Katakura Silk, which put it into series production.

Figure 15.4   A 1909 Fongers military folding bicycle (collection of RHC Groninger Archieven).

The late 1950s saw the first of a great wave of European small-wheelers. The popularity of such machines grew during the 1960s and lasted into the 1980s. Most of them had 20-inch wheels and could be folded or separated to fit into a car's trunk. They became popular in many Western European countries. There were various open-frame designs, most of them from French, German, Italian, and Dutch makers, but over time a few variants, most with simple U frames or H frames, became dominant. In the 1970s, many cheap small-wheelers were imported from Eastern Europe.

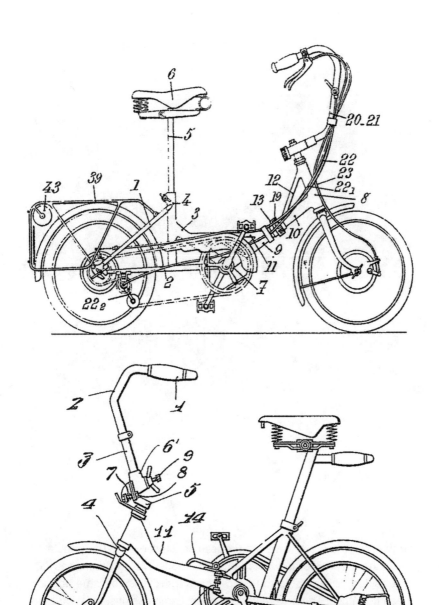

BRITISH SMALL-WHEELERS, 1960S–1980S

In the 1960s, British small-wheelers developed in relative isolation, partly because Britain imported very few Continental bicycles, and partly because of the influence of the Moulton bicycle. Its creator, Alex Moulton, was an engineer with a background in steam power, aeronautical engineering, automotive suspension, and rubber technology. He was well known for designing the rubber suspension used on the 1959 Mini automobile.

It was the Suez crisis of 1956, which led to gasoline rationing in the UK, that stimulated Moulton's interest in bicycle design. Thought not a bicycle maker or a cycle historian, he was aware of the lack of development of the diamond-frame bicycle since the 1890s. He decided "to take the evolution of that most remarkable device beyond its classical form" and "to produce a bicycle which was more pleasing to have and to use." His background in rubber technology enabled him, in collaboration with Dunlop, to demonstrate that well-designed narrow-section 14-inch and 16-inch tires inflated to 50 pounds per square inch or more could match the rolling resistance of standard lower-pressure roadster tires on a smooth surface. To eliminate the rough ride that high-pressure small-diameter tires gave, Moulton added suspension. This not only gave a generally smoother ride than a conventional bicycle; it also reduced the loss of momentum on rough surfaces. Although rarely used for sporting purposes, Moultons have performed well in point-to-point record attempts, in time trials, in solo and four-man pursuit, in criterium, in ultra-marathons, in triathlons, in Audax, and in HPV races, and have been successfully used in transcontinental touring.

Introduced in 1962, the Moulton bicycle was initially a great success. Production peaked at over 1,000 units a week at a time when the British cycle industry was in steep decline. Other cycle makers were quick to jump on the bandwagon but could not easily circumvent Moulton's patents. Raleigh (which had rejected the Moulton) initially responded with the RSW16, a bike that looked superficially like a Moulton but which had low-pressure balloon tires instead of high-pressure tires with suspension. The RSW16 was cheaper than the Moulton and was

Figure 15.5   Above: A later version of Le Petit Bi, designed in 1944 (patent drawing). Below: A Porta Cycle, designed in 1951 (patent drawing).

promoted by a massive advertising budget. Other makers, including Dawes, Royal Enfield, and subsequently Raleigh, produced open-frame utility bikes with 20-inch wheels, commonly referred to as "shoppers." They focused on what had become Moulton's core market, ignoring his more exotic racing and touring models. The competition hit Moulton hard, and in 1967 Raleigh bought him out. Raleigh then concentrated its efforts on the Raleigh 20 range of H-frame 20-inch-wheel machines. In 1975, the Raleigh 20 was the company's best-selling line, with 140,000 sold in the UK alone. Raleigh 20 machines were exported to North America and made under license in New Zealand.

"Shoppers" with 20-inch wheels accounted for a significant percentage of Britain's bicycle production until the 1980s. In contrast with mainland Europe, the vast majority of British small-wheelers produced from the 1960s to the 1980s weren't folders. Continental-style U-frame or H-frame folders were rarely seen in Britain until the 1970s, when imports from Austria and Eastern Europe began making inroads.

Figure 15.6   Left: A 1963 Moulton Deluxe (courtesy of the artist, Paul Grogan). Right: A 1981 Raleigh 20 Shopper (National Cycle Library).

FOLDERS

Dawes and Raleigh both produced portable versions of their 20-inch-wheel bikes, but these, like the Continental folding bikes, were relatively cumbersome. Some designers sought to produce lighter, more compact machines. Raleigh considered manufacturing one designed by David Newland of Cambridge University, but decided that it would be too expensive.

The breakthrough design was the Bickerton Portable, launched in 1970. Designed by the aeronautical engineer Harry Bickerton, it was built of aluminum alloy and almost entirely bolted and dowelled together. In its lightest form, it weighed 20 pounds or less and packed down to 30 × 20 × 10 inches. With its long, thin aluminum handlebars and seat post, it was inherently flexible. Nonetheless, it was adopted by tourists who wished to integrate cycling with public transport, and was manufactured intermittently in the UK and in Australia for more than 25 years. A Bickerton was even ridden across the United States, coast to coast, by an English grandmother who hitherto had not been a long-distance cyclist (Miller 1980).

Another notable folder was the Transit Compact, based on a design by a Suzuki engineer named Shoji Iwai and produced by Bridgestone during the 2000s. The Transit Compact was a "stick" folder—when folded, it formed a long, thin package, and still rolled easily on its wheels.

Graham Herbert's Airframe (US patent 4,296,940A of 1981), another bike that folded into a relatively long and thin package, had 16-inch wheels and an folding aluminum diamond frame. It was put into series production in the 1980s and again in the 2000s, selling poorly both times (probably because it didn't find a niche in the market). Although ingenious and relatively light, it wasn't as compact or easy to fold as the Brompton, nor was it significantly easier to propel or cheaper.

Another interesting stick folder was the Zoombike. Developed over many years by the German industrial designer Richard Sapper, it was put into production in 1998 by an Italian company called Electromontaggi. It wasn't a big commercial success, and production soon ceased. The 14-inch wheels were supported on one side only. The front wheel was suspended by a trailing arm. Drive was by chain and a three-speed derailleur, all housed within the main beam of the frame. Lighting was built into the frame members.

Perhaps the best-known and most enduring stick folder was the Strida, created by the British designer Mark Sanders. Like the Zoombike, it had wheels supported on one side only. This minimized width when the two wheels were stowed side by side; it also made repairing punctures and changing tires easier. The Strida was first produced in 1987 and, despite some breaks in production, was still available in the 2010s. It bore a striking resemblance in its general arrangement to an 1897 design by Otto Spiess of Berlin (German patent 110,963 of 1897).

Figure 15.7 Shoji Iwai's design for a folding bike, which won second prize in a 1974 International Cycle Design Competition in Japan (*International Cycle Design Competition: Report on Prize-Winning Projects*, Koichi Ishida, 1974).
Figure 15.8 Richard Sapper's Zoombike in folded and ready-to-ride modes (© Bernhard Angerer).

Figure 15.9 Left: A 2011 Strida (catalog photo). Right: A remarkably similar design by Otto Spiess of Berlin (German patent 110,963 of 1897).

The Brompton folder was the result of an effort by one Andrew Ritchie, not to be confused with the cycle historian of the same name. Ritchie (like David Newland and Alex Moulton, an alumnus of Cambridge University) was inspired by the Bickerton Portable to produce a better compact folder. He sought to create a machine that would be more rigid to ride and that would fold more easily and more compactly. After five years of prototyping, he filed his first patent application in 1976 (British patent 1,580,048 of 1980). A particularly novel feature of the Brompton was the rear wheel was carried in a hinged sub-frame that doubled as a suspension arm, acting on an elastomer spring. The main frame was also hinged, and the handlebars folded down. A Brompton could be folded down to 22 × 21 × 10 inches. The steel frame was much more rigid than that of the Bickerton Portable, although the first Bromptons were about 9 pounds heavier than a Bickerton. (Subsequently, the weight of the basic model was reduced by about five pounds.)

Raleigh rejected the Brompton. Andrew Ritchie made a few in 1981 and 1982, but uninter-rupted and ongoing production didn't begin until 1988. By that time, the bike had won the Best Product award at the 1987 Cyclex show in London. Since then, the Brompton company has grown steadily. At the time of writing, it was the largest firm still producing bicycles in the UK. (Raleigh was no longer making anything in the UK and was no longer British owned.)

The Brompton bicycle, having undergone many incremental improvements and refine-ments, is generally regarded as the folder that offers the best combination of easy folding, compactness, lightness, and ride quality. It has had many challengers, however. The American inventor David Hon first applied for a patent for a folding bicycle two weeks after Andrew Ritchie. Hon's first design (US patent 4,067,589 of 1978) was very different from Ritchie's. His patent focused particularly on the frame hinge and the telescopic seat post. Hon's company, Dahon, became the most commercially successful maker of folding cycles, with numerous and frequently changing models, many of them badge-engineered for other cycle manufactur-ers. From 1982 to 2012, Dahon produced more than 2 million folding bicycles. Since 2011,

Figure 15.10   Left: A Bickerton Portable (Mike Hessey). Center: A Brompton (Guy Chapman, Wikipedia Commons). Right: A Dahon folder of the 1980s, the Getaway V (Mike Hessey).

Dahon has faced competition from Tern, a breakaway company founded by David Hon's estranged wife Florence Shen and their son Joshua Hon.

HIGH-PERFORMANCE SMALL-WHEELERS

Alex Moulton resumed production of bicycles in 1983 at the low-volume upscale end of the market. His new models had space frames rather than the original "lazy F" frames of the 1960s. Most space-frame Moultons were separable for ease of transport, but portability wasn't the main objective; that was, as before, "to create a better bicycle." But whereas the Moultons of the 1960s cost only about 25 percent more than equivalent conventional machines, the space-frame Moultons cost considerably more.

Figure 15.11   Left: A space-frame Moulton (Alex Moulton). Center: An H-frame Bike Friday, with a trailer doubling as a transit case for the folded bike (Bike Friday). Right: An Airnimal (Airnimal).

Bike Friday of Eugene, Oregon has been making high-performance small-wheelers (most of them unsprung) since 1991. A British-based company called Airnimal Designs has been producing them (most with rear suspension) since 2000. Moulton, Bike Friday, and Airnimal all have produced some bikes with 406-format tires (nominally 20 inches in diameter but actually varying between 18.3 and 20 inches, depending on cross-section). Most Moultons have been fitted with the company's own 17-inch-format tires (designed to be interchangeable with 18-inch sew-ups), whereas some Bike Fridays have had 451-format tires (nominally 20 inches, but bigger than the 406 format). Most Airnimals have narrow-section 520-format tires (nominally 24 inches, but typically 22½).

ULTRA-SMALL WHEELS

Exceptionally small wheels, while making for a compact fold and light weight, present particular design problems.

In 1919, Charles Haskell Clark of New York took small-wheeled bikes to new extremes with a radical design intended for city use (US patent 1,381,281 of 1921). His machine had wheels only about 9 inches in diameter, an overall length of little more than 2 feet, and a choice of tiller or under-seat steering. The A-shaped frame was so compact that it didn't have to be foldable. When Clark took his bike to the Manhattan offices of *Scientific American*, he simply brought it onto the crowded passenger elevator (Herlihy 2004, 314–315). Clark's bike didn't achieve commercial success, nor did any of the later bikes with very small wheels find much commercial success.

A British engineer named John Barnes developed an interesting prototype in 1967. Barnes's aim was to make it easy to "dump the car, scoot down the road a few hundred yards by bike, hop on a bus, etc." He built a working prototype with 6-inch-diameter solid-tired wheels, a normal wheelbase, and a two-stage chain drive. A provisional specification filed in 1967 didn't proceed to full patent status. The design wasn't commercially exploited, but tiny wheels and two-stage drive have been seen in later designs (Hadland and Pinkerton 2006, 89–91).

The MDEbikes Mini125, a micro-folder designed by Giuseppe and Paolo Ganio of Turin, had roller-ski wheels about 4 inches in diameter. Introduced in 2003, it didn't remain in production long.

The British inventor Sir Clive Sinclair has worked on micro-folders since the 1980s. His A-bike, developed with a design engineer named Alex Kalogroulis, became available in 2006. It folded down to 27 × 16½ × 8 inches and weighed less than 14 pounds. The wheels had high-pressure

Figure 15.12 Center: Charles Clark and his tiny bike (*Scientific American*, December 27, 1919) Above left: A 2006 Pacific Cycles CarryMe (Pacific Cycles Inc.). Below left: a 1986 MicroBike (patent drawing) Top right: A 2006 Sinclair A-bike (Sinclair Research Ltd.). Below right: A Tresoldi & Casiraghi Pocket Bici, circa 1963 (© Bernhard Angerer).

Figure 15.13 Alessandro Belli's cable-tensioned ultra-compact folding bike (Alessandro Belli).

pneumatic tires. Early versions had 6-inch wheels, but in 2010 a model with 8-inch wheels was introduced.

In 2006, Pacific Cycles of Taiwan introduced the CarryMe, a micro-folder designed by the company's president, George Lin. It has 8-inch pneumatic tires and is available in a range of models. By early 2008, Lin, then 70 years old, had ridden his own CarryMe more than 2,000 miles (Wang 2008).

Around 1963, an Italian company called Tresoldi & Casiraghi introduced a micro-folder called the Pocket Bici, which had wheels about 12 inches in diameter. The wheels and most of the other components folded into the frame and were protected by it. About 2,500 units were produced. The Pocket Bici was heavy and didn't ride well (Embacher 2011, 174–175).

One of the more successful attempts at a micro-folder was the MicroBike, created in 1986 by the Swedish designers Otto Linander and Sven Hellestram (US patents 4,895,386 and Des. 306,841 of 1990). With 12½-inch wheels and folding down to 42 × 19 × 14 inches and weighing about 20 pounds, it was one of the lightest and most compact folders. It won design awards in Tokyo (1988) and New York (1990) and was in series production for a while (Hadland and Pinkerton 1996, 93–95). A more recent 12-inch-wheel micro-folder was the Mobiky Genius, a French design launched in 2006.

Ingenious designers continue to invest considerable effort in super-compact, ultra-light folding bicycles. Alessandro Belli's "Minimum Vehicle" research project was funded by the European Union's Life Program. Working with the University of Florence's Business Incubator department, Belli prototyped a cable-tensioned bicycle that, when folded, took up only one-fourth as much space as a folded Brompton. Belli's use of cables to keep elements of the frame in tension is unusual, though not altogether unprecedented; the Slingshot mountain bike, designed by Mark Groendal circa 1991, substituted a spring-loaded tension cable for the downtube of the diamond frame. Belli's prototype, sponsored by the international plastics company Ticona and made mostly of thermoplastic composites, won a commendation in the 2008 Compasso d'Oro design awards. However, the plastics proved impracticable for a production model.

BMX

BMX (bicycle motocross) started in the late 1960s when some California youngsters on bicycles began emulating off-road motorcycle racers. Ten-year-olds began racing 20-inch-wheel Schwinn Sting-Rays on dirt courses. Amateur customization of bikes for BMX competition soon

Figure 15.14   A Raleigh Team Mag, a typical mass-produced BMX bike of the mid 1980s (Raleigh).

arose. By 1974, there were 130,000 BMX bikes in California alone and 100 BMX tracks. Soon makers all over the world were producing BMX bikes. Mongoose bikes (made by BMX Products, Inc., a company founded in 1974 by Skip Hess in Simi Valley) came to dominate the market.

BMX became an enduring success. The bikes were simple, with squat diamond frames and rugged wide-section 20-inch wheels. Strength and nimble handling were important. The frames were reinforced with gussets. The unicrown fork, with the blades welded directly to the steerer tube, was adopted. Proper BMX bikes had to be strong enough to survive stunt riding by athletic young men in their teens and twenties. (BMX was no longer just for kids.)

As a result of BMX's international popularity, tires in the North American 20-inch (406) format became widely available all over the world. Although early 406 tires were "fat" (between 1½ and 2¼ inches wide), narrower ones were introduced. By the 1990s, narrow-section 406 tires for road use, with actual diameters as small as 18.3 inches, were available. These were widely used on recumbents, on folding bicycles, and on high-performance small-wheelers made by Bike Friday and by Moulton.

SMALL-WHEELED BICYCLES TODAY

Quite a few types of specialized small-wheeled bicycles are available today. There are compact folders (such as the smaller Dahons, the Brompton, and the Strida), high-performance small-wheelers (such as Bike Fridays, Airnimals, and Moultons), machines that fall somewhere between the compact folders and the high-performance small-wheelers (such as the Riese & Müller Birdy), micro-folders (such as the Sinclair A-bike and the Pacific Cycles CarryMe), sporty Mini Velos (such as those made by Kuwahara and by Fuji), simple 20-inch-wheel H-frame and U-frame utility bikes (widely used in some Asian cities), and BMX bikes.

RECUMBENT BICYCLES

16

The rider of a recumbent bicycle occupies more space horizontally than vertically. The seat back of a fully recumbent bicycle is at an angle of 30° or less to the horizontal.

The French-style velocipedes of the 1860s were, technically, semi-recumbents. The upright riding position now regarded as standard evolved with the high-wheeler, as it wasn't possible both to pedal and to steer the high wheel unless the rider was over the steering axis. When the high-wheeler became accepted as the "ordinary" bicycle, the upright riding position became regarded as normal and was therefore retained for the safety bicycle.

In still air, the aerodynamic drag on a bicycle and its rider is proportional to the square of their velocity. It is the biggest form of resistance that the cyclist wishing to ride fast has to overcome. For this reason, recumbents, with their reduced frontal area, can have a significant aerodynamic advantage.

EARLY RECUMBENTS

Geared recumbents, as distinct from early front-drivers, first appeared in the 1890s, soon after the pneumatic-tired safety bicycle. Charles Challand, a professor in Geneva, built what
was probably the first geared recumbent (Swiss patent 11,429 of 1895, British patent 6,748
of 1896). He called it the Normal Bicycle, because the rider's posture was more normal that
that of a stooped-over rider on a standard bicycle. The rider sat directly over the standard-size
back wheel, directly steering the smaller front wheel. The crank axle was a few inches behind
the steering head. The patent drawing shows a skid-shoe brake, and Paul von Salvisberg mentioned this brake in his report on a lightweight timber-framed version of the Normal Bicycle
displayed at the Swiss National Exhibition of 1896 (von Salvisberg 1897, 47–48). The American
consul in Geneva was so impressed by Challand's machine that he sent a drawing of it to the
State Department. According to a report published in the *New York Times* on October 25, 1896,
the bike had been tried in the streets of Geneva and had made a favorable impression. In 1897
a tubular steel version, weighing about 26 pounds, was shown at the Paris Salon du Cycle.

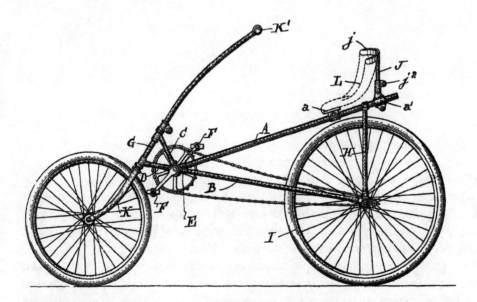

Figure 16.1: Challand's Normal Bicycle (patent drawing).

Irving Wales of Rhode Island applied for a patent for a recumbent bicycle in 1896 (US patent 577,895 of 1897). Wales's machine had wheels of equal size and, like the Normal Bicycle, had its cranks behind the steering head. In addition to the standard pedal drive, there was hand drive, which the rider used in the same way as a rowing machine, pulling back and releasing sliding handgrips linked to the cranks by cables. (Arm power is a recurring theme in recumbent design but has never proved popular.)

In 1901, an American named Brown took a long-wheelbase recumbent called a Sofa Bicycle to England to promote it. The Sofa Bicycle had been designed by Harold Jarvis of Buffalo (US patent 690,733 of 1902). Weighing about 30 pounds, it had a standard-size rear wheel and a smaller front wheel, which was steered indirectly by means of a chain-and-sprocket linkage. The seat was ahead of the rear wheel, rather than over it, and the cranks were completely behind the steering head. Hugh Dolnar reviewed the Sofa Bicycle in *The Cyclist*. Though he admitted that it was easy to mount and maneuverable, and that it pedaled and coasted well and was a good climber, Dolnar (1902) ridiculed and dismissed it.

In 1905, P. W. Bartlett of Richmond, England promoted his short-wheelbase recumbent as being "comfortable as a rocking chair." Its rear wheel was of standard size, its front wheel

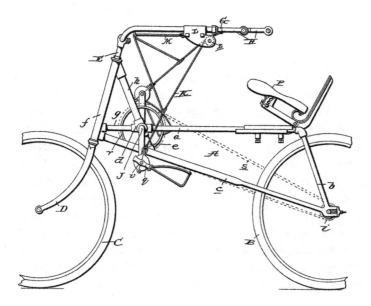

Figure 16.2 A patent drawing of Wales's recumbent, showing drive-cable linkages from the handlebars to the cranks.

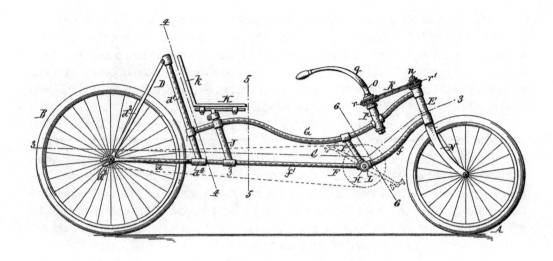

Figure 16.3 Jarvis's Sofa Bicycle (patent drawing).

much smaller (about 16 inches). Its unique selling point was a chair-like, softly sprung saddle. *Scientific American* took note of it in the August 1905 issue. The design had been patented in 1902 by Ernest Ames of London on behalf of Leslie John Hamilton Leslie-Miller, an engineer based in Soerabaya, Java (British patent 14,541 of 1902). The machine is of historic significance for its early implementation of under-seat steering. However, it wasn't the first machine to be steered in that fashion. The 1896 Humber Open Front ladies' bicycle (not a recumbent) had had under-seat steering, and the steering system of the Ames/Bartlett recumbent may have evolved from the Humber's.

In 1914, an Italian named Guglielmo took his long-wheelbase recumbent to Paris to promote it. In general layout that machine was similar to Brown's Sofa Bike; however, instead of handlebars, it had a steering wheel, which was connected to the steerer tube by a universal joint. The outbreak of World War I put a stop to promotion of this machine, but after the war it was mentioned in *Scientific American* and in the French periodical *Le Commerce Automobile* (Schmitz 2010, 57–59).

In 1914, a long-wheelbase recumbent bicycle, perhaps made by Peugeot, was introduced in France. It had a 26-inch rear wheel, a 22-inch front wheel, and a front end resembling that

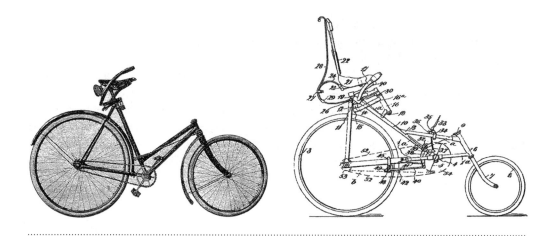

Figure 16.4 Left: Humber's Open Front ladies' model of 1896 (National Cycle Library). Right: The "rocking chair" recumbent patented six years later by Ernest Ames (patent drawing).

of a diamond-frame safety, complete with bottom bracket. But the handlebars were where the saddle of a safety would have been; they were linked to the steerer by bridle rods. The rear of the machine had a low-slung frame with a low seat ahead of the rear wheel.

In 1921, an Austrian aeronautical engineer named Paul Jaray (then living in Friedrichshafen, Germany, where he worked for the Zeppelin company) applied for a patent for a treadle-driven recumbent. (A British patent, number 186,948, was granted in 1922.) Jaray also obtained French and Dutch patents and registered several designs in Germany. Among the options that Jaray proposed were a wrap-around clip-on "skirt" and a removable canopy.

Jaray's first prototype, built in 1920, had two 26-inch wheels. At first the treadles were linked to the rear wheel by steel cables with return springs, but this was changed to a system in which the cable from the left treadle lever wound several times around a left drum on the rear hub, then onto a horizontal pulley, and then onto a right drum, connecting after several winds to the right treadle lever; this did away with the dead-center problem.

Jaray's second prototype, built soon after the first, was broadly similar but had a smaller front wheel (about 20 inches) and a much shallower head-tube angle. About 1,300 miles of test riding was done on it. In 1921 the J-Rad was put into production under license in Stuttgart.

About 2,000 were made by Hesperus-Werke GmbH, a subsidiary of the Lufft barometer company. The production version, similar in most respects to the second prototype, weighed about 44 pounds, the comfortable seat contributing about 9 pounds. The treadles usually had three steps, giving the effect of three drive ratios (due to the differing leverage) without the complexity of multi-speed gears.

The J-Rad appealed to an educated middle-class clientele rather than to aspiring racers. Comparative measurements by a German physician named Gmelin showed that a rider on a J-Rad had a heart rate about 10 to 12 beats per minute slower when climbing than a rider on a safety bicycle with a four-speed hub gear, even though the J-Rad was about 13 pounds heavier. The British *CTC Gazette* mocked the machine, but it sold quite well in the Netherlands. Many thousands were produced, but production ceased in 1923 after a decline in build quality and a fatal accident (Lessing 1998).

THE RECUMBENT BOOM OF THE 1930S

In the mid 1930s there was a wave of interest in recumbents, particularly in Europe.

In 1933, Ernesto Pettazzoni, an engineer from Bologna, applied for a British patent for an ultra-short-wheelbase semi-recumbent machine, the Velocino (US patent 2,007,725 of 1935). It resembled a wheelchair chopped in half, with the seat over the normal-sized rear wheel. The tiny front wheel was about 10 inches in diameter. The handlebar was reversible, giving the option of under-seat steering. Mussolini is said to have commissioned the Velocino as a compact, easily stored urban vehicle. The project attracted a lot of attention but was canceled after Italy entered World War II.

In 1964, a Dutch manufacturer called Union produced 1,000 examples of a Velocino-inspired design called the Strano, which had been designed by Bernard Overing of Deventer (Dutch patent 286,409 of 1965). The following year, a German inventor named Emil Friedman

Figure 16.5   A J-Rad (Graziella Pellicci).
Figure 16.6   Left: A patent drawing of a Velocino showing steering options. Right: A British cigarette card of the 1930s showing a Velocino. Inset: A catalog picture of a 1964 Dutch copy of a Velocino, the Union Strano (Dutch Bicycle Group).

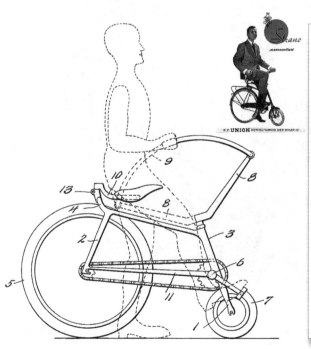

ITALIAN VELOCINO BICYCLE

exhibited a somewhat similar machine, the Donkey cycle). In 2011, an Italian company called Abici introduced a twenty-first century version of the Velocino. Less well known is the stretched Velocino of 1935, which had a very low seat ahead of the rear wheel, with indirect steering linking to inverted drop handlebars, just ahead of the seat squab. There is an example in the Collezione Genazzini.

In 1934, F. H. Grubb Ltd of Brixton introduced the Kingston, a long-wheelbase recumbent, with under-seat steering and 20-inch wheels. It had a welded "stretched" diamond frame with a low seat ahead of the rear wheel. Freddie Grubb then built (at his works in Wimbledon) a prototype of a recumbent designed by W. E. Gerrard of Kennington. Completed in the summer of 1936 and called the Velocycle, it had a single main tube instead of a triangulated frame, 20-inch wheels, and a weight of 33 pounds (*The Bicycle*, July 28, 1936). This was the first bicycle closely to resemble a modern recumbent, having all the elements of the later Avatar 2000: a

Figure 16.7 A Grubb recumbent of the 1930s being ridden by Brian Cottrell during Alex Moulton's research into riding positions, circa 1960 (Alex Moulton).

long wheelbase, small wheels, under-seat steering, multiple gears, and rim brakes. But its influence on later designs is doubtful.

The Moller Auto-Cycle, designed in 1935 by Holger Møller of Copenhagen (US patent 2,125,644 of 1938), was manufactured in very small numbers under license by Triumph in England (Cox 2012). The patented aspect of the machine was its indirect steering system. It had a steering wheel, a universal joint linking the steering column to the steerer, a self-centering coil-spring steering damper, a medium-length wheelbase, wheels about 20 inches in diameter, wide-section tires, and leading-link front suspension. The seat was fairly high, ahead of the rear axle. The cranks were at a normal height, midway between the wheels.

The Ravat Horizontal was a French recumbent developed by Henri Martin and built by the Ravat-Wonder factory in Saint-Étienne. Described by Arnfried Schmitz as looking "like the father of all modern short-wheelbase recumbents," the 1935 sports version had a 28-inch rear

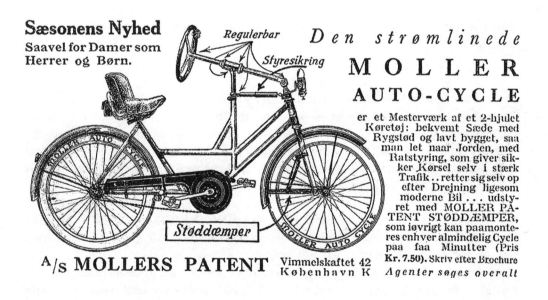

Figure 16.8   An advertisement for the Moller Auto-Cycle (Brian Rosenberg).

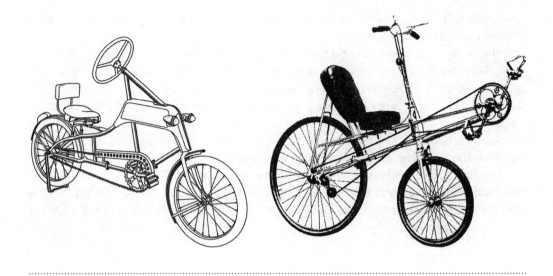

Figure 16.9   Left: A Boynton Pedi-Plane (patent drawing). Right: A Ravat Horizontal (Arnfried Schmitz).

wheel and a 20-inch front wheel (nominal sizes) and a frame of Reynolds lightweight tubing. The seat was ahead of the rear wheel and close to the relatively upright head tube. Steering, by means of high handlebars, was direct. The cranks were well ahead of the head tube and the front wheel. In the UK, this machine was sold in very small numbers under the name Cyclo-Ratio (Schmitz 2010, 60–61; Grützner 2012). A number of modern short-wheelbase recumbents, including the Lightning P-38, are similar in configuration.

Another recumbent of the mid 1930s, unusual in that it was American, was the Pedi-Plane, designed by Earl Boynton of New Jersey (US patent Des. 100,684 of 1936). This was a long-wheelbase machine with a low riding position, wheels about 20 inches in diameter, and a complex indirect steering mechanism with a steering wheel.

Charles Mochet's Vélo-Vélocars were the most successful and influential recumbents of the 1930s. Mochet started his company in 1920 to build sporty two-seat gasoline-powered cyclecars. After building a pedal-powered version for his son, he began to manufacture similar machines. They were so successful that Mochet then introduced a range of models for adults. Mochet's pedal cars, called Vélocars, sold for about the same price as a motorbike but were cheaper to run and maintain. Mochet produced about 6,000 Vélocars, some with four wheels and some with three, between 1925 and 1944.

Mochet tried to promote the Vélocar by racing it at velodromes, but neither the four-wheel version nor the three-wheel version handled well on a velodrome's banking. So he decided to make a recumbent bicycle that would be, essentially, a four-wheel Vélocar cut in half down the middle. He called it the Vélo-Vélocar. In 1932, the Vélo-Vélocar was awarded the Grand Prix Lepine for its patented "indirect steering for recumbent cycles." In the autumn of 1932, through the Union Vélocipedique de France, Mochet sought confirmation from the Union Cycliste Internationale that the Vélo-Vélocar complied with UCI regulations. The reply was affirmative. The next summer, Francis Faure, a second-rate rider, broke the 5-kilometer, 10-kilometer, 20-kilometer, 30-kilometer, 40-kilometer, and 50-kilometer records and the hour and half-hour records on an unfaired, fully recumbent racing version of a Vélo-Vélocar (Schmitz 2000, 19–22).

It is significant that development of the Vélo-Vélocar arose from "the need for speed," whereas previous recumbent bicycles appear to have been designed primarily for comfort. Francis Faure's speed records clearly demonstrated that the Vélo-Vélocar was significantly faster than a conventional bicycle. In February of 1934, the UCI set up a committee to define and enforce a new definition of the bicycle. The barely hidden agenda was to ensure the exclusion of recumbents. On April 1, 1934, the UCI's committee published its definition of a racing bike. It stated that the bottom bracket could not be more than 10 centimeters ahead of the nose of the saddle, thus ensuring that only upright bicycles could be raced under UCI rules. Charles Mochet died soon afterward (Schmitz 2000, 26–28).

Charles Mochet's widow and son and one of Charles's cousins kept the firm going. In 1934, Manuel Morand put in impressive performances on a Vélo-Vélocar in six road races: Paris-Angers, Paris-Vichy, Paris-Troyes, Paris-Soissons, Paris-Limoges, and Paris-Contres. In a major 1934 endurance event, the Concours des Pyrenées du Touring Club de France, one of Mochet's workers, Henri Martin, demonstrated that, even though his eight-speed touring Vélo-Vélocar weighed nearly 45 pounds, he could outperform many riders of conventional bikes in the mountains. Martin went on to develop the Ravat Horizontal (Schmitz 2000, 41–47; Cordon Champ 2004, 24).

Vélo-Vélocars were in production from 1932 until 1940. About 400 are thought to have been produced. There were standard, touring, and track versions, most with equal-sized wheels 18–22 inches in diameter. Balloon tires were used on all but the track versions. The wheelbase was relatively long. The cranks were behind the steering head. The frames were of seamed and welded 40-millimeter steel tubing. The first models had an expensively made bevel drive between the steering column and the steerer. In 1933, seeking a cheaper alternative, Charles Mochet applied for a patent for a simple universal-joint linkage (French patent 765,263 of 1934). This was used in the Vélorizontals, a budget range of Vélo-Vélocars supposedly built under license but in fact made by Mochet's company. A Vélorizontal had a single

Figure 16.10 Top: A Vélo-Vélocar—the Standard Luxe model (Arnfried Schmitz). Below: Francis Faure on a Vélo-Vélocar in 1934 (Arnfried Schmitz).

chain in place of a Vélo-Vélocar's two-stage drive with countershaft. Some Vélorizontals had a larger 26-inch rear wheel (Schmitz 2010, 48–56; Cordon Champ 2004, 24–28).

The Vélo-Vélocar's race-bred technical refinement and sporting successes made it the most influential of the 1930s' many recumbent designs. Its influence was far greater than the relatively small production figures might suggest. Many of the designs mentioned above, including the Ravat Horizontal, the Grubb Kingston, and the Gerrard Velocycle, were inspired by it. The Swiss record breaker Oscar Egg responded by building a streamlined recumbent, hoping to become the first cyclist to exceed 50 kilometers in an hour. But it was Francis Faure, in a streamlined Vélo-Vélocar, who first achieved that, in March of 1939 (Wilson 1995, 115–116).

In the April 6, 1934 issue of Cycling, A. C. Davison argued that the Vélo-Vélocar should not be banned: "If it does not live up to its reputation, riders will soon cease to try for records and no harm will be done; if it does prove speedier the public, who are the final arbiters, will call it a bicycle whether the legislators approve or not, and will go to see it ridden." Davison also addressed the question of what bicycles of this kind should be called in English. He concluded that, rather than "low-bike" (which he detested), people should call the new machine a "bicycle"; a new name would then have to be found for the conventional machine (much as the name "ordinary" had been coined for the previously dominant type, the high-wheeler).

In Cycling's issue of August 10, 1934, Davison revealed his ideas for what he now called "a recumbent bicycle." Built almost entirely from standard parts, it should have 20-inch wheels with balloon tires, a wheelbase of 62 inches, a low seat ahead of the rear wheel, and underseat steering. Davison pleaded for some British manufacturer to take up his ideas and "try to get ahead of the foreign manufacturers for once" (Davison 1934, 151, 168).

RECUMBENTS AFTER WORLD WAR II

In 1946, Jack Fried of New York applied for a patent for a compact recumbent (US patent 2,482,472 of 1949) but his design doesn't appear to have been put into production. For several decades, there was little development of recumbents in the West. But work on recumbents continued in East Germany after 1948. Paul Rinkowski worked for a state-owned rubber manufacturer and had an opportunity to develop his own radial-ply tires for lower rolling resistance. His short-wheelbase recumbents, with wheels of equal size, were not unlike the Ravat Horizontal in general arrangement. An early prototype with 22-inch wheels combined conventional pedal-and-chain drive with arm-operated levers, but Rinkowski soon dispensed with the complications that the arm drive added and settled on 20-inch wheels. In 1953, to protect the design, he applied for an East German patent. Patent 9,127 was granted in 1955. Rinkowski proposed mass production of these machines to the East German state, but his suggestion was turned down; the bureaucrats didn't think the public would accept the design (Wagenknecht 1997).

As readers of the first edition of Whitt and Wilson's *Bicycling Science* will recall, an American experimenter, Captain Dan Henry, built a long-wheelbase recumbent with sprung 27-inch wheels in 1968. Henry's use of a full-size front wheel was unusual, even on a long-wheelbase machine. A short-wheelbase recumbent typically has a small front wheel because the rider's legs or feet are above the wheel yet must reach the ground when the machine is stationary. Most long-wheelbase recumbents also have a small front wheel. As Wilson explains (1995, 116), there are two reasons:

> Although smaller wheels *prima facie* have higher rolling resistance, this is proportional
> to load, and the front wheel of a long-wheelbase recumbent is lightly loaded.
> Smaller wheels are lighter, have less air resistance, and provide nimbler steering.

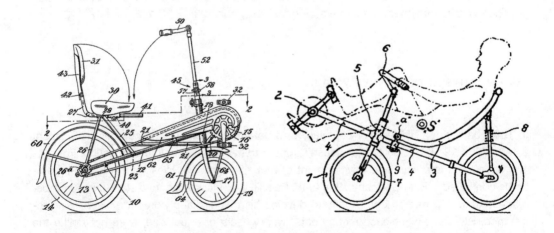

Figure 16.11 Left: Jack Fried's 1946 design (patent drawing). Right: Paul Rinkowski's 1953 design (patent drawing).

THE RECUMBENT REVIVAL OF THE 1970S AND ITS AFTERMATH

In 1967, David Gordon Wilson organized a cycle-design competition in conjunction with the British journal *Engineering*. First prize, announced in 1968, went to the Bicar, a recumbent designed by W. G. Lydiard (Wilson 1967, 1968). In 1972, this stimulated H. Frederick Willkie II of Berkeley, California to build a short-wheelbase recumbent called Green Planet Special 1, which he based on an outline design by Wilson. Although neither Willkie nor Wilson was aware of it at the time, Green Planet Special 1 was much like the Ravat Horizontal of the 1930s. Willkie's observations during test riding led to a revised design with lower cranks, the small front wheel moved back to clear the rider's heels, and under-seat steering. Wilson modified this further, changing the seat, the wheelbase, and various aspects of the machine's geometry. The third version, called the Wilson-Willkie, was fitted with a fiberglass trunk. Ridden thousands of miles, it attracted much interest (Wilson 1995, 117). Perhaps stimulated by Wilson's work, Josef Müller of Prien am Chiemsee, in West Germany, built a short-wheelbase recumbent of his own design in 1975.

As was noted in chapter 12, the most significant factor in the rebirth of recumbent bicycle development after 1975 was the establishment and influence of the International Human Powered Vehicle Association. Wilson was an early supporter of the group and became one of its original directors. In 1975, eight recumbents were entered in the IHPVA's first International Human-Powered Speed Championship. In the next few years, interest in recumbents grew exponentially. Between 1975 and 1980, dozens of other recumbent bicycles and tricycles were raced in HPV events.

Wilson continued developing the Wilson-Willkie with Richard Forrestall of Fomac, Inc. In 1978 it was put into commercial production under the name Avatar 1000. A long-wheelbase version, the Avatar 2000, was introduced the following year (US patent 4,283,070 of 1981). The Avatar 2000 tracked better than the 1000 in ice and snow, owing to the lower loading on the front wheel, and it braked better (Wilson 1995, 118–123).

In 1980, Wilson took an Avatar 2000 to the European Cyclists' Federation's Velo-City conference in Bremen. Richard Ballantine, author of *Richard's Bicycle Book*, saw it there and subsequently bought an Avatar. Derek Henden modified Ballantine's machine for racing, fitting it with a fairing. In 1982, Tim Gartside rode that machine (which had been dubbed *Bluebell*) in the International Human-Powered Speed Championships in Irvine, California. At the time, the Vector, a streamlined tricycle designed in 1980 by Dan Fernandez, John Speicher, Doug Unkrey, and Al Voigt (US patent 4,410,198 of 1983), was the machine to beat in HPV races, and most of its competition came from low-slung streamlined tricycles inspired by it. But after the 1982 successes of *Bluebell* and another streamlined recumbent bicycle, the Easy Racer,

Figure 16.12 Professor David Gordon Wilson on a Fomac Avatar recumbent (Len Phillips, MIT News Office). Inset: An Avatar 2000 (patent drawing).

the fashion changed, and streamlined recumbent bicycles became dominant in HPV racing (Wilson 1995, 123–124).

The Easy Racer was designed by Gardner Martin, whose first HPV, built in 1975, was a recumbent that put the rider in a prone position. Such a position had been tried in 1917, and perhaps earlier. In 2012, Graeme Obree experimented with a similar design. In 1976, with his wife Sandra, Gardner Martin began developing a recumbent with a more practical riding position. This became the Easy Racer, a long-wheelbase small-wheel recumbent. Fred Markham set several new HPV world speed records on Easy Racers. The Martins also marketed an everyday version called the Tour Easy. Partially faired Tour Easy machines won the 1982 and 1983 practical-vehicle contests at the International Human Powered Speed Championships (Wilson 1995, 124–126). Riding an Easy Racer Gold Rush, Fred Markham won the $25,000 DuPont Prize for the first HPV to exceed 65 miles per hour. Today he owns Easy Racers Inc., one of the two Californian recumbent manufacturers that participated in the International Human Powered Speed Championships in the 1970s and are still extant today. The other surviving manufacturer is Lightning Cycle Dynamics, founded by Tim Brummer.

In 1979, three students at the Northrup Institute of Technology in Inglewood, California— Tim Brummer, Don Guichard, and Chris Dreike—built the first version of their Lightning recumbent. Two years later, Brummer won the Abbott Prize for the first human-powered vehicle to exceed the highway speed limit of 55 miles per hour, riding the Lightning with a 700C back wheel, a 20-inch front wheel, the crank ahead of the front wheel, and direct front-wheel steering with conventional handlebars. In 1986, the Lightning exceeded 64 miles per hour at sea level before the Easy Racer achieved 65 mph at an altitude of 7,000 feet. In 1989, the Lightning placed first in the Argus Tour, a 65-mile race around the cape of South Africa, ahead of 15,000 other machines, many ridden by professional cyclists. Brummer's cycles have held world records and have won the HPV Race Across America, beating the Easy Racer while averaging more than 25 miles per hour for 2,200 miles (Abbott and Wilson 1995).

The commercially produced Avatar, Tour Easy, and Lightning recumbents had many imitators. Although no recumbent has ever achieved mass-market popularity, and although Avatars are no longer made, there is a wide choice of specialist machines. Recumbents are manufactured in the United States, in Australia, in Germany, in the Netherlands, in Switzerland, in Poland, in Taiwan, and in the UK.

One reason why recumbent cycling didn't really come of age until the early twenty-first century was that certain technological developments were needed. For example, the seats of many early machines was less than ideal, whereas today's glass-fiber and carbon-fiber moldings are close to perfection. The wide-range indexed gears that were developed for mountain bikes certainly helped, too. But arguably the most important technological development was the clipless pedal—on some recumbents, undoing a toe trap while riding was virtually impossible.

Whereas diamond-frame safety bicycles varied relatively little from one another, by the early 2000s recumbents came in many shapes and sizes, and there were marked regional differences. In the United States, where the modern recumbent movement started, the long-wheelbase design was still by far the most popular, but in Europe long-wheelbase recumbents weren't often seen. Recumbent bicycles were especially suitable for the Netherlands, a country with strong winds, no mountains, and many cycle paths. A cyclist in a velomobile (a fully enclosed three-wheeler) could go twice as fast as a traditional Dutch bicycle and not get cold or wet.

Most recumbents of the early twenty-first century were short-wheelbase derivatives of the Ravat Horizontal, but there were quite a few other designs, including "high racers" with twin 700C wheels, "traditionals" with 20-inch front wheels and 26-inch rear wheels, and "low racers," often with the same wheel configuration as a "traditional" but a longer wheelbase to allow the seat to be mounted lower. Also catching on around the world were low unfaired three-wheelers, once rarely see outside the UK.

Figure 16.13   G. A. Phillips's 1917 prone recumbent (National Cycle Library).

Much of the growth in the popularity of recumbents could be traced back to the first international HPV speed trials, held in England in 1980, and the subsequent media coverage, which sparked interest in Germany and the Netherlands. It was estimated that by 2006 there were 50,000 recumbents in the latter country.

Early-twenty-first-century recumbents could be broadly classified into three main categories: long-riders, short-riders, and low-riders. A long-rider is a long-wheelbase machine with either above-seat or under-seat steering and usually with a chain driving the rear wheel. Long-riders (which can be traced back as far as Harold Jarvis's patent, applied for in 1901) were revived in the 1970s in the forms of the Avatar 2000 and Tour Easy. A short-rider has a shorter wheelbase and either above-seat or below-seat steering. Most short-riders have chain drive to the rear wheel, but some drive the front wheel by means of a flexing chain or cranks that move with the steering. The Ravat Horizontal of the 1930s was a classic early short-rider. Thomas Traylor's 1982 design (US patent Des. 277,744 of 1985) was an early front-drive short-rider.

Figure 16.14 Thomas Traylor's front-drive recumbent (patent drawing).

Low-riders typically have seat backs at 30° or less to the horizontal. Most have a medium-length wheelbase and cranks ahead of the front wheel.

Not all recumbents fit neatly into these categories. For example, the Burrows Ratcatcher, launched in the late 1990s, is somewhere between a short-rider and a low-rider. In its standard form it was faster than most recumbents yet fine for day-to-day riding. On the other hand, it wasn't particularly suitable for urban cycling or for speed-record attempts.

A few recumbents can be folded for portability. For example, in the 1980s Linear offered two models with folding frames, one called the SWB Sonic and one called the LWB. One of the best-known folding recumbents of recent years was the Bike Friday SatRday, which could be bought with either under-seat or above-seat steering. A conversion kit was produced to convert a Brompton folding bicycle into a recumbent.

If recumbents have manifest technical advantages, why are so few of them sold? One reason is that cyclists, as Vélocio pointed out (1911), "follow each other like sheep." The vast majority are still accustomed to the conventional riding position. Another reason is that it is widely thought that recumbents are more difficult for motorists to see in traffic, and that therefore recumbent riders are at more risk than riders of conventional bicycles. This view is fiercely contested by many advocates of recumbents, who point out that the eye level of a recumbent's rider is typically quite close to that of someone driving a sedan. Nonetheless, the suspicions of the cautious may be reinforced by the sight of recumbent riders using pennants on masts to make themselves more conspicuous. But whether or not recumbents are as visible to motorists as conventional bicycles, the fact remains that they are widely thought to be less conspicuous.

APPENDIX A:

....

DEBUNKED PRIORITY HOAXES

The event that appears to have started cycling historiography was the closure of an old cemetery in the German city of Karlsruhe that contained the mortal remains of Karl Drais, the inventor of the two-wheeler principle. German cycling societies and clubs began collecting money in 1890 for the exhumation of Drais's remains and the erection of a tombstone in the new cemetery. France, defeated by Germany in the Franco-Prussian War twenty years earlier, observed this with annoyance, and Louis Baudry, a journalist who had awarded himself nobility by adding "de Saunier" to his name, quickly wrote a 336-page *Histoire Générale de la Vélocipédie* (Baudry 1891). The book went through four editions in the first year. The dedication of the new Drais tomb in 1891, and a Drais monument in the center of Karlsruhe in 1893, inspired the erection of a Michaux monument by the French in Bar-le-Duc in 1894. Ten years earlier, in 1884, the city of Coventry had unveiled a monument to its "father of the cycle trade," James Starley, three years after his death.

During the safety-bicycle boom of the 1890s, bicycle magazines began to open their pages to cycle history, and the cycle clubs needed historical "firsts" to commemorate in their street parades. One should not forget that the Western countries were fighting an economic war among themselves at the time. The cycling press began to cater to readers' patriotic emotions, often publishing unsubstantiated letters pertaining to priority. The history of technology was not yet established as an academic discipline, and later it neglected the bicycle. It is, therefore, no wonder that priority tales proved hard to kill. It appears to be necessary to present the dominant myths, and to debunk them. We shall do so in chronological order.

THE "RIGID CÉLÉRIFÈRE OF COMTE DE SIVRAC 1791"

In his book, Baudry wrote:

> The Frankfurt treaty made the French think and led them quickly to this correct thought: Could a brain from the other side of the Rhine have conceived the draisine? Is that plausible after all? . . . The Badenian was merely a thief of ideas just as his descendants were thieves of clocks. (Baudry 1891, 14, translated)

Bad memories of the Franco-Prussian War must still have been present after two decades.

From the fact that Baudry usually gave sources for the illustrations in his booklet but didn't do so here, one may conclude that he himself scribbled the animal-headed, rigid two-wheelers called "célérifères" that he alleged were already in use in 1791 and which he credited to a Comte Dédé de Sivrac (Baudry 1891, 4). He chose the date 1791 because his book would then appear just at the centennial. Since one could not disprove this in Germany, Drais was merely regarded from then on as the inventor of a steerable two-wheeler. But a non-steerable two-wheeler could not be balanced for long, particularly by an inexperienced rider. An unpublished linguistics thesis written in 1950 by a Canadian at the Sorbonne showed that the terms "célérifère" and "vélocifère" referred to four-wheeled diligences (public stagecoaches) (Jeanes 1950, 44). A coachmaker in Marseille, Jean-Henri Sievrac, was granted an import license for a British diligence called a "célérifère" on June 30, 1817. It is to his credit that Jacques Seray dug up this information and published it in the French cycling media (Seray 1976). Yet even today, schoolbooks repeat the two-stage velocipede fiction, drawing credibility from analogies with Otto Lilienthal's "unsteerable" hang glider and the Wright brothers' later steerable airplane. However, the rigid two-wheelers existed only as fakes on paper. In fact, in the 1860s there are some examples of Frenchmen calling their draisine "mon célérifère," but presumably this was ironic.

Figure A.1   Above: Jean Sievrac's Célérifère of 1817 and Baudry's fantasies thereof (patent drawing; Baudry 1891). Center: The Stoke Poges church window (photo by Renate Lessing) and the forged drawing (Duncan 1928). Below: Fischer's velocipede dates from 1869, not "1855"; Artamanov's velocipede, claimed to be from 1802, fits better into the 1870s (Lessing 2010; Street 1992).

THE "STOKE-POGES BICYCLE WINDOW OF 1642"

Sketches of the so-called bicycle window of the parish church in Stoke Poges, Buckinghamshire, west of London, appeared in cycling gazettes after a club visited the site in 1884 (Bowerman 1988b). A faithful sketch also appeared in a book (Griffin 1890). Although the original window comprises fragments of stained glass, dismantled and reassembled in different order, the fragment of interest remains unchanged. It depicts a rather adult-looking cherub on a one-wheeled contraption. An adjacent fragment carries the date 1642. In France, in 1894, the cycling magazine *Révue Encyclopédique* published a line drawing alleged to represent the church window. The cherub now sat on what appeared to be a rigid two-wheeler, flanked by two cavaliers in Renaissance costumes. Inspection of the actual window reveals that there is no second wheel, but rather a skid as on a wheelbarrow, and not a single cavalier can be seen. The faked drawing was included in the privately printed book *World on Wheels* (Duncan 1936), from which it has been widely copied.

The knotted string as a surveyor's tool shown in the window, as well as similar allegorical illustrations from Renaissance books, suggest a one-wheeled way-wiser (with a skid), commonly referred to nowadays as a surveyor's wheel (Whitt 1971). Discussion following the review (Bowerman 1988b) revealed that the unknown glass painter may have copied very similar strapwork from grotesque ornamental designs by the Flemish artist Cornelis Floris. In short, the church window has nothing to do with a bicycle.

THE "MACMILLAN VELOCIPEDE OF 1838"

With hindsight, James Johnston, a corn trader and a member of the Glasgow Tricycling Club, claimed that he began in 1888 "to prove that to my native country of Dumfries belongs the honour of being the birthplace of the invention of the bicycle" (*The Gallovidian*, no. 4, 1899). Yet the earliest newspaper report on Johnston's campaign was in 1892, so this could well have been another reaction to Drais's new tombstone of 1891. From a series of oral histories sworn by descendants, Johnston claimed to prove that his distant relative Kirkpatrick MacMillan, who was working at the Vulcan foundry in Glasgow (Dodds 1993), was the inventor of a foot-lever driven velocipede resembling McCall's velocipede (see figure 2.17 above) of 30 years later (*English Mechanic*, May 14 and June 11, 1869).

Without proof, Johnston connected MacMillan with a report of a velocipede incident in Glasgow (*Glasgow Argus*, June 9, 1842), ignoring the conflicting sentence that "it moved on wheels turned by the hand by means of a crank." Moreover, the artisan MacMillan would not have been termed a "gentleman from Dumfriesshire" as in the *Glasgow Argus* (Dodds 1993).

Other presumed builders—among them Gavin Dalzell, James Charteris, and Alexandre Lefebvre—also can't be documented by solid period proof (Herlihy 2004, 66). A recent attempt to establish MacMillan again relies on unwavering cycle-magazine editors' being absolutely non-patriotic and committed to historical truth (Ritchie 2010). The jury is still out, but there are good reasons to think that all these foot-lever two-wheelers followed rather than antedated the foot-cranked front-driven velocipede from Paris. For instance, some of them feature the straight-stick handlebar provided to wind up the brake string (patented by the Michaux company in 1868), yet without using it for that purpose. This allows dating those velocipedes after 1868. Sadly, Thomas McCall rebuilt his velocipede as a "MacMillan," at the behest of Johnston, for exhibition at the 1896 Stanley Show—presumably because he needed the money (Clayton 1987a).

THE FISCHER VELOCIPEDE "OF 1855"

A letter to the editor of *Radfahrhumor*, a German cycling magazine, sufficed in 1895 to antedate a self-built foot-cranked velocipede with similarities to the one from Paris. The letter from a town councilor and member of the local Schweinfurt bicycle club mentioned the Michaux monument of 1894 and "ascertainably" dated a velocipede made by Philipp Moritz Fischer to the period 1850–1855. At that time, the Michaux velocipede was believed to date from 1859. Yet a local chronicle of 1869 reports that velocipedimania had come to the town and that an elderly citizen had suffered an accident—this perfectly fits Fischer. So his do-it-yourself velocipede can be safely dated to 1869, not earlier. Several replicas of his "first bicycle" were built, and when donating one to the emerging Deutsches Museum in Munich in 1905 the magistrate of Schweinfurt decided to date it "of 1853" (Lessing 1995). A new tombstone for Fischer was erected; it was inscribed "inventor of the pedal-crank bicycle—his son Friedrich later founded the ball-bearing industry in Schweinfurt." Though one of us was able to keep the Fischer velocipede "of 1853" from appearing on a series of German postage stamps in 1986, the PR department of the ball-bearing company SKF in Schweinfurt still appears to insist on Fischer's supposed priority.

THE "YORKSHIRE HOBBY-HORSE OF 1815"

This item owes its existence to the fiftieth anniversary of the Cyclist's Touring Club. The commemorative volume (Lightwood 1928) showed a drawing, allegedly from a lost 1815 diary of a schoolmaster at Bedale, of a draisine with coiled springs under the seat. "The noticeable feature," the book states, "is the provision of springs before and aft, a provision of the rider's comfort which does not seem to have occurred to M[onsieur] Drais." Yet coiled springs were unknown in coach building then, and the unproven priority claim, four years before the draisine arrived in England, can be confidently dismissed as wrong (Roberts 1991, 6). Lightwood also misread other documents to claim that the French velocipede was in use in Liverpool in 1867 rather than in 1869 (ibid., 32). His predating of velocipede use in England has led to many misunderstandings in later texts.

"ARTAMANOV'S IRON GRAND-BI OF 1801"

According to a claim that appeared in volume 2 of the *Great Soviet Encyclopedia* of 1950, a serf named E. M. Artamanov had ridden a self-made "Grand-bi" from the Urals to the Czar's wedding at Moscow in 1801. This was alleged to be the world's first bicycle, already perfect with pedal cranks, seven decades before such machines existed in Western Europe (Roberts 1991, 27). A replica was exhibited in a museum in Moscow. In post-USSR times the claim has been researched by Russian authors; they have concluded that it cannot be confirmed by authentic archive material. Roger Street quoted them as follows in a 1992 article in *The Boneshaker*: "The widely used story about this invention is a literary version and cannot be used as a real fact in historic investigations."

"LEONARDO'S BICYCLE OF 1492"

In 1949, in a French sports magazine, an Italian writer named Curzio Malaparte mused:

> In Italy, the bicycle belongs to the national art heritage in the same way as the Mona
> Lisa by Leonardo, the dome of St. Peter's or the Divine Comedy. It is surprising that

it has not been invented by Botticelli, Michelangelo, or Raffael. Should it happen to you, that you say in Italy that the bicycle was not invented by an Italian you will see this: all miens turn sullen, a veil of grief descends on the faces. (translated from Malaparte 1949)

Two decades later, this shortcoming was remedied. At the Frankfurt Book Fair of 1974, a collaboration of international publishers presented a book titled *The Unknown Leonardo* (Reti 1974). The third volume (edited by Augusto Marinoni, then a lexicographer at the Catholic University of Milan) showed, in an appendix, a crude sketch from the *Codex Atlanticus* showing something similar to a modern bicycle with pedals and a chain. Though in a style definitely not from Leonardo's hand, it was swiftly declared to be the work of Leonardo's apprentice Salai, and to be based on a lost plan by the master himself. This was argued on extremely shaky grounds, and it was criticized early on (Roberts 1991, 29). Marinoni was invited to the second International Cycling History Conference, held at Saint-Étienne in 1992. His agility was impressive, but he could not convince the audience (Marinoni 1995).

As a proof of Leonardo's mental authorship and previous use of chain transmissions, Marinoni produced a drawing of fountain buckets on chains from the *Codices Madrid*, rediscovered in 1967. He claimed that any potential fabricator could not have seen these before 1974, when the facsimile edition of the *Codices Madrid* was published.

At the eighth International Cycling History Conference, held in Glasgow, one of us was able to show that this very drawing of the bucket chains went around the world in 1967, accompanying the news of the rediscovery of the *Codices Madrid* (Lessing 1998). An unknown joker in Italy must have been inspired by this to create, by archival intervention, a non-steerable Leonardo chain-drive bike. However, an independent catalog of the restored *Codex Atlanticus* by Carlo Pedretti, art historian at UCLA, showed what he could see on the backside of glued-on sheet 133 with the aid of a strong lamp in 1961: two unconnected circles and some arcs (Pedretti 1978). (See figure A.2 here.) During restoration, sometime between 1966 and 1969, a joker must have transformed the two circles into wheels and the arcs into a frame and a mudguard, and added pedals and a chain.

Though Marinoni always contended that only he and the restorers (monks at the Grottaferrata cloister, near Rome) had access to the *Codex Atlanticus*, in reality many others did, including the clerks of the Ambrosiana library in Milan, one of whom tried to sell stolen Leonardo sheets (Pedretti 1972), and the staff of the reprographics specialist employed on the facsimile. Speculation as to who created the fake thus inevitably centered on Marinoni (in the view of the late expert Ladislao Reti) or on the monks. This was unfortunate, as it prevented an official debunking; the Vatican, as the possessor of the *Codex Atlanticus*, felt itself to be under attack (*New Scientist*, October 18, 1997).

In 1998, Carlo Pedretti told a French journalist by phone that an age test that had been performed on the non-sealed sheet 133 proved that the materials of the sketch stemmed from the

133 VERSO. New. Black chalk.

Scribbles, including the word 'salaj', not by Leonardo, probably not from Leonardo's time. Self-explanatory.

SEE f. 132 VERSO, to which this sheet was originally joined. When I examined the original sheets in 1961, holding them against a strong light so as to detect elements of their (at that time) hidden versos, I noticed the presence of scribbles in black chalk as well as light traces of circles in pen and ink, which appeared to be the beginning of some geometrical diagrams.

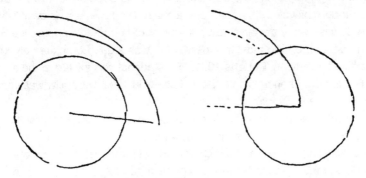

Fig. c.

Author's record of geometrical diagrams on f. 133 VERSO as seen from the RECTO in 1961.

While I was denied permission to study the Codex Atlanticus, a library attendant was stealing some of its folios, trying to sell them for about twenty dollars each in a bar next to the library! Cf. *La Nazione*, November 13, 1968.

Figure A.2 The scribble, due to a compass opening itself as seen in 1961, did not form a bicycle (Pedretti 1978). The footnote reproduced below thwarts the inaccessibility myth (Pedretti 1972).

nineteenth and twentieth centuries, not "from 1492." Unfortunately, a quotable source was not given. Italy finally took notice when the historian of science Federico di Trocchio published an article on the case (*L'Espresso*, March 4, 1999). A letter to the editor of *L'Espresso* from Marinoni's widow revealed that, when editing the facsimile of *Codex Atlanticus*, he mostly worked at home from color photographs. Nevertheless, full-size replicas of the fake machine—though obviously unrideable—were built from the sketch and are still exhibited in Leonardo exhibitions worldwide. The Italian cultural bureaucracy has not given in and still upholds "Leonardo's bicycle."

The other side of the argument, Marinoni's position, could until recently be read on the website of his home town, Legnano. It was then removed, but it has re-appeared, with Reti's indiction "L'hai fatta tu" ["you did that"] edited out, on an American website that doesn't allow critical responses (http://sansfrontieres.wordpress.com).

Marinoni's rhetoric in this piece is based largely on a faulty German newspaper report (*Berliner Morgenpost*, October 17, 1997), translated on the website of an Italian Leonardo fan (available at http://www.bclaudios.net). Marinoni simply assumed that comments made in the newspaper were Hans-Erhard Lessing's statements or opinions. Marinoni's "maledizione," indicting six supposed errors by Lessing, is reprinted below, with interspersed italicized comments by Tony Hadland:

1. That the "ink" of the sketch came into use only during the nineteenth century (although the sketch in question is a brown charcoal drawing, and Lessing himself speaks of a "brown crayon" drawing).

The modernity of the marks was verified in 1998 by an unreleased age test (Prof. Pedretti and Prof. Galuzzi, in a personal communication to Lessing and Serge Lathière of "Science et Vie Junior" Jan. 1988.)

2. That during the 1960s, a group of monks "from the Catholic University of Milan" restored the *Codex Atlanticus* under the guidance of Professor Marinoni (although we know that the *Codex Atlanticus* left the Ambrosiana to be restored at Grottaferrata).

This was an error in the Berliner Morgenpost *article.*

3. That the sketch was a forgery produced by the monks.

This was not stated by Lessing but by the New Scientist *(October 18, 1997.)*

4. That in 1974 Marinoni announced the discovery while delivering the fourteenth "Lettura Vinciana," saying that "his" monks had discovered it.

This was another error in the Berliner Morgenpost *article. In his desire to exclude the possibility of any archival intervention, Marinoni maintained that access was only feasible to himself and the monks.*

5. That Marinoni himself produced the "forgery" during the restoration at Grottaferrata.

This was another error in the Berliner Morgenpost *article.*

6. That Marinoni himself (as Lessing realized that the former version was clearly impossible) produced the "forgery" after the return of the *Codex* to the Biblioteca Ambrosiana, that is to say, during the time when Marinoni could work only from the photographs(!).

This was the accusation by the late Leonardo expert Ladislao Reti: "L'hai fatta tu," which could be read hitherto on the Legnano website. Lessing himself considered that Marinoni could have been an uninitiated discoverer, rather than the perpetrator.

But regarding this last version, Prof. Lessing himself gives unquestionable proof against what he said before, in a note of October 17, 1997, taken up by the magazine *New Scientist* in an article, "On yer bike, Leonardo" of October 18, 1997, by Jonathan Knight (available at http://www.newscientist.com).

He says that "chemical analysis of the brown crayon marks (in the article no mention is made of 'ink') that make up the sketch could provide conclusive proof." But unfortunately the restored pages have been sealed away in plastic to preserve them. He doesn't realize that this thin layer of "plastic preservation" makes it impossible for anybody to make additions of any kind to the sketch of Folio 133v, or to any folio whatsoever of the manuscript.

Only damaged sheets have been sealed, but crucially not Folio 133 (Prof. Pedretti, personal communication to Lessing)

This "proof" backfires on Prof. Lessing and demolishes his version of a "forgery after the restoration of Grottaferrata."

Many people had access to the Codex Atlanticus *even before, e.g. the clerk at the Biblioteca Ambrosiana who tried to sell stolen Leonardo sheets to Pedretti.*

These absurd fantasies need no comment; a serious scholar bases his assertions on real evidence and tries, at least, to be coherent and consistent with himself.

In spreading the myth that all sheets were sealed, Prof. Marinoni undermined his own case.

APPENDIX B:

The distinguished British mathematician Thomas Stephens Davies (1794–1851) became a mathematics master at the Royal Military Academy of Woolwich in 1834. His new system of spherical geometry earned him a place in the list of well-known mathematicians. The following manuscript (the original of which is held by Trinity College Library at Oxford) dates from three years later. Presumably it is the text of a lecture delivered to the Academy. The figures mentioned are no longer with the manuscript.

Mr. Chairman and Gentlemen,

There was a little machine invented some years ago by a German gentleman named the Baron Carl von Drais, which many persons now present have seen, and will recollect, and which went by various names, but the most appropriate was perhaps that of the velocipede.[1] The inventor, Baron v. Drais, published, in Germany, a pamphlet describing his invention, with a print representing its construction, which was (appeared) heavier than those since used in this country, and some parts were of wood that were afterwards made here of iron. He called it Laufmaschine, which signifies the running machine, and in his pamphlet printed out the uses to which it might be applied. Soon after the publication of this pamphlet, a German gentleman, with whom I was acquainted, named Mr. Bernhard Seine, a native of the City of Mannheim, came to England, about twenty years ago, bringing with him the pamphlet, and he

Figure B.1   Thomas Stephens Davies. From obituary in *The Expositor* (1, 1851, 284).

frequently rode about the streets of the city of Bath upon a velocipede made after construction of the original invention. Mr. Seine did not hesitate to run on his veloci-pede at a violent rate down some of the steepest streets in that city over the pitching of the road, but I never heard of his meeting with any accident.

The invention soon became known in London, and many persons now present can, no doubt, remember, how quickly this novelty was adopted by the public. The equality and swiftness of the motion when compared with walking which it so much resembled, recommended velocipedes to many persons who disliked the trouble and expense of keeping a horse, and the rapidity which could be acquired bore some resemblance to skating. The novelty and ingenuity of the idea quickly brought this invention into common use: in the New Road they might be seen in great numbers running every fine evening especially near Finsbury Square, and the top of Portland Road, where they were let out for hire by the hour. Rooms for practice were opened in various parts of the town, and several expert riders made it their business to exhibit them in the principal cities of England.

I am acquainted with individuals who went with their velocipedes from twenty to thirty miles in a day on excursions into the country, and many young men were in the habit of riding sixty miles or more in the course of a week. It is easy to see how beneficial this exercise must have been to the health of the riders, who were generally inhabitants of cities and often occupied during the day in sedentary pursuits con-nected with the business.

The original velocipede consisted of two wheels, one running behind the other; the prongs in which these wheels revolved were fastened to a wooden perch, upon which was placed the saddle of the rider, sometimes on springs, but too often deficient in that respect, and then he motion along a rough road became jerking and dangerously irregular. In front of the rider was placed a cushion supported from the perch, to sus-tain his arms and enable him to balance the machine; before this cushion, technically called the rest, was the handle, connected with the front wheel, and enabling it to turn it to the right or the left.

In the original Laufmaschine of Baron von Drais, the stays that fixed the axis of the hind wheel to the perch, were of wood; and, to support the front wheel, besides a prong, a curved piece of wood was fixed to the perch, against which another similar piece of wood worked, connected by stays with the axis of the wheel. These stays to the front wheel were evidently intended to strengthen the prong, and enable it to resist any accidental shocks the front wheel might encounter.[2]

With a velocipede constructed in this manner, as long as the rider went on a smooth level, he could always go much faster than a man could walk. When he came to a hill he was obliged to dismount and walk at the side of his machine, holding the handle in his right hand, and balancing it by holding the end of the rest with his left; which is little more laborious than walking freely, for the support that the velocipede gives is a greater assistance than any walking stick would be, and greatly alleviates the labour of going up the hill. But on descending a slope, the skill of the rider and swiftness of the velocipede were seen to much advantage. The man lifted his feet from the ground and permitted the velocipede to run down the hill, which it did, with a rapidity proportioned to the steepness of the descent; the rider balancing all the while without touching the earth with either foot, and the faster he went the more easy it was to preserve the balance, for when a loop is set running down a hill, everybody knows that the more swiftly it is propelled the more steadily it maintains its upright position, but when the velocity slackens, it begins to totter, and as it loses its force, the motion becomes irregular and it falls. When the rider had acquired a certain velocity it became extremely difficult to turn the machine to the right or left, or even to touch the earth with either foot without instantly oversetting; and this difficulty of checking or stopping the machine when at full speed ended in many accidents. If the velocipede ran against a post or wall, the front wheel received the blow, and the rider, when prepared for the shock, was usually only overturned, though the prong of the front wheel, or even the perch, was sometimes broken off short. This difficulty of stopping or checking the motion was a great imperfection[3] in the original machines, as a scientific old gentleman once mournfully observed to me, after he had dragged the remains of his velocipede out of a ditch at the bottom of a steep hill. "Ah!" said the venerable gentleman with a deep sigh, "If I had devised some spring to check the motion of the wheels, I should not have been rolled just now into that bed of nettles and thistles."

Though the velocipede then employed was imperfect, and ill-constructed in many respects, especially to some details to which I hope presently to call your attention, yet it may be useful to look a little into the mechanical principles of the machine and into the advantages that arise from employing it to accelerate motion, and which caused it, among other titles, to be named the accelerator.

The first advantage gained by employing the velocipede appears to consist in this, - a considerable weight is taken off the legs and placed upon wheels. If a human body, without the legs, weighs one hundred pounds as it frequently does; when the legs have to be support and carry these hundred pounds twenty or thirty miles in the course of a day, the man is fatigued, but if these hundred pounds which constitute the weight of the body are taken off the legs and laid upon a pair of wheels, the legs are spared the labour of carrying them, and can consequently go the same twenty or thirty miles with less fatigue. This appears to have been the chief object of the inventor Baron von Drais and as far as it goes may be considered a very happy idea.

Besides this, there was also a second mechanical advantage; a man's usual step or pace seldom exceeds or even equals the length of a yard; but when moving on a velocipede, his step is lengthened by progressive motion on the machine; as it goes along the space is sometimes six feet after the right foot has been raised from the ground before the left foot touches the earth; and though the step in walking is not more than three feet in length, by placing the man on wheels this step is lengthened to six feet ore more showing a difference of two to one in favour of the velocipede. So if a man can walk twenty miles in a day, when each of his steps is doubled in length by using a velocipede, it appears he could go twice as far, or forty miles a day, with the same labour. Thus two mechanical advantages resulted from using the velocipede, a man had not to carry the weight of his body, which was placed upon wheels, and his step was doubled, ore more than doubled in length, by the onward motion of the machine as it ran. So obvious were these advantages that, at first, every person of a mechanical turn was pleased with the ingenuity of the idea and surprised that it had never occurred to himself to invent such a contrivance. All that could ride agreed the velocipede much accelerated the motion of walking. It was found by repeated trials that a person travelling on foot could go many miles farther in a day with his velocipede than without its aid.

Several foreign writers were of opinion that such machines might afflict the march of bodies of infantry, by enabling the soldier not only to get over ground more rapidly and easily, but also to carry his arms, provisions and ammunition, with less trouble or inconvenience, and when it is considered that the arms, provisions, and ammunition of an infantry soldier, on the march, amount to a weight of more than sixty pounds, and that a day's march extends from twenty to thirty miles, the advantage of taking this weight from the shoulders of the man and placing it upon two wheels appears obvious.

It has been suggested to me, gentlemen, that I ought to apologize to you for bringing before you a subject, that may appear to some persons too trifling to merit the attention of the members of this institution and which they may regard as obsolete, - quite gone by, and out of date. It is true, gentlemen, that it is with some diffidence I venture to call your attention to this little invention, but as I have had the honour on two several occasions to bring mathematical subjects before you, and been favoured by your kind attention, I confide in your indulgence now; being convinced that to no others than practical men would it have been prudent to offer any suggestions on this subject; and I am persuaded that many of you will think with me, that a new machine ought not to be laid aside and forgotten, until its principle or theory has been fairly enquired into, and closely examined, and until this theory had received every improvement which the assistance of the science of mechanics can give it. For many isolated ideas of ingenious men are started, which for want of fair examination and development, are, as it were, nipped in the bud, and either lost or left for years, and sometimes for centuries, before they are brought to bear, and made practically useful to mankind. Besides, everything is not trifling which appears trifling: when the boy saw the old gentleman earnestly engaged in blowing soap bubbles and watching them as they rose in the air and burst, the boy fancied the old gentleman was out of his wits, - in something beyond second childhood; and yet that old gentleman happened to be no other than Sir Isaac Newton, busily engaged in making some experiments on light and colours and entering upon a path of science which few philosophers have since been able to explore much farther than he went. It is remarkable how long a new idea or suggestion in science has sometimes lain dormant before it was turned to account for the benefit of the public. You all know that the steam engine was for many years employed in the drudgery of pumping water out of the mines of Cornwall, until Mr. Watt found out that it was able to do something better. In like manner, Apollonius of Verga who lived about two centuries and half before the Christian era wrote his book on Conic Sections, which for more than thousand nine hundred years laid buried in oblivion, known only to the learned, and but to few even of them, until Sir Isaac Newton observed that the planets moved in Conic Sections and that their orbits are elliptical; upon this his friend Dr. Halley took the pains to translate the work of Apollonius from the Greek and they were instantly applied to the Newtonian theory and published at Oxford. These examples are sufficient to show that an original ideal should not be lost sight of, for, if the inventor himself does not see the full extent and application of it, those who come after him may.

But, as usually the case with every remarkable invention, it was not long before an outcry was raised against velocipedes. The old ladies remarked: "They are such foolish looking things." Now it was very natural the old ladies should say so, for old ladies cannot ride velocipedes, they could not share in the enjoyment or participate in the advantages of them; they looked upon velocipedes in much the same way as savages look upon shirts, as a useless, worthless expensive luxury that the wise never think of indulging in. The old ladies could no more see any good in velocipedes that Hottentots can see any good in shirts. But people do yet continue to wear shirts even though the Hottentots and New Zealanders cannot see the use of them.

However, the old ladies were not entirely wrong, for when quietly disposed people saw a velocipede come rattling towards them down a steep hill, rush by like a thunderbolt, going every moment faster and faster, and finally behold the rider terminate his furious career by plunging with frantic desperation, headlong into a deep ditch up to his eyes in mud, respectable people were at a loss to account for this violent conduct, and in their own minds ascribed it to mental alienation, - a sort of temporary insanity brought on by velocipedes; while others could not help thinking of a certain herd of swine, that under satanic influence ran violently down a steep place into the sea, and perished among the waters.

But other evils arose; if velocipedes ran on the foot pavements of the streets which they should not do, they got in the way of the children, or the children got in the way of them[4] and alarmed the ladies' maids. Rash and heedless riders ran unluckily against fat people, and all fat men and old women cried out that velocipedes took up too much room on the pavement, especially if it was a narrow one. Worse than all this arose the outcry of danger, the great danger, gentlemen, of riding velocipedes; but when any new invention appears, accidents always happen, until people get aware of the good and evil attending the new discovery. You may fancy the accidents, gentlemen, when men first caught wild horses and got upon their backs; you may imagine the falls, the broken necks and fractured limbs, before men succeeded in training horses to the service of the human race. Even now in his domestic state, and carefully trained from his birth, how often does the horse cause the sacrifice of human life, in spite of all the precautions that can be taken. Yet these evils have not caused the horse to be discarded, for it is found that the good derived from his services is greater than the evil that results from employing him.

Again, gentlemen, when the steam engine was applied to boats, how often did we hear of boilers bursting, and scalding, maiming and drowning the passengers. The loss of life was very great, and yet modes of preventing those evils have been found, and a person need only look over the parapet of London Bridge into the pool to see the estimation in which the application of steam to navigation is held, after all the dangers and loss of lives that occurred upon its first application to boats.

The motion of the velocipede has been compared to that of skating, but it is not as dangerous as a pair of skates. The average motion of a velocipede is not more rapid or uncontrollable than the average motion of a good skater. A skater has but two points of support; - a velocipeder has four, his two feet and the two wheels; - and the skater has the risk of being drowned by the breaking of the ice, besides the heavy falls he usually gets in learning to skate.

Some cases were presented for admission at the public hospitals, arising from mismanagement and falls; and I have been told that at one time St. George's Hospital contained many patients from the abuse of these machines: but if a young man who

never crossed a horse in his life, should walk down to Tattersall's and providing himself with a fiery quadruped, should set off and ride up to Hampstead, then go along
the flat and come full gallop down Highgate Hill, he might get home safe or he might
not, but I fear he would meet with some serious accident. Young men who never had
learned to ride the velocipede attempted exploits as dangerous as this and when they
met with misfortunes instead of blaming themselves they laid the blame entirely on
the wood and iron that carried them; - and very right, too - if it had not been for the
attractions of that seductive machine they would not have returned home as I have
sometimes seen them, with one half of their coat tails torn off by the hind wheel of the
velocipede, presenting a spectacle to all beholders, and a warning to them never to
ride on a contrivance that took such whimsical liberties with people. Men who might
have been perfectly secure if they had been content to go at an easy pace at first, until they got accustomed to the motion, would mount and try to run as rapidly as possible along a gravely road full of loose stones, and suffered from the violent exertion.

     The rabble also took part against the old velocipede, and they were led on and
abetted by the great men of that day who may have been in poor and needy circumstances and glad to raise a few shillings in any way they could - I do not know,
gentlemen, whether they were or not but they may have been, for they gave orders
that those who rode velocipedes should be stopped in the streets and highways and
their money taken from them. This they called putting down the velocipede by fines.
The constables therefore, supported by the fat men, the watchmen, the old women,
the great men, the rabble, the King's ministers, and the horses united to put them
down. What could resist such a compact phalanx? Acting all in concert, as they did?
Why the steam engine itself never could have stood against so powerful and united a
body, all in one mind too and acting together with an unanimity truly wonderful; and
they succeeded so completely that a velocipede is as rare as a black swan, and the
young people now rising up scarcely know what it is, even by report.

     But when anything is very much persecuted, people are apt to suspect that there
may be some very good points about it, to excite so much animosity and virulence,
and when the uproar is over and the persecution abated we may again recur to the
invention. It may now be useful to enquire why the velocipede did not answer, what
were the real defects in its construction, and why the principles of doubling the step
and relieving the weight of the rider did not ensure the permanent use of the machine.
The causes that impede and stop machines in motion are the resistance of the air and
the friction of the machines on the earth or of the parts among themselves. With these
impediments all machinery has to contend, and while these exist the problem of the
perpetual motion must remain unsolved. The greater the velocity of our machines the

greater will ever be the resistance of the air opposed to them, and therefore all that is left for us to do is to increase force and diminish friction, and the more one can gain in these two points the faster and the more easily the machine will move or run. In the velocipede the force appears fixed, and there seem no means of increasing the impulse given by the foot of the rider, all that can be done is to remove friction and diminish useless weight.

The old velocipede weighed in many instances about forty lbs, some of a large size as much as fifty lbs, and others between forty and thirty lbs, but perhaps the average was about forty lbs. Of these forty lbs when the machine was going, ten pounds may have been acting in the wheels to continue the motion, and the remaining thirty pounds were dead weight, which added to the hundred lbs that the rider's body, without the legs may be supposed to weigh, made 130 lbs to be overcome, and moved along; to this may be added the resistance occasioned by the friction of the wheels. The double advantage of taking a step of five or six feet in length and of carrying the body upon wheels, was thus counterpoised by having so heavy a mass as 130 lbs or more to move along, and being required to exert muscular force sufficient to overcome the resistance or inertness of this mass.[5] Now some parts of this weight were absolutely useless, and the friction caused by making the wheels of wood, with the axis working in a box, impeded the motion very much though this evil was sometimes lessened by employing friction rollers.[6] The width also of the edge of the wheels was often too great, a quarter of an inch is wide enough to support the weight, and by reducing the width we reduce the friction of the wheel on the road, and thus remove an impediment to the motion. Persons who are continually employed in constructing machines of one particular class, are very apt to make any other machine they are called upon to construct upon the same principles, and as nearly as possible in the same way, overlooking the different end the new machine is intended to answer. The men who made velocipedes were generally coachmakers or wheelwrights who were accustomed to make carriages, carts, and wagons, intended to carry weights of from several hundred pounds to many tons, so they usually made the wheels of a velocipede which can carry but one man, strong enough to carry twenty times the weight it could possibly be required to sustain. If a man's weight is 120 lbs and that weight is divided between two wheels - if each wheel is made strong enough to carry 60 lbs and to resist accidental strains, it is quite enough, and we may make our wheels much larger without being heavier than before, especially if they are made of iron and brazed at the joints. Now an essential advantage of a large wheel is that the friction on the centre of axis is diminished as the size of the wheel is increased. Thus, if a wheel is two feet six inches in diameter, and makes two turns or revolutions in 15 5/7 ft, when this wheel is increased to five feet in diameter it will make only one turn in that distance; and the friction at the centre of the large wheel would be just half the friction at the centre of the small one; therefore as regards the friction at the centre, only, the forces sufficient to drive the large wheel 15 ft 8 in will only suffice to drive the small wheel 7 ft 10 in; consequently, looking only to the friction at the centre of the wheels, the force sufficient to drive a velocipede with 30 in wheels twenty miles, will suffice to drive a velocipede with 60 in wheels forty miles.

Many people saw at first, how advantageous it would be to enlarge the hinder wheel, and some actually did construct velocipedes, with large hinder wheels; and these wheels being made of wood in the old way, and very heavy, especially in the box at the centre, whatever advantage was gained by the size of the wheel was usually lost by the encumbrance of its additional weights, and the friction on the centre by the axis working in a box remained little better than before. The steel axis on which the wheel of the old velocipede turned was made like that of a coach wheel; it was strong enough and large enough to carry nearly fifty times the weight placed upon it, being frequently six inches long and at least half an inch in diameter; working in a box it presented a surface of many square inches upon which it and the box came in contact; thus securing plenty of friction at the centre of each wheel and impeding the exertions of the rider at every instant.

But by enlarging the wheels, gentlemen, and loading the circumference of them we develop a power which was feeble in the small wheels formerly employed. The long radius and heavy circumference makes it act like what is called in other machines a fly wheel, that is a heavy wheel which acts as a receiver of all superfluous force, and when the impelling force ceases, this fly wheel continues to revolve and keep up the motion of the machine for some time longer. The use of a fly wheel is now so generally admitted that not only are they essential to stationary steam engines, but you may see them in seed mills and other mills of small size. Thus by lengthening the radius of our wheels and making the circumference of each heavy they begin to act as fly wheels and to carry on the motion as well as to render it uniform.[7] To examine what additional advantage this gives let us consider a five foot wheel, with a circumference made of a rod of a pound to the foot; the length of such a circumference will therefore be 15 5/7 ft and its weight nearly 16 lbs. Now as the wheel runs along, if the centre goes five miles in an hour the 16 lbs in the circumference not only goes these five miles but as they also turn round the centre, they go farther than this centre represents the wheel (show figure) and this wheel rolls along till it has made one complete revolution on its axis a point at the bottom of the wheel has first risen up to the top and then sunk down again to the bottom. If it is a five-foot wheel and the circumference consequently 15 5/7 in length, while the centre has gone 15 5/7 ft this point in the circumference has performed this curve (show curve). But this is a curve known by the name of cycloid, and it is such that the distance the point in the circumference has traversed is four times the length of the diameter of the wheel or twenty feet. The demonstration of this fact, gentlemen, depends on a problem in the differential calculus, which might not be generally understood if I were to enter into it. While, therefore the centre has gone 15 5/7 ft every point in the circumference has gone 20 feet; or nearly 5 feet while the centre has gone 4 feet.

In like manner if the fore wheel is 3 ft in diameter, circumference will be 9 3/7 ft in length but the fore wheel should be stronger than the hinder one, because it has to endure ruder shocks when by accident it runs against a stone or other obstacle, and also because it has to carry a greater weight; for as the riders weight is placed nearer to the centre of the fore wheel than to the centre of the hinder one, the fore wheel carries more weight in proportion to the distance of the rider from the centre of the hinder wheel. The front wheel also has the weight of the fore part of the perch to carry and also to sustain the pressure arising from the impulse given by the rider. There is also a direct advantage in loading the circumference of the front wheel, its force as a flywheel is increased, and thus it may be made equal in this respect to the force of the other. If then the circumference of the front wheel is made of iron two pounds to the foot, the weight of this circumference will be 18 6/7 lbs or nearly 19 lbs; and while the centre travels five miles these 19 lbs will have gone by their compound motion over a space of 6 4/11 miles.

Therefore while the machine goes 5 miles the sixteen pounds of large wheel and the nineteen pounds of the small one have gone each over a space of 6 4/11 miles, and multiplying their united weight by this number the result 222 8/11 expresses the force that the fly wheels exert to keep up the motion of the machine, and this equivalent to a weight of forty four lbs and 6/11, going at the rate of 5 miles an hour. Therefore as long as the friction of the wheels on their axes, and on the road, combined with the resistance of the air, does not amount to a resistance of more than forty four lbs and ½, the rider may expect to get along with very little exertion on his part.

But to this loading of the circumference there is a limit, and the heavier the wheels are made the more difficult it becomes to go up hill, therefore the weight of the wheels should be proportioned to the strength and weight of the rider. A strong and heavy rider will run rapidly when the rim of each wheel is made heavy in proportion to his muscular force and weight; but decidedly stout men, unless extremely skilful, should never trust their velocipedes on any but smooth and level ground, and then only at a moderate pace.

That part of the old velocipede technically named the rest was not very well adapted to the purpose for which it was designed. In the machine before you, gentlemen, another form is adopted, which gives more support to the forearm and in consequence more firmness and security in the saddle. It was usually with the end of the rest that the riders of the original velocipedes annoyed passengers as they went along the pavement.

I need not explain to so well informed a body as the members of this Institution what is meant by the centre of gravity of a machine; but some persons may not be aware that it is a point so situated that if this point is supported the whole body is supported. Now in the old velocipede the centre of gravity appears to have been somewhere between the rider and the front wheel, and much lower than the centre of gravity of the man, which is in the loins; but it would be desirable to place the centre of gravity of the machine as near to that of the rider as it can be, thus (.man.machine) for if two bodies are going in the same direction and one is intended to urge the other forward; that which give the impulse should be placed so as to give it with the greatest possible effect. By enlarging the wheels we elevate the centre of gravity and bring it nearer to that of the man. For as the centre of gravity of the man is at a fixed height, the higher we raise the centre of gravity of the machine the more the man and machine when in motion will act as one body.

A very important defect, and one that went a long way towards lowering the velocipede in public estimation, was that there was no contrivance for stopping or checking the motion when the machine was in its full career down a steep hill.[8] In consequence of this imperfection the rider was sometimes dashed against a post or wall. A young friend of mine came up one day; saying - "Had a misfortune last Sunday morning." How? said I. "Upset into a barber's shop just before church time. Velocipede ran down the hill like the wind, - could not possibly stop it, - just managed to point it at a door, - door better than wall - door flew open and in I went with a crash." But what did the barber and his customers say to you? "Too busy shaving to say much, saw it was an accident, - picked me up and I carried away the pieces of the velocipede."

When the various deficiencies that I have endeavoured to point out, are effectually remedied, and a spring applied to check the too rapid motion of the wheels, it may possibly be found that the velocipede is not so useless an invention as it has been sometimes fancied; though after all the trials given to the machine and all the opposition made to it in its old form; most of its advocates were inclined to admit that it did not answer the expectations it had raised and that the advantages of the old machine were not equal to counterbalance the inconveniency. When the velocipede first came out, twenty years ago, people expected too much from it; some went so far as to fancy it was to supersede horses; and truly if the land that supplies food for such kinds of horses as are kept for display and pomp, and not for use, were employed for raising food for men, there might be fewer complaints now made that horses are fed while men are starved. But as to the comparison so often drawn between the veloci-pede and the horse, it is generally admitted, that a man on foot can tire down a horse, going day after day a long distance, and that no horse could have gone a thousand hours as Captain Barclay and several others have done. If then a man on foot can tire down a horse, he should be able to go yet farther with a well constructed velocipede on a good road. The notion of machines superseding horses appears to have a very slight foundation in fact. The steam engine itself has not superseded horses even in America where locomotive engines are most numerous, nor is the steam engine ever likely to supersede them. A horse has his peculiar sphere of usefulness and certain facilities which no machine can compete with; he can cross a stony, rocky or sandy country, leap over fence or ditch, and run along a sea beach covered with loose pebbles which no machines can ever be expected to do. It is only with the riding or the carriage horse that the velocipede is in any way suited to compete and with no other classes of horses is it ever likely to interfere; and the uses of the velocipede will in many respects be quite distinct from those of the riding horse or carriage horse, for though it can run on any good horse road, it can also run on a foot path in a field, and cross parts of the country where horses can not well be taken. For by taking the machine in two, which may be done in a moment, each separate part may be lifted over any gate, and afterwards as rapidly joined together and set in motion again.

This machine has several advantages over a horse, especially in point of ex-pense. A riding horse costs perhaps forty pounds, and afterwards at bad 30 or 40 pounds a year to keep, and with the expense of a stable, and a man to look after him, often much more than twice that sum. If he lives to thirty years, this expense added to his first cost amounts to more than £1700 that a horse costs from first to last. If, in-stead of a horse, the same person had kept a velocipede for the same length of time, the first cost and repairs would not have amounted to more than twenty pounds. But at the end of that time, gentlemen, the horse is dead, but the machine is a machine still, and with needful repairs will go on again as well as ever.

But so distinct are the uses of machinery from those of animal power that we may argue if the steam engine cannot supersede the employment of horses much less could the velocipede even if it became ever so common. Indeed good roads seem es-sential to all locomotive machines, and without a railroad the steam engine itself loses much of its locomotive power. Some years ago when the velocipede was in common use the roads were much more rough and bad than they are at present; the system of breaking up the great stones on the roads has removed an impediment not only to carriages of a large size but to velocipedes as well, and the great stones on the roads in many parts of England about 1819 were the causes of most of the oversets that befell the riders of velocipedes.

During the time they were in favour about 18 or twenty years ago many gentlemen of my acquaintance of various ages and weights employed velocipedes constantly in the hilly country about the city of Bath; many ran distances of twelve or fourteen miles out and back again before dinner, and I have heard some affirm that they could go six or seven miles an hour. It was not unusual to run thirty or forty miles in a day on the old velocipedes and yet nobody was killed, no arms or legs were broken and no surgeon was wanted, indeed I never heard an any accident among them that could not be cured with vinegar and brown paper.

Such, gentlemen, are the uses and applications of which the velocipede appears capable, whether they will suffice to make it practically useful remains to be proved. It is certain, that cities are unfit for velocipedes, - the pitching of the road is too rough, and the pavements are too crowded for them to run with comfort to themselves or others. No courteous or well-bred rider likes to run the risk of going over people's toes, - it causes too much friction to be pleasant to either party. But in an open country road the velocipede displays its useful qualities, especially when we descend a gentle slope of a mile or two in length balancing all the way without touching the ground with either foot, and with a rapidity like the swiftness of an arrow; this makes the journey appear short, and the rest obtained in this manner relieves the fatigue of going many previous miles.

The velocipede appears best suited to the use of that class of society that is perhaps the most numerous and active of all, - men possessing the full use of their limbs, to whom horses would be a trouble and an encumbrance, but who delight in locomotion, and who do not shrink from bodily exercise. To such, the velocipede gives the power of going from place to place at a small expense and with sufficient rapidity; if broken it is easily repaired, and when no longer wanted it takes up but little room leaning against the wall. When using it, the rider depends for safety upon his own care and skill, and not as the horseman does, upon the pleasure of an animal, frequently ill trained and often timid or vicious. Whether the machine will again become common it is hard to foresee, but if tried in this form no doubt many farther improvements will be suggested; nor need we be surprised at any clamour that has been raised or that may hereafter be raised against this machine; as long as there continues to exist that class of animated creation on whom nature for some wise purpose has bestowed the faculty of braying, they must bray and they will bray. When umbrellas were first brought out, they brayed at them, and when the steam engine got common they raised with one content a bray so loud that it was heard across the Atlantic and re-echoed back from North America; but the umbrella and the steam engine were too useful and too strong to be put down by that sonorous body. We need not be surprised at their exertions nor alarmed by their clamour, knowing from what source all that clamour comes.

I regret, gentlemen, that there is not room in this Institution, to show fully the working of the machine; perhaps nothing less than a run of twenty or thirty miles would be sufficient to show clearly its use; but however this may be, I may be permitted on quitting the subject to express my thanks to you gentlemen for the patient attention you have been so kind as to give, to suggestions that I fear have been too dry and too closely connected with calculation to have been laid before any others than the members of an institution who are capable of judging and deciding upon them.

The defeat of the Dandy or Hobby-horse in 1819-20 was reported as follows by Charles Spencer, early manufacturer of cranked velocipedes in Britain, in his hard-to-obtain booklet *Bicycles and Tricycles* (London 1883):

The Dandy or Hobby-horse was known and ridden in England as long back as between sixty and seventy years ago, and though its career was a short one, owing to the ridicule cast upon it by some of the eminent caricaturists - Cruikshank, Rowlandson, and others, yet it made its mark at the time, and, as events have proved, was destined in another shape to achieve a popularity which may almost be described as unparalleled.

Why, it may be asked, should Cruikshank trouble his head about the matter, or concern himself to bring into ridicule a practice which, if not graceful, was at least harmless? The answer to this question is to be found in the fact that the artist, who was himself disposed to patronize the new sport, having once been placed in a somewhat ridiculous position by his unskilful use of the machine, thenceforward became its most determined opponent, and brought to bear upon the practice the powerful battery of his wit, and, by placing the Hobby-horse and its rider before the public in an absurd aspect, he rendered riders afraid of encountering the jeers of the general public, and thus retarded by at least fifty years the progress of the art. Thus it happened.

[Robert] Cruikshank was on very friendly and intimate terms with his publisher James Sidebetham, and on one occasion, in the winter of 1819, the two cronies, dressed in the extreme of the preposterous fashion of the day, set forth an excursion, mounted each on his hobby-horse. (Cruikshank's earlier caricatures were published by his friend, James Sidebetham, at the shop of the latter, 287 Strand, whose widow [he died after what follows; HEL] afterwards removed to Burlington Arcade, where many of them were exhibited in the window, to the exquisite delight of the public, and the extreme annoyance of the beadle, who found perpetual difficulty in clearing the space opposite Mrs Sidebetham's shop.).

All went well for a considerable distance, but when coming down Highgate Hill at full speed - at a rate of nearly ten miles an hour - the riders "cannoned," or "collided," to use the expressive Americanism, and away they went, each falling with considerable violence on an opposite side of the road, the result being that the machines sustained serious injuries, while they themselves were severely shaken. Mr Cruikshank was led by his friend, who was the less injured of the two, into the Archway Tavern, where they obtained as much consolation as was possible under the circumstances, finally returning to London on one of Wiber's coaches.

This unlucky accident was really the main reason of the loss of popularity sustained by the Hobby-horse. Instead of riding their hobbies, Messrs Cruikshank and Sidebetham devoted themselves henceforth to turning the sport into ridicule, the ingenious and fantastic imagination of the former inspiring him in the execution by his facile pencil of numberless droll sketches of mournful-looking individuals, attired in the extreme of the fashion of the period, mounted upon Dandy or Hobby-horses, upon which they appeared alike uncomfortable and ridiculous. These were exhibited in Mr Sidebetham's window in the Strand, and promptly excited the risibility of passers-by to such an extent that it became positively unsafe to appear in public on a Hobby-horse, so loud and universal was the laughter at the resemblance between the rider in the street and his caricature in the shop window.

NOTES TO APPENDIX B

1. Drais himself could have chosen the name "vélocipede" for his French patent of 1818. See chapter 1 and figure 2.3. —HEL
2. What Davies erroneously identified on the plate as additional stays are the stands that Drais provided to be let down for parking the machine. See figure 1.7. —HEL
3. Unlicensed copies of Drais's design lacked the back-wheel brake that Drais had hidden intentionally behind the rider's leg. Only the string to actuate it from the armrest could be seen—see figures 1.5 and 1.6. —HEL
4. According to Davies, as the velocipedes ran along the roads, skittish horses sometimes shied away from them, and evidently even steady old chaise horses eyed them with astonishment and horror.
5. This argument suggests that an additional 130 pounds have to be accelerated. In reality the body mass has to be accelerated even when walking or running; thus only the 40 pounds of the velocipede have to be accelerated in addition. —HEL
6. This is the earliest mention of bearings in a two-wheeler. —HEL
7. Today it is clear that this is provided already by the inert mass in linear motion. Quite the reverse, the wheels are given the smallest possible moment of inertia. See box. 2.2. —HEL
8. See note 3.

APPENDIX C:

....

BICYCLE AESTHETICS

In this book, we have deliberately made few references to aesthetics. Our primary aim has been to concentrate on the invention and development of the engineering aspects of bicycles. Our contention is that most of a bicycle's aesthetic characteristics derive primarily from engineering, which is one of the reasons why bicycles are such pleasing creations. We feel, however, that we should include some brief mention of aesthetics.

FORM FOLLOWS FUNCTION

"Form ever follows function" was a phrase coined by the American architect Louis Sullivan in 1896. In an article in *Lippincott's Magazine* titled "The Tall Office Building Artistically Considered," he wrote:

> It is the pervading law of all things organic and inorganic, of all things physical and metaphysical, of all things human and all things superhuman—of all true manifestations of the head, of the heart, of the soul—that the life is recognizable in its expression, that form ever follows function. *This is the law.* (Sullivan 1896)

The innovative pneumatic-tired diamond-frame safety bicycle was enjoying great popularity at that time and illustrated the truth of Sullivan's observation. Indeed, the diamond frame is such a widely recognized functional form that, more than a century later, it is instantly recognizable to the general public in many countries. Hence, bicycle-related traffic signs across the developed world employ simple depictions of a diamond-frame safety bicycle. Similarly, certain other classic bicycle designs have characteristic forms that are easily identified, even in caricature. One such is the high-wheeler. Another is the Brompton folding bicycle, easily recognized by the curve of its main beam. That curve results solely from the functional requirement of compact folding: the main tube curves tightly around the small rear wheel when the bike is folded.

The derivation and the variety of aesthetic features other than those stemming directly from engineering functionality can be considered under several headings.

COSMETIC FINISHES

As surface coatings, cosmetic finishes serve two primary functions: to protect components (primarily from deterioration due to moisture, road debris, pollutants, and general wear and tear) and to make the machine more visually attractive. (The latter is also, of course, useful in marketing.)

An early finishing technique used on steel bicycle frames was japanning. As the name suggests, it emulated the appearance of Japanese lacquer work. In the industrialized West's interpretation of the process, resin-based varnishes were used. They were applied by dipping or brushing. Each coat was heat-dried, then polished to a high gloss. The color used most often was black. To relieve the dark coloring, gilding was applied; by the early twentieth century this was almost always done by leaf transfer (Oddy 1995). Japanning was used by manufacturers of sewing machines, some of whom became bicycle manufacturers, and John Marston's Sunbeam bicycle company had its roots in Wolverhampton's japanning industry.

The first colored enamels had to be applied with a brush, layer by layer, and each layer had to be dried at low heat. These enamels gave a rougher, softer, and less durable finish than black enamel. But by the mid 1890s, improved colored enamels were developed that gave bright, smooth, glazed, hard-wearing surfaces. Subsequently, sprayed and stove-hardened enamels were widely used on bicycle frames.

Powder coating, developed after World War II, is now widely used on bicycle frames. Unlike traditional paints, powder coating doesn't require a solvent to keep the binder and the filler in liquid suspension. The coating is usually applied electrostatically, then heated to allow it to flow and form a skin before curing hard. Among the advantages of power coating are lower environmental impact, reduced health risks for operatives, greater thickness and durability, reduced wastage, and reduced capital and plant operating costs.

Until the 1920s, nickel plating was widely used to give steel components, such as wheel rims, hubs, brakes, and handlebars, a bright, shiny finish. But nickel plating was by no means universal, and for some decades it was common to find these components finished in black enamel. Often the customer was given a choice of black or nickel.

Chromium plating became widespread in the 1930s and soon replaced nickel plating. Very occasionally, a bicycle's entire frame would be chromed; this was usually done only on a special edition. More commonly, certain components of upscale bikes, such as the fork tips or the chain stays, were chromed.

Poorly applied chromium plating could easily pit, crack, or even flake off, allowing the underlying steel to rust. The more the plating pitted, the more the steel substrate would corrode. The prevalence of low-grade chromium plating in the 1960s was one reason it went out of fashion. Good chromium plating, however, such as that used for many decades on Sturmey-Archer hub gears, could be very durable.

Early aluminum-alloy bicycle components had the advantage over steel of not being subject to rusting, but surface oxidation could occur. Anodizing, developed in the 1920s to protect seaplanes' fuselages from the corrosive effects of sea water, improved aluminum's resistance to corrosion; it also facilitated dyeing. Since the second half of the twentieth century, colored anodized aluminum has been widely used as a material for bicycle components.

Polished stainless steel frames have been produced from time to time.

BADGES, LETTERING, AND LINING

Badges and lettering are often used to identify the make and model of a bicycle. At one time, head badges (i.e., those fitted to the conspicuous forward face of the head tube) were pressed or molded from steel or some other metal, then soldered, glued, or riveted to the head tube. In the 1960s, self-adhesive plastic badges were widely adopted.

Lettering on a bicycle's frame, usually applied in the form of decals, might include the model name, further information about the maker (such as an address), patent or registered design information, and safety warnings.

Decorative lining (striping) of frame tubes and fenders was popular for many years. Sometimes it consisted of decals, but on some upscale machines it was applied with a hand-held lining wheel, fed with paint from a small-built-in reservoir, which was run along a guide rail fitted around the frame tube. Gold leaf lining was far superior to bronze, a cheaper alternative.

EMBELLISHMENT OF FUNCTIONAL ELEMENTS

There are several ways in which functional elements of bicycles have been embellished for aesthetic and branding reasons. The tops of seat stays, where they join with the seat tube, were sometimes fluted for aesthetic effect; they might even taper and join together while wrapping around the top of the seat tube. Frame lugs and fork crowns were sometimes manufactured with elaborately cutaway sections, and in some cases further refined by hand filing. The lugs of the Hetchins Magnum Opus, an upscale bicycle introduced in the 1950s, were sometimes picked out in a color contrasting with the rest of the frame or edged in gold paint.

Very occasionally, a maker modified the generic profile of the diamond-frame bike to make his machines more easily identifiable. For example, some Hetchins models had curved chain stays, curved seat stays, and even curved seat tubes. Some classic British lightweights made by Bates had a distinctively shaped double curve (flattened S) fork, a registered design called the Diadrant. Dubious claims of improved shock absorption were sometimes made to justify such designs.

A pressed steel chainwheel could easily be given a decorative motif, such as Peugeot's lion or Raleigh's heron head.

DECORATIVE NON-FUNCTIONAL ELEMENTS

Sometimes bicycle makers added decorative features that were purely stylistic and had no function other than to create some kind of distinctive image or fantasy. For example, some Draisines and at least one early French velocipede had, forward of the steerer, a figurehead suggesting a dragon or a sea monster. From the 1930s into the 1950s, some bicycles (notably Schwinns) had false gasoline tanks resembling those of motorcycles.

FASHION

Materials come into fashion and go out of fashion, but that happens at different times in different cultures. In the 1960s, when British roadsters and sports light roadsters invariably had chromium-plated steel components, Belgians were buying roadsters with aluminum-alloy parts. Forty years later, fashionable roadsters sold in Rome came with chromed steel components similar to those favored by Brits in the 1960s.

Sometimes the customer is less concerned with the actual materials than with their visual characteristics. Raleigh proved this in the 1990s when it successfully used large-diameter steel tubing to mimic the look of bikes with oversize aluminum tubes, then popular with British adolescents.

The shapes of components are also subject to the whims of fashion. For example, when the flat "all-rounder" handlebar became popular on post-World War II British sports light roadsters, prewar roadster bars became very unfashionable, even though many of the older bars were ergonomically superior.

Typefaces used in lettering on frames and on head badges also go in and out of fashion. The very modern fonts and graphic styles that Alex Moulton used on his all-new bicycle brand in the 1960s marked a significant departure from the British cycle industry's traditional approach to graphics. In other cases, an old concept was subtly and almost imperceptibly updated, as with the packaging of favorite consumer food brands. A good example is Raleigh's heron-head motif, which has been revamped many times over the course of more than 100 years.

IN CONCLUSION

This has been by no means a comprehensive survey of bicycle aesthetics, merely a brief introduction. It is a fascinating subject, and you can read more about it in various papers published in the proceedings of the International Cycling History Conferences. We hope, with this short appendix, to have offered some insights into the subject while also explaining why we haven't gone into the matter in greater detail in the chapters. This book is basically about engineering, and we're with Louis Sullivan.

APPENDIX D:

THE PARTS OF A BICYCLE

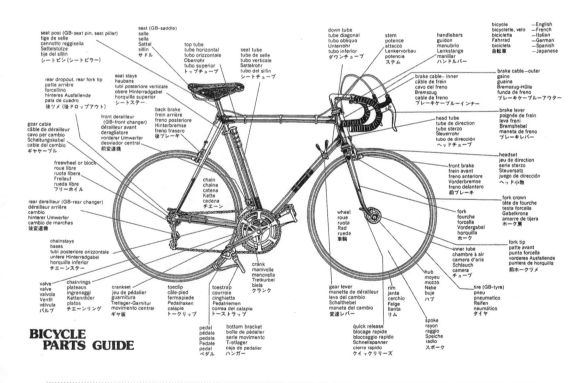

Figure D.1 A diagram identifying the parts of a typical diamond-frame bicycle (Howard Sutherland).

SELECT LITERATURE

....

CYCLING BIBLIOGRAPHIES

Clayton, Nick. 2001. "Index of British Cycling Periodicals." *The Boneshaker* 155: 30–35. Also includes holdings of libraries.

Déon, Bernard, and Seray, Jacques. 1996. *Les révues cyclistes*. Saint-Étienne: Association des amis du Musée d'Art et d'Industrie de Saint-Étienne. Bibliography of French cycling magazines.

Kobayashi, Keizo. 1984. *Pour une bibliographie du cyclisme 1818–1983*. Paris: Fédération Française du cyclotourisme. Yearly updates, 1985–present: *Bibliographie Cycliste.* Saint-Étienne: Association des amis du Musée d'Art et d'Industrie de Saint Étienne.

Luebbers, David J. 1977. *The 1950–1972 Bicycle Bibliography.* Denver: Silers.

Schultz, Barbara, and Schultz, Mark. 1979. *Bicycles and Bicycling: A Guide to Information Sources.* Detroit: Gale Research.

Sokoll, Alfred H. *Fahrrad und Radsport.* 1985. Munich: Alkos-Verlag. German bibliography; includes periodicals.

Truelsen, Erling. 1977. *Litteratur om cykler, cykling og cykeltrafik.* Copenhagen: Dansk Cyklist Forbund. Danish 1868–1976; Norwegian, Swedish, and English 1965–1976.

Ulreich, Walter. 2003. "Historische deutsche Fahrradzeitschriften." *Der Knochenschüttler* 28: 14–15. German periodicals; includes holdings of libraries.

Williams, Edward. 1993. *A Bibliography of Cycling Books.* Kings Heath: National Cycle Archive.

PATENT ABRIDGEMENTS AND LISTINGS, AND GENERAL CYCLE HISTORY ARCHIVES

Allen, James Titus. 1892. *Digest of Cycles or Velocipedes, with Attachments Patented in the United States from 1789 to 1872*. Two volumes. Washington: US Patent Office.

USPO Supplements: *Patents and References*. 1789–July 1893.

USPO periodical: *Cycle Patents Monthly*. 1892–1896.

Anonymous. 1869–70. "Liste chronologique des brevets relatifs à la vélocipédie." *Le Vélocipède Illustré* (December 9, 23, and 26, 1869; May 26 and 29, 1870).

Herzog, Ulrich. 1984. *Fahrradpatente*. Kiel: Moby Dick.

National Bicycle History Archive of America, Davis, California. Available at http://www.nbhaa.com.

National Cycling Library Digital Archive, Llandrindod Wells, Powys. National Cycle Collection. Available at http://www.cyclemuseum.org.uk.

Phillips, Robert Edward. 1886/87. *Patents for Inventions. Abridgements and specifications relating to velocipedes*. Two volumes. London: Iliffe.

BICYCLE SCIENCE

Abbott, Allan V., and Wilson, David Gordon. 1995. *Human-Powered Vehicles*. Champaign: Human Kinetics Publishers.

Appeltauer, Peter. 2013. *Das Kleingedruckte beim Radfahren. Physikalische Hintergründe Ihres Rennalltags*. Leipzig: Maxime-Verlag.

Glaskin, Max. 2012. *Cycling Science: How Rider and Machine Work Together*. University of Chicago Press.

Gressmann, Michael. 2005. *Fahrradphysik und Biomechanik*. Tenth edition. Bielefeld: Delius-Klasing Verlag.

Pooch, Andreas. 2009. *Wissenschaft vom schnellen Radfahren*. Windeck: LD-Verlag.

Sharp, Archibald. 1896. *Bicycles & Tricycles. An Elementary Treatise on Their Design and Construction*. London: Longmans, Green. Reprinted in 1977 by MIT Press.

Wilson, David Gordon, with Papadopoulos, Jim. 2004. *Bicycling Science*. Third edition. Cambridge: MIT Press.

BICYCLE DESIGN, AESTHETICS, AND LITERATURE

Astié, Charles. 2003. *Musée Virtuel du Vélocipède 1817–2000*. Toulouse: Cépaduès-Éditions. Computer-rendered pictures of bicycle landmarks.

Burrows, Mike, and Hadland, Tony. 2004. *Bicycle Design: The Search for the Perfect Machine*. Second edition. Hereford: Pedal.

Embacher, Michael. 2011. *Cyclepedia. A Century of Iconic Bicycle Design*. San Francisco: Chronicle Books.

Heine, Jan, and Pradères, Jean-Pierre. 2008. *The Competition Bicycle: A Photographic History*. Seattle: Bicycle Quarterly Press.

Heine, Jan, and Pradères, Jean-Pierre. 2009. *The Golden Age of Hand-Built Bicycles*. New York: Rizzoli.

Isendyck, Jürgen. 2013. *Über Fahrräder und Fahrradteile*. Aurich: VSF Akademie.

Klanten, Robert, and Moreno, Shonquis. 2010. *Velo: Bicycle Culture and Design*. Berlin: Gestalten Verlag.

Klanten, Robert, and Ehmann, Sven. 2013. *Velo—2nd Gear: Bicycle Culture and Style*. Berlin: Gestalten Verlag.

Lessing, Hans-Erhard. 1995. *Ich fahr' so gerne Rad. Geschichten von der Lust, auf dem eisernen Rosse dahinzujagen*. Munich: Deutscher Taschenbuch-Verlag.

Newson, Alex. 2013. *Fifty Bicycles That Changed the World*. London: Design Museum.

Roy, Robin, with Cross, Nigel. 1983. *Bicycles: Invention and Innovation*. Milton Keynes: Open University Press.

Schenkel, Elmar. 2008. *Cyclomanie. Das Fahrrad und die Literatur*. Eggingen: Edition Isele.

Starrs, James E. 1997. *The Literary Cyclist. Great Bicycling Scenes in Literature*. New York: Breakaway Books.

Sumner, Philip, and Osbahr, Alan. 1966. *Early Bicycles*. London: Hugh Evelyn.

Tenberge, Katharina. 2011. *Klassische Fahrräder des 20. Jahrhunderts*. Bielefeld: Moby Dick.

teNeues Verlag. 2012. *The Bike Book: Lifestyle—Passion—Design*. Kempen.

HISTORIOGRAPHIC CYCLE PERIODICALS

The Boneshaker. 1955 to date. Thrice-yearly magazine of the Veteran-Cycle Club (UK). Index 1–150 in autumn 2000 issue.

Cycle History. Proceedings of International Cycling History Conferences, 1994–present. The first three volumes had different titles, but are usually quoted as follows. *Cycle History 1: 1st International Conference of Cycling History*. Glasgow: Museum of Transport, 1991. *Cycle History 2: Actes de la deuxième conférence internationale sur l'histoire du cycle*. Ville de Saint-Étienne, 1995. *Cycle History 3: 3. Internationale Konferenz zur Fahrradgeschichte*. Neckarsulm: Deutsches Zweiradmuseum, 1993. A keyword index of volumes 1–23 is available at http://www.cycling-history.org—click on Proceedings in the menu.

The Wheelmen. 1970-present. Half-yearly magazine of The Wheelmen (US). Bulletin #26 is an index to magazines #1–63/2003.

Les Dossiers de la Vélocithèque #1/1986-present, ed. Gérard Salmon. Vélocithèque, 69590 Le Bois, France. Occasional publications by various authors.

Het Rijwiel 2010–present, formerly: *De Oude Fiets* 2001/1–2009/4. Dutch quarterly of Historische Rijwielvereniging De Oude Fiets. Index at http://oudefiets.nl.

Der Knochenschüttler. Bimonthly magazine of Historische Fahrräder e.V. (Germany). #1/1995-present. Separate index: *Gesamtverzeichnis 1995–2006*.

Vintage Bicycle Quarterly (2002–2006), renamed *Bicycle Quarterly* (2006–). Published in Seattle by Bicycle Quarterly Press.

GENERAL CYCLING HISTORIES

Antila, Kimmo, ed. 2007. *Velomania!* Tampere: Museum Centre Vapriikki.

Dodge, Pryor. *The Bicycle*. 1996. Paris: Flammarion.

Durry, Jean. 1982. *L'Encycl(e)opédie.* Lausanne: Edita.

Herlihy, David. 2004. *Bicycle: The History*. New Haven: Yale University Press.

Geist, Roland C. 1978. *Bicycle People*. Washington: Acropolis Books.

McGurn, Jim. 1999. *On Your Bicycle*. Second edition. York: Open Road.

Norcliffe, Glen. 2001. *The Ride to Modernity: The Bicycle in Canada 1869–1900*. University of Toronto Press.

Pridmore, Jay, and Hurd, Jim. 1995. *The American Bicycle*. Osceola: Motorbooks International.

Ritchie, Andrew. 1975. *King of the Road: An Illustrated History of Cycling*. Berkeley: Ten Speed.

Ritchie, Andrew. 2011. *Quest for Speed. A History of Early Bicycle Racing 1868–1903*. El Cerrito: Cycle Publishing.

Roberts, Derek. 1991. *Cycling History: Myths and Queries*. Erdington: Pinkerton. (V-CC correction notes by Nick Clayton, 1991.)

Seray, Jacques. 1988. *Deux Roues. La véritable histoire du vélo*. Rodez: Éditions du Rouergue.

Smith, Robert A. 1972. *A Social History of the Bicycle.* New York: American Heritage.

CYCLING HISTORIES BY EPOCH

Besse, Nadine, and Henry, Anne, eds. 2008. *Le Vélocipède—the velocipede. Objet de modernité—a modern object.* Exhibition catalog. Saint-Étienne: Musée d'Art et d'Industrie.

Burgwardt, Carl F. 2001. *Buffalo's Bicycles.* Orchard Park: Carl Burgwardt.

Kobayashi, Keizo. 1993. *Histoire du Vélocipède du Drais à Michaux 1817–1870. Mythes et Réalités.* Tokyo: Bicycle Culture Center.

Lessing, Hans-Erhard. 2003. *Automobilität—Karl Drais und die unglaublichen Anfänge.* Leipzig: Maxime-Verlag.

Reynaud, Claude. 2008. *Le Vélocipède illustré . . . et déjà la bicylette!* Two volumes, paginated throughout. Domazan: Éditions Musée Vélo-Moto.

Reynaud, Claude. 2011. *L'Ère du Grand-Bi en France 1870–1890*. Domazan: Éditions Musée Vélo-Moto.

Street, Roger. 2011. Dashing Dandies - the English Hobby-Horse Craze of 1918. Christchurch: Artesius

CYCLE MANUFACTURERS' INDEXES

Cranked velocipedes

Clayton, Nick. 1987a. "An index of makes & Makers of Boneshaker cycles." *The Boneshaker* 115 (winter): 15–18.

Kielwein, Matthias. 2006. "Velozipede in Deutschland, Fabrikanten und Händler." *Der Knochenschüttler* 37: 2–7.

Reynaud, Claude. 2009. "Les constructeurs français." In *Le vélocipède illustré*. Domazan: Muséé du Vélo.

High Wheelers

Reynaud, Claude. 2011. "Liste de constructeurs, fabricants et monteurs de grands-bis, tricycles et accessoires en France entre 1871 et 1890." In *L'Ère du Grand-Bi*. Domazan: Muséé du Vélo.

Stockdale, Glyn, and Clayton, Nick. *Index of Makes and Makers of Bicycles*. Supplement to *The Boneshaker* 106 (autumn 1984).

Safeties

Hetzel, Charles. 1981. "Bicycle Brand Directory of American Safeties 1890–1900." In G. Donald Adams, *Collecting & Restoring Antique Bicycles*. Blue Ridge Summit: TAB Books.

UK in general

Miller, Ray. 2009. *Encyclopedia of Cycle Manufacturers up to 1918*. Second edition. Birmingham: John Pinkerton Memorial Fund.

US in general

Hetzel, Charles. *List of American Bicycle Brands Prior to 1918*. May be available at http://www.thewheelmen.org (site under construction at time of writing).

Germany in general

Baumann, Chris, and Schöla, Ottokar. 2000. *Deutsche Fahrradmarken von A–Z*. Langenhagen: Historische Fahrräder.

Papperitz, Frank. 2003. *Markenware Fahrrad*. Pirna: Hochland-Verlag.

CYCLE INDUSTRY AND MANUFACTURER MONOGRAPHS

Aidn, Werner. 2010. *Diamant. Fahrräder-Motorräder-Radsport.* Leipzig: Maxime-Verlag.

Bäumler, Ernst. 1961. *Fortschritt und Sicherheit. Der Weg des Werkes Fichtel & Sachs.* Munich: Mercator Verlag.

Cotter, John-Baptist. 1994. *From Turkish Bath to Motor Carriages: The Concise History of the Crypto Car and Cycle Co 1894–1994.* London: Yelling Cycling.

Crown, Judith, and Coleman, Glenn. 1996. *No Hands: The Rise and Fall of the Schwinn Bicycle Company, an American Institution.* New York: Henry Holt.

Epperson, Bruce D. 2010. *Peddling Bicycles to America. The Rise of an Industry.* Jefferson: McFarland.

Evans, David E. 2007. *Mr. Pedersen: A Man of Genius.* Stroud: The History Press.

Facchinetti, Paolo, and Rubino, Guido. 2008. *Campagnolo: 75 Years of Cycling Passion.* Boulder: Cordee.

Hadland, Tony. 1981. *The Moulton Bicycle: The Story from 1957 to 1981.* Erdington: Pinkerton.

Hadland, Tony. 1987. *The Sturmey-Archer Story.* Erdington: Pinkerton.

Hadland, Tony. 2010. *The Spaceframe Moultons.* Berlin: LIT-Verlag.

Hadland, Tony. 2011. *Raleigh: Past and Presence of an Iconic Bicycle Brand.* San Francisco: Cycle Publishing.

Heine, Jan. 2012. *René Herse: The Bikes—the Builder—the Riders.* Seattle: Bicycle Quarterly Press.

Henshaw, David. 2011. *Brompton Bicycle.* Second edition. Wakefield: Excellent Books.

Krach, Martin. 2001. *NSU-Fahrräder 1886–1963.* Second edition. Neckarsulm: Krach.

Land, Nigel. 2011. *Elswick-Hopper of Barton-on-Humber: The Story of a Great British Bicycle Maker.* Barton-on-Humber: Fathom.

Marchesini, Daniele. 2008. *Bianchi. Una bicicletta sola al comando.* Azzana San Paolo.

Mertins, Michael. 2001. *Die Geschichte der Anker-Fahrräder.* Langenhagen: Historische Fahrräder.

Moffitt, John. 2003. *The Ivel Story.* Driffield: Japonica.

Nöll, Jürgen. 2001. *Opel-Fahrräder. Fünf Jahrzehnte Fahrradbau in Rüsselsheim.* Bielefeld: Delius-Klasing Verlag.

Pinkerton, John, and Roberts, Derek. 1998. *A History of Rover Cycles.* Edington: Pinkerton.

Pinkerton, John, and Roberts, Derek. 2002. *Sunbeam Cycles: The Story from the Catalogues, 1887–1957.* Erdington: Pinkerton.

Pridmore, Jay, and Hurd, Jim. 1996. *Schwinn Bicycles.* Osceola: Motorbooks International.

Rosen, Paul. 2002. *Framing Production: Technology, Culture, and Change in the British Bicycle Industry.* Cambridge: MIT Press.

Shimano, Keizo. 1975. *History of Shimano.* Osaka: Shimano Industrial Co.

Ulreich, Walter. 1995. *Das Steyr-Waffenrad.* Graz: Weishaupt-Verlag.

SPECIALIZED FORMS OF CYCLING; CYCLE PARTS AND THEIR HISTORY

Berto, Frank J., Shepherd, Ron, and Henry, Raymond. 2009. *The Dancing Chain: History and Development of the Derailleur Bicycle*. Third edition. San Francisco: Van der Plas.

Berto, Frank J. 2009. *The Birth of Dirt: Origins of Mountain Biking*. San Francisco: Van der Plas.

Caidin, Martin, and Barbree, Jay. 1974. *Bicycles in War*. New York: Hawthorne.

Dodds, Alastair. 1999. *Scottish Bicycles and Tricycles*. Edinburgh: NMS.

Euhus, Walter. 2003. *Die Geschichte der Fahrradbereifung*. Langenhagen: Historische Fahrräder.

Grützner, Michael. 2009. *Kettenlose Fahrräder. Die Geschichte der kettenlosen Fahrräder in Deutschland ab 1890: von Adler bis Woerner*. Rickmansworth: Fidibus.

Hadland, Tony, and Pinkerton, John. 1996. *It's in the Bag!* Erdington: Pinkerton.

Rohloff, Barbara, ed. 2010. *Stories*. Kassel: Rohloff.

Schmitz, Arnfried, with Hadland, Tony. 2000. *Human Power: The Forgotten Energy 1913–1992*. Coventry: Hadland.

Schmitz, Arnfried, with Hadland, Tony. 2010. *Cyclists Cycling Cycles & Cycle Parts*. Faringdon: Hadland.

Way, R. John. 1973. *The Bicycle: A Guide and Manual*. London: Hamlyn.

COLLECTIONS OF ARTICLES, ILLUSTRATIONS, OR ADVERTISEMENTS FROM CYCLING MAGAZINES

Joseph, Lionel, ed. 1997. *The First Century of the Bicycle and Its Accessories. Compiled from the archives of the Cyclists' Touring Club*. Godalming: CTC. Illustrations, advertisements.

Kielwein, Matthias, and Lessing, Hans-Erhard, eds. 2005. *Kaleidoskop früher Fahrrad- und Motorradtechnik. Vollständige Artikelsammlung aus Dinglers Polytechnischem Journal 1895–1908*. Two volumes. Leipzig: Maxime-Verlag. Reviews with illustrations.

Noguchi-san. 2002. *The Data Book. 100 Years of Bicycle Component and Accessory Design*. San Francisco: Van der Plas. Illustrations.

REFERENCES

....

Abbott, A. V., and Wilson, D. G. 1995. *Human Powered Vehicles*. Champaign: Human Kinetics.

Barrett, R. 1982. Photograph of Sharrow CC. *The Boneshaker* 99.

Bartleet, Horace Wilton. 1928. "Spokes." *The Motorcyclist*, June. Reprinted in *The Boneshaker* 119.

Bartleet, Horace Wilton. 1931. *Bartleet's Bicycle Book*. London: Burrow & Co. Reprinted in 1983 by Pinkerton.

Baudry de Saunier, Louis. 1891. *Histoire de la Vélocipédie*. Paris: Paul Ollendorff.

Baudry de Saunier, Louis. 1899. *L'automobile théorique et pratique*, 1. tôme. Paris: Baudry de Saunier. German edition reprinted in 1989 by Zentralantiquariat der DDR.

Baudry de Saunier, Louis. 1925. *Ma petite bicyclette. Sa pratique*. Paris: Flammarion.

Bauer, Johann Christian Siegesmund. 1817. *Beschreibung der v. Drais'schen Fahrmaschine und einiger daran versuchter Verbesserungen*. Nuremberg: Steinische Buchhandlung. Reprinted in 2001 as *Das erste Zweirad fuhr in Mannheim* by Quadrate-Buchhandlung.

Berruyer, Alfred. 1869. *Manuel du Véloceman, ou notice, système, nomenclature, pratique, art et avenir des vélocipèdes*. Grenoble: Allier.

Berto, Frank J. 1998. *The Birth of Dirt*. San Francisco: Cycling Resources.

Berto, Frank J. 2009. *The Dancing Chain*. Third edition. San Francisco: Cycle Publishing.

Besse, Nadine, and Henry, Anne, eds. 2008. *Le Vélocipède—Objet de modernité*. Saint-Étienne: Musée d'Art et d'Industrie (bilingual French-English)

Boore, James Percy. 1951. *The Seamless Story: The Story of the Mannesmann and the Stiefel Piercing Patents*. Los Angeles: Commonwealth.

Bottomley-Firth, J. F. 1869. *The Velocipede, Its Past, Its Present and Its Future*. Reprinted in 1995 by National Cycle Archive, Warwick.

Bouglise, Georges de la. 1868. *Note sur le vélocipède à pédales et à frein de M. Michaux (par un amateur)*. Paris: Lainé & Havard.

Bowden, Frank. 1913. *Cycling for Health and Points for Cyclists*. London: Criterion.

Bowerman, Les. 1988a. "Paul de Vivie (Vélocio)." *News & Views* (Veteran-Cycle Club), April/May: 24.

Bowerman, Leslie. 1988b. "The Stoke-Poges window updated; a non-cycle (& nonsensical) saga." *The Boneshaker* 117.

Bowerman, Les. 1992. "Lewis Gompertz and his addition to the velocipede." In *Cycle History* 3. (On *Cycle History*, see the explanation in "Select Literature" above.)

Bowerman, Les. 1994. "John Keen—The life of a cycling pioneer." In *Cycle History* 4.

Boys, Charles Vernon. 1884. "Bicycles and tricycles in theory and practice." *Nature*, March 20.

Briese, Volker. 2008. "Children as bicycle passengers." In *Cycle History* 18.

Brun, Jean-François. 2010. "Incorporation of the bicycle into the French Army (1889–1914)." In *Cycle History* 19.

Burrows, Mike. 2000. *Bicycle Design*. York: Company of Cyclists.

Campbell, Peter. 1903. Letter to the editor. *The Cyclist*, April 22.

Camus, Charles. 1722. *Traité des forces mouvantes*. Paris: Claude Jombert.

Card, Peter W. 2006. *The Electric-Powered Bicycle Lamp, 1888–1948*. Birmingham: John Pinkerton Memorial Publishing Fund.

Card, Peter W. 2008. *Early Vehicle Lighting 1868–1948*. Second edition. Ramsbury: Crowood.

Chaussinand, Bernard. 2010. "Capitaine Robert's *La Percutante* [The Striker]." In *Cycle History* 19.

Chen, Patrick. 2002. "The bicycle in war: Vietnam 1945–1975." In *Cycle History* 12.

Clayton, Nick. 1987a. "The first bicycle!" *The Boneshaker* 113.

Clayton, Nick. 1987b. "An index of makes & makers of boneshaker bicycles." *The Boneshaker* 115.

Clayton, Nick. 1991. "The Meyer-Guilmet bicycle—1869 or 1879." In *Cycle History* 1.

Clayton, Nick. 1992. "The development of the suspension wheel." In *Cycle History* 2.

Clayton, Nick. 1993. "Hans Renold and the birth of the cycle chain." In *Cycle History* 3.

Clayton, Nick. 1997. "Who invented the penny-farthing?" In *Cycle History* 7.

Clayton, Nick. 1999. "William Jackson—A forgotten pioneer of the modern tricycle." In *Cycle History* 9.

Clayton, Nick. 2005. "Willard Sawyer—a reassessment." In *Cycle History* 15.

Clayton, Nick. 2006a. "James Hastings and the High Peak Velocipede Club." In *Cycle History* 16.

Clayton, Nick. 2006b. "Getting a handle on Michaux." *The Boneshaker* 172.

Clayton Nick. 2008. "William Blood's Dublin Tricycle." In *Cycle History* 18.

Clayton, Nick. 2010a. "The mysterious McCammon." In *Cycle History* 19.

Clayton, Nick. 2010b. "The Rover Safety bicycle—the three pattern problem." In *Cycle History* 20.

Clayton, Nick. 2012a. "Who invented the Bowden cable?" In *Cycle History* 21.

Clayton, Nick. 2012b. "A tale of two dwarfs—The Facile and the Kangaroo." In *Cycle History* 22.

Cordon Champ, Bob. 2004. "Bicycle of the future—The cycles of the Rue Roque de Filliol." *The Boneshaker* 165.

Cox, Peter T. 2009. *Energy and the Bicycle—Human powered vehicles in perspective*. Chester: University of Chester.

Cox, Peter. 2012. "Human-powered-vehicles in Britain, 1930–1980." In *Cycle History* 21.

Coventry Machinists' Company. 1880. *Coventry Machinists' Company Catalogue*. Coventry Machinists' Co.

Crown, Judith and Coleman, Glenn. 1996. *No Hands: The Rise and Fall of the Schwinn Bicycle Company, an American Institution*. New York: Henry Holt.

Cycling. 1909. *Variable Gears and All About Them*. London: Cycling.

Davies, Thomas Stephens. 1837. "On the velocipede." Manuscript R.1.68, Library of Trinity College, Cambridge.

Davis, A. 1868. *The Velocipede and How to Use It*. London: Davis. Reprinted in 1994 by National Cycle Archive.

Davison, A. C. 1934a. "Is the Velocar a bicycle?" *Cycling*, April 6.

Davison, A. C. 1934b. "A design for a recumbent bicycle." *Cycling* (August 10).

Davison, A. C. 1939. "Actual experiences with some freak bicycles." *Cycling*, June 31).

Deharme, Ernest. 1874. *Les merveilles de la locomotion*. Paris: Hachette.

Demarest. Undated catalogue in Pryor Dodge Collection.

Desaguliers, John. 1744. *A Course of Experimental Philosophy*. London: W. Innys.

Dixon, Leon. 2007. *The 1960 Bowden Spacelander*. Davis, California: National Bicycle History Archive of America. Available at http://www.nbhaa.com.

Dodds, Alastair. 1993. "Kirkpatrick MacMillan—Inventor of the bicycle: Fact or hearsay?" In *Cycle History* 3.

Dodds, Alastair. 1999. *Scottish Bicycles & Tricycles*. Edinburgh: NMS.

Dodds, Alastair. 2001. "Dunlop and the pneumatic bicycle tyre—the Edinburgh connection." In *Cycle History* 11.

Dodge, Pryor. 1996. *The Bicycle*. Paris-New York: Flammarion.

Dolnar, Hugh. 1902. "An American stroke for novelty." *The Cyclist*, January 8.

Drais, Karl. 1816. "Ein Wagen, der ohne Pferde läuft, erfunden von dem Freiherrn von Drais in Mannheim." *Neues Magazin* (Leipzig) 3, no. 3. Written in 1813. Facsimile on pp. 118–119 of Lessing 2003a.

Drais, Karl. 1817a. "LODA, eine neu erfundene Fahrmaschine." *Badwochenblatt für die Großherzogliche Stadt Baden*, July 29. Facsimile on p. 145 of Lessing 2003a.

Drais, Karl. 1817b. "Die Fahrmaschine des Großherzogl. Badenschen Forstmeisters Herrn Freiherrn Karl von Drais in Mannheim." *Allgemeiner Anzeiger der Deutschen* no. 279, October 17. Facsimile on pp. 150–155 of Lessing 2003a.

Drais, Karl. 1817c. *Die Laufmaschine des Freiherrn Karl von Drais*. Mannheim: Schwan & Götz. Facsimile on pp. 182–186 of Lessing 2003a.

Drais, Karl. 1818. *Le Vélocipède du Baron Charles de Drais*. Mannheim. Facsimile on p. 283 of Lessing 2003a.

Drais, Karl. 1820. "Draisinen." *Journal für Literatur, Kunst, Luxus und Mode*, June. Facsimile on pp. 326–339 of Lessing 2003a.

Drais, Karl. 1832. "Drais' Improved Velocipede." *Mechanics' Magazine*, September 29.

Drouen, H. 1993. *Vouwen of Delen*. Nijmegen: Velorama.

Duncan, Henry O. 1928. *The World on Wheels*. Paris: Duncan.

Dunham, Norman L. 1956. The Bicycle Era in American History. Thesis, Harvard University.

Durry, Jean. 1982. *L'Encycl(e)opédie*. Lausanne: Edita.

Dyer, Herbert. 1940. *How to Work Sheet Metal*. London: Percival Marshall.

Eckermann, Erik. 1998. *Die Achsschenkellenkung und andere Fahrzeug-Lenksysteme*. Munich: Deutsches Museum.

Epperson, Bruce D. 2010. *Peddling Bicycles to America: The Rise of an Industry*. Jefferson: McFarland.

Euhus, Walter. 2003. "Die Geschichte der Fahrradbereifung." In *Schriftenreihe zur Fahrradgeschichte 4*. Langenhagen: Euhus.

Evans, David E. 1992. *The Ingenious Mr. Pedersen*. Stroud: Alan Sutton.

Fairburn, John. 1819. *Accurate Description of the New Pedestrian Carriage*. London: Fairburn. Facsimiles on pp. 301–305 of Lessing 2003a and pp. 200–212 of Street 2011.

Firth-Bottomley, Joseph. 1869. *The Velocipede: Its Past, Its Present, and Its Future*. London: Simpkin Marshall.

Fisk, Fred C., and Todd, Marlin W. 2000. *The Wright Brothers, from Bicycle to Biplane*. Dayton: Fred Fisk.

Fitzpatrick, Jim. 1998. *The Bicycle in Wartime*. Washington: Brasseys.

Flink, James J. 1988. *The Automobile Age*. Cambridge: MIT Press.

French, Anne, et al., eds. 1985. *John Joseph Merlin—the Ingenious Mechanick*. Greater London Council.

Fuss, Nicolaus. 1798. *Versuch einer Theorie des Widerstandes zwey- und vierrädriger Fuhrwerke*. Copenhagen: Brummer.

Garcin, Jean. 1813. *Le Vrai Patineur, ou prinipes sur l'art de patiner avec grâce*. Paris: Delespinasse.

Gardellin, Angelo. 1941. *Storia del velocipede et dello sport ciclistico*. Padova: Tipografia.

Garnet, Jeremy M. 2008. Ergonomics of Direct-Drive Recumbent Bicycles. Available at http://www.hupi.org.

George, B., and Surber, H. 1995. "Swiss military cyclists and their cycles." *The Boneshaker* 138.

Gerstner, Franz Josef von. 1813. *Zwey Abhandlungen über Frachtwägen und Strassen*. Prague: Haase.

Ginzrot, Johann Christian. 1830. *Die Wagen und Fahrwerke der verschiedenen Völker des Mittelalters und der Kutschen-Bau neuester Zeiten*. Four volumes. Munich. Reprinted in 1979, in two volumes, by Olms.

Gobert, Jean-Baptiste. 1870. "Étude générale sur les Vélocipèdes." *Portefeuille économique des machines* 171.

Gompertz, Lewis. 1821. "Addition to the velocipede." *Repertory of Arts, Manufactures, and Agriculture* 39, series 2.

Graber, Jacques. 2002. "The Lefèbvre bicycle." In *Cycle History* 12.

Griffin, Harry H. 1887. *Bicycles & Tricycles of the Year 1887*. London: Upcot Gill. Reprinted in 1971 by Olicana Books.

Griffin, Harry H. 1890. *Cycles and Cycling*. London: George Bell.

Grosser, M. 1981. *The Gossamer Odyssey*. Boston: Houghton Mifflin.

Grützner, Michael. 2008. "The chainless bicycle craze in Germany around 1900." In *Cycle History* 18.

Grützner, Michael. 2009. *Kettenlose Fahrräder. Die Geschichte in Deutschland ab 1890 von Adler bis Woerner*. Rickmansworth: Fidibus.

Grützner, Michael. 2012. "Ravat Wonder and Cycloratio: The first short wheel-base recumbent." In *Cycle History* 21.

Hadland, Tony. 1981. *The Moulton Bicycle*. Erdington: Pinkerton.

Hadland, Tony. 1987. *The Sturmey-Archer Story*. Erdington: Pinkerton.

Hadland, Tony. 1994. *The Spaceframe Moultons*. Coventry: Hadland.

Hadland, Tony. 1997. "Small wheels for adult bicycles." *Cycling Science*. Available at http://hadland.wordpress.com.

Hadland, Tony. 2011. *Raleigh: Past and Presence of an Iconic Bicycle Brand*. San Francisco: Cycle Publishing.

Hadland, Tony, and Pinkerton, John. 1996. *It's in the Bag!* Erdington: Pinkerton.

Hamer, Nick. 2005. "Brimstone and Bicycles." *New Scientist*, January 29

Harrison, A. E. 1977. Growth, Entrepreneurship and Capital Formation in the UK's Cycle and Related Industries 1870–1914. PhD thesis, University of York.

Henry, Raymond. 1998. *Du Vélocipède au Dérailleur Moderne*. Saint-Étienne: Association des Amis du Musée D'Art et D'Industrie.

Herlihy, David. 1994. "Who Invented the bicycle—Lallement or Michaux?" In *Cycle History* 4.

Herlihy, David. 2001. "Choosing the strongest Michaux invention claim." *The Boneshaker* 157.

Herlihy, David. 2004. *Bicycle: The History*. New Haven: Yale University Press.

Herlihy, David. 2010. "Mind the gap. An explanation for the primitive bicycle's surprisingly low profile from 1864 to 1867." In *Cycle History* 20.

Hillier, G. Lacy. 1891. *The Badminton Library of Sports: Cycling*. London: Longmans, Green.

Hoerner, Sighard F. 1965. *Fluid Dynamic Drag*. Bricktown: Hoerner Fluid Dynamics.

Houckgeest, Andreas E. 1798. *Reise der Gesandtschaft der Holländisch-Ostindischen Gesellschaft an den Kaiser von China*. Leipzig: Heinsius.

Hounshell, David A. 1984. *From the American System to Mass Production, 1800–1932*. Baltimore: Johns Hopkins University Press.

Hult, Jan. 1992. "The Svea (1892) and the Itera (1982)—two unsuccessful Swedish bicycle projects." In *Cycle History* 3.

Hurbin, J. d'Horta. 1894. "Henri Gourdoux et la pédale." *L'Industrie vélocipédique*, December.

ICDC. 1974. *International Cycle Design Competition. Report on Prize-Winning Projects*. Tokyo: Koichi Ishida.

Jeanes, Richard Walter. 1950. Des origines du vocabulaire cycliste français. Thesis, Sorbonne.

Jones, Bernard E. 1913. *Cycle Repairing and Adjusting*. London: Cassell.

Kanigel, Robert. 1997. *The One Best Way—Frederick Winslow Taylor and the Enigma of Efficiency*. New York: Viking.

Kielwein, Matthias. 2010. "The velocipede in Germany 1868 to 1870: Sport, design and manufacturers." In *Cycle History* 19.

Kielwein, Matthias, and Lessing, Hans-Erhard, eds. 2005. *Kaleidoskop früher Fahrrad- und Motorradtechnik*. Two volumes. Leipzig: Maxime.

Kobayashi, Keizo. 1993. *Histoire du Vélocipède de Drais à Michaux 1817–1870. Mythes et Réalités*. Tokyo: Bicycle Culture Center.

Kobayashi, Keizo. 2008. "Le vélocipède Michaux." In *Le Vélocipède—objet de modernité*, ed. Nadine Besse and Anne Henry. Saint-Étienne: Musée d'Art et d'Industrie.

Koike, Kazusuke. 2013. "The early Japanese pedal tricycle and its origin." Reference to be completed in page proofs.

Krausse, Joachim, and Lichtenstein, Claude. 1999. *Your Private Sky: R. Buckminster Fuller: The Art of Design Science*, volume 1. Baden: Lars Müller.

Kron, Karl [Lyman H. Bagg]. 1887. *Ten Thousand Miles on a Bicycle*. New York: Karl Kron. Reprinted in 1982 by Emil Rosenblatt.

Krünitz, Johann Georg. 1850. "Velocipede." In *Ökonomisch-Technologische Enzyklopädie*, volume 203. Berlin: Pauli (1970 microfiche from Olms).

Kyle, Chester R. 2001. "Bicycle aerodynamics and the Union Cycliste Internationale." In *Cycle History* 11.

Kyle, Chester R. 2007. "Racing cyclists and the birth of aviation." In *Cycle History* 17.

Kyle, Chester R., Crawford, C., and Nadeau, D. 1974. "What affects bicycle speed." *Bicycling Magazine*, July.

Kyle, Chester R., and Edelman, W. 1974. "Man powered vehicle design criteria." In *Proceedings of Third International Conference on Vehicle System Dynamics*.

Lambert, Johann. 1778. "Über die vierrädrigen Wagen." *Archiv der reinen und angewandten Mathematik* 5.

Land, Nigel. 2010. *Elswick-Hopper of Barton-on-Humber*. Barton-on-Humber: Fathom Writers Press.

Lankensperger, Georg. 1818. *Bewegliche Achsen und andere Verbesserungen an Wagengestellen*. Munich: Zeller.

Lawrence, Scotford. 2005a. Vianzone Wooden Bicycle (dimensioned drawing and notes). Llandrindod Wells: National Cycle Museum.

Lawrence, Scotford. 2005b. Itera Moulded Plastic Bicycle (dimensioned drawing and notes). Llandrindod Wells: National Cycle Museum.

Lessing, Hans-Erhard. 1991. "Karl von Drais' two-wheeler: What we know." In *Cycle History* 1.

Lessing, Hans-Erhard. 1994. "The reception of the front-wheel-driven velocipede in Germany." In *Cycle History* 4.

Lessing, Hans-Erhard. 1995. "Around Michaux: Myths and realities. Towards a new chart of early bicycle history." In *Cycle History* 2.

Lessing, Hans-Erhard. 1996. "Cycling or roller skating: The resistible rise of personal mobility." In *Cycle History* 5.

Lessing, Hans-Erhard. 1998. "The evidence against 'Leonardo's bicycle.'" In *Cycle History* 8.

Lessing, Hans-Erhard. 1999. "The J-Wheel." In *Cycle History* 9.

Lessing, Hans-Erhard. 2000. "An early patent of a two-wheeler on rails." In *Cycle History* 10.

Lessing, Hans-Erhard. 2001. "What led to the invention of the early bicycle?" *Cycle History* 11.

Lessing, Hans-Erhard. 2003a. *Automobilität—Karl Drais und die unglaublichen Anfänge*. Leipzig: Maxime.

Lessing, Hans-Erhard. 2003b. "The velocipede of 1819 in America." In *Cycle History* 13.

Lessing, Hans-Erhard. 2007. "Balancing while cranking was new in 1865, not the crank." *The Boneshaker* 175.

Lessing, Hans-Erhard. 2008. "Adolph Schoeninger, the Henry Ford of the bicycle?" In *Cycle History* 18.

Lessing, Hans-Erhard. 2010. "From Paris to Mannheim: A German velocipede rider pioneers the gas automobile." In *Cycle History* 19.

Lessing, Hans-Erhard. 2012. "The origin of the two-wheeler. A solution for the climatic crisis of 1816." In *Cycle History* 22.

Leupold, Jakob. 1725. *Theatrum Machinarum*, volume 5: *Schauplatz der Heb-Zeuge*. Leipzig: Gleditsch. Facsimile reprint published by VDI in 1981.

Liesegang, J., and Lee, A.R. 1978. "Dynamics of a bicycle: Nongyroscopic aspects." *American Journal of Physics* 46, no. 2.

Light Dragoon, A. 1870. *Wheels and Woes. Words of Warning to Would be Velocipedists*. London: Ward & Lock.

Lightwood, James T. 1928. *The Cyclist Touring Club. Romance of 50 Years of Cycling*. Godalming: CTC.

Lilienthal, Otto. 1894. "Über die Geheimnisse des Vogelflugs." *Polytechnisches Zentralblatt* 56.

Malaparte, Curzio. 1949. "Les deux visages de l'Italie." *Sport Digest* (Paris) 6.

Manoury, Paul. 1894. "La Genèse du Cyclisme." *Le Figaro* (September 30).

Marchegay, Alphonse. 1874. *Essai théorique et pratique sur le véhicule bicycle (vélocipède)*. Lyon: Pitrat.

Marinoni, Augusto. 1995. "Leonardo da Vinci's bicycle." In *Cycle History* 2.

Marks, Edward Charles Robert. 1903. *The Manufacture of Iron and Steel Tubes*. Second edition. Manchester: Technical Publishing Company.

Maystrov, Virginski, et al. 1983. [Title unknown.] In *Voprosy Istory Estestvoznania I Techniki* 1/1983 and 1/1989.

Meijaard, J. P., Papadopoulos, Jim, Ruina, Andy, and Schwab, Arend. 2011. Historical Review of Thoughts on Bicycle Self-Stability. Available at http://hdl.handle.net/1813/22497. For a short review see van Dijk 2007

Merki, Christoph Maria. 2008. *Verkehrsgeschichte und Mobilität*. Stuttgart: Verlag Eugen Ulmer.

M.H. 1983. "Cads on Castors, part 1." *The Boneshaker* 104.

M.H. 1984. "Cads on Castors, part 2." *The Boneshaker* 105.

Microbac Laboratories, Inc. 2007. *Preliminary Results: Poly Chain Versus Chain Efficiency*. Denver: Gates Corporation.

Miller, Christian. 1980. *Daisy, Daisy—A Journey across America on a Bicycle*. London: Routledge & Kegan Paul.

Millward, Andrew. 1999. Factors Contributing to the Sustained Success of the UK Cycle Industry, 1870–1939. Thesis, University of Birmingham.

Moed, Gertjan. 2008. "Netherlands." In *Le Vélocipède—Objet de modernité*, ed. Nadine Besse and Anne Henry. Saint-Étienne: Musée d'Art et d'Industrie.

Moghaddass, Amir. 2003. "The bicycle's long way to China." In *Cycle History* 13.

Montague Corporation. 2011. Our History. Available at http://www.montaguebikes.com.

Mouhot, Henry. 1876. *La Rinkomanie*. Paris: Amyot.

Moulton, A. E, Hadland, A., and Milliken, D. L. 2006. "Aerodynamic research using the Moulton small wheeled bicycle." In *Proceedings of the Institution of Mechanical Engineers, Part A: Journal of Power and Energy* 220, no. 3.

Muir, Andrew. 1869. *The Velocipede: How to Learn and How to Use It*. Manchester: Andrew Muir. Reprinted by National Cycle Archive.

Needham, Joseph. 1991. *Science and Civilisation in China*, volume 1. Cambridge University Press.

Nieswizski (a.k.a. Neveu), Sam. 1991. *Rollermania*. Paris: Gallimard.

Nonweiler, Tony. 1957. The Air Resistance of Racing Cyclists. Report 106, College of Aeronautics, Cranfield Institute of Technology

Norcliffe, Glen. 2001. *The Ride to Modernity: The Bicycle in Canada 1869–1900*. University of Toronto Press.

Norden, Gilbert. 1999. "Passing fashions but no sustainable market—A history of roller-skating in Austria before 1914." *International Journal of the History of Sport* 3, no. 16.

Oddy, Nicholas. "The machine aesthetic: Marketing the bicycle in the late 19th and early 20th centuries." In *Cycle History* 2.

O'Donovan, Gerald. 1995. Handbuilding Bicycle Frames and Forks. Internal document, Raleigh Industries, Nottingham.

Oliver, Smith Hempstone, and Berkebile, Donald H. 1974. *Wheels and Wheeling: The Smithsonian Cycle Collection*. Washington: Smithsonian Institution Press.

Olivier, Aimé de Sanderval. 1892. "Le vélocipède—aperçu historique." *La Nature*, August 6.

Olivier, René. 1869. "Note pour MM. Olivier frères contre M. Michaux." Manuscript produced by a clerk from Olivier's handwriting for his lawyer. Collection de Sanderval, Archives du Calvados.

Ovenden. 1775. A New Machine to Go without Horses. Flyer. Copy in London Science Museum.

Ozanam, Jacques. 1696. *Récréations Mathematiques et Physiques*. Paris: Jean Jombert.

Palmiéri, A. 2007. Available at www.artsetmetiers.net/pdf/DEPJ-evolution-tech-bicy.pdf

Paulin-Désormeaux, A.-O. 1853. *Patinage et Récréations sur la glace*. Paris: Roret.

Pedretti. Carlo. 1972. *Leonardo da Vinci—The Royal Palace at Romorantin*. Cambridge: Harvard University Press.

Pedretti, Carlo. 1978. *The Codex Atlanticus of Leonardo da Vinci: A Catalogue of Its Newly Restored Sheets*. New York: Johnson Reprint Co.

Pickering, Tony. 2009. "Pickering & Davis—The American velocipede." *The Boneshaker* 179.

Pinkerton, John, et al. 2002. *Sunbeam Cycles*. Erdington: Pinkerton.

Pinkerton, John, and Roberts, Derek. 1998. *A History of Rover Cycles*. Erdington: Pinkerton.

Playfair, William. 1822. *A Letter on our Agricultural Distresses, Their Causes and Remedies*. London: W. Sams.

Porter, Luther H. 1892. *Wheels and Wheeling*. Boston: Wheelman.

Porter, Luther H. 1898. "Evolution of the cycle." *League of American Wheelmen Bulletin* 27.

Post, John D. 1977. *The Last Great Subsistence Crisis in the Western World*. Baltimore: Johns Hopkins University Press.

Pratt, Charles E. 1883. "Pierre Lallement and his bicycle." *Outing and the Wheelman*, October. Reprinted in 1992 by Lallement Memorial Committee, Boston.

Radford, Michael. 2010. "Puffs Corner." *The Boneshaker* 181.

Rankine, William John Macquorn. 1870. *Théorie du Vélocipède*. Paris: Gauthier-Villars.

Rauck, Max. 1943. "Der erste Benzwagen." *Automobiltechnische Zeitschrift*, August 25.

Rebour, Daniel. 1976. *Cycles de Compétition et Randonneuses*. Paris: Technique et Vulgarisation.

Reissinger, Elisabeth. 2011. *Kutschmuseum Auerstedt. Die historischen Kutschen der Großherzöge von Sachsen-Weimar und Eisenach*. Munich: Deutscher Kunstverlag.

Reti, Ladislao, ed. 1974. *The Unknown Leonardo*. New York: McGraw-Hill.

Reynaud, Claude. 2003. *La genèse de la moto ou le véloce qui va tout seul*. Domazan: Musée Vélo-Moto.

Reynaud, Claude. 2008. *Le Vélocipède Illustré*. Two volumes paginated throughout. Domazan: Musée Vélo-Moto.

Reynaud, Claude. 2010. "1871, Viarengo de Forville Made the First Bicycle". In *Cycle History* 19.

Reynaud, Claude. 2011. *L'Ère du Grand Bi en France 1870–1890*. Domazan: Musée Vélo-Moto.

Reynaud, Claude. 2012. "New light on the origins of the pedal velocipede." In *Cycle History* 22.

Ritchie, Andrew. 2002. "The velocipede of Alexandre Lefebvre and problems of historical interpretation." In *Cycle History* 12.

Ritchie, Andrew. 2010. *The Origins of the Bicycle—Kirkpatrick Macmillan, Gavin Dazell, Alexandre Lefebvre*. Birmingham: John Pinkerton Memorial Publishing Fund.

Roberts, Derek. 1991. *Cycling History: Myths and Queries*. Erdington: Pinkerton.

Robin, Francis. 2010. *Traité de Cyclonomie. Les principaux noms des deux-roues en France avant 1900* (Dossier de la Vélocithèque 42). Pomeys: La Vélocithèque.

Rolt, Lionel Thomas Caswall. 1965. *Tools for the Job*. London: Science Museum.

RRA. 1965. *Road Records Association Handbook 1965*. Middlesex: RRA.

Salmon, Gérard. 2012. "The rise of the velocipede in Lyon." In *Cycle History* 22.

Sanderson, Gary W. 2009. "Velocipede-mania in the USA (1868–1869)." In *Cycle History* 19.

Sanderson, Gary W. 2012a. "The Hay & Willits Manufacturing Company of Indianapolis, Indiana (USA): Two ambitious men try to make their fortune in the bicycle boom of the 1890s." In *Cycle History* 21.

Sanderson, Gary W. 2012b. "Albert F. Rockwell, Edward D. Rockwell and the 'New Departure Companies': From bells to brakes and beyond in the 1880s, 1890s, and 1900s." In *Cycle History* 22.

Sauvaget, Roland. 2000. "Michaux v. Lallement: The conclusion." *The Boneshaker* 152. Amplified by "Michaux Lallement again." *The Boneshaker* 160.

Schmitz, Arnfried. 2000. *Human Power—the Forgotten Energy*. Coventry: Hadland.

Schmitz, Arnfried. 2010. *Cyclists, Cycling, Cycles and Cycle Parts*. Faringdon: Hadland.

Scholes, Brent. "William Winterborne of Isleworth and the freewheel." *The Boneshaker* 187.

Schulze, Hans-Georg. 1936. *Flug durch Muskelkraft*. Frankfurt: Fritz Knapp.

Seray, Jacques. 1976. "Naissance de la vélocipédie et d'une polemique." *Cyclisme Magazine* 4. English translation in *The Boneshaker* 85. See also Seray 1988, 14.

Seray, Jacques. 1988. *Deux Roues. La véritable histoire du vélo*. Rodez: Éditions du Rouergue.

Seyfert, Otto Erich. 1912. *Die deutsche Fahrradindustrie*. Leipzig: Borna.

Sharp, Archibald. 1896. *Bicycles & Tricycles. An Elementary Treatise on Their Design and Construction*. London: Longmans, Green. Reprinted in 1977 by MIT Press.

Sheldon, J. A. 1955. "Origin of the Sidecar." *The Motor Cycle* 94.

Shields, Lorne. 2012. "What did you call that thing that just went by?" *The Boneshaker* 188. Bedford: Veteran-Cycle Club.

Silberer, Victor. 1885. *Handbuch des Bicycle-Sport*. Second edition. Vienna: Verlag Allgemeine Sport-Zeitung. Reprinted in 2004 by Maxime.

Spencer, Charles. 1883. *Bicycles and Tricycles*. London: Griffith & Farran.

Starley, John Kemp. 1898. "The evolution of the bicycle." *Journal of the Royal Society of Arts*, May 20. Reprinted in *The Boneshaker* 114.

Steinheil, G. 1892. "La roue tension." *Le Cycle* 65 (November 19). Translated in *The Boneshaker* 149.

Steinmann, Gustav. 1870. *Das Velocipede—seine Geschichte, Konstruktion, Gebrauch und Verbreitung*. Leipzig: J. J. Weber. Reprinted in 2008 by Hyperion.

Street, Roger. 1979. *Victorian High-Wheelers*. Christchurch: Artesius.

Street, Roger. 1990. "The celebrated Rantoone." *The Boneshaker* 122.

Street, Roger. 1992. "The end of Artamanov." *The Boneshaker* 130.

Street, Roger. 1998. *The Pedestrian Hobby-Horse*. Christchurch: Artesius.

Street, Roger. 2000 "One small step for mankind." In *Cycle History* 10.

Street, Roger. 2006. "The manupedes of Charley Townley." *The Boneshaker* 170.

Street, Roger. 2010. "The *Alert* bicycle: A cycle dealer's view." In *Cycle History* 19.

Street, Roger. 2011. *Dashing Dandies—the English Hobby-Horse Craze of 1819*. Christchurch: Artesius. Second amplified edition of Street 1998.

Strictland, Margaret. 1843. *A Memory of Edmund Cartwright*. Manuscript. Reprinted in 1971 by Adams & Dart.

Sturmey, Henry. 1879. *Sturmey's Indispensable Bicyclist's Handbook*. Weymouth: H. Wheeler.

Sturmey, Henry. 1881. *Tricyclist's Indispensable Annual & Handbook 1881*. London: Iliffe.

Sturmey, Henry. 1885. *Indispensable Handbook to the Safety Bicycle*. London: Iliffe (reprint).

Sturmey, Henry. 1887. *Sturmey's Indispensable Bicyclist's Handbook*. Weymouth: H. Wheeler.

Sullivan, Louis H., 1896. The tall office building artistically considered. *Lippincott's Magazine* 57 (March).

Tietze, Hans. 1925. *Das vormärzliche Wien*. Vienna: Schroll.

Trapmann, A. H. 1901. "The cycle in warfare: Its potency and tactical factor." *Journal of the Royal United Services Institution*.

Tredgold, Thomas. 1835. *A Practical Treatise on Railroads and Carriages*. London: Nichols.

Treue, Wilhelm. 1986. *Achse, Rad und Wagen*. Second edition. Göttingen: Vandenhoeck & Ruprecht.

Tripp, Basil H. 1956. *Renold Chains—A History of the Company and the Rise of the Precision Chain Industry 1879–1955*. London: Allen & Unwin.

Tulla, Johann. 1813. "Gemeinschaftliches Gutachten des Oberbaudirektors Weinbrenner und des Majors Tulla die von dem Forstmeister von Drais nachgesuchte Erteilung eines Monopols für seine Fahrmaschine betreffend." In *Generallandesarchiv Karlsruhe 236/6735–6*. Karlsruhe. Reprinted in Lessing 2003a.

Ulreich, Walter. 1993. "Anton Burg and Son—the Viennese hobby-horse maker." In *Cycle History* 3.

Ulreich, Walter. 1999. "Three recently discovered Draisines in Austria." In *Cycle History* 9.

van Dijk, Tomas. 2007. "Bicycles made to measure. Delft researchers unravel the bike's operating principle." *Delft Outlook*. July. Available at http://bicycle.tudelft.nl/schwab/Bicycle/DO-07-3-2bicycles.pdf.

Van Helden, B. 2011. *Condorclub Holland*. Available at http://www.benvanhelden.nl.

Vélocio. 1911. "De l'influence de la hauteur des roues." *Le Cycliste,* January.

Velox. 1869. *Velocipedes, Bicycles and Tricycles. How to Make and Use Them*. New York. Reprinted in 1994 by National Cycle Archive.

von Salvisberg, Paul. 1897. *Der Radfahrsport in Bild und Wort*. Munich: Academischer Verlag. Reprinted in 1980 by Olms.

Wackernagel, Rudolf H. 2002. *Wittelsbach State and Ceremonial Cariages*. Two volumes. Stuttgart: Arnoldsche.

Wagenknecht, Tilmann. 1997. "Paul Rinkowski—ein Fahrradgenie." In *Wegbereiter des Fahrrads*, ed. Volker Briese et al. Bielefeld: BVA.

Wang, S. 2008. "For avid bike-fan, keeping fit comes naturally." *The Straits Times*, January 23.

Warring, Charles B. 1891. "What keeps the bicycle upright?" *Popular Science Monthly*, April. Also see "Letter to the Editor" in December issue.

Way, R. John. 1973. *The Bicycle: A Guide and Manual*. London: Hamlyn.

Whitt, Frank. 1971 "What is that cherub doing?" *CTC Gazette*, April/May.

Whitt, Frank Rowland. 1977. "Tyre and road contact." *Cycletouring*, February/March.

Whitt, Frank Rowland. 1979. "Variable gears: Some basic ergonomics and mechanics." In *Developing Pedal Power*. Milton Keynes: Open University Press.

Wilson, David Gordon. 1967. "A plan to encourage improvements in man-powered transit." *Engineering* (London) 204.

Wilson, David Gordon. 1968. "Man-powered land transport." *Engineering* (London) 207.

Wilson, David Gordon. 1995. "The development of modern recumbent bicycles." In *Human Powered Vehicle*s, ed. Allan Abbott and David Gordon Wilson. Champaign: Human Kinetics.

Wilson, David Gordon. 2002. "Bicycle design, safety, and product-liability litigation." *Human Power* 53.

Wilson, David Gordon. 2004. *Bicycling Science*. Third edition. Cambridge: MIT Press.

Wolf, Wilhelm. 1890. *Fahrrad und Radfahrer*. Leipzig: Otto Spamer. Reprinted in 1979 by Harenberg.

Zindel, Christian Siegmund. 1825. *Der Eislauf*. Nuremberg: Campe. Reprinted in 1980 by Dausien.

INDEX

558

INDEX